WildTHINGS

D1089173

Landscapes of Childhood

GENERAL EDITOR:
Elizabeth N. Goodenough,
Residential College, University of Michigan

EDITORIAL BOARD

Joan Blos
Children's Author
1980 Newbery Medal

Louise Chawla
Kentucky State University

Robert Coles
Harvard University

Donald Haase
Wayne State University

Gareth Matthews
University of Massachusetts

Martha Minow
Harvard University

Robin Moore
North Carolina State University

Michael Nettles
University of Michigan

Valerie Polakow
Eastern Michigan University

Eugene Provenzo
University of Miami

Pamela Reynolds
Johns Hopkins University

John Stilgoe
Harvard University

Marcelo Suarez-Orozco
Harvard University

Jack Zipes
University of Minnesota

WildTHINGS

CHILDREN'S CULTURE
AND ECOCRITICISM

Edited by

SIDNEY I. DOBRIN and
KENNETH B. KIDD

Wayne State University Press
Detroit

Copyright © 2004 by Wayne State University Press,
Detroit, Michigan 48201. All rights are reserved.
No part of this book may be reproduced without formal permission.
Manufactured in the United States of America.
08 07 06 05 04   5 4 3 2 1

Cataloging-in Publication Data

Wild things : children's culture and ecocriticism / edited by Sidney I. Dobrin and Kenneth B. Kidd.
        p.   cm.
Includes bibliographical references.
ISBN 0–8143-3027-4 (cloth) — ISBN 0-8143-3028-2 (pbk.)
1. Children's literature, English—History and criticism.   2. Nature in literature.
3. Children—Books and reading—English-speaking countries.   4. Children's literature,
American—History and criticism.   5. Conservation of natural resources in literature.
6. Environmental protection in literature.   7. Wilderness areas in literature.
8. Landscape in literature.   9. Ecology in literature.   10. Ecocriticism.   I. Dobrin,
Sidney I., 1967–   II. Kidd, Kenneth B.
PR143.W55 2004
809'.9336—dc22

                                                                      2003028060

∞ The paper used in this publication meets the minimum requirements of the American
National Standard for Information Sciences—Permanence of Paper for Printed Library
Materials, ANSI Z39.48–1984.

"It's Not Easy Being Green" words and music by Joe Raposo, © 1970 by Jonico Music,
Inc. Copyright renewed. Rights in the U.S.A. administered by Green Fox Music, Inc.
Used by permission of the Estate of the late Joe Raposo.

This one's for Teresa
Always

To Mr. Nature

In memory of
Chuck Chamberlin

Contents

Acknowledgments

We wish to thank all those who made it possible for us to put together this collection, including Carla Blount, whose continual support makes it possible for us to engage in such projects. We would also like to thank the reviewers of this project for their thorough and helpful suggestions for revisions. We are grateful to each of the contributors for participating in this collection. We also acknowledge the advice and support of Liz Goodenough. We are deeply indebted to Jane Hoehner for her support of this project and to the editorial staff at Wayne State University Press.

Introduction: Into the Wild

Sidney I. Dobrin and Kenneth B. Kidd

> If facts are the seeds that later produce knowledge and wisdom, then the emotions and the impressions of the senses are the fertile soil in which the seeds must grow. The years of childhood are the time to prepare the soil.
> RACHEL CARSON, *The Sense of Wonder*

> All education is environmental education.
> DAVID W. ORR, *Ecological Literacy*

We title our introduction "Into the Wild" to highlight what this collection of essays is most fundamentally about: the interplay of children's texts—literary, multimedia, cultural—and children's environmental experience. We also allude to John Krakauer's book *Into the Wild*, which recounts Christopher McCandless's fatal venture—inspired by nature writing, particularly Henry David Thoreau's *Walden*—into the Alaskan wilderness. McCandless, an Emory graduate student in his twenties, renamed himself "Alexander Supertramp." In search of a more natural way of life, he abandoned all trappings of civilization—his clothes, his cash, his car, the new friends he had made along the trail. In September 1992, a hunter found McCandless's emaciated body inside a bus shelter. There were no identifying papers, only a brief diary of his final days. Krakauer's initial magazine article about McCandless generated responses ranging from sympathy to ridicule. At issue in this tragic story is the character and legitimacy of the search for identity in nature or, alternately, the effort to shake identity, to lose oneself through exposure to an allegedly purer, if not always a kinder and gentler, nature.

It's easy, perhaps too easy, to read McCandless's story as a cautionary tale of idealism gone awry, even though Krakauer's book guards against such a simple understanding. And certainly, in *Wild Things: Children's Culture and Ecocriticism,* we often sound the opposite alarm, that children are often denied or discouraged from outward-bound forms of nature experience (even from reading about nature). We allude to Krakauer to acknowledge the complexities and ambivalences of our expectations about the natural world as represented in and mediated through our cultural production. Close contact with nature can be dangerous, but so, too, can our evasion and denial of it. Perhaps if children are encouraged to explore nature from the beginning, they will not need the encouragement of nature writers or seek "extreme" experiences; perhaps such thinking is itself problematic, in that it takes McCandless's story as too representative of our cultural moment. In any case, we hope neither to idealize nature recklessly nor to deny its allure and its centrality to our lives. That dialectic, as much as anything, inspires this volume.

Our book title, of course, invokes Maurice Sendak's classic 1963 picture book, *Where the Wild Things Are*, which tells the story of young Max venturing into the land of the wild things, becoming their king, and finally returning safely home—where he finds his supper waiting for him, still hot. Here again, we appeal to the text in a dual way, at once celebrating the excitement of adventure and discovery but also acknowledging that adventure and discovery owe much to problematic practices. The very canonicity of Sendak's book points to the complicity of adventure tale and colonialist metaphor. Thus Jennifer Shaddock reads *Where the Wild Things Are* as indebted to adventure and imperialist narrative, as the book recycles all the classic tropes of the nineteenth-century adventure story for boys: the sea voyage, the lush tropical landscape, the docility of the natives (not to mention the reluctant white monarch). Put simply, the "wild" is hardly a neutral concept but an ever shifting rhetorical and political term in need of specific elaborations. Neither are terms like *nature* or *the environment* free-floating or self-evident, as the following essays demonstrate.

We don't mean to imply in this study that children's culture is our field and ecocriticism our methodology; in fact, several essays in this volume examine ecocriticism as a field through the critical lens of children's literature and what scholars now call "children's studies." The term *ecocriticism* was introduced in 1978 by William Rueckert in his essay "Literature and Ecology: An Experiment in Ecocriticism" but did not become popularly used until the 1989 meeting of the Western Literature Association, when Cheryll Glotfelty employed the word as a part of a vocabulary for a critical approach to studying nature writing. The term has since become more widely used, though its definition remains ambiguous. In the collection *The Ecocriticism Reader*, Glotfelty explains:

"Simply put, ecocriticism is the study of the relationship between literature and the physical environment. Just as feminist criticism examines language and literature from a gender-conscious perspective, and Marxist criticism brings an awareness of modes of production and economic class to its readings of texts, ecocriticism takes an earth-centered approach to literary studies" (xviii).

At its core, "ecocriticism takes as its subject the interconnections between nature and culture, specifically the culture artifacts of language and literature . . . as a theoretical discourse, it negotiates between the human and non-human" (Glotfelty xix). Glotfelty's foundational understanding of ecocriticism is strategically wide-ranging; in fact, she appeals to the importance of interdisciplinary work or "cross-fertilization" among literary studies, work in ecology, and "related disciplines such as history, philosophy, psychology, art history, and others" (xvii–xix). Ecocritical work has, in fact, been productively varied and eclectic, but like any other academic discourse, it has its own troubling orthodoxies, some of which are challenged in this volume.

Wild Things: Children's Culture and Ecocriticism provides scholars and teachers with essays that offer readings both of literary texts and of historical and theoretical paradigms. Thus far, children's culture studies and ecocriticism have been largely separate undertakings. While this collection is the first book-length project to address their intersection(s), we do want to acknowledge earlier efforts to bring these fields together. For instance, the spring 1995 issue of the *American Nature Writing Newsletter* (a precursor to the journal *Interdisciplinary Study of Literature and Environment* [ISLE], a publication of the Association for the Study of Literature and Environment (ASLE), is devoted to the special topic "Children's Literature and the Environment." The issue includes several intriguing articles, notably an essay by Naomi Wood, also a contributor here. The winter 1994–95 issue of the *Children's Literature Quarterly*, guest-edited by Betty Greenaway, is similarly devoted to "Ecology and the Child." This work, too, is quite useful; Carolyn Sigler's "Wonderland to Wasteland," for instance, is an overview of three hundred years of nature representation in children's literature. Equally invaluable is the winter 1995 special issue of *The Lion and the Unicorn* titled "Green Worlds: Nature and Ecology," edited by Suzanne Rahn. Thanks to such scholarship, we can begin to envision the mutual history of children's literature and environmental writing and activism.

Suzanne Rahn's introduction to the December 1995 "Green Worlds" issue of *The Lion and the Unicorn* suggests a particular beginning point for environmentally conscious children's literature in America. Rahn points out that *St. Nicholas: A Magazine for Young Folks,* the most important American periodical for children in the nineteenth century, regularly featured illustrated articles about natural history subjects and even addressed the extermination of certain animal species by humans. Rahn identifies Charles Frederick Holder's article "How Some Animals Become Extinct," which appeared in *St. Nicholas* in 1887, as evidence of the emergent conservation ethic of this period. As she points out, the first issue of *Audubon Magazine* appeared the same year, addressed specifically to "young folks" (cited in Rahn, 155). Bird protection led in turn to other forms of wildlife conservation, and children were understood from the start as vital to this movement. Rahn links the articles in *St. Nicholas* to the proliferation of "wild animal stories" in America especially and of stories about children living in harmony with nature (published on both sides of the Atlantic), such as Kipling's *The Jungle Book* (1894), Stratton-Porter's *A Girl of the Limberlost* (1909), and Burnett's *The Secret Garden* (1911). As several of the essays in our collection demonstrate, classic children's literature has long been preoccupied with natural history, ecology, and human-animal interaction.

Recent years have seen a proliferation of academic research and writing on nature and childhood within and across specialties other than children's literature and ecocriticism. Much of this scholarship responds to E. O. Wilson's claim in *Biophilia* that the human species shows an "affinity for life and lifelike processes" (81), an affinity ostensibly rooted in our evolutionary and genetic makeup. The various essays included in *Children and Nature,* as editors Peter H. Kahn Jr. and Stephen R. Kellert explain in their introduction, make clear the need for science "to embrace the dialectic between theory, concepts, and empirical data" (xviii). In his polemical but persuasive contribution to the volume, "Political Economy and the Ecology of Childhood," David W. Orr attributes the decline of environmental awareness to the success of corporate capitalism, which in his view compromises not just that awareness but indeed our physical and emotional health. As evidence he points to class-inflected child obesity, to the preponderance of chemicals in our food and water, and to other consequences of "a century of promiscuous industrial chemistry" (281). In other publications, Orr links our sorry political economy with what he calls "biophobia." Peter H. Kahn Jr. takes a somewhat more critical view of the biophilia hypothesis in *The Human Relationship with Nature,* arguing that some evolutionary paradigms supporting biophilia subscribe to an overly mechanistic model of brain functioning. Still, he underscores the problem of "environmental generational amnesia" (110), even suggesting that postmodern theory justifies such amnesia or at least refuses a rationalist faith in environmental preservation and enrichment.

Much of this scholarship emphasizes the physical and psychological resemblances of children and animals. So long after Darwin, notes Gene Myers in *Children and Animals*, we've yet to come to terms with our own animality, preferring to see animals as really human. Working primarily with preschoolers, Meyers studies the interactional dynamics between children and animals in pursuit of what he calls "the relational nature of the self" (3). Responding to the classic question about feral children—does their isolation from humans turn them into animals?—Meyers asks instead: can a child provided with human contact but denied interactions with animals achieve his or her full developmental potential? In *Why the Wild Things Are*, social psychologist Gail F. Melson reports on her fascinating research on children's bonds with animals both real and imagined. Adapting Wilson's biophilia hypothesis, Melson speculates that "[b]ecause animals were the most salient aspects of the environment of human evaluation, the human mind may be prewired to vibrate to *animal* as an innate category of thought and emotion" (146).

As these and other studies make clear, childhood experiences in, of, and with the natural world are often deeply formative. Many scholars write movingly about their own such experiences and their attempt to assure contact with nature for future generations. In *The Geography of Childhood*, Gary Paul Nabhan and Stephen Trimble document and interpret children's need for wild places; in his individual essay, Nabhan also stresses the use-value of first-person narratives as a form of environmental education. Two recent special issues of the *Michigan Quarterly Review* edited by Elizabeth N. Goodenough explore along similar lines both the natural and artificial "secret spaces of childhood," emphasizing the significance of sanctuary and retreat. No doubt we overlook other important work. As the essays in our collection demonstrate, scholarship in the larger field is diverse and stimulating, and in a sense, these essays introduce our concerns more ably than we can here. We hope that this volume, which concentrates on issues of language and representation, will complement these cross-disciplinary scientific investigations into biophilia and biophobia.

With respect to literary representation, it seems to us that our society's understanding of the relationship between children and nature is, at the most general level, twofold. On the one hand, there is the belief that children are innocent and/or virtuous, in keeping with the

romantic philosophy of Rousseau and other advocates of "original innocence." Wordsworth's 1807 "Ode: Intimations of Immortality" is rou-
tinely cited as a baseline for this perspective on childhood. Children are
still presumed to have a privileged relationship to nature, thanks largely
to the legacy of romantic and Victorian literature, which emphasized—
often to the point of absurdity—the child's proximity to the natural
world and consequent purity. The child is positively pastoral in the
Anglo-American literary tradition, from William Blake's oppressed and
angelic chimney sweeps through Charles Kingsley's water babies and
beyond. Even the American Bad Boy and the rebellious tomboy are
admirable, thanks to time spent in the great outdoors, away from the civ-
ilizing influences of home (and the misery of urban child labor). The
pastoral, of course, often has a decidedly social agenda—hence the political history of the child-nature link long before conservation was a
"movement" and biophilia a scientific hypothesis or conceit.

Or consider the secret garden tradition in children's literature, from
Frances Hodgson Burnett's urtext *The Secret Garden* onward. Here the
child is situated in his or her ostensibly natural habitat, even if the garden represents a compromise of sorts, at once domestic and wild, outside the home but nearby—at once familiar and new. The garden is not
only the classic Judeo-Christian space of renewal but also a literalization
or emplotment of the child's organic innocence. As Maude Hines makes
clear in her contribution to this volume, children have long been likened
to plants and child rearing to plant nurture, such that James Kincaid
identifies the "child botanical" (90) as one of the major tropes of childhood that we've inherited from the Victorians. In his study *Secret Gardens,* Humphrey Carpenter proposes that the garden pastoral allowed
children's writers to disavow Christianity and/or construct secular
utopias; Carpenter argues, in effect, that this allegedly apolitical space is
a subversive narrative conceit. More reason, in other words, to be at least
somewhat dubious about understanding the child as nature as well, as
innocence embodied; this association drives not only the field of children's literature but indeed much ecocriticism.

On the other hand, the child is still assumed to be devoid of content, in keeping with John Locke's empiricist faith. The child thus has
no necessary connection with nature, no experience or understanding of
it, so it's our task to educate young people into nature appreciation and
analysis. As with the innocent-child-as-nature tradition, there are variations on this blank slate or empty vessel theme. Thus in 1997, the U.S.

Department of Education Office of Educational Research and Improvement distributed a pamphlet entitled "What Can I Teach My Young Child about the Environment?" arguing that environmental education should begin during the earliest years of life. The writers of the pamphlet maintain that "such experiences play a critical role in shaping lifelong attitudes, values, and patterns of behavior toward natural environments" (3). The department's belief in environmental education is based on two premises. First is the assumption that children who are not exposed to the natural environment and its concerns at an early age risk never acquiring the respect and value of nature that society deems appropriate. Second is the more fundamental notion that interaction with the environment is an important part of healthy child development in general, which will enhance learning and the quality of life in the years to follow. The department lists the following "guidelines" that can be used as a "framework for developing and implementing" a preschool environmental education program: (1) begin with simple experiences; (2) provide frequent positive experiences outdoors; (3) focus on "experiencing" rather than "teaching"; (4) demonstrate a personal interest in and enjoyment of the natural world; and (5) model caring and respect for the natural environment. The department suggests that opportunities such as these are the "essence of environmental education and can help children form solid bonds with the natural world around them" (3–4).

We agree that many children have limited opportunities for such experiences. Many of the activities that occupy the time of young children take place in settings that isolate them from the natural world or present only simulations of that world. The impact of this may very well be that considerable numbers of children may never develop the positive attitudes toward the environment that are so crucial to its preservation. They may never achieve the familiarity with nature that is vital to environmental planning and activism. Here again, we recognize the ideologies in and around children and nature because we live those ideologies as well as subject them to scrutiny. We believe both that children are naturally close to nature and that nature education, even intervention, is in order. But through this collection we also try to acknowledge the ongoing debates about what constitutes sufficient or appropriate nature education and about the mediating role of representation. The essays included here underscore the consensus belief across narrative genres that even if the child has a privileged relationship with nature, he or she must be educated into a deeper—or at least different—awareness.

Another dialectic endemic to children's culture obviously informs this collection: that of instruction and entertainment. Scholars argue that the nineteenth century ushered in a kinder, gentler mode of children's literature, with a greater emphasis on recreation and amusement; Edward Lear and Lewis Carroll, among others, are credited with breaking from the didactic tradition. Of course, dating the break with sentimentality in children's literature is a bit like dating the rise of the middle class in social history. Put another way, writers and critics have been disavowing the sentimental for perhaps the entire history of children's literature, such that this disavowal could be understood as one of the field's foundational gestures. In any case, the essays gathered here take up the relation of instruction and entertainment in a variety of genres and contexts. We hope that the diversity represented suggests the even wider richness of the field. Although the term *children's culture* is potentially problematic, suggesting as it does some organic reality, we prefer it to *children's literature* as a subtitle, since four of our essays reckon with extra-literary texts.

Recognizing that there are many ways to arrange this volume, we have grouped the essays roughly according to period and genre, beginning with literature, from the nineteenth century to the present. We then offer studies of music and television, concluding with an examination of Disney's Animal Kingdom. In the first chapter, Maude Hines addresses how plants have been depicted as sentient and speaking creatures long before *The Little Shop of Horrors*. Examining materials in the Baldwin Library of Historical Children's Literature at the University of Florida, Hines identifies three major genres of "botanical" literature for children in the nineteenth century in the wake of the Industrial Revolution. In the first, plants speak of their painful experiences so that children may sympathize with the oppression and exploitation of the natural world as well as of human subjects. In the second genre, plants are not anthropomorphized but rather furnish object lessons for nature instruction. The third botanical genre likens girls to flowers, at once affirming familiar social hierarchies and urging adults to treat children more gently. Hines speculates that this third genre has survived because such stories are less disconcerting than more animistic stories of suffering plants. As Hines shows, botanical literature for children is at least as concerned with human nature and culture as with the botanical world.

In chapter 2, Kaye Adkins examines (after Rahn) *St. Nicholas*, a nineteenth-century magazine that, according to Adkins, "recognized [children's] natural curiosity and intelligence and their special ways of learning about the world." *St. Nicholas* was intended by its publishers to "improve society, provide moral and ethical guidance, and help the growing middle class, as well as immigrants, share the values of 'patriotism, respect for the family, hard work, self-reliance, and social concern' in addition to connecting religion and science." Adkins provides a history of *St. Nicholas,* accounting for its environmentally conscious agendas. In examining how children's texts have engaged the natural world, such historical accounts are crucial to our understanding of the tradition of children's literature and ecological literacy.

Peter Pan, of course, is one of the most familiar figures of children's literature. In chapter 3, M. Lynn Byrd explores the history of the Peter Pan stories, examining some of the more popular incarnations of its characters and looking specifically at four versions of Peter Pan and Neverland: two of J. M. Barrie's novels and the two most recent film versions. Byrd initiates these critiques from an ecocritical perspective, arguing that these four versions of the Peter Pan myth are ecocritical, or perhaps ecorhetorical, texts themselves. Byrd aligns these texts with Cheryll Glotfelty's definition of ecocriticism, claiming that each of the Peter Pan myths "takes as its subject the interconnections between nature and culture, specifically the cultural artifacts of language and literature" (Glotfelty xix). According to Byrd, J. M. Barrie's versions of the Peter Pan stories and both film versions (Disney and Spielberg) "grapple with the intersections of the social sphere, the natural world, and the imagination," and Neverland ultimately "parodies the ecological problems inherent in literature and criticism today."

In chapter 4, Marion W. Copeland fills a critical gap by examining the works of Gene Stratton-Porter and Beatrix Potter from an ecofeminist perspective, focusing on their attention to nature writing, animals, and landscape. For Copeland, ecofeminism's "condemnation of the domination of nature and of all animals, wild and domestic, human and nonhuman, lies at the heart of the work of both women." Since, as Copeland points out, many ecofeminists argue that the very sorts of oppression that are leveled against women and other groups are directly linked to the oppression of the natural world, children's texts become a crucial place in which to detect and combat cultural hegemony. Copeland shows how the works of these two authors were designed "not to elicit sentimental clichés, but to move audiences to actively engage in dialogues with nonhumans . . . and to become advocates of conservation strategies." Apart from Copeland's specific analysis of Stratton-Porter and Potter's work, it is critical to recognize that any ecocritical look at children's literature must include ecofeminist perspectives.

The overlooked contributions of Arthur Ransome, the British author of the twelve *Swallows and Amazons* books, to the celebration of the English Lake District is Karen Welberry's subject in chapter 5. While scholars have considered the influence of the district on Ransome's life and writing, Welberry goes further in addressing his rather interventionist refashioning of the district in these children's books. It is precisely Ransome's status as a children's writer, she points out, that has kept his environmental vision out of the popular and critical conversation. Whereas in the effort to make the district into a national park, Wordsworth and Ruskin have been praised (even "indigenized") for their conservationist vision of the Lakes, Ransome has been overlooked, not only because he wrote for children but also because his perspective on the district is more populist and less paranoid about development and mass tourism. In fact, Ransome works more from colonialist discourses of exploration and seafaring than from the solipsistic, meditative aesthetic of Wordsworth, which is at once more custodial and more socialist or "green." Welberry thus points to the conservatism of conservationism (be it essentialist or strategic) and to the tension between romantic ideology and children's literature (against the usual narrative of continuity). Of late, she concludes, the literature on the Lake District has been more sociologically oriented and thus less invested in this weirdly territorial ethic-aesthetic of conservation.

E. B. White's *Charlotte's Web*, suggests Lynn Wake in chapter 6, is not so much a simple children's pastoral as a "comedy of survival" and an "invitation to life's dance," a text that celebrates the web of life and the proximity of life and death.(As to the latter, she reminds us that his 1948 sketch "Death of a Pig" anticipates *Charlotte's Web*). Focusing on this famous text but also addressing his other writings for children, Wake urges us to consider White as (to borrow Thoreau's phrase) a "scribe of all nature," pointing to White's lifelong love for animals. Here, as elsewhere, we see the centrality of Thoreau's *Walden,* of which White said in 1953, "Every man, I think, reads one book in his life, and this one is mine." Wake suggests links between White's nature appreciation and his devotion to simplicity in composition, in effect treating *Elements of Style* as a companion book of sorts to *Charlotte's Web.*

In chapter 7, Nicole M. DuPlessis examines C. S. Lewis's *Chronicles of Narnia* from an ecocritical perspective—a perspective she admits is not usually associated with this author. "Although Lewis would not have allied himself explicitly with protoenvironmental movements," she writes, "the rhetorical force of a text may reach beyond the strict intentions of its author," and Lewis's "appreciation of the beauty of nature and concern for the transience of nature and often for humanity's part in nature's demise" is evident from his diaries and scholarly writing. Lewis turns to environmental settings and characters as a means of developing metaphors in his fantasy writings. But as DuPlessis also notes, "while Narnia is utopian, its environmental troubles are meant to translate to the real world." DuPlessis argues further that Lewis uses animal exploitation to protest colonial expansion and the displacement of indigenous people.

For many, the environmental movement in children's literature began in 1971 with Dr. Seuss's *The Lorax*. The book, apparently Seuss's own favorite, has become the canonical text of literary environmentalism and thus also the object of study in educational settings ranging from third-grade classrooms to university programs. In chapter 8, Bob Henderson, Merle Kennedy, and Chuck Chamberlin turn specifically to pedagogical applications of *The Lorax*, asking a series of important questions: "How best to present *The Lorax* in environmental education or social studies classes? How might the story itself provide for a respectful and generous hearing of both the entrepreneurial Once-ler and the environmental Lorax, one in which they are both moved in new directions of thought and action? How, for example, to move beyond the rhetoric of the Lorax and the Once-ler to ask who benefits from acting on each of these positions and how do these two frames of reference answer ontological questions of 'Who am I?' and 'Who am I becoming?' for children and adults?" In provisional answers, the authors offer both a useful discussion of pedagogy and an equally useful annotated bibliography of children's texts that might be taught alongside *The Lorax*.

Tara L. Holton and Tim B. Rogers offer in chapter 9 a nuanced analysis of the changes and continuities in nature representation in the Canadian children's periodical *Owl Magazine*, founded in 1976. Sampling one hundred issues from a twenty-year period, Holton and Rogers identify seven major themes or ideological emphases in the magazine, four of which have evolved or shifted over the years and three of which have remained fairly stable. For example, *Owl* has consistently emphasized the scientific study of nature and its alleged objectivity, even as there's been a marked decrease of what we might call the "wonder" or appreciation model of nature experience. At the same time, of late there's been a greater emphasis on caretaking and conservation. Holton and Rogers attempt to account for what appear to be contradictory messages for children and adults; for instance, children are encouraged to study nature while adults are urged to explore its beauty. At the essay's end, they express concern that scientific exploration has replaced embodied experience of nature for children—that, in short, reason has supplanted passion.

Arlene Plevin turns her attention in chapter 10 to the American nature magazine *Ranger Rick* and its ethic of "modulated anthropocentric stewardship." Examining the magazine's covers as well as its regular columns and articles, Plevin holds that *Ranger Rick* has been a forerunner of ecocriticism, particularly in its strategic attempt to emphasize the interdependence of human and animal life while also respecting the specificity—even the inaccessibility—of the latter. In the year 2000, Ranger Rick himself—that lovable raccoon—become more cartoonlike, more like a comic strip character; Plevin suggests that this shift represents an attempt to make the character more accessible to contemporary child readers. The magazine at once disrupts the "privilege of humanism" and positions nature within a more contemporary sort of humanism.

Kamala Platt's important essay, chapter 11, makes a dual contribution to this volume, challenging the consensus understanding of ecocriticism while offering fascinating readings of environmental justice books for children written outside of the States. Platt begins by pointing out the contributions of Chicano studies and feminism especially to a broader sociopolitical understanding of ecology, drawing together environmental concerns with work on social justice and human rights. Here again we see the importance of studying the legacy of racism and colonialism alongside the emergence of the so-called new world order. Her three texts are *The Story of Colors/La historia de los colores: A Folktale from the Jungles of Chiapas*, by the Subcomandante Insurgente Marcos of Mexico's Zapatista National Liberation Army (a text that received much publicity when the NEA rescinded its grant for political reasons); *The People Who Hugged the Trees*, an environmental folktale that motivated the Chipko movement in India; and *Rani and Felicity: The Story of Two Chickens*, an Indian environmental justice story that criticizes corporate capitalist agriculture, published by the Research Foundation for Science, Technology, and Natural Resource Policy in New Delhi. Platt acknowledges the challenge that each text takes up: how to represent troubling histories of cultural and environmental devastation "without shattering a sense of hope" among young readers.

Mothers, as Naomi Wood reminds us in chapter 12, are not always warm or reassuring, as popular conceits and some ecofeminist literature would have us believe. The icy northern mother is a staple of classic folktales and children's fantasy; she "is beautiful, frequently clad in furs, travels rapidly by flying or in a sled or some combination, and offers the child sublimity, rarified love, and power." Unlike the warm and nurturing earth mother, the cold mother demands submission, challenging but often sustaining humanity through her severity. But we should understand her not merely as some sort of archetype. As Wood explains, she arises as a trope as part of the Western imperialist project, alongside arctic exploration and "boreal" figuration, at once testifying to the warmer realities of culture and offering escape from them, a purer (necessarily more painful) form of nature contact. Drawing from Deleuze's *Coldness and Cruelty*, Wood reinterprets Hans Christian Andersen's Snow Queen, Charles Kingsley's Mother Carey, and the icy mothers—one true, one false—of Philip Pullman's *Dark Materials* trilogy, which develops an environmentalist atheology.

Michelle H. Martin's meditation on children's environmental music as a form of "eco-edu-tainment" in chapter 13 reminds us of how useful other cultural genres can be in helping children experience nature. Emphasizing the debts of such music to both American folk music and certain genres of children's writing, Martin offers close readings of songs that are alternately problematic and exemplary in their balance of instruction and amusement. Martin inveighs against more heavy-handed or didactic examples, arguing that the most successful such music—for example, the later work of the Banana Slug String Band—at once empowers children as agents of social change yet is more biocentric than anthropocentric in emphasis.(While reading, please feel free to sing along.)

Borrowing the familiar title "It's Not Easy Being Green" from the song made famous by Jim Henson's Kermit the Frog, Sidney I. Dobrin argues in chapter 14 that various Jim Henson projects, ranging from *Sesame Street* to *The Dark Crystal* to *Fraggle Rock* have done much to teach children (and adults) about their relationships with the natural world. Dobrin contends that Henson maintained an agenda of ecological literacy throughout his work. Dobrin reviews a number of Henson's more well-known works and offers an ecocritical/ecorhetorical glance at the ways in which Henson spread his message of ecological awareness via his Muppets—despite (or perhaps because of) their anthropomorphized depiction of animals, creatures, and monsters.

Susan Jaye Dauer, in chapter 15, considers how *Captain Planet and the Planeteers*—an "ecofictional cartoon series that was one of the most popular shows for children in the early 1990s"— "uses ecological fantasy to teach children about their responsibilities to the world, staking its claim to the didactic and giving its violence a moral purpose." Dauer reviews the ecological mission of the show, in terms of both its themes and its invitation to viewers to participate in local and global environmental activism. Specifically, Dauer explores the ways in which *Captain Planet and the Planeteers* teaches secondary lessons with each explicit lesson. According to Dauer, what is taught is empowerment. "The Power Is Yours," according to one of the series' mottos; individual action really matters. Dauer concludes: "If children are the last line of defense, teaching them to care and hoping that they will have, find, or create 'the Power' are inescapable extrapolations"—even if, as she notes, it's unfair and perhaps even dangerous to assume that they will clean up our mess.

Chapter 16, concluding our volume, is Kenneth B. Kidd's treatment of Animal Kingdom, the most recent theme park addition to the Walt Disney World resort in central Florida. Kidd reads the park as a contemporary exercise in colonialist storytelling, linking the "theming" of nature in multimedia and theme park formats to classic strategies of animal and human exhibition. The theme park more generally, he points out, at once imitates and evacuates the public sphere; Animal Kingdom in particular privatizes the public zoo but (like the zoo) keeps simple botanical and zoological education. He ends with an analysis of the most anomalous section of the park, DinoLand USA, drawing from the work of Joseba Gabilondo to suggest that perhaps imperialist-style "theming" may not always be the best way to represent or think critically about the wonderful world of corporate nature work.

Wild Things: Children's Culture and Ecocriticism examines the ways in which literature, media, and other cultural forms for young people address but are also shaped by nature, place, and ecology. We imagine our book as a cousin of sorts to collections such as Glotfelty and Fromm's *The Ecocriticism Reader* and Kahn and Kellert's *Children and Nature*. It is our hope that the essays gathered here provide an initiation or return to the wild places of childhood—both real and imagined.

WORKS CITED

Carpenter, Humphrey. *Secret Gardens: The Golden Age of Children's Literature.* London: Unwin Hyman, 1987.

Glotfelty, Cheryll. "Introduction: Literary Studies in an Age of Environmental Crisis." In *The Ecocriticism Reader: Landmarks in Literary Ecology,* ed. Cheryll Glotfelty and Harold Fromm. Athens: University of Georgia Press, 1996.

Goodenough, Elizabeth, ed. Parts 1 and 2, *Michigan Quarterly Review* (spring 2000); (summer 2000). Special issue: "Secret Spaces of Childhood."

Greenaway, Betty, ed. *Children's Literature Quarterly* 19:4 (1994–95). Special issue: "Ecology and the Child."

Kahn, Peter H., Jr. *The Human Relationship with Nature: Development and Culture.* Cambridge: MIT Press, 1999.

Kahn, Peter H., Jr., and Stephen R. Kellert. *Children and Nature: Psychological, Sociocultural, and Evolutionary Investigations.* Cambridge: MIT Press, 2002.

Kincaid, James. *Child-Loving: The Erotic Child and Victorian Culture.* New York: Routledge, 1992.

Krakauer, John. *Into the Wild.* New York: Doubleday, 1996.

Melson, Gail F. *Why the Wild Things Are: Animals in the Lives of Children.* Cambridge: Harvard University Press, 2001.

Myers, Gene. *Children and Animals: Social Development and Our Connections to Other Species.* Boulder, Colo.: Westview Press, 1998.

Nabhan, Gary Paul, and Stephen Trimble. *The Geography of Childhood: Why Children Need Wild Places.* Boston: Beacon Press, 1994.

Orr, David W. *Ecological Literacy: Education and the Transition to the Postmodern World.* Albany: State University of New York Press, 1992.

———. "Political Economy and the Ecology of Childhood." In *Children and Nature: Psychological, Sociocultural, and Evolutionary Investigations,* ed. Peter H. Kahn Jr. and Stephen R. Kellert, 279–303. Cambridge: MIT Press, 2002.

Phillips, Anne K., Carolyn Singer, and Naomi J. Wood, eds. *The American Nature Writing Newsletter: A Biannual Publication Devoted to the Study of Writing on Nature* 7:1 (1995). Special issue: "Children's Literature and the Environment."

Rahn, Suzanne. *The Lion and the Unicorn* 19 (December 1995). Special issue: "Green Worlds: Nature and Ecology." 149–70.

Rueckert, William. "Literature and Ecology: An Experiment in Ecocriticism." *Iowa Review* 9 (winter 1978): 71–86.

Sendak, Maurice. *Where the Wild Things Are.* New York: Harper, 1963.

Shaddock, Jennifer. "*Where the Wild Things Are*: Sendak's Journey into the Heart of Darkness." *Children's Literature Association Quarterly* 22 (winter 1997–98): 155–59.

Sigler, Carolyn. "Wonderland to Wasteland." *Children's Literature Association Quarterly* 19 (winter 1994–95):148–53.

U.S. Department of Education. *What Can I Teach My Young Child about the Environment?* Washington: Office of Educational Research and Improvement, 1997.

Wilson, E. O. *Biophilia.* Cambridge: Harvard University Press, 1984.

"He Made *Us* Very Much Like the Flowers"

Human/Nature in Nineteenth-Century Anglo-American Children's Literature

Maude Hines

In 1822, a London publishing company introduced *The Blue Flower; or, Henry's Shirt,* a book marketed to children. While the question-and-answer format that begins the book—a Socratic conversation between schoolboys and their teacher about the origin of linen—is typical of the period, the central story line is far from typical. The story narrates a flax plant's enslavement, its repeated torture, and its rebellion against being made into a shirt. It is the shirt/plant itself, rather than the boys or the teacher, who tells the story. The flax plant is a speaking subject who can feel pain and who identifies himself as a "slave." The story evokes sympathy for the plant through a first-person narrative in which the plant speaks to an audience addressed as "you." The second-person address is directed at the boys in the story's framing narrative, but at the same time it interpellates readers.[1] Those who wear linen "use" the flax plant at the expense of its suffering: "You may think I had already suffered enough, but I do assure you I had much more than this to endure before I became useful to you" (15–16).

In giving voice to its botanical narrator, *The Blue Flower* employs a rhetorical strategy that continues to be powerful today. The importance of "voice"—reclaiming voice, giving voice, achieving voice—has been stressed repeatedly in recent decades. This is especially true in discourse interested in the abolition of oppression in its various forms. A signal example is bell hooks's *Talking Back,* in which she proposes that the move "from silence into speech" is a "movement from object to subject": "Moving from silence into speech is for the oppressed, the colonized, the

16

exploited, and those who stand and struggle side by side a gesture of defiance that heals, that makes new life and new growth possible. It is that act of speech, of 'talking back,' that is no mere gesture of empty words, that is the expression of our movement from object to subject—the liberated voice" (9). Ecocritic Christopher Manes extends this logic to plants, arguing that a nature that is silenced is ripe for exploitation. Manes places nature within a framework that includes relationships between people by building on Michel Foucault's analysis of the rhetorical structure of power, adding nature to "silenced speakers such as women, minorities, children, prisoners, and the insane" (16).

This essay looks at depictions of relationships between children and nature in children's literature of the nineteenth century, in which plants are often given a voice in one way or another. Keeping in mind a central idea in Horkheimer and Adorno's *Dialectic of Enlightenment*—that the domination of nature is a model for the domination of human beings—I trace the routes through which the lessons these texts present about children's place in relation to nature extend to lessons in power and relationships between people.[2]

Nineteenth-century botanical children's literature connects two of the primary obsessions of the preceding romantic period: nature and children. Produced in the wake of the Industrial Revolution during a period of environmental devastation and deplorable child labor practices, these narratives depict beautiful nature, free children, and an intricate connection between them—a connection through language, through sympathetic analogy, and through botanical models for child rearing. In the pages that follow, I look at exemplary texts from this period, tracing the complicated (and intensely ambivalent) ways they negotiate the tensions between often harsh social realities and utopian child rearing and environmental visions through representations of the relationships between nature and children. Those relationships, in turn, extend to social place. From stories that seek to improve children by improving their treatment of plants and insects to those that narrate incredibly violent treatment of anthropomorphized plants to botanical imagery that classifies children by envisioning them as plants, connections between human beings and the rest of the natural world proliferate in nineteenth-century children's literature. By placing the botanical metaphors that pervade Golden Age "classics" in the context of other treatments of nature in children's literature of the period, this essay suggests new ways of reading those metaphors.

I begin here by examining stories that explicitly aim to instruct children in how to treat nature. Often, these books present children learning about nature from adult instructors. In *The Village Flower Show; or, Self-Denial in Little Things* (1877), a girl named Julia chases and angrily crushes a butterfly that "did not wish to be caught," despite her mother's having "forbidden her to catch and torment insects" (49). By the end of the story, Julia learns that it "is the very essence of cruelty, to torment an innocent creature for your amusement; and it is very sinful to torture any of God's creatures" (53). Julia's conversion is multivalent: she moves from disobedient to obedient, from heedless of the "wish[es]" of insects to respectful of them and, signally, from cruel to sympathetic. *The Village Flower Show* teaches sympathy for insects through Julia's conversion.

Garden Amusements: For Improving the Minds of Little Children (1816), chronicles a garden walk three children take with their teacher, who compares people and plants to teach lessons in human relationships and social ethics (for example, a vine leans against the wall as we lean against each other). The teacher emphasizes the importance of not making prisoners of "pretty creature[s]" or "put[ting them] to pain" (13). How the children treat plants and insects is an indication of their moral character. The narrator notes his pleasure in observing "the tenderness expressed by my little companions" and expresses a "hope that all my young readers will feel a like disposition towards all helpless creatures; for it is among the highest ornaments of our nature to be humane and kind" (13). Kindness here "ornaments" the child characters (as well as the "young readers" to whom the lesson is explicitly extended).

In a discussion of the "pornography of pain" in eighteenth- and nineteenth-century reform literature, Karen Halttunen points to reformers' belief that cruelty endangers the moral sensitivity of its perpetrators. She cites the nineteenth-century reformer Lyman Cobb, who wrote that "'children should not witness the butchering or slaughtering of animals' because 'it *hardens* their fine and originally kind feelings'" (323). In *Garden Amusements* and *The Village Flower Show*, children are saved along with insects and plants, their "originally kind feelings" preserved, their characters "ornament[ed]." These stories reflect the message of contemporaneous reform movements by cautioning children not to be cruel, saving children through the cultivation of their sympathetic faculties, and thus extending kindness toward butterflies to human beings. The stories further connect people with the rest of the natural world rhetorically: *Garden Amusements* extends the lesson in sympathy to "all helpless creatures"; *The Village Flower Show* extends it to "any of God's creatures" (13, 53).

While the plants in these stories are unfeeling (the teacher in *Garden Amusements* informs his pupils that "everything you behold here in the garden is full of life; though it is not conscious of feeling, as you and I are"[6]), other stories showed the helplessness of plants that feel, talk, suffer, and even plot revenge. These stories connect botanical and human suffering at the same time as they teach a paternalistic sympathy toward plants. "Coming Out," a story in the 1875 collection *Little Blue-Eyes and Other Field and Flower Stories,* begins with a conversation between anguished flowers that have been violently popped open by a spoiled boy before they were ready to bloom. The end of the story makes a clear comparison between the flowers' "coming out" and the boy's: "Yet it was some satisfaction to think, as [the Poppy] drooped, and faded, and died a failure of a flower, that it was possible that the same thing might happen to the meddlesome little boy. If they cut short his 'getting-ready time' and made him come out too soon, he might turn out just as ugly, and distorted, and unnatural a thing, he might be 'a failure of a boy.' Revenge is sweet, you know, even if it ought not to be" (102). The relationship between children and plants here is complex. "Coming Out" instructs children to be kind to flowers, equates children and flowers, and pits them against one another. It uses plants to access a "natural order," which is then applied to children. Plants here slip from wards to competitors to objects of study to analogies to surrogates to models.

The Blue Flower, the tale I outlined at the beginning of this essay, is among the most interesting of the stories presenting plants in these contradictory roles. Early in the narrative, the flax plant becomes the "slave of a Dutch merchant" who, as the plant tells it, "sold me [and put me and my] brothers and sisters, with all our friends and relations, and many thousands of our neighbours, into very large bags, in which we were tied up as close as possible. In this uncomfortable situation we had so little air, that no English boy or girl could have breathed . . . and after our last journey in Holland, we were put on board a ship, sent down to the darkest part of it, and never suffered to stir from our places until we got to England" (8–10). Although the flax plant is taken from Holland, its journey invokes the middle passage of African slaves through the enslavement of "thousands" of its neighbors, the darkness of the hold, and the ship's crowded and unhealthy conditions. Although they are Dutch, the flax plants' ability to survive in "so little air, that no English boy or girl could have breathed" recalls European notions about hardy Africans.

Even more bizarre and disturbing than the speaking and feeling plant's middle passage is the extreme pain and torture it endures as its story unfolds. The plant is "chained to [one] spot," "put between the teeth of a giant, who broke my bones to pieces," "beaten till I lost all my bones, and had nothing but skin left," and "drawn through [the] teeth" of "a great thing, stuck full of large spikes" (15–16). The torture is psychological as well as physical: "My master was pleased to say that I was nothing but outside, and that the only good part of me was my skin" (15). Paradoxically, then, this speaking subject is psychologically abused by a master who characterizes it as having no inside. This relationship mirrors the experience of African American slaves of the same period, who were valued for physical labor and denied interiority. And it exposes a central paradox of raciological slavery: privileging the outside—conferring object status to subjects—places value on the body, which is the very thing devalued in the first place. The metaphorical connection to human slavery is continued as the plant is sold from master to master: "My tormentors being tired of inflicting tortures, bound me up together, and let me rest in a very compact state. But I seldom stayed very long in the possession of one master" (16). Indeed, it is only through analogy with *American* chattel slavery that we can understand the plant's strange reference to England—the country in which it is enslaved—as "this happy land of liberty" (10).[3]

The Blue Flower ends with a violent battle of wills between the plant and some human beings, after which the plant becomes "Henry's shirt":

> The only thing I could do in my own defence was, to stir up a white froth, which came up to their elbows, flew over some of their aprons, and sometimes hid me from their sight. But, they to be revenged on me, put me into a pan and boiled me, hung me on thorns in the open fields to be blown about by the wind, then passed hot irons all over me, and left me by the fire till your mother took me away, and put me into her draw, where I remained until Sunday, when the maid washed you, and combed you, and put me on your back, and called me *"Henry's shirt."* (24)

The flax plant's story, as we have seen, is modeled on a general history of American chattel slavery, with its middle passage, quelled rebellion, torture, and bodily expenditure for the economic gain of the "master." The final "master," we can assume, is Henry himself—who can now count his own shirt among his servants. By the end of the story, the shirt has become "white," and the question that prompts the flax plant's story ("the lady . . . asked them how they thought shirts became white") is answered (7). The white/washed product at the end of the tale replaces the flax plant, erasing the labor that produced the commodity, at the same time as the plant's story restores that labor to memory. If the commodity replaces labor metaphorically, it replaces the plant directly, repeating in microcosm the effects of the Industrial Revolution on the natural environment.

Still, it would be a stretch to celebrate *The Blue Flower* as an unproblematic cautionary tale about the evils of commodity fetishism, industrialization, and slavery: the story domesticates slavery by inflicting it on plants rather than people, and Henry is happily wearing his shirt at the end of the book. More important, the plant's suffering is entertaining, if sadistic. In this way, *The Blue Flower*'s connection between botanical and human suffering is generic as well as metaphorical. *The Blue Flower* engages in a complex rhetorical play that toggles between caricature of and sympathy with slaves. By giving the flax plant a voice, the story gives it subject status. By representing the horrors of slavery being inflicted on a plant, it obscures the subject status of human slaves, in much the same way as that subject status was obscured by a pro-slavery rhetoric that referred to adult slaves as children.

The Blue Flower and stories like it participate in what Karen Halttunen has shown to be the other side of nineteenth-century reform literature's cultivation of sympathy, "the pornography of pain." Throughout reform literature's exhortations to kindness, "a wide range of victims—including British soldiers, American sailors, schoolboys, convicts, the insane, and African slaves—were endlessly flogged" (320). Like *The Blue Flower*, this reform literature was deeply ambivalent: "Humanitarian reform was a major cultural vehicle for the growing unacceptability of pain; it was also, inescapably, an expression and even a demonstration of the new obscenity of pain. Apologize though they might, the reformers were caught up in the same cultural linkages of revulsion with desire that fueled a wide range of popular literary explorations of pain" (330). The violence and ambivalence of reform literature directed at adults made its way into children's literature, transformed into representations of the relationships between children and plants or insects. Stories of plants in pain appealed to sympathy in children—themselves a target of humanitarian reform literature and low on the social order—in much the same way as stories of the pain of children and other human groups appealed to adult readers. These narratives share a rhetorical indebtedness that also extends to literature aimed at preventing cruelty to animals.

Attention to the humanitarian context in which children's stories of painful plants are produced illuminates connections between the suffering of plants, animals, and people in stories that do not make the connections as directly. *The Flower People,* published in 1862 by Horace Mann's wife, Mary Mann, presents the gathering of bouquets as intensely painful to flowers. In a conversation with a little girl, the flowers complain of another girl who "used to tear us up by handfuls, and carry us into the house where we could not see the sun nor drink the dew, but stood in glass vases many days, and there died for want of food" (12). The flowers compliment the human heroine, telling her, "you and your mamma are very kind, for you never pluck us from the bosom of our mother Earth, but let us live and die together here" (9). Granting the flowers a voice gives them subject status: they are able to narrate their preferences as well as dictate what is natural for them. At the same time, it elicits sympathy from readers and connects them with nature: flowers too have a mother, from whom they do not want to be separated.

Little Blue-Eyes and Other Field and Flower Stories, the collection in which "Coming Out" appears, contains several stories of plants that narrate their own pain. In "Little Blue-Eyes Down the Lane" a bird asks flowers to keep the location of her nest a secret from obnoxious boys who throw stones in attempts to disturb the fledglings and thereby locate and destroy the nest. Although the "brown hand" of one of the boys "came diving in among the flowers, and one of our little friends was all crushed up, and never lifted its head anymore . . . the Blue-eyes did not tell; in fact, they looked supremely unconscious" (9). In the same collection, "The Little Berry Boys" describes yellow berries who are at the mercy of "sharp beaks [that] pierce and peck, and pinch, and wound without paying the smallest attention to those wee, tiny, plaintive cries, which are the only way the flowers have of expressing pain. Indeed, those sounds are so infinitely tiny, that there are few ears . . . that ever hear them. Some people would persuade us that we are only fancying them, which people we do not condescend to answer" (26–27).

These stories, in which suffering plants "look . . . unconscious," cry out with "infinitely tiny" voices, or speak to characters only when emotionally moved, represent nature as voiced while explaining why readers might not hear talking plants. Even *The Blue Flower* presents the narrator's voice as anomalous: the flax plant says that its "parents, who have been dead many years, were . . . brought up and taken care of [in Holland], and, like the people of that country, they were very silent. Some people say, that my mother never spoke a word in her whole life" (8). The absence of plant sounds, these stories suggest, is not conclusive evidence of the absence of plant voices, and plants may speak in the world of child readers as well as in the world of the story. Indeed, conferring and then silencing voice is a powerful rhetorical move: it creates the possibility of imagining nature as voiced without the problem of human projection. Giving voice to plants, by granting them subject status, represents them as worthy of protection. The deleterious effects of silence were well recognized in the nineteenth century: the Society for Prevention of Cruelty to Animals called their organ *Our Dumb Animals,* evoking sympathy based on the inability of animals to speak in ways we recognize.

Humanitarian politics address the denial of conditions of selfhood. By giving nature a voice and then explaining why it can't be heard, these stories present one way of understanding plants as deserving of human sympathy and cooperation. The representations of the voices and pain of plants connect them ambivalently with human suffering: they call for humanitarian reform of subjects who can't speak for themselves while parodying human suffering by inflicting it on plants.

The lesson is further bifurcated as the stories teach child readers a paternalistic sympathy toward plants while conveying their dominant position over plants. Berries in "The Little Berry Boys" are persecuted not only by birds but by a boy who "was the doom of those beautiful Berries." The briars vow to "defend" the berries, while nettles vow to "avenge" them, both to no avail. The narrator has "a sort of impression that those scratched hands, though they are a great deal bigger now, would run the risk of worse things than scratches for the sake of pleasing that same younger sister" (28). The tone of the narrator's "impression" is clearly one of sympathy with the boy's noble act, a sympathy that renders the berries' silent pain simultaneously comical and disturbing:

> Poor little round Berries, they went home in a very resigned state of mind, for they knew that it is never of any use to grumble; that in fact, when you are in the power of one stronger than yourself, there is nothing better than to be silent and still. . . . They were torn apart, and pulled off their stalks. . . . And then—and oh, that was far the worst—they were stabbed through the very heart, and the dagger twisted round and round, until, when it came out at last, you could have seen all the secrets written on their minds—if they had any—as easily as possible. (28–29)

"The Little Berry Boys" is a highly ambivalent text. While the boy is a hero in the story, he is also characterized, however humorously, as a "tormentor"; while the berries are portrayed as having no "minds," they are capable of memory and repeatedly compared to readers: "And their tormentor never thought a bit about the heart-ache of each little yellow fellow. Let us hope they soon forgot it themselves, and never thought any more of the hedge, nor of their friends . . . nor of their own stalks, nor anything. When we are turned out of our old life, and old home, the best thing, if we want to be comfortable, is to forget it, isn't it? I am not quite sure, to tell the truth" (30). "The Little Berry Boys," like *The Blue Flower*, connects the mock suffering of plants to the real suffering of human beings, both by its generic connection to reform literature for adults and by its connection to readers through the use of the first-person plural. The narrator's ambivalence—"I am not quite sure"—makes the story's line of sympathy unclear.

The line of sympathy is clearer in "The Fight." Here two crabs fight to the death, losing claws and arms along the way, while a piece of sea-weed laughs at them until it is pulled and torn away to the depths of the ocean. While the seaweed is capable of laughter, it "didn't mind a bit if the little live creatures came and nibbled at it. Almost all things, except human things, are made to be eaten, some alive, some after they are dead, and they don't grumble, any of them. No more than did the Sea-weed" (50).

This notion of having been "made" (as in "made to be eaten") per-vades this literature, and is an important ingredient in a hierarchy that extends to relationships between people, an extension that renders *The Blue Flower*'s treatment of slavery that much more troubling. In *The Village Flower Show*, the protagonist's mother tells her, "He who made you able to run made the insect to fly; the same sun shines for both of you; you breathe the same air, in one sense, we may say that birds and insects are more especially the objects of God's care, as He himself feedeth them, while you, for example are fed and cared for by others under Him, and not directly by God" (53). Since Julia dissects the butterfly at the end of the story and not the other way around, readers are likely to extrapolate that while birds and insects are privileged "in one sense," humans are privileged in all others.

The hierarchical relationship between nature and humankind is more explicit in *The Blue Flower*, where the master-servant relationship is discussed at length with reference not just to one plant but to the earth itself. Earth, the flax plant's "nurse," also speaks in the first person:

> Indeed I have been so much abused by man, that my disposition is very much changed. I was originally formed to be his servant, but he, without any fault of mine, made me his master; and, in the struggle which has taken place, in

order to make man acknowledge no master but him that made him, I have been overflowed with water, and disturbed by fire. But notwithstanding all this, it is my unwearied endeavour to do him good, and I do no harm to any one who does not make a bad use of me. (11–12)

This section extends the relation between Henry and his shirt to "man" and the earth, with the latter triply subordinate: as female, as servant, and, importantly, as natural—below us in a hierarchy reminiscent of the Great Chain of Being. "Man," being superior to (and indeed separated from) the rest of nature, is meant to control a female earth—"Mother Nature"—an earth "formed [by God] to be his servant." Giving the earth a voice here naturalizes a hierarchy in which man is superior, and his superiority is further naturalized through God's will. If, as Adorno and Horkheimer assert, men want to learn how to use nature "in order to dominate it and other men" (4), these children's stories show that domination of the earth is natural, as is the domination of certain groups of people. At the same time, they encourage the kind treatment of nature and, by extension, of people.

Hierarchies naturalized by notions of being "made for it," God's will, and "natural" taxonomies extend to human beings most explicitly in stories where plants appear as metaphors rather than characters. Like "Coming Out," the tale in which the boy spoils flowers as his parents spoil him, these stories use plants as indicators of a child's character— and often of his place. In a brief survey of Victorian child-rearing manuals, James Kincaid shows that what he calls "the child botanical" was a central model for child rearing in Victorian culture. Little "budding" adults were endlessly "cultivated" in "nurseries," where they "bloomed" and "blossomed." For Kincaid, the trope of the "nursery" was a "model . . . for evacuating 'the child' and exalting 'the parent'":

> We see the term [nursery] everywhere: "Home is the grand nursery for virtues"; or, more extensively, "We would rather consider the nursery as a garden into which trees and flowers of various kinds have been transplanted in their wild state, to be developed into all the beauty of which their nature, and the highest perfection of cultivation make them susceptible." We notice in this last analogy, otherwise so pleasing, a buried but noxious suggestion that the child/plant has a "nature," an inner being we can only help perfect. Such a suggestion is, happily, quite uncommon in this widespread connection of children with plants, a connection so pervasive that the same word, nursery, can be used for the place where both are brought up and managed. (90)

Perhaps this suggestion is "quite uncommon" in manuals for parents, but in children's fiction it is par for the course. If botanical metaphors proliferated in nineteenth-century child-rearing manuals, they grew like weeds in fiction, bringing with them the problems and ambivalence of other literature that taught children about their relationship to the natural world. They also accessed the sympathetic treatment of nature in these texts, extending that sympathy through analogy and metaphor to children. Contrary to Kincaid's claims about child-rearing manuals, botanical children's fiction from the period happily used plants to describe the "nature" of children—especially as that nature suggested the social places in which they belonged. Attention to how the botanical trope works in children's literature leads to a reading of Kincaid's quote that places more emphasis on the "various kinds" of children as "trees and flowers" than Kincaid does: botanical children in fiction were by no means "evacuated," if they were in child-rearing manuals. To paraphrase the famous phrase, botany was destiny.

The Wayside Flower (1877) is the story of poor Cora, who is a "daisy" of a girl, and her relationship to the rich but deathly ill Nettie, who is a "rose" of a girl. Nettie's doctor tells Cora, "I would call you a tiny flower growing along the wayside . . . if they are fresh and sweet, almost everyone loves them. God made them, Cora, as well as the roses and more splendid flowers. He made *us* very much like the flowers: some of us are rich and some poor; some high and some low, but *we can all blossom for God*" (25). The doctor's direct analogy between flowers and girls extends his artificial floral taxonomy of splendor to Cora and Nettie: Nettie is "more splendid" than Cora as roses are "more splendid" than daisies. The hierarchy we saw in *The Blue Flower* (in which the earth is "formed to be [the] servant" of God's "favourite creature, man") is here figured as one in which the rose is favored—apparently by consensus— above the daisy. This hierarchy is used in turn as a model for the domination of some people by others: "some of us are rich and some are poor; some high and some low" (25), and this difference is as falsely natural as the difference between the appearance of different types of flowers. The floral metaphor naturalizes class distinctions.

The plot of the story reads like a chapter of Janeway's *Token for Children*: Cora reads for Nettie and they become friends (at least to the extent that Nettie no longer insists that she be called "Miss Nettie"). Nettie gets well, but Cora gets sick and dies, having "bloomed very patiently in [her] little spot by the wayside." On her deathbed, "she turned her eyes toward the window, as if to take a last look at the green fields. . . . The little wayside flower had gone to bloom for ever in God's heavenly garden" (59). Cora learns her lessons through botanical models and is rewarded in heaven, if not on earth.

Made for It; or, The Wild Flower Transplanted (inscribed 1906), is about a girl who "was a wild flower, and flourished amid all the changing humours of nature, who, however rough, was to her kind and motherly, just as the untended children of the earth—weeds let men call them, if they will—grow healthily in their native soil" (7). The poor girl gets "transplanted" into a rich woman's home but finds herself unsuited for the life of a "garden flower." Her benefactors take her back to the impoverished life for which she is better suited, taking more care with a second transplantation: "We must loosen the earth, and remove it gently, with just a little of this soil it has been growing in of late around it. Now that the rose has been in the conservatory so long, we must shelter it a little on first setting it again in the open air" (82–83).

This text, printed around the time of the first child labor bill, uses botanical taxonomies to naturalize class differences in human beings, class differences that likely reflected the economic distance between child readers of these stories and those described in them. The "wild flower transplanted" learns not to blame the rich for poverty, telling those of her class who "grumble in her hearing about the pride of the rich . . . and their carelessness of the poor" that "you would not like their kind of life better than they would like yours. You would feel fettered and chained and burdened by many things you envy in the distance. I was not, and you are not, *made for it*" (87; italics in original). This notion of being "made for it" echoes the doctor's sermon in *The Wayside Flower* ("He made *us* very much like the flowers: some of us are rich and some poor") and is rendered even more troubling in its taxonomic claims by attendant metaphorical references to slavery. These stories simultaneously place humans above nature and use botanical metaphors to naturalize divisions among humankind, a naturalization that hearkens back to the enslaved flax plant-become-servant in *The Blue Flower*. Another function of the botanical metaphor is to gender the subject, referencing the Victorian feminine language of flowers through a coding of girls as plants and flowers. The protagonists in stories that use botanical models are almost exclusively girls, while those who pick and mutilate the flowers tend to be boys.[4]

We find botanical children not only in obscure stories like *The Wayside Flower* and *Made for It*; they also populate what we've come to think of as "classics" of the period. Louisa May Alcott's *Rose in Bloom* (1876) and Margaret Sidney's *The Five Little Peppers and How They Grew* (1881) compare children to plants in their very titles, and the metaphors continue in the texts. Alcott's *Jack and Jill* (1880) is full of botanical children, exemplified by the character Merry, who is "a tea-rose in a field of clover and dandelions" (87). In Frances Hodgson Burnett's *The Secret Garden* (1911), the child characters blossom along with the garden they bring back to life, as the boy in "Coming Out" fails like the flowers he opens too soon. In Kate Douglas Wiggin's *Rebecca of Sunnybrook Farm* (1902), Rebecca needs sunshine and dirt in order to grow. The list goes on and on—indeed, it extends to contemporaneous adult fiction.[5] This brief survey of lesser-known texts suggests that the botanical metaphor, more than a description, is shorthand for assumptions about class and character.

While the botanical models in Golden Age children's literature might seem insignificant today, attention to tropes in now forgotten texts that were familiar to the original readers of those classics shows us the power, ubiquity, and ambivalence of those models. Perhaps the stories in which nature and children are connected only metaphorically survived as "classics" because they are more comfortable for later readers than the animistic ones, which forced readers to think of themselves as actually connected, at least through language, to their environments.[6] Botanical models access and borrow both from sympathy for plants encouraged by anthropomorphic representation of speaking nature in stories like *The Blue Flower* and from imperatives to treat plants and insects gently in stories like *Garden Amusements* to encourage the same sympathy for (and in) children. This follows the path of real-life reform movements, where animal rights reform tended to precede human rights reform. Indeed, as Kincaid's research suggests, tending animals and raising gardens made the idea of "tending" children thinkable in the first place.[7]

On the other hand, this literature that advocated treating the natural world gently was written in tandem with increasing devastation of the natural world—a kind of compensatory romanticism. Literary analogies between children and plants taught children their places in the world, often problematically. These places were taught to readers not only as children but also as classed, raced, and gendered subjects, as plant taxonomies extended to human beings. This literature suggests that children should be treated delicately, *like* flowers, while indicating that some children are naturally poor and unsuited for a better life. The texts collectively show a real ambivalence about the nature/nurture relationship as well as of the nature/human relationship. The plants in these texts are talking (or perhaps more accurately ventriloquizing) even when they are silent—the treatment and characterization of plants speak volumes about the treatment and characterization of human beings.

NOTES

I want to thank Rita Smith and the Baldwin Library of Historical Children's Literature at the University of Florida for access to primary sources for this project. Thanks to Kenneth Kidd, Maria DePriest, Ann Marie Fallon, Malini Schueller, Patricia Schechter, Peter Carafiol, Jennifer Ruth, Marcia Klotz, Leerom Medovoi, Greg Jacob, and Rayna Kalas (who was nearly to blame for this piece being called "Stamen Alive") for their valuable suggestions. Thanks also to Ashlie Miller, a student in my Golden Age of Children's Literature class at the University of Florida, whose research project brought *The Blue Flower* to my attention.

1. I am referring here to the Althusserian notion of interpellation, in which we are hailed as certain types of subjects—in this case as linen-wearers (and by association as the most recent masters of the plant). See Althusser 168.

2. In *Dialectic of Enlightnment*, "nature" works in the dual sense of human nature and the natural world. Throughout this essay, I make a distinction between human beings and "nature," or "the natural world" to emphasize the separation between the two, paradoxically implied in these texts by the use of metaphors and analogies that link them.

3. At the time of *The Blue Flower*'s publication, English audiences welcomed stories of escaped American slaves, for whom England was indeed, by comparison, a "happy land of liberty."

4. Even in "Coming Out," the comparison of plants and children is gendered female: the boy hears a girl accused of coming "out too soon" before the same complaint is levied against him, at which point he objects that "boys don't come out." In *The Flower People*, a rich girl picks and kills flowers, while a poor one is more sympathetic—reflecting, like the gendering of floral comparisons, a connection between nature and humans low on the social order.

5. The "hothouse flower" is an especially common attribution, although Crane's "Maggie, a Girl of the Streets" "blossom[s] in a mud puddle" (141), and despite her eponymous simplicity, James's Daisy Miller is not regarded "as a wholly unspotted flower" (762–63).

6. *The Wonderful Wizard of Oz* and *Through the Looking Glass* are two Golden Age "classics" that have talking plants. Carroll's flowers and Baum's trees cause their female protagonists to lose their way.

7. Complicatedly, these texts use plants to create sympathy for children, who are at the same time encouraged to be sympathetic to plants. This circular logic reflects the class disparity between literate child readers of these texts and children whose conditions made them targets for reform movements. It follows the pattern of animal reform movements, which appealed to human beings from some groups while paving the way for movements to reform the treatment of others. Halttunen demonstrates that efforts to prevent animal cruelty tended to precede similar efforts toward humanitarian reform in slavery, child rearing, and education (319). Notably, the first court case of an adult tried for physical abuse of a child was brought forward by the founder of the Society for Prevention of Cruelty to Animals, an organization that predated similar societies organized on behalf of children—Henry Bergh, who founded the SPCA in 1866, began the Society for the Prevention of Cruelty to Children (SPCC) on behalf of Mary Ellen Wilson in 1874, the year the New York Supreme Court tried her case.

WORKS CITED

Alcott, Louisa May. *Jack and Jill.* Boston: Little, Brown, 1928 (1880).

——. *Rose In Bloom.* Boston: Little, Brown, 1927 (1876).

Althusser, Louis. "Ideology and Ideological State Apparatuses (Notes toward an Investigation)." In *Lenin and Philosophy and Other Essays.* London: New Left Books, 1971.

Baum, L. Frank. *The Wonderful Wizard of Oz.* Belmont, Calif.: Wadsworth, 1991 (1900).

The Blue Flower; or, Henry's Shirt. London, 1822.

Burnett, Fances Hodgson. *The Secret Garden.* New York: Penguin, 1993 (1911).

Carroll, Lewis. *"Alice's Adventures in Wonderland" and "Through the Looking Glass."* New York: Oxford, 1998 (1865).

Crane, Stephen. "Maggie, a Girl of the Streets." In *Great Short Works of Stephen Crane.* New York: Harper, 1968 (1893).

Garden Amusements: For Improving the Minds of Little Children. New York: Samuel Wood & Sons, 1816.

Halttunen, Karen. "Humanitarianism and the Pornography of Pain in Anglo-American Culture." *American Historical Review* 100:2 (1995): 303–34.

Harrison, Jennie. *The Wayside Flower.* New York: Dodd, Mead, 1877.

hooks, bell. *Talking Back: Thinking Feminist, Thinking Black.* Boston: South End Press, 1989.

Horkheimer, Max and Theodore Adorno. *Dialectic of Enlightenment.* Trans. John Cumming. New York: Continuum, 1993 (1944).

James, Henry. *Daisy Miller.* In James H. Pickering, ed., *Fiction 100.* New York: MacMillan, 1988 (1903).

Kincaid, James. *Child-Loving: The Erotic Child and Victorian Culture.* New York: Routledge, 1994.

Little Blue-Eyes and Other Field and Flower Stories. London: Seeley, Jackson, & Halliday, 1875.

Made for It; or, The Wild Flower Transplanted. London: James B. Knapp, [1906?].

Manes, Christopher. "Nature and Silence." In Cheryll Glotfelty and Harold Fromm, eds., *The Ecocriticism Reader: Landmarks in Literary Ecology.* Athens: University of Georgia Press, 1996 (15–29).

Mann, Mary. *The Flower People.* Cambridge: Cambridge University Press, 1862.

Sidney, Margaret. *The Five Little Peppers and How They Grew.* New York: Books Inc., 1940 (1881).

"The Village Flower Show; or, Self-Denial in Little Things" and Other Stories. Edinburgh: Oliphant, 1877.

Wiggin, Kate Douglas. *Rebecca of Sunnybrook Farm.* New York: Random House, 1957 (1902).

"Foundation-Stones"

Natural History for Children in *St. Nicholas Magazine*

Kaye Adkins

St. Nicholas: A Magazine for Young Folks was not the earliest magazine for children, but many critics have argued that it was the best in the nineteenth century. Parents and children apparently agreed: during the last quarter of the nineteenth century, it was one of the most widely read and circulated children's magazines. The magazine was founded in 1873 along principles its editor, Mary Mapes Dodge, laid out in an article in *Scribner's Monthly. St. Nicholas* aimed to offer children a magazine that recognized their natural curiosity and intelligence and their special ways of learning about the world ("Children's Magazines" 352).

In a eulogy for Dodge that appeared in *St. Nicholas* in 1905, her assistant William Fayal Clarke remembered that Dodge had always loved writing. She was the daughter of James J. Mapes, an influential member of New England literary circles whose friends included Horace Greeley and William Cullen Bryant, and in her teens she had helped her father ("a scholar, and inventor, a scientist, and an author") with his essays and educational pamphlets (1060). To support herself and her sons after the death of her husband, Dodge began writing professionally, first publishing essays and stories for adults, then stories for children. In 1870, following the success of her children's book *Hans Brinker; or, The Silver Skates,* she became associate editor in charge of the juvenile department of *Hearth and Home,* a weekly family newspaper. Under her guidance, the department became a prominent feature of the paper, and circulation grew (Clarke 1063).

When the publishers of *Scribner's* decided to develop a magazine for children, they sought Dodge's advice. They wanted a children's periodical that would share *Scribner's* view that magazines were more than commercial ventures—they should improve society, provide moral and ethical guidance, and help the growing middle class, as well as immigrants, share the values of "patriotism, respect for the family, hard work, self-reliance, and social concern" in addition to connecting religion and science (Gannon and Thompson 104–5). They asked Dodge to send them a letter describing her vision of a children's periodical. As Dodge wrote the letter, it became a manifesto declaring children's preferences and needs in literature.

In the letter, which appeared in *Scribner's* in July 1873, Dodge argues that a good children's magazine should show its readers the world accurately, without distortions or heavy-handed moralizing. Children's magazines suffered because "we edit for the approval of fathers and mothers and endeavor to make the child's monthly a milk-and-water variety of the adult's periodical. But in fact the child's magazine needs to be stronger, truer, bolder, more uncompromising than the other" ("Children's Magazines" 352). Dodge believed that children were naturally curious and eager to learn, but that a magazine must be entertaining if children were to learn anything from it. In his eulogy for Dodge, Clarke remembered that she wanted "to make child-readers happy first, and through this happiness to lead them on to higher and nobler living,—this was her aim and work" (1060). Dodge declares that there should be "no sermonizing, no wearisome spinning out of facts, no rattling of the dry bones of history" (353). Instead, the "cheer" of a children's periodical "must be the cheer of birdsong, not of condescending editorial babble" (352). Dodge argues that children are as interested in the modern world as adults and need preparation for it, but they do not read and respond to information as adults do. They need to feel that they are in their own world, where they are free to find "odd bits and treasures" of information on their own (353). To this end, everything in a good children's magazine must be as accurate and realistic as possible. This means that "harsh cruel facts" must be presented truthfully, even as the emphasis remains on pleasant things (354). Dodge believed that children would welcome a magazine that was not condescending, that gave them credit for intelligence, wit, and imagination. She sums up her philosophy this way: "Wells and fountains there may be in the grounds [of the world of the young], but water must be drawn from the one in a right, trim, little bucket; and there must be no artificial coloring of the other, nor great show cards about it, saying, 'Behold! a fountain!' Let its flow and sparkle proclaim it" (354).

Scribner's publishers were so impressed by Dodge's philosophy and her work at *Hearth and Home* that they asked her to edit their new magazine. She chose the name *St. Nicholas* because, as she explained in the opening letter to her readers, the magazine would, like St. Nicholas himself, be "the especial friend of Young Americans," treating subjects "fair and square" and seeking to cast "a light upon the children's faces that lasts from year to year" ("Dear Girl and Boy" 1). Her philosophy, emphasizing a child's natural curiosity, had broad appeal: as *St. Nicholas's* circulation reached 70,000, but actual readership was much higher, as Dodge urged children, parents, and teachers to share the magazine.

As editor of *St. Nicholas*, Dodge exercised control over every aspect of the magazine, from layout to detailed planning of the contents to negotiating with authors and artists. The contributors *St. Nicholas* attracted include many of the most prominent authors of the nineteenth century—from both sides of the Atlantic. Through her own reputation and the reputation of the magazine itself, Dodge was able to convince writers like William Cullen Bryan, Henry Wadsworth Longfellow, John Greenleaf Whittier, and Alfred Lord Tennyson to contribute. One of her policies was to serialize longer works over a year, so that when the bound annual volumes were sold for Christmas, they would contain at least one complete novel. These serials included Louisa May Alcott's *Eight Cousins,* Frances Hodgson Burnett's *Little Lord Fauntleroy,* and Mark Twain's *Tom Sawyer Abroad.* Other authors for *St. Nicholas* included Theodore Roosevelt, Bret Harte, John Burroughs, Sarah Orne Jewett, and Jack London. Dodge also insisted on excellent illustrators— Howard Pyle, Maxfield Parrish, and Frederick Remington were among the artists whose work she published. When Rudyard Kipling asked Dodge if he could write for the magazine, she replied, "Do you think you are equal to it?" He responded to the challenge with "Rikki-Tikki-Tavi" and "Toomai of the Elephants," eventually contributing many other stories and poems.

Dodge realized that the success of the magazine would increase with the direct involvement of its young readers, so she invited their participation in puzzles and letter writing. Certificates and cash rewards for excellent writing were given to young contributors; Robert Benchley, Stephen and William Benét, William Faulkner, F. Scott Fitzgerald, Ring Lardner, Eudora Welty, E. B. White, and Rachel Carson are among those whose first published works appeared in *St. Nicholas.*

St. Nicholas is noteworthy for its additions to the usual mix of stories, poems, and inspirational biographies. To prepare children for life in the modern world, each issue contained articles on travel, history, geography, biography, science, and practical matters. Natural history articles are prominent, in part because of Dodge's interest in natural history and in encouraging children to learn science through experience. Children are encouraged to be open to the world around them at all times and to find ways to enjoy nature.

The importance of experiencing the world, as opposed to merely reading about it, is emphasized by many writers. The nature essays of John Burroughs, for example, one of the most popular writers of the late nineteenth century, encouraged people to go on long rambles, and his articles on ornithology helped make bird-watching a popular hobby. In one article, Burroughs explains the importance of "Observing Little Things." He offers examples of the kind of observation that he wishes children to practice. Close observation can help children make connections and understand evolution. For example, Burroughs notes that the young of the bluebird have speckled breasts like those of the thrush, and its song is like that of the olive-backed thrush. From this, he suggests that the birds may be related. Burroughs was best known for his knowledge of birds, but to make his point about small details, "Observing Little Things" focuses on spiders. He describes his observations of the wolf spider and the sand spider and how they interact with their environment. He explains the precautions he takes to avoid being bitten; describes an experiment with a wolf spider he kept for a few days to see how it reacted to flies, wasps, and grasshoppers; and outlines how he studies the reactions of these small animals in their habitats. These examples make his point that much can be learned by observing the smallest things in nature. To illustrate that "hasty observations" can be misleading, he dispels the myth that the number of spider webs in the grass in the morning can be used to predict the weather. (It was popularly believed that many webs indicated coming good weather.) Burroughs points out that careful observation reveals that the number of webs does not change but the amount of dew on the webs, which makes them visible, does. He admonishes, "We all need to be on our guard against hasty observations and rash conclusions. Look again, and think again, before you make up your mind" (763). Close scientific study can help children learn the truth about nature.

In a later article about wildflowers, Burroughs gives other reasons for looking closely at the natural world: "Most young people find botany a dull study. So it is as taught from the text-books in the schools; but study it yourself in the fields and woods, and you will find it a source of perennial delight" ("Wildflowers" 583). Burroughs also suggests a practical reason for studying nature: "When one is stranded anywhere in the country in the season of flowers or birds, if he feels any interest in these things, he always has something ready at hand to fall back upon. . . . The tedium of an eighty-mile drive which I lately took was greatly relieved by noting the various flowers by the roadside" (585).

Ernest E. Thompson contributed several articles to *St. Nicholas*. Thompson wrote and illustrated *Wild Animals I Have Known* and many similar books for children under the name Ernest Thompson Seton. A friend of Teddy Roosevelt, he founded the Woodcraft Indians, which became the model for the Boy Scouts. In a typical article, he encourages children to take up fly-fishing, especially for bass since they are more common than trout. The value of this activity for boys and girls (the illustration shows a girl fishing while boys stand by with a net) is partly in its enjoyment but even more in its opportunity for studying the habits of animals such as birds or muskrats ("Fly-Fishing" 787). Thompson encourages children to practice quiet, careful observation while they are fishing.

Thompson's "Tracks in the Snow" shows children how to learn about the lives of animals through indirect observation. He includes illustrations of tracks with explanations of what they are and what they mean, pointing out that they are "a record, not only of the animals, but of their actions" (339). For example, one set of tracks tells the story of a deer walking, pawing for acorns, and listening to sounds with one foot lifted. Another set reveals the rather dramatic tale of a hare running back and forth in panic and then being killed. The tracks indicate that the predator was an owl. More detective work reveals that the bird has settled on a nearby branch.

Articles by naturalists explain how children can become naturalists themselves, using observation as an important tool. In 1877, William Howitt, a British naturalist and explorer, published "A Letter to a Young Naturalist." At this time, "naturalists" gauged themselves by the number of specimens they had collected and preserved. The larger their collections, the better their skills. Children were usually limited to collecting butterflies and other insects. For many children, it could be difficult to amass the large collections of specimens that nineteenth-century naturalists did, but Howitt does not want this to discourage them. The true rewards of the study of nature are not physical specimens but "the consciousness of all the freshness, loveliness, and indescribable harmonies of the magnificent world in which God has given them places to live for our mutual pleasure and advantage" (155). Howitt encourages children to become amateur naturalists, arguing that the study of natural history does not require special training. "I do not make collections of any kind of natural history objects. If I can be called a naturalist at all, it must be a very *natural* one, for I never studied any branch of natural history in books, excepting botany, and only the botany of the British Isles" (154). But that study provides him healthy exercise and fresh air, as it does for children, while the ability to recognize British plants allows "a good guess" at foreign plants in his travels. He has made himself familiar with the appearance, habits, and songs of birds, a practice that children should adopt: "I never hear a song or a twitter of one, as I am walking, anywhere, but I recognize it as the voice of an old friend, to the great astonishment of my human friends. Such are the pleasures of an habitual intimacy with the works of God in their wonderful world." Perhaps for the benefit of parents and the goals of *Scribner's,* Howitt suggests that "in classifying and preserving . . . various specimens [children will] keep alive in [their hearts] all the poetry of nature connected with these innumerable and charming inventions of the Great Mechanist" (155).

Howitt's examples are drawn from all over the world, from South America and Australia as well as Europe. The treasures of nature are illustrated with a story of finding a nest of "splendid warblers" while looking for gold in South America. He and his companions are so entertained by the birds that they decide to wait until the young have left the nest rather than disturb it to dig for gold. When he returns to the site, someone else has been there and dug out sixteen pounds of gold, but Howitt writes that "we did not regret it, for [the birds] had given us more than the amount in amusement" (156). Following Dodge's emphasis on speaking directly to children instead of down to them, Howitt closes with the article with a direct appeal: "May you live, learn, enjoy, and make known much of the hidden knowledge of God's humble creatures.—Your friend, William Howitt" (157).

Mary Mapes Dodge did not intend for children to be merely passive observers of the world around them. She wanted to encourage their active curiosity and experimentation. She wanted them to feel comfortable asking questions. To encourage this, she worked with Harlan Ballard to found the Agassiz Association, announcing it in *St. Nicholas* in 1880. Named for Louis Agassiz, a well-known Harvard professor who popularized science through his lectures, the Agassiz Association offered a regular column in the magazine, a place for children to send questions about nature and to share their observations of the natural world. Local chapters of the association were set up all over the country and beyond, and by May 1883, the organization reported that it had five thousand members in places ranging from Brunswick, Maine, to Dallas, Texas, to Greeley, Colorado, to Valpariso, Chile. Experts, such as a botanist from Salt Lake City, a mineralogist from Webster Groves, Missouri, a zoologist from the American Museum of Natural History, and an entomologist from the Academy of Natural Sciences in Philadelphia, volunteered to answer children's questions in the feature. Readers were instructed in proper methods of collection and identification of specimens, and in how to set up experiments to answer questions like "Can insects hear?" ("Report" 558). The association is often mentioned in articles in the magazine, as when Ernest E. Thompson notes, "Those readers who are members of the Agassiz Association will have learned that no one can safely undertake to identify any strange bird or beast, without having it in hand to measure and to examine; but it must not therefore be forgotten that valuable knowledge may be acquired by watching the living creatures from a distance, by means of a telescope" ("Pintail" 826). The Agassiz Association eventually outgrew *St. Nicholas* and founded a publication of its own.

Of course, children did not have the far-reaching opportunities to make firsthand observations that adults did, and since Dodge's goal was to prepare them for life in the modern world, *St. Nicholas* includes articles about unfamiliar animals and plants. These articles are also models for the kind of work done by good naturalists. They are characterized by accuracy, detail, and appropriate use of scientific language. The descriptions of animals are written from observations of specimens in collections as well as from field observations of their behavior, while the illustrations of many of the exotic animals, such as manatees, aardvarks, and chimpanzees, are drawn from live models in the Central Park Zoo.

When children are introduced to unfamiliar animals such as the hornbill, care is given to provide accurate, scientific descriptions, making these clear to children. For example, describing the bird's most prominent feature, its bill, the author notes that "though seemingly heavy and unwieldy, the bill of the hornbill is very light, being composed of light cellular tissue, resembling in this respect the skull of the elephant; and the walls of thin bone are so fragile, that in dried specimens it may be crushed in the hand. The edge of the mandibles or beaks are very sharp, frequently breaking off and being renewed" (Beverly 151). Notice the use of language like "cellular tissue," the comparison to the elephant's skull, which had been described in a previous article, the description of study of a specimen (crushing the bill) and of the bird in nature (breaking off and renewing the beak). Writers are careful to separate fact from speculation; for example, the statement "It is said that the age of the bird may be ascertained from the wrinkles on its bill, as the age of a cow is sometimes told from the wrinkles of her horns" is clearly labeled as supposition, not fact.

Other articles describe animals that are common but often overlooked, like "The Water-Bear" or tardigrade. As with articles about larger animals, the article about the microscopic water bear is based entirely on observation. It opens with a description of how the author finds these creatures, making it clear that they are accessible to children. Once at a freshwater pond, "all that the successful hunter needs is a stout stick (a forked one is best), to pull the plants that harbor [the water bear] from the pond, and a supply of vials to hold the water and plants" (Treat 274). The author explains how to mount slides for observation of the animals and describes their appearance and behavior in detail. She includes one story that bears out John Burroughs's warnings about the importance of careful observations and avoiding hasty conclusions. She notes that water bears slip out of their skins as they outgrow them, but that she did not learn this immediately. "For a time I was completely puzzled on seeing these old dresses standing about as if inflated, and thought they must be skeletons—that the body had decomposed and left only the skin; but after awhile I caught one slipping out of his dress, and the mystery was explained." In keeping with the policy of accuracy and honesty, Treat admits that the illustration that accompanies the article is not completely accurate. "The portrait does not look quite natural; he would not keep still long enough to have his portrait taken, and so had to be held fast between two glasses, and this flattened him somewhat." Instead of "improving" the drawing to make it more lifelike, the author draws directly from observation, in the process showing children the problems a naturalist might encounter when studying microscopic life.

The natural history articles in *St. Nicholas* not only include detailed descriptions of animals and of how they interact with their environment, many of the articles go one step further to explain how animals adapt to their environments, drawing on Darwin's theories to explain how they are formed by their environments and to examine their place in the ecosystem. For example, the belted kingfisher is built "to be a fisherman," with small feet to perch on twigs that hang over water, a large heavy head that "serves to balance and carry him with great swiftness in his downward, arrow-like plunges," and a long, rough-edged bill that helps to hold fish (Smith 810). Another article describes how vireos in one area adapted a strategy of building nests in two levels to foil cowbirds. They would build their hanging nests, wait for the cowbird to lay its egg, and then build a second layer above the first in which to lay their own eggs ("Curious" 527). Several articles appear over the history of *St. Nicholas* that show how birds have adapted their nest building to industrialization and urbanization, with illustrations of nests in the trusses of bridges or on the ledges of buildings. While these sites might be unusual, they are also effective choices. "It is not always a mere whim that causes a pair of winged builders to violate the usual fashions of bird-architecture, or to select a site for their home that might well make respectable bird-society gossip and stare . . . the thing which made it peculiar, as bird's nests go, was the very thing that made is more safe or more comfortable than birds' nests usually are."

Occasionally, articles appear that describe entire ecosystems. For example, an early issue includes a description of the llanos of Venezuela. The article opens with a general description of the geography, the flora, and the fauna, followed by an in-depth discussion of the importance of the annual cycle of rain and drought in maintaining the geological and biological makeup of the region. The author notes that plants and animals have not only adapted to this cycle, but that they depend on it (Gale).

Throughout *St. Nicholas,* there is a sense that these articles could comprise a somewhat unsystematic course in natural history. References to other articles are common, sometimes indirectly, as we have already seen in the elephant skull illustration from the hornbill article. At other times, readers are directed to specific articles, as in an article about penguins of the antarctic that encourages children to refer to the previous month's article about auks of the arctic circle (Worstele). Especially noteworthy is a series of nineteen articles by William Temple Hornaday. Hornaday was well known as the director of the Bronx Zoo and for his many articles advocating preservation of wildlife. He has since been recognized for introducing the practice of displaying mounted specimens in groups, posed naturally (he became chief taxidermist for the Smithsonian). *Quadrupeds of North America,* which appeared from January 1894 through March 1896, was intended to be a thorough course in natural history for children.

The first article in the series, "A Bird's-Eye View of the Animal Kingdom," outlines his philosophy and goals; Hornaday opens the series with a discussion of the importance of an education in natural history

and of learning how to observe and understand the world. He argues for
the systematic study of zoology in the schools; without it, we lack understanding of "our neighbors . . . the other animals of the world" (231).
Children lack this knowledge because "those whose business it is to publish magazines and books for the young have either forgotten or neglected
to lay for them a series of foundation-stones on which they might build
intelligently all the rest of their lives. The publishers of *St. Nicholas* have
decided to do now what has been so long and so universally left undone."
Hornaday aims to give children "a foundation on which they can build
zoological knowledge with regularity and precision."

Hornaday is reacting to works like Alphonso Wood's *First Lessons
in Botany*, published in 1856. Wood suggests that botany is an appropriate study for children because it is "gentle" and "involves no cruelty."
At the same time, he urges teachers to use the study of botany to develop
mental discipline. Wood emphasizes the memorization of appropriate
scientific labels for plants and their parts as a way of training young
minds in logic. This approach was still being encouraged in books like
James Johonnot's *Neighbors with Wings and Fins*, a natural history published in 1888. Johonnot believes that the study of animals and birds is
valuable for the "mental activity" it offers. He argues that children should
learn about nature through a "mingling of science, story, and song" (6).
Although Johonnot mentions science in his preface to teachers, the
book's organization takes children from the familiar (chickens) to the
exotic (peacocks) without much concern for how the animals are related.
Other books that address natural history for children bury scientific
information in animal stories, which often have an Aesop-like moral
(Gatty, Hooker, and Kelly are examples). While Hornaday's series was
meant to encourage children's curiosity, it was also designed to provide
parents and teachers with a model of an appropriately challenging
approach to educating children about the natural world.

In the familiar tone of *St. Nicholas*, Hornaday invites children into
his imaginary study, pointing out the sign that hangs over the door (and
is set off from the text by white space and a box): "ALL JAW-BREAKING
NAMES ABANDON, YE WHO ENTER HERE!" (231). Although he will
introduce the notions of order, family, genus, and so on down to sub-
species and will introduce children to the Latin nomenclature, he does
this to explain how scientists communicate to each other about their
subjects. He does not want to bore or intimidate his readers. He also suggests that a lack of knowledge is an opportunity to learn from others by

welcoming the contributions of the best American museums, zoological gardens, artists, and engravers to his articles.

Through text and illustrations, the first article also offers an overview of the animal kingdom, so that future articles on quadrupeds, birds, reptiles, and fishes of North America can be understood in their proper relationship to each other. Hornaday notes that the previous natural history articles in *St. Nicholas* have been informative; he often refers to them throughout the series. He sometimes refers to an earlier *St. Nicholas* piece by another writer, suggesting that it explains an animal so well that it would be a waste of time for him to do so. Excellent as the previous natural history articles have been, however, they have been presented as "miscellaneous studies" that suggest that the animal kingdom is "an animated crazy quilt" when it is, instead, "one long, unbroken chain, . . . the unity and beauty of which are seen to be most complete when you follow it up or down, link by link" (231). This understanding of the connections between all living things, including humans, is central to Hornaday's articles. These connections are depicted in a series of charts that begin by showing the relationship of natural history to other sciences and end with showing humankind's relationship to the other primates.

Throughout the series, Hornaday meticulously describes various species, including their physical appearance, habitats, diet, and behavior. He presents his observations and the observations of others, explains how those observations are made, and describes how specimens are taken. He often connects the physical development of an animal with its environment, as when he describes the armadillo. He points out that in the treeless areas where it lives, there is very little cover from its enemies, so it has developed a "suit of bony plate-armor" for protection ("Lowest" 424). Hornaday describes the stomach contents of a Bighorn sheep he killed ("Buffalo" 680) and the way an opossum plays dead ("Lowest" 428). The illustrations, drawn from specimens, show animals as they appear in life or show skeletons and skulls, and the articles are often accompanied by maps outlining an animal's range. Hornaday's goals in this series are to teach children to see the world around them and to show adults how to encourage children's natural curiosity to help them understand the natural world ("Lowest" 429).

Mary Mapes Dodge encouraged this understanding from the first issue of *St. Nicholas.* She felt that it was vital to provide children with a sense that they had the power to change the future and to provide them with the information about the world that they would need to improve it (Gannon and Thompson 155). Believing that responsible treatment of the natural world was an important part of the future, Dodge drew on her love of nature and her interest in natural history to publish works by highly regarded nature writers.

In the early years of the magazine, the natural history articles reflect traditional ways of appreciating nature and presenting it to children. Some of the articles about animals include moral lessons like those found in fables (one of the approaches to natural history that Hornaday decries at the beginning of his series). Including this kind of lesson in scientific articles can produce dissonance. For example, an 1874 article about manatees includes an accurate description of the animals, sketches taken from a specimen in the Central Park Zoo. However, the author is also careful to point out that manatees have "lovely traits of character." They use their "hands" to crawl on land, to hold their babies, and they help each other. Children can learn about cooperation and compassion from their example. "When a harpoon is thrown into one of the party, all the rest crowd around and try to pull it our or to bite off the rope that holds it" (Miller 201).

One value traditionally accorded to nature is as a resource. From the earliest explorations of the New World through the 1890 Census Bureau's declaration that the frontier was closed, settlers "rejected everything in nature that was not of immediate and practical use" (Huth 5). Some of this utilitarian value of nature also appears in early natural history articles in *St. Nicholas*. Plants like the date palm or the water chinquapin bean are described chiefly as sources of food and textiles or as building materials (Feudge; "Sacred Bean"). An early article about the zebra notes that although it is not very useful because it can't be tamed to the harness or saddle, it is beautiful in menageries ("Zebra" 9). Fish hawks are valued by farmers because it is believed that the "noble" fishhawks help keep the "greedy" eagles from killing poultry (Ruff 81).

However, the natural history articles in *St. Nicholas* introduce readers to other ways in which nature is valuable, reflecting the thinking of preservationists. Nature is accorded an aesthetic value simply for its fascinating variety. This interest in all of nature is accompanied by calls for an ethical relationship with the natural world. Often reflecting the work of George Perkins Marsh, the earliest natural history articles regularly note the effect that humans have had on their environment. Marsh's *Man and Nature*, published in 1864, reversed contemporary geologists' and geographers' emphasis on how nature shapes humans. Marsh argues that physical nature does not have as great an impact on human society as human progress has on nature. He suggests that it was possible that humans could make earth uninhabitable through continued exploitation of natural resources. In *St. Nicholas*, concern for the human impact on nature often leads to calls for more ethical treatment of animals. The first issue includes a story about the practice of "robbing the roost"—knocking young passenger pigeons (squabs) to the ground from the nests so they can be caged and fattened. "So many of these birds are killed every year for the New York and other markets, that it seems as if they must gradually disappear" ("Passenger"). In 1873, when this article appeared, there was some question as to whether this could really happen, "but they multiply very fast and Audubon, the naturalist, thought that nothing but the destruction of our forests could lessen their number." The article leaves the reader with the feeling that although the possibility of extinction for the passenger pigeon is small, it does exist, and should be a concern.

An article in the second month's issue follows this topic with a much stronger argument for the conservation of birds. C. C. Haskins announces: "I have been thinking for a long time of writing a plea for a large family of our friends who are wantonly destroyed and abused by impulsive persons without good reason, and, very often, thoughtlessly" (72). Haskins is referring to birds—all birds "from the eagle and the vulture down to the tiniest hummingbird." Birds such as the sparrow, hawk, crow, and phoebe are described and their habits noted. Haskins describes why people object to them and kill them and explains that this is shortsighted because of the benefits they offer. Haskins, using the resources of *St. Nicholas*, proposes to "raise an army" in defense of all birds. Using example, argument, and information, enlisting the help of children (and their parents), Haskins hopes to change the treatment of birds, encouraging children to adopt this resolution:

> *Whereas*—We, the youth of America, believing that the wanton destruction of wild birds is not only cruel and unwarranted, but is unnecessary, wrong and productive of mischief to vegetation as well as to morals, therefore,

> *Resolved*—That we severally pledge ourselves to abstain from all such practices as shall tend to the destruction of wild birds; that we will use our best endeavors to induce others to do likewise, and that we will advocate the rights of birds at all proper times, encourage confidence in them, and recognize in them creations of the great Father, for the joy and good of mankind.

Haskins's call was successful, and the Bird Defenders was formed, with Dodge including the names of those who joined the organization and reporting its activities in subsequent issues of the magazine.

The ethical treatment of nature is a theme that appears throughout *St. Nicholas*. One article notes that wild birds do not make good pets and are difficult to rehabilitate, noting the death of a young fish hawk when the author tries to nurse it back to health after it breaks its wing (Ruff 80). Readers are warned about the danger to whole species; manatees, for example, although gentle and harmless, are in danger because they have "good meat on their bones; and men hunt them to get it for their own use" (Miller 201). Theodore Roosevelt explains the plight of the buffalo, even as he describes a hunting trip along the Brazos. While praising the experience as "healthy, as well as pleasant and exciting," he also notes that the vast herds have dwindled and are in danger; the southern herds have been destroyed because of hunting and encroachment (143). Writing just a few years after Roosevelt, William Temple Hornaday declares that "in a wild state, the American Bison, or Buffalo is practically, though not quite wholly, extinct" ("Buffalo" 674). Like other writers for *St. Nicholas*, he blames "man's inborn greed and destructiveness" but holds out hope for the future if "the boys of the rising generation [learn] more sense and more humanity in the preservation of our beasts and birds than we have yet shown; and the girls should stop wearing dead birds, and birds' wings right *now!*" (676). This philosophy is consistent with most of the natural history articles that appeared in *St. Nicholas*.

In the final article of his series, Hornaday laments that his natural history has not had much influence on science education: "It seems as if our high school boys and girls have time, place, and opportunity to learn something of everything save the living creatures that God has made so wonderfully, and put before us to teach us valuable lessons, supply our wants, or provoke us to industry. Will the time ever come when a little systematic knowledge of the inhabitants of this earth will be considered essential to every person who would consider himself fairly educated? Let us hope so" ("Lowest" 429). Hornaday's evaluation may have been too narrowly focused on the classroom, for his series was part of a growing understanding and appreciation of nature. By the 1890s, interest in the outdoors had encouraged wilderness camping, scouting, summer camps, and tourism to the American West. There was a proliferation of gardening clubs and birding societies. The parks and playground movements, with their emphasis on improving health through physical activities in fresh air, had gained wide support, and the preservationist movement, led by John Muir, was gaining recognition. *St. Nicholas* could not claim to be the only factor influencing this new appreciation of nature, but the adults of the 1890s had probably read the magazine as children and were probably reading it with their own children. *St. Nicholas* introduced children to influential voices for nature preservation, like Burroughs, Hornaday, Howitt, and Roosevelt. Through the natural history articles, *St. Nicholas* showed children how to observe nature, learn about it, and love it. It provided one of the "foundation-stones" for public acceptance of preservation of the natural world.

WORKS CITED

Beverly, Fred. "The Hornbill." *St. Nicholas: A Magazine for Young Folks,* January 1875, 151–52.

Burroughs, John. "Observing Little Things." *St. Nicholas: A Magazine for Young Folks,* August 1888, 763–65.

———. "A Talk about Wildflowers." *St. Nicholas: A Magazine for Young Folks,* September 1891, 581–86.

Clarke, William Fayal. "In Memory of Mary Mapes Dodge." *St. Nicholas: A Magazine for Young Folks,* October 1905, 1059–71.

"Curious Items about Birds." *St. Nicholas: A Magazine for Young Folks,* May 1883, 527–34.

[Dodge, Mary Mapes]. "Children's Magazines." *Scribner's Monthly,* July 1873, 352–54.

———. "Dear Girl and Boy." *St. Nicholas: A Magazine for Young Folks,* November 1873, 1.

Feudge, Fannie R. "The Date and Some Other Palms." *St. Nicholas: A Magazine for Young Folks,* December 1873, 60–62.

Gale, Ethel C. "Seas of Grass." *St. Nicholas: A Magazine for Young Folks,* December 1874, 77–78.

Gannon, Susan R., and Ruth Anne Thompson. *Mary Mapes Dodge.* New York: Twayne, 1992.

Gatty, Mrs. Alfred. *Parables from Nature.* London: George Bell & Sons, 1887.

Haskins, C. C. "For the Birds." *St. Nicholas: A Magazine for Young Folks,* December 1873, 72–74.

Hooker, Worthington. *The Child's Book of Nature.* New York: Harper & Brothers, 1857.

Hornaday, William Temple. "A Bird's-Eye View of the Animal Kingdom." *St. Nicholas: A Magazine for Young Folks,* January 1894, 231–37.

———. "The Buffalo, Musk-ox, Mountain Sheep, and Mountain Goat." *St. Nicholas: A Magazine for Young Folks,* June 1895, 674–82.

———. "The Lowest of Our Quadrupeds." *St. Nicholas: A Magazine for Young Folks,* March 1896, 424–29.

Howitt, William. "A Letter to a Young Naturalist." *St. Nicholas: A Magazine for Young Folks,* January 1877: 154–57.

Huth, Hans. *Nature and the American: Three Centuries of Changing Attitudes.* Rev. ed. Lincoln: University of Nebraska Press, 1990.

Johonnot, James. *Neighbors with Wings and Fins: And Some Others, for Young People.* New York: D. Appleton, 1888.

Kelly, Meriba Ada Babcock. *Leaves from Nature's Story Book.* Boston: Educational Publishing, [c. 1893].

Marsh, George Perkins. *Man and Nature: A Physical Geography.* New York: Scribner, 1864.

Miller, Harriet M. "The Manatee." *St. Nicholas: A Magazine for Young Folks,* February 1874, 200–201.

"Passenger Pigeons." *St. Nicholas: A Magazine for Young Folks,* November 1873, 15.

"Report of the Agassiz Association." *St. Nicholas: A Magazine for Young Folks,* May 1883, 557–58.

Roosevelt, Theodore. "Buffalo Hunting." *St. Nicholas: A Magazine for Young Folks,* December 1889, 136–43.

Ruff, M. D. "Fish-Hawks and Their Nests." *St. Nicholas: A Magazine for Young Folks,* December 1873, 79–82.

"The Sacred Bean." *St. Nicholas: A Magazine for Young Folks,* December 1873, 92.

Smith, DeCost. "Halcyon Days and Halcyon Ways." *St. Nicholas: A Magazine for Young Folks,* September 1883, 810–12.

Thompson, Ernest E. "Fly-Fishing for Black Bass." *St. Nicholas: A Magazine for Young Folks,* June 1883, 784–87.

———. "The Pintail." *St. Nicholas: A Magazine for Young Folks,* September 1888, 826–27.

———. "Tracks in the Snow." *St. Nicholas: A Magazine for Young Folks,* March 1888, 338–41.

Treat, Mary. "The Water-Bear." *St. Nicholas: A Magazine for Young Folks,* March 1875, 274–75.

Wood, Alphonso. *First Lessons in Botany: Designed for Common Schools in the United States.* Boston: Crocker & Brewster, 1856.

Worstele, Mary V. "Almost a Quadruped." *St. Nicholas: A Magazine for Young Folks,* April 1892, 386–88.

"The Zebra." *St. Nicholas: A Magazine for Young Folks,* November 1873, 9–10.

ADDITIONAL READING

Buell, Lawrence. *The Environmental Imagination: Thoreau, Nature Writing, and the Formation of American Culture.* Cambridge: Harvard University Press, 1995.

Ekrich, Arthur A., Jr. *Man and Nature in America.* New York: Columbia University Press, 1963.

Klassen, Kenneth. "The School of Nature: An Annotated Index of Writings on Nature in *St. Nicholas Magazine* during the Editorship of Mary Mapes Dodge, 1873–1905." Ph.D. diss., University of Kansas, 1989.

Nash, Roderick. *Wilderness and the American Mind.* 3d ed. New Haven: Yale University Press, 1982.

Roe, E. P. "Some Stories about 'The California Lion.'" *St. Nicholas: A Magazine for Young Folks,* September 1888, 814–18.

Saler, Elizabeth C., and Edwin H. Cady. "The *St. Nicholas* and the Serious Artist." In *Essays Mostly on Periodical Publishing in America: A Collection in Honor of Clarence Gohdes,* ed. James Woodress. Durham, N.C.: Duke University Press, 1973, 163–70.

St. Nicholas Correspondence. De Grummond Collection, University of Southern Mississippi. http://www.lib.usm.edu (September 5, 2000).

Weiss, Erica E. *Children's Periodicals in the United States during the Nineteenth Century and the Influence of Mary Mapes Dodge* (fall 1999). Online Archive of Nineteenth-Century U.S. Women's Writings. http://www.facstaff.bucknell.edu (September 5, 2000).

Somewhere outside the Forest

Ecological Ambivalence in Neverland
from *The Little White Bird* to *Hook*

M. Lynn Byrd

Stories and images of Peter Pan are well known and widely promulgated. Pop star Michael Jackson named his ranch Neverland. An American peanut butter brand and a London bus company share the sprite's name. Both Disneyland and Disney World have rides dedicated to Peter Pan, and Disney released a 2002 sequel to its 1953 animated film.[1] Peter Pan syndrome has even become a pop psychology term.[2] Popular culture continues to play with and on these images. Joel Schumacher's 1987 film *The Lost Boys* takes its name from Peter's band. The 2002 *Prairie Home Companion Annual Joke Show* has a Peter Pan airline joke: you never never land; and in a December 2000 "The Family Circus" cartoon the daughter reads *Peter Pan,* and compares his storybook fighting with his "real life" peanut butter making.

The pull of fantasy and escapism in the Peter Pan story is obvious, as is the allure of youth and youthfulness; however, it is also interesting to examine other cultural mores and attitudes that are embedded in the story. Jacqueline Rose has written a massive study of Peter Pan and the "impossibility" of children's literature; one might propose another study—on Peter Pan and the impossibility of nature. To start that endeavor, this chapter examines four versions of Peter Pan and Neverland (two of Barrie's own novels and the two most recent film versions) under an "eco-conscious" lens. In response to Cheryll Glotfelty's definition of ecocriticism as "the study of the relationship between literature and the physical environment" and in response to her question "should place become a new critical category?" (xix), this study investigates Neverland and Peter Pan along ecocritical lines. Each of the myth's incarnations, from Barrie's inception to Spielberg's response, matches

Glotfelty's definition of ecocriticism; each "takes as its subject the inter-connections between nature and culture, specifically the cultural artifacts of language and literature." Barrie, Disney, and Spielberg grapple with the intersections of the social sphere, the natural world, and the imagination. Furthermore, in an ecocritical reading, Neverland parodies the ecological problems inherent in literature and criticism today. While pointing out that criticism uses terms like *boundary, field, intersect, map, frontier,* and *space,* William Howarth recognizes that literature itself "dwells Nowhere." He cites Greenblatt and Gunn: "The odd thing, in fact, about literature as an imagined territory is that there are apparently no natural limits—and hence, it would seem, there are apparently no natural limits to the field of literary criticism" (cited in Howarth 77).

This study argues that each of these Pan texts, while playing with ideas of nature and the natural, actually—and perhaps inevitably—superimposes the human imagination over nature. Not only are nature and natural space constructed entities and confined spaces, but also the idea of nature is distorted into domestic or fantasy spheres that ultimately elide nature itself. Each of these versions of the Peter Pan myth desires a return to values and family, but the values are the same old Enlightenment values—recast in distinctly colonialist terms—that privilege humans, human thought and language, and social realms over nature. Peter Pan may have evolved into the ultimate adventure story and, as Richard Phillips points out in his study of the genre, such stories "contain" and can teach many interrelated social concepts and precepts, including power relations based on conservative, imperial constructions of nationality, gender, race, religion, and language (17).

The examination starts with *The Little White Bird* (1902), Barrie's first rendition of the Peter myth.[3] In this novel, Peter is only a small aspect of the 350-page story, which recounts an old man's friendship with a young boy that allows him to subtly court the boy's nanny. His tale forms a rather roughly sketched four-chapter centerfold. Based on the premise that all humans were once birds, Peter is depicted as a wild child, a liminal character who, although human, gets lost as an infant and returns to the "wild" of the park, Kensington Gardens. Because he waits too long to go home, he finds that his way back inside the house (through the window) is barred. His mother has a second child whom she tries to keep inside. Peter is thus forever locked out of full human and family life.

Peter fits nowhere. In fact, his first three chapters set up the difficulties he has. Fairies flee from him, and birds fly away from him. He finds "[e]very living thing . . . shunning him" (163). Solomon Caw, the bird who guards the garden mound, finally names Peter: "You will be a Betwixt-and-Between" (166). Through the construction of Peter, Barrie creates an interesting triangular relationship between humanity, nature, and make-believe; Peter becomes a new nature god: Faunas or Pan. "Oh, he was merry. He was much merrier than you, for instance, as you are merrier than your father. Sometimes he fell, like a spinning-top, from sheer merriment. Have you seen a greyhound leaping the fences of the gardens? That is how Peter leaps them" (188). The narrator claims that Peter is forever one week old. This characteristic makes Peter an image not of youth, but of agelessness and unnaturalness. He is jollier than human boy or adult. Although unclothed, Peter is not "cold or unhappy" (167). Like the earlier Pan, Peter is unrestricted. Free in this world, Peter demarcates the natural (real) and the constructed (fantasy and fear) space between life and death.

His connection to humanity is all that troubles Peter. In *The Little White Bird*, the ambivalence shows best when Peter meets Maimie, an early version of Wendy. He asks her to marry him but decides that he cannot steal her away from her mother, who might bar the door and not let her back. Maimie does go home, but she and her mother return to the gardens and give Peter an imaginary goat.[4] The fairies are able to make the animal real: "so that is how Peter got the goat on which he now rides round the Gardens every night playing sublimely on his pipe" (249). The narrator insists that although Peter recovers, he misses Maimie and his earlier human state: "Though Peter still remembers Maimie he is become as gay as ever, and often in sheer happiness he jumps off his goat and lies kicking merrily on the grass. Oh, he has a joyful time! But he has still a vague memory that he was a human once, and it makes him especially kind to the house-swallows when they revisit the island for house-swallows are the spirits of little children who have died" (249–50). Peter's negotiation of the realms of life and death and his pacification of human fears are clearest in *The Little White Bird*'s last portrait of him as funeral director for dead children. The Peter story and the main narrative intersect as the narrator explains how David leaves flowers on the tiny graves that Peter Pan built for two infants who fell from their perambulators and died in the park. The narrator closes the Peter saga: "I do hope that Peter is not too ready with his spade. It is all rather sad" (252). Death is made a story.

Throughout the novel the central conflict is the narrator's competition with David's mother for the boy's affection and attention. In fact, the narrator's invention of Peter was designed to keep David from mother and nanny. Although Peter is left on this strange note in the center of the novel in the center of Kensington Gardens, the narrator and David move on. They continue to walk and play in the gardens, but the scope of their imagination branches out. The narrator begins to take David on their own adventures.[5] As David matures, the narrator has to struggle to come up with even more real and narrative adventures to entice the boy from his mother and from his peers.

Fearing he is losing David, the narrator takes the boy and his friend Oliver "exploring." They move (narratively speaking) from the gardens in London to the South Pacific, from land to sea. Because the older boy, Oliver, had already invented the idea of "Wrecked Islands" that was popular throughout the gardens, the narrator invents his own exotic island, Patagonia.[6] The last adventure, actually a colonial tale in miniature, is the narrator's final attempt to hold the boys' interest as they turn their thoughts toward Pilkington School. "With wrecked islands I did it. I began in the most unpretentious way by telling them a story which might last an hour, and favoured by many an unexpected wind it lasted eighteen months. It started as the wreck of the simple Swiss family . . . , but soon a glorious inspiration of the night turned it into the wreck of David A—— and Oliver Bailey" (305). The narrator builds art from art: "I spent much of my time staring reflectively at the titles of the boys' stories in the booksellers' windows, whistling for a breeze, so to say, for I found that the titles were even more helpful than the stories" (305). Through artifice, the narrator transforms the gardens into a place of high adventure: "As we walked in the Gardens I told them of the hut they had built" (306). While the real park is now ordinary, the fantasy island is enchanting. The island is complete with exotic wildlife and savage cannibals who threaten to boil and tattoo the wrecked Englanders.

Through his linguistic and narrative abilities, the narrator enthralls the boys, encourages their patriotism, quiets their fears, and reinforces the value of home and family. His inventions establish and maintain the status quo. At the end of *The Little White Bird*, however, the exploits in the park and on the island give way to a more powerful story. David's mother has a new baby girl. Oliver goes to Pilkington, and David prepares to do so. The narrator lets David's mother set him up for a blind date. Thus, as Jack sums up the novel, the "mother proves herself both the prime creator (by having a child) and the superior writer" (104). She has trapped the narrator, and thus all his stories, into her larger tale of family life.[7]

The narrator knew all along that he would fail. He admitted early on that around the age of eight, "children fly away from the Gardens, and never come back. When next you meet them they are ladies and gentlemen holding up their umbrellas to hail a hansom" (30). In terms of an ecological vision, this becomes one of the most poignant images of the book, as the narrator paints a picture of adults cumbersomely attempting to control nature with umbrella, carriage, and domesticated horse. This image reveals that in this earliest version of the Peter Pan myth, the loss of nature and the loss of imagination are simultaneous and related. As critic Martin Green notes, the fantasy itself was always "firmly limited and located within a highly civilized social setting and is motivated by the parents' life, . . . full of stresses" (19).

The novel's final romantic and domestic resolution was actually foreshadowed in all of the narrator's stories. The island exploits included David's rescuing damsels. Furthermore, in that story, families had to be shipwrecked so that the boys would not be separated from them. Thus, even in the guise of shipwreck, domesticity prevails. As Richard Phillips notes, in adventure stories the distant and exotic lands only seem disconnected to home and civilization. The foreign spaces are actually "vehicles for reflecting upon and (re)defining domestic, 'civilised' places" (13). Furthermore, conservative and stereotypic gender constructions often accompany and carry the colonial themes (51). They, to use Phillips's phrase, actually "map masculinities in relation to geography" (45).

The island adventures reinforce the theme from the earlier Peter Pan stories. Even Peter himself tried to get back into his home; and when that attempt failed, he tried to set up a new home with Wendy. Thus Peter, rather than resisting domestication, actually navigates the way. All of the stories in *The Little White Bird,* including Peter's story—and the language in which they are told—actually negotiate the journey from infancy to maturity. The narratives, whether about the park or an imaginary island, are ideologically successful. These adventure stories temporarily disrupt and even subvert the "home," only to restore a reinforced and more secure status quo.

Domesticity's inevitable triumph is reinforced by setting. Even the wildness of Peter's dwelling is an illusion; there is very little difference between the children's park and the adult streets of London. One of the central Peter Pan images to explore under an ecolens is that of Kensington Gardens itself.[8] Although it serves as the antithesis of the family home, the park is already also tamed space. Illustrations from the

Fireblade edition of *The Little White Bird* reveal the park's domesticated nature.

In the frontispiece illustration, both boy and man are nattily dressed, with a well-trained St. Bernard by their side. The hedges are clearly marked; the paths, clean. The pond is artificial; model boats sail on it, and a watchful seat for parental observers is set close by. In a second illustration, placed in chapter 13, children run pell-mell down a lane. However, the path is clean and clear. The fences are well maintained and prominently placed in the foreground; they even appear larger than the children. The bordering trees and hedges are also clearly landscaped. An adult follows behind the children. The park thus provides the illusion of wildness within the confines of domesticity.

The park, like other English gardens at this time, had evolved from an enclosed space and style into a version of the Italian Renaissance garden, with formal influences from the French and Dutch traditions. Although considered natural, they were at this time highly stylized.[9] They were also markers of wealth and power.[10] What park visitors see today, "a round pond, formal avenues, and sunken Dutch garden, and an orangery,"[11] is similar to what Barrie would have seen. A third illustration from *The Little White Bird* demonstrates how well documented and "civilized" was the park of Peter Pan and introduces the idea of mapping and map reading that will be troped throughout subsequent versions. The symbolism of the literal maps within the various versions underscores the power of the narratives to contain and explain not only physical but also metaphorical or social space. As Phillips explains, "[a]dventure stories constructed a concrete (rather than purely abstract) cultural space that . . . mapped a social totality in a manner that was imaginatively accessible and appealing to the people" (12).

While enchanting, the park is also educational. Society is made and measured here. Authority is present inside the park, and domesticity surrounds it. The park is presided over by the ominous figure of Pilkington, the schoolmaster who will evolve into Hook. The garden is also surrounded by perambulators, and all the paths, nooks, and crannies are mapped and labeled. Peter's island, in fact, is only a small mud mound in the middle of Kensington Gardens. Significantly, the island and garden imagery will be expanded and developed in later versions of Peter Pan. As the narrator moves David metaphorically from the gardens to the faraway island in *The Little White Bird,* so the story of Peter Pan itself will expand and encompass more territory. As the limits of civilization

The Stick Boat on the
Round Pond. I. Appleton
Clark. Frontispiece, *The
Little White Bird,* 1912 ed.

are felt, as cultural ennui sets in, the exoticism of the landscape and the
intricacy of the design will increase. As the maps of experience pale, the
maps of imagination intensify.

In Barrie's *Peter Pan* (1906), the issues of human hierarchy and dominance are more rigidly established and consequently less fully explored.
The two separate stories (Peter Pan and the wrecked boys) and families
(the narrator's and David's) from *The Little White Bird* are all merged.[12]
Although the fusion and simplification of the story lines make the narrative more fluid, it always sublimates the tension between nature and
culture. R. D. S. Jack's manuscript analysis illuminates this change. He
notes that while later versions of Peter Pan still explore the connections
between nature and imagination and between timelessness and muta-

The Broad Walk, Illustration, *The Little White Bird*, 1912 ed.

bility, they do so "neither so exhaustively nor so explicitly." Jack thus finds later versions less "adult in focus" (104).

The real split in Peter Pan now lies not between nature and culture or society, but between social reality and imagination. Jack demonstrates how the setting symbolizes the conflict. In Kensington Gardens "gates clang shut in the evening, dividing those who have chosen the enclosed freedom of eternal youth from those who have chosen the different freedom of aging in the outside world. . . . Those who stay outside are prisoners of time and place, never again to know the transcendental freedom of the childish imagination" (104). Jack suggests that Barrie argued with himself about the role of imagination in the human situation. The critic claims that while reality won in *The Little White Bird*, myth and imagination win in *Peter Pan* (105). Sarah Gilead would concur. Her study of fantasy endings finds that Peter Pan "acts in a tragic mode that reveals, without an assuring sense of mediation, both the seductive force and the dangerous potentiality of fantasy" (278).

Battle lines are now drawn within domestic space, between adult restraint and childish abandon, between practical daylight and dreamy nighttime, and between master and domesticated animal. It is Nana's

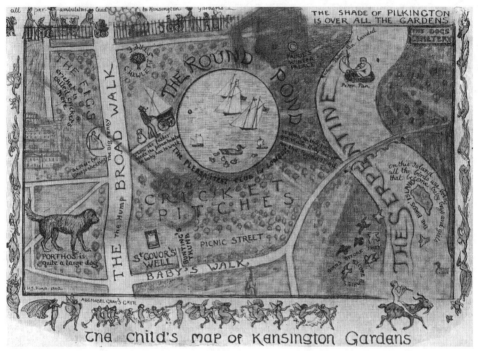

"The Child's Map of Kensington Gardens," *The Little White Bird,* Scribner ed., chapter 13.

transformation that starts the conflict. The dog fails to perform her job of nursery maid to the father's satisfaction. She refuses to drink his medicine, placed into her bowl as a prank, and the children and mother sympathize more with Nana than with the father. This confrontation sets up the conflict that will continue throughout the play as the father and Nana "ex-change" places. At the end of the novel, the father even lives in the doghouse as a punishment for his earlier lack of understanding toward his pet and his children. In no way, however, is this reversal an endorsement of equality between humans and animals. Mr. Darling's action underscores the master/pet relationship; it simply insists that the master treat his property properly.

Nana's banishment allows Peter, or imagination, to enter the room, and it permits him to lure the Darling children away. They go, not to Kensington Gardens, but to Peter's new primary place of residence, Neverland. The new hybridized version of *The Little White Bird*'s local park and Patagonia Island is a still a literary construct. It is a map of a child's mind, and so it varies; however, it is insistently not English. "[T]he Neverland is always more or less an island, with astonishing splashes of colour here and there, and coral reefs and rakish-looking craft in the offing, and savages and lonely lairs, and gnomes who are mostly tailors, and caves through which a river runs, and princes with six elder brothers, and a hut fast going to decay, and one very small old lady with a hooked nose" (213). This mix drops nature and privileges both imagination and society. The island can only become real as children look for it, and society makes the order: even the exotic Tinker Bell gets her name from mending pots and kettles (238).[13] Thus the fantasy island is a mocking mirror of family life, with the Lost Boys living in (tree)houses and yearning for mothers.

Barrie's earlier ambivalence and uncertainty about nature's role is resolved; nature itself is omitted from this equation. Through the treatment of females this elision can be most clearly seen. Wendy is Persephone (Gibson 177). She is lured from her mother to go to Neverland to mother the boys. Once there, she lives underground and washes, cooks, sews, and darns for the boys. Furthermore, Wendy's actions set up a cycle that extends to her daughter Jane and to Jane's daughter Margaret, as each agrees to visit Peter yearly.

Although the archetype begins to crystallize, Gibson observes that it ultimately fails. Barrie reduces the archetype to stereotype, and the Demeter/Persephone story loses its ability to resonate (Gibson 178) as Tinker Bell, Wendy, and Tiger Lily compete for Peter. Gibson's arguments are insightful, but an ecocritical reading suggests that the archetype also fails to resonate because Barrie has removed the nature behind the Persephone myth. Spring, for Peter, for Wendy and her female descendants, and for Peter Pan fans, is reduced to spring-cleaning, a domestic ritual of organization and capital management rather than the natural cycle of animal birth and plant renewal that the Greek and Roman myths explore. The Darling children's choice of turning away from Neverland and returning home solidifies the family and its social values. The "appropriateness" of their choice is reinforced with the decision of the six Lost Boys to join them and "fit" into the Darlings' drawing room (366).

The propriety of a civilized family is underscored by the introduction of "uncivilized" Native Americans. They also expand *The Little White Bird*'s earlier flirtation with eco-colonial themes. The narrator calls the Native Americans "redskins" and paints them stereotypically: "They carry tomahawks and knives, and their naked bodies gleam with paint and oil" (260). Even the narrator's commendations are superficial and limiting. They "pass over fallen twigs without making the slightest noise" (260), and they are valiant fighters who do not fear death: "No more would they torture at the stake. For them the happy hunting-grounds now" (323).

Of greatest concern, however, is the narrator's nationalistic racism. A pejorative Jamaican Creole term for blacks is used to name the tribe: "Strung around them are scalps, of boys as well as pirates, for these are the Piccaninny tribe, and not to be confused with the softer-hearted Delawares or Hurons" (260). The narrator is also sanguine about the extermination of the tribe—brought about by their defense of Peter's band. "It is no part of ours to describe what was a massacre rather than a fight. Thus perished many of the flower of the Piccaninny tribe" (323). The text—which has already transcended nature—treats the genocide of a people as child's play and evolutionary casualty. The text thus condones the U.S. westward expansion in which land and indigenous populations were erased through a callow and callous nationalistic imagination.

Words rather than make-believe fights are what accomplish these dangerous disappearing acts. *Peter Pan* continues *The Little White Bird*'s self-conscious play with narrative power and with the seductiveness of storytelling. Peter is mesmerized by Wendy's stories about him. The Lost Boys are mesmerized by her stories of mothers. It is, in fact, at the very moment that the narrator introduces Neverland and the Indians that his voice most prominently breaks into his story: "Feeling that Peter was on his way back, the Neverland had again woke into life. We ought to use the pluperfect and say wakened, but woke is better and was always used by Peter" (257). He makes obvious that Neverland is his creation through his depiction of circling natural hierarchy: "The lost boys were out looking for Peter, the pirates were looking for the lost boys, the red-skins were out looking for pirates, and the beasts were out looking for the redskins. They were going round and round the island, but they did not meet because all were going at the same rate" (257). The narrator even invites readers at this moment to "pretend to lie" in the pretend world to see better (258). Throughout the rest of the story, the narrator includes the audience in his royal first-person "we." He simultaneously claims and mitigates his control.

In Disney's *Peter Pan* (1953), the distortion of ecological systems is most graphic. The power of the human mind to alter, interpret, control, and re-create nature is what is celebrated—both through animation and

interpretation. Make no mistake, however: Barrie is the one who dena-
tured nature; Disney just vulgarized and trivialized the process. The
1953 *Peter Pan* film opens with a caricature of the already silly struggle
for dominance between human and pet. The St. Bernard Nana is
straightening alphabet blocks. While the kids and later the father tum-
ble through them, she vigorously but unsuccessfully attempts to maintain their order. This framing is significant because Nana can order the
blocks as A, B, C, but she cannot control the alphabet. Without linguistic control, she is relegated to a subservient position.[14]

Once again, Nana is sent outside; her being chained allows the
children to leave. In Disney the children fly through a cartoonish park
and water-ski with swans on the Serpentine canal on their way to Neverland. Disney's Neverland—influenced by the nineteenth-century
American Southwest humorists—is now "naturalist and primitive"
(Green 19).[15] Although Nana attempts, in this version, to come along,
she is denied imagination as well as language. Michael sprinkles magic
dust on her, and Nana lifts off the ground; but, chained by her position,
she hangs, a dog-balloon, in midair.

The dual forms of caricature and sentimentality affect animals
and humans alike. The Lost Boys' animal skins look like Halloween
costumes. A seagull's bottom is accidentally shaved by Smee as the bird
nests in Hook's towels. The Native American alliance with nature is
parodied as they "wear" fir trees as a disguise. Furthermore, following
Barrie's own lead in conflating different ethnic groups, Disney's Native
Americans live in an eastern woods setting but dwell in western
prairie–style tepees. Disney makes the Native Americans figments of
a cruelly comic imagination. They are a band of slouching, stupid, sloppy
people who smoke pipes, yell "how," and sing that their skin color
resulted from the blush of "braves" kissing "maidens" a million years ago.

The island itself—first seen covered by rainbows on a sunny day—
contains too varied an assortment of vegetation for its territory. The
children's trek through the forest reveals impossible anomalies; a hippo,
an orangutan, a rhinoceros, and a bear appear in quickly changing landscapes. All of the island's landforms are divided into anthropomorphized
territories—Cannibal Cove, Mermaid Lagoon, Skull Rock, Peg-Leg
Point, and Blindman's Bluff—and attention is drawn over and over to
Hook's weathered map of the island. The pirates "search" and "mark"
Peter's hiding place.

Even the oceangoing crocodile, another manifestation of Barrie's
own imperialism (as a distinct species in some areas of New Zealand and
Australia), is made silly; its eyes and tail tick in time. The crocodile's

clock is the most obvious marker of human imagination and its control of space and time. Although designated as a threat to Hook, the clock also symbolizes narrative control as a way of keeping time that does not rely on natural cycles. The clock also functions as a symbol of marking time with imagination and stories. The clock's importance is primary. Unlike novels, which can be put down and picked back up, the uninterrupted film experience controls its viewers.[16]

The increasing role of technology changes the look of *Peter Pan* but not the impetus. Disney, as Green recognizes, shares a kinship with Barrie (20). Green suggests that Barrie's cult of boy charm and Disney's *Peter Pan* push actually sell the same capitalistic and nationalistic values to opposite ends of the social spectrum, with Barrie reaching out to the privileged and Disney grabbing the middle and lower classes (25). Ironically, the union of Barrie and Disney in Green's analysis matches Lynn White's critique of the union of science and technology: "[S]cience was traditionally aristocratic, speculative, and intellectual in intent; technology was lower-class, empirical, action-oriented. The quite sudden fusion of the these two, towards the middle of the nineteenth century, . . . tended to assert a functional unity of brain and hand" (5–6). In its many variations and progressions, *Peter Pan* may, in fact, illustrate what Lynn White sees as a "widespread practice of the Baconian creed that scientific knowledge means technological power over nature" (4). Disney only amplified and extended Barrie's original ideas.

White writes that the term *ecology* did not enter the English language until 1873, but that its roots go far back in our culture (5). He claims that ecological practice is fundamentally informed by beliefs about "our nature and destiny—that is, by religion" (9). The Christianity that White sees underlying both Western science and technology is anthropocentric, relying on a dualistic view of humankind sharing God's transcendence of nature and of human beings exploiting nature for their own use (9–10). This is the hidden impetus of both Barrie and Disney's *Peter Pan*. Peter remains a viable cultural myth because while he cannot replace, he does represent lack. The many bridges that critics see Peter spanning—from childhood to adulthood, from irresponsibility to maturity, from life to death—are all bridges based on humans' relationship to nature. Peter limns and thus belies human uncertainty.

Thus, in both content and use, the Peter Pan myth retains the remnants of animistic pagan religions. Characters like Solomon Caw, the mermaids, and the fairies, who all guard their territories, can actually be seen as *genii loci*, guardian spirits. The Roman version of Pan himself,

Faunas, was said to speak to humans through the voice of nature or the vision of their dreams. However, Barrie turns Pan and his other characters into cartoons, even before Disney animates and caricatures them. Just as the myth of Persephone and Demeter is reduced, so are the symbols of nature's communicative power made silly and silent. Barrie's fairies and mermaids retain the characteristic of the guardian spirits without their function. They are relics of a pagan nature-based religion. They are obsolete: present without purpose—except entertainment value.

Peter Pan remains neither boy nor animal, but consolation prize. He serves as the marker for human satisfaction, almost an atonement figure for humanity's indifferent destruction of nature. Christopher Manes's discussion in "Nature and Silence" actually supports White's radical assertions. Manes claims: "Nature is silent in our culture (and in literate societies generally) in the sense that the status of being a speaking subject is jealously guarded as an exclusively human prerogative" (15). This aspect of dominance/colonization explains why Peter Pan is a narrative construct and why the story itself is so enmeshed in its own art.

Manes's analysis reveals that not only narrative but also language itself endorses these dangerous, seemingly progressive Enlightenment goals and conveys the global destruction. "The language we speak today, the idiom of Renaissance and Enlightenment humanism, veils the processes of nature with its own cultural obsessions, directionality, and motifs that have no analogues in the natural world" (15). Like White, Manes looks to earlier animistic cultures for solutions. He admires cultures that view the natural world as "inspirited," in which "not just people but also animals, plants, and even 'inert' entities such as stones and rivers are perceived as being articulate and at times intelligible subjects, able to communicate and interact with humans for good or ill." Manes points out that such cultures recognized two languages, human and natural. He notes that ignoring the natural voice imperiled the human one.

The connection between voices remains; it is the recognition of it that is missing. Peter Pan, of course, is *not* the voice of nature. However, he *is* the figure that negotiates the nature/culture matrix, and ignoring him may prove dangerous. He marks the discomfiture of both realms when one voice is silenced, dominated, and destroyed by the other. Thus the Pan myth, in addition to its other roles, becomes an inadvertent marketing ploy, selling first and foremost complacency and acceptance. Serving first British, then U.S., and finally a transglobal capitalistic drive, Peter Pan reconciles economic productivity and natural exploitation. As the liminal figure between culture and nature, Peter Pan shoulders the burden of loss for both realms.[17]

It is small wonder that the latest rendition of the myth deliberately and self-consciously plays with and upon Peter's nexus role. In *Hook* (1992), Peter—now Peter Banning—has become the ultimate capitalist pirate, an acquisitions lawyer. He tells Wendy, upon his return to London after ten years away, that he is "in mergers and acquisitions" and that he has begun "dabbling in some land development." Furthermore, the only business discussed in the movie involves conservation. The concerns of industry and expansion meet head-on the concerns of ecological preservation. When he is notified by cell phone in London that it may fall through because of the "cozy blue owl," his response is telling, "Wait a minute. You're telling me a ten-inch owl has a fifty-mile mating radius. Why don't they just fornicate somewhere else?" He continues, "There have always been casualties in evolution. Ask them if anyone misses the Tyrannosaurus Rex."

At this crucial moment, as Peter tells his wife that he must take the call to "fix" this, she replies, "No, you've got to fix your family first." She throws the cell phone out the window and the family sheepdog, the newest incarnation of Porthos/Nana, buries it in the snow. Thus *Hook*— as the previous versions of *Peter Pan*—becomes primarily a domestic drama, its environmental potential refused. The main conflict lies between the father and son, as the son, Jack, challenges the father, Peter, for his lack of attention to the family. Even Hook's stealing the children reinforces this conflict because Hook tries to steal Jack's affection and lure him from his father.

The question never arises, however, as to whether the domestic drama can be played out in nature. Barrie's *Peter Pan* initiated the direct move to fantasy that both Disney and Spielberg follow. Nature in this film is self-consciously—even flamboyantly—colonized and directed. *Hook* "corrects" the cartoonish depiction of the story. Recognizing the importance of the symbol, this film presents a spectacular, postindustrial, suprareal Neverland. There is no natural turf. Nature is completely reformed and defined as domestic fantasy. Two central scenes are set on baseball fields; one of those fields is drawn on the decks of two ships. Neverland is a theme park, with the Lost Boys riding roller coasters that resemble early coal-mining trolleys.

Attempts are even made to "correct" the earlier narratives' colonial aspects. The Lost Boys have swelled in number and now form a markedly multicultural band. Although their inclusion may be read as an amelioration of Barrie and Disney's racism, it might also be seen as an admission that due to such imperialism and colonialization, everyone is indeed in the same boat. Although the Lost Boys have the trappings of "wildness," they are artificially wild. They garb themselves in bamboo and spider-web armor and fight with natural weapons like egg and pea shooters, tomato catapults, and reflective mirrors; yet they create their food with their imaginations. The new leader, Rufio, cannot fly; he is adroit at skateboarding.

The island is too small for its variegated landforms and vegetation. Artificially large and vibrant flowers form and bloom instantly as Peter moves—sneezing—from one to next. All of the animals are domestic. From the mermaid lagoon, Peter is hoisted to a rocky seashore, then dropped down a snow slide into a tropical forest. Peter trains in a cypress swamp, in rain and snow, and in a desert. Each different landscape has a different season. There are two moons over the island.

The anachronisms in nature are paralleled in society as technology takes center stage. The pirate village resembles a nineteenth-century Cockney London street mall, and all the ships are docked. Turning nature into a rhyming game and playing as much on alliteration as imagery, Smee introduces Hook as the "cunning kingfish, barring barracuda, and stunning stingray." Clocks, still symbolizing narrative and technological control, have been collected and are displayed in a museum. Significantly, Hook has broken them. Peter's pocket watch, given to his son back in London, is ironically and nostalgically the only one working. The importance of this moment and of this incarnation of Peter Pan is emphasized in the stopping of the clocks. Even the crocodile has been stuffed and formed into a huge outdoor grandfather clock, symbolizing the conflation and final castration of both nature and culture by humankind.

Technology now, like nature earlier, waits on its self-proclaimed master; and that master's precariousness is evident as Peter's daughter, Maggie, sets the clocks to drive him crazy, and as the crocodile clock falls and devours him. Both events symbolize potential ecological developments. Hook is the agent of his own destruction. What he thought was conquered is what comes back to kill him. Hook loses everything, including sympathy. The dead crocodile lets out a lengthy and satisfied belch.

The fate of Peter is also tenuous. Because the overt ecological discussions are dropped after the opening of the film, Peter's task seems largely psychological. He has to recover a psychological construct: his inner child.[18] The sprite from earlier versions has—for love of a woman—forfeited his identity and forgotten who he was. Wendy even asks him, "Peter, don't you know who you are?" When Peter appears in Neverland with only a checkbook and legal threats to rescue his children, Hook observes, "You're not even a shadow of your former self."

This postcapitalist Peter is merely a shadow of an already imaginary being. Peter cannot use natural images. He first identifies Tinker Bell as a "firefly from hell" and then asks if she is related to Mighty Mouse. He is afraid of flying and of heights. In one of the most humorous reality scenes, he screams at his son for banging on the window of their plane. In another Neverland scene, Peter cannot even rescue the children because he is too afraid to let go of the rope to reach out.

Peter does reconnect with himself and his family; his love for his children and their love for their mother restore him. Instead of making these connections within or through nature, however, he uses and bypasses that realm. As Peter begins to use his imagination under the Lost Boys' tutelage, he sees his reflection in a clear island stream. However, his reflection magically is that of his youth, and his shadow imaginatively breaks loose and lures him underground to recover his past and claim his future.

Unlike Hook's demise, Peter's fate is representative of and both important and meaningful to the audience with whom he is identified; and to determine what that future is, a close look must be taken at the film's inversion of Peter's famous words about death. It is here that the silent and silenced nature returns. The obsolescence of nature is an important and underexplored element in the film's struggle for individuality and family unity. These issues, however, haunt *Hook*'s other restorations and resolutions. Ghostlike, ecological questions hang unformed at the end of the film as Peter proposes a toast to the family: "To live will be an awfully big adventure."

This statement directly reverses Peter Pan's words in earlier versions. Although the restored Peter does not address environmental sustainability overtly, the toast to life implicitly contains that concern. The toast serves as promise and plea, because the pledge is undercut by Peter's preceding analogy between flying and throwing the cell phone out the window. Perhaps ending with a balanced individual and a happy family suggests that further balance will be restored; perhaps subordinating questions of ecoimperialism and capitalist conquest to individual and family recovery suggests that hope for ecological recovery is gone. It is hard to muster much optimism. Certainly, precedent suggests that this return to family, like those in Disney and Barrie before it, is resistant and conservative.

Peter Pan thus remains a pivotal—and ambivalent—figure at this millennial juncture. Always the inadvertent emblem of civilization's disease, through the artifice and foolishness of Barrie, the caricatures of Disney, and the confusion and confoundment of *Hook,* Pan provides a figure for ecological consideration and reflection. The evolution of Peter Pan reflects the increasing colonial power and concerns of first world territorial and technological expansion. However, if Peter Pan has been an enduring and expanding character, he has become ironically also a tired symbol, overfull of Western ideology of mind over matter, humanity over nature, and industry/technology's imaginative superiority over reality.[19] A century-old symbol of the rift between nature and culture, Peter Pan stands now, ironically, not as an ecological prophet, but as ecology's errant poster child.[20] Peter Pan has been captured and contained in Disney's stage and animated images. Furthermore, the domestication of his image mirrors the domiciliation of his audience. As a poster child, Pan's image is finally fixed. Tellingly, Disney's resurrection of the animated Pan in 2002 produced a movie poster entirely in verdant, tropical greens, with a faceless, shadowed silhouette of Peter standing in the middle: his head is cocked slightly down. His legs are spread; his arms, akimbo. The pose could be read as challenging or playful. It is probably not intentionally reflective.

However, this latest project demands reflection. The studio's film, *Return to Neverland,* sets a spin-off story in World War II London. Wendy's daughter, Jane, is mistakenly kidnapped by Hook as bait for Peter and, of course, Peter responds to the challenge and adventure ensues. However, Disney's attempt to revive the image fuses Neverland with the Caribbean world of *The Little Mermaid.*[21] The story itself is insubstantial and trite; the film, in most reviewers' estimation, a flop.[22] Peter's 1950s image is no longer as appealing as it once was. He is now indeed only a shadow of his former self. Overburdened with ideology, his image is faded. This story is a tired replay.

There is nowhere left to travel. No new territory. No interiority. Barrie, Disney, and Spielberg's versions of Peter Pan all offered a false freedom. What Disney cannot recapture now is the magic of its audience's investment in its own innocence and naiveté. The dead-end *Return to Neverland* exposes the harsh realization that Peter Pan's journeys are, and always were, fantasies of fantasy. Even if Peter will never grow up, it is possible that his audience finally has. However, it may be too late. Our obsession with Peter Pan and with a fantasy freedom has ensured our complacency and trapped us as surely as it has trapped the sprite: somewhere outside the forest.

Notes

1. The sequel took some time to make. One story claims that Disney "clipped the wings" of the sequel and sent it back to development ("Disney Sends Idea for *Peter Pan* Sequel Back to Drawing Board").

2. While Vladimir Golstein cites Dan Kiley's book, *The Peter Pan Syndrome: Men Who Have Never Grown Up* (New York: Avon, 1983), he also chooses to extend the definition to describe Anna Karenina's "dominant feature . . . her inability or refusal to grow" (31).

3. R. D. S. Jack finds a 1901 picture book, *The Boy Castaways of Black Island*, by Barrie that suggests the author's interest in adventure stories (101). Gillian Avery, however, notes that "*The Little White Bird* contains the first sketches for the play *Peter Pan* performed two years later." The critic states that the story's "evolution as a book was gradual," with *Peter and Wendy*, the story of the play's creation and evolution, appearing in 1911 and with many other "retellings and reductions of the text" appearing even after that (173).

4. Peter, who resolves conflicts in the larger narrative, also resolves conflicts within his own tale. When Maimie gives Peter the goat, she can no longer use this imaginary beast to frighten her younger brother at night.

5. The two of them have a sleepover. They visit the pantomime and meet the clown, and the narrator spins a manners competition between his dog, Porthos, and David. The narrator even turns Porthos into a human, William Patterson, and tells of this gentleman's mysterious visit.

6. The narrator creates scientific names for the island's fauna and flora: there is the *Psittacidnae*, with its multicolored plumage, the *yucca filamentosa*, and the *cocos-nucifera*.

7. The Cinderella romance—which was scornfully introduced earlier as the "only" story that David's nurse knew—wins over all adventures.

8. Kensington Gardens, which originally belonged to the palace of the same name, is situated to the west of Hyde Park in London. The gardens were laid out for Queen Caroline by Henry Wise and Charles Bridgeman and were first opened to the public in the mid-eighteenth century. Class and dress determined admission. Sailors and servants, as well as members of the military, were denied entrance, and those allowed access were required to wear formal dress. Only after Queen Victoria came to the throne was the public given unrestricted access to the park.

9. Bridgeman, the designer of the gardens' Round Pond, was royal gardener from 1728 to 1738. Wise designed "a series of parterres and a mount which have been replaced by a modern 'Dutch garden'" (http://www.gardenvisit.com).

10.   Tom Turner, citing Roy Strong's history of Renaissance gardens, claims that from the accession of Henry VIII in 1509 to the accession of George I in 1714, gardens symbolized "the power and prestige of the court."

11.   http://www.gardenvisit.com.

12.   While Peter remains Peter, the schoolmaster Pilkington, only hinted at in *The Little White Bird*, becomes Hook. The wrecked boys of Patagonia, David and Oliver, are "othered" as the Lost Boys. The male dog, Porthos, actually becomes caretaker and is renamed Nana.

13.   The island can only be seen "by children who believe and go out looking" for it. (250).

14.   Green states that Nana's being made to "to skid and smash just like every Disney animal" is an affront (20). He believes it is essential to Barrie's scheme that Nana maintain her dignity to convey his conceit that beneath an animal like a servant is a servant treated like an animal.

15.   Green believes Disney shares these humorists' "love of exaggeration, particularly of size and speed, and their obsession with aggression and violence" (19).

16.   Obviously, when Disney released *Peter Pan* there were no home video releases. Green also uses the metaphor of time to find another similarity of Barrie and Disney; he believes both creators come at the end of the line in their cultural traditions. Barrie is the end of British adventure tales, infantilism, indirection, and sweetness, and Disney represents the end of the line in American pop taste (25). Green places both men within a "cult of nationalist complacency" and states—suggestively for this study—that the critics of Disney are "no doubt to be found in ecological communities, baking their own bread and refusing to go to the movies" (26).

17.   The issues of Disney's marketing and imperialism, especially, have been addressed by many different scholars—some admiring, others critical. Critical investigations of Disney's empire and influence include Byrne and McQuillan, Giroux, Schweizer and Schweizer, and Hiaasen. Both Giroux and Schweizer and Schweizer record Disney's emphasis on the family market and on "traditional" family values (Schweizer and Schweizer, 138–39), with Giroux identifying a "conventional, white, middle-class, heterosexual family" drawn to Disney's staging of "commodified space as a transnational shopping mall" (41). According to Giroux, Disney's realism relies on programming out unwanted elements of both nature and history and replacing them with positive and celebratory images. Giroux considers Disney's approach a "pedagogy," not about "the power of the imagination to recognize the benefits and limitations of reality," but rather "a fantasy world grounded in a promotional culture and bought at the expense of citizens' sense of agency and resistance" (55). In his critique of Disney World, Carl Hiaasen also eloquently condemns Disney's simultaneous erasure of nature and escalation of profits: "To do what Eisner's Team Rodent does, and do it on that scale, requires a degree of order that doesn't exist in the natural world. . . ."What Team Rodent has recreated in Orlando . . . has been engineered to fit the popular image and to hold that charm for tourist cameras. Under the Eisner regime, nothing in the real world cannot be copied and refined in the name of entertainment, and no place is safe" (79).

18.   See Patricia Pace for a fuller analysis of the psychological construct of the "inner child" and *Hook*.

19.   In his little-known 1989 postmodern novel, *The Peter Pan Chronicles*, Charles Frye tackles this ideology and tropes the underbelly of the sprite. Frye carries the Peter

Pan myth out of childhood and extends it to its logical conclusion. He explores the adult world fostered by the myth and mentality of Peter Pan. He selects as his epitaph ominous passages from Barrie's *Peter Pan*:

> They do seem to be emerging . . . don't they the little people of the play, all except that sly one, the chief figure, who draws farther and farther into the wood as we advance upon him? He so dislikes being tracked, as if there were something odd about him, that when he dies he means to get up and blow away the particle that will be his ashes. . . . He often wanders away alone with [his] weapon, and when he comes back you are never absolutely certain whether he has had an adventure or not. He may have forgotten it so completely that he says nothing about it; and then when you go out you find the body. (Frye, ix)

Frye uses these passages as backdrop for his exploration, not of freedom, but of restraint and oppression, as he laments the (im)possibilities of psychological portrayal and of identity for African American males within America's surveillance society and consciousness. Frye's is the first Peter Pan narrative to successfully pull the subplots of racism, colonialism, and entrapment into the main story line. In Frye's narrative, Peter Pan's forest is a metaphor for escapism: a conflation of madness, drug hallucinations, and sexual fantasy; the forest also serves as the image of judgment and punishment as a science fiction courtroom. The only literal "flights" in the *Chronicles* are the fall of paratroopers and the suicide of a young girl who jumps from a three-story building. As Frye's *Chronicles* reveal, Peter's flights are really for tracking and containment; as the narrative states, the "[f]orest sojourn ha[s] become psychohistory of modern man" (91).

20.   Ann Yeoman's Jungian analysis of Peter Pan also identifies him as an important contemporary cultural symbol. "Peter Pan provides a metaphor for the unknown. . . . rootless consciousness is the dis-ease of contemporary society as it a faces an uncertain future. The radical uncertainty of our future finds its own metaphor in our rapidly evolving electronic technology" (175). Other writers have underscored a similar importance for symbolism and metaphor in ecological debates. For instance, White claims that "our present science and our present technology are so tinctured with orthodox Christian arrogance toward nature that no solution for our ecological crisis can be expected from them alone" (14). He continues: "Since the roots of our trouble are so largely religious, the remedy must also be essentially religious, whether we call it that or not. We must rethink and refeel our nature and destiny" (14). While White proposes that St. Francis, who "tried to depose man from his monarchy over creation and set up a democracy of all God's creatures," serve as patron saint for ecologists (13–14), that saint's figure may be too closely tied to a specific spiritual tradition.

21.   Screenwriter Temple Matthews also wrote *The Little Mermaid II: Return to the Sea.*

22.   See "Overviews and Reviews of *Return to Neverland.*"

Works Cited

Avery, Gillian. "The Cult of Peter Pan." *Word and Image* 2 (April–June 1986): 173–85.

Barrie, J. M. *The Little White Bird; or, Adventures in Kensington Gardens.* New York: Charles Scribner's Sons, 1902.

————. *The Little White Bird; or, Adventures in Kensington Gardens.* Fireblade Fiction ed. Jerry Stratton, web master. http://www.hoboes.com.

————. *Peter Pan.* 1906. Classic Library ed. London: Anness, 1999.

Byrne, Eleanor, and Martin McQuillan. *Deconstructing Disney.* Sterling, Va.: Pluto Press, 1999.

"Disney Sends Idea for Peter Pan Sequel Back to Drawing Board." *Capitol Times,* September 1999. http://www.capitoltimes.com (November 26, 2000).

Ford, H. J. *"A Child's Map of Kensington Gardens."* Illustration. In *The Little White Bird; or, Adventures in Kensington Gardens.* New York: Charles Scribner's Sons, 1902.

Frye, Charles. *The Peter Pan Chronicles.* Charlottesville: University of Virginia Press, 1989.

Gibson, Lois Rauch. "Beyond the Apron: Archetypes, Stereotypes, and Alternative Portrayals of Mothers in Children's Literature." *Children's Literature Association Quarterly* 134 (winter 1988): 177–81.

Gilead, Sarah. "Magic Abjured: Closure in Children's Fantasy Fiction." *PMLA* 106 (March 1991): 277–93.

Giroux, Henry. *The Mouse That Roared: Disney and the End of Innocence.* Boston: Rowman and Littlefield, 1999.

Glotfelty, Cheryll. "Introduction: Literary Studies in an Age of Environmental Crisis." In *The Ecocriticism Reader: Landmarks in Literary Ecology.* Ed. Cheryll Glotfelty and Harold Fromm. Athens: University of Georgia Press, 1996, xv–xxxvii.

Golstein, Vladimir. "Anna Karenina's Peter Pan Syndrome." *Tolstoy Studies Journal* 10 (1998): 29–41.

Green, Martin. "The Charm of Peter Pan." Children's Literature *Annual of the MLA Division on Children's Literature* 9 (1981): 19–27.

Hiaasen, Carl. *Team Rodent: How Disney Devours the World.* New York: Ballantine, 1998.

Hook. Directed by Steven Spielberg. Columbia Tri-Star, 1992.

Howarth, William. "Some Principles of Ecocriticism." In *The Ecocriticism Reader: Landmarks in Literary Ecology.* Ed. Cheryll Glotfelty and Harold Fromm. Athens: University of Georgia Press, 1996, 69–91.

Jack, R. D. S. "The Manuscript of Peter Pan." *Children's Literature* 18 (1990): 101–13.

Manes, Christopher. "Nature and Silence." In *The Ecocriticism Reader: Landmarks in Literary Ecology.* Ed. Cheryll Glotfelty and Harold Fromm. Athens: University of Georgia Press, 1996.

"Overview and Reviews of Return to Neverland." Rotten Tomatoes, July 7, 2002. http://www.rottentomatoes.com.

Pace, Patricia. "Robert Bly Does Peter Pan: The Inner Child as Father to the Man in Steven Spielberg's Hook." *The Lion and the Unicorn* 20.1 (1996): 113–20.

Phillips, Richard. *Mapping Men and Empire: A Geography of Adventure.* London: Routledge, 1997.

Rackham, Arthur. *Illustrations. The Little White Bird; or, Adventures in Kensington Gardens.* 1902. New York: Charles Scribner's Sons, 1912.

Return to Neverland. Directed by Robin Budd, Donovan Cook, and Ian Harrowell. Buena Vista Pictures, 2002.

Rose, Jacqueline. *The Case of Peter Pan; or, The Impossibility of Children's Fiction.* London: Macmillan, 1984.

Schweizer, Peter, and Rochelle Schweizer. *Disney: The Mouse Betrayed.* Washington, D.C.: Regnery, 2001.

Turner, Tom. English Garden Design (1998). http://www.gardenvisit.com.

Walt Disney's Classic Peter Pan. Directed by Hamilton Luski, Clyde Geronimi, and Wilfred Jackson. Walt Disney, 1953.

White, Lynn, Jr. "The Historical Roots Of Our Ecologic Crisis." In *The Ecocriticism Reader: Landmarks in Literary Ecology.* Ed. Cheryll Glotfelty and Harold Fromm. Athens: University of Georgia Press, 1996, 3–14.

Yeoman, Ann. *Now or Neverland: Peter Pan and the Myth of Eternal Youth: A Psychological Perspective on a Cultural Icon.* Studies in Jungian Psychology 82. Toronto: Inner City Books, 1999.

The Wild and Wild Animal Characters in the Ecofeminist Novels of Beatrix Potter and Gene Stratton-Porter

Marion W. Copeland

As more books and articles about ecofeminism emerge from academic and popular presses, readers will be looking at literary works with new eyes. Inevitably, this will be true of readers of Gene Stratton-Porter (1863–1924) and Beatrix Potter (1866–1943), especially since little of the criticism devoted to either focuses on their nature writings or on animals and landscape in their fictional works. Ecofeminism's concern with the domination of nature and of all animals, wild and domestic, human and nonhuman, lies at the heart of the work of both women.

Potter and Stratton-Porter experienced enough oppression in their lives and careers to be drawn to ecofeminism's linking of the oppression of women and the domination of nature.

> In 1896, Beatrix Potter came face-to-face with . . . ignorant prejudice. The soon-to-be-famous children's author and illustrator was hounded out of biology by the closed ranks and narrow minds of London's top scientific institutes. Their members, all male, refused to accept Potter's evidence that lichens . . . were made up of not one but two organisms in intimate alliance. . . .
>
> A century after the stifling of Beatrix Potter's search for natural truths and her final retreat into voluntary exile, we can now celebrate her radically new view of life. (Wakeford 15)

Stratton-Porter met the same resistance from publishers, who considered the first draft of *Freckles* too focused on the great Limberlost Swamp and its wild denizens. Although she capitulated to her publisher's demand for a happy ending for the novel's human characters, renaming the novel (originally titled *The Black Feather*) to reflect the publisher's anthropocentric bias, Stratton-Porter insisted on retaining the original's "realistic descriptions" and drawings of the swamp and its creatures. Read with an ecofeminist eye, they evoke a power that reaches well beyond the "sentimental characterization of the boy hero" (Natov 248).

The original novel, even more than the published version now available, "depicted the urgency of conservation" (Phillips 156). "[E]ven then, Porter could foresee the end of the Limberlost" (Perkins vii). In both versions, the effects of logging and draining are clearly illustrated. As a result, the novel can fairly be said to be "a story about nature . . . [whose] hero, in many ways, is the swamp itself and [whose] . . . central theme is its destruction" (Natov 247). The original ending, the death of the young hero under a tree felled by loggers, was meant to emphasize that "the total destruction of the swamp [was] inevitable once the country had been won over to the promises of capitalism and industrialization" (Richards 34).

When Beatrix Potter became established as a children's author, she bought a farm in the Lake District, where so many of her stories had been set, determined to preserve the area's natural balance. To do so, she became a breeder of "[n]ot just any sheep, but Herdwicks, a rare breed that had grazed the fells of the Lake District for 1,000 years." The recent danger posed to the descendants of Potter's herds by foot-and-mouth disease has sharpened appreciation for Potter's realization that "[u]nlike other sheep that feed solely on grass, the Herdwicks eat the bracken and scrub that otherwise would clog the countryside. Herdwicks are not found anywhere else, nor can their natural landscaping techniques be duplicated by other animals—or humans" (Cullen).

Potter's "last book, *The Fairy Caravan*, featured the charismatic animals" and responds, as does Stratton-Porter's *Freckles*, to an ecofeminist reading. Unlike the early little tales, *The Fairy Caravan* has a complex structure that joins nearly a dozen separate tales through a frame tale. All the caravan's performers, having eaten the fern seeds indigenous to the district and become invisible to humans, roam the countryside, performing for farm animals not free to wander at will. The main protagonist, Tuppence, a longhaired guinea pig, escapes from the cage humans keep him in, joins the fairy caravan, and encourages other domestic animals to tell their stories.

Pony Billy, who pulls the driverless caravan, is related to the wild ponies of the fell whose mysterious dance is said to have inspired Potter to write the novel. She records having seen them: "In the lonely wilderness behind the tableland of Troutbrook Tongue; cantering round . . . a stunted thorn. Round and round, then checked and turned; round and round reversed; arched necks, tossing manes, tails streaming. . . . Who had taught them? . . . These half wild youngsters had never been handled by man" (quoted in Taylor 165). The novel suggests that the ponies are practicing for the performances the fairy caravan brings to reconnect domestic animals with the wild.

Although most of the tales are narrated by farm animals actually identifiable as belonging either to Potter or her neighbors, the wild characters of her earlier and more famous little tales are also present. A memorable illustration for a Christmas Eve tale told in chapter 14 shows "[a]nimals treading a circle in the snow round 'a very small spruce, a little Christmas tree some four feet high,' its branches 'wreathed with icicles and chains of frost' and shining with a clear, incandescent light" (Taylor 165). The characters dancing around the tree, as the ponies dance around the thorn on the fell, are familiar: Peter Rabbit and his clan, Mrs. Tiggy Winkle, Squirrel Nutkin, Jemima Puddleduck, Jeremy Fisher (the frog), and Mrs. Tittlemouse, virtually all of Potter's wild animal characters except for Mr. Tod. None of the domestic animals share in the magic of this midnight hour.

Potter meant to help her readers "find a magic that humans have lost" (Blount 139). But to Potter's scientifically oriented mind, real "magic" is the delicate balance created by the community of creatures and plants that share and maintain a habitat like the Lake District's. *The Fairy Caravan* posits that the loss of the "wild" drains the magic from the worlds of both human and nonhuman animals, much as logging and agriculture drain Stratton-Porter's great swamp. It is that magic that both of these early and influential ecofeminists sought to retain through their art as they watched the wild places of their worlds being absorbed by the same patriarchal powers that were, then as now, severing wild and domestic animals and humans from the community of the wild.

Oppression and domination of the individual as well as of nature find expression in the fiction written by Potter and Stratton-Porter. Equal rights under the law for women is the theme of Stratton-Porter's *A Daughter of the Land* (1918). Nonhumans, wild and domestic, suffer at the hands of despots like Potter's Farmer McGregor in *Peter Rabbit* and Stratton-Porter's Farmer Shane in *The Strike at Shane's*. The latter novel, almost unknown today, was published anonymously by the American Humane Society in 1893 as a reinforcement of the American publication of Anna Sewell's *Black Beauty*.

Potter, unlike Stratton-Porter, experienced a childhood restricted by stern middle-class Victorian parents. Although many of Potter's animal characters are wild, others are familiar domestic animals—dogs, cats, pet rodents, and farm animals like Herdwick sheep, horses, and pigs. Like the guinea pig protagonist in *The Fairy Caravan,* they suffer the restraints of domestication. Only Statton-Porter's *Strike* makes a similar plea for the welfare of domestic animals. Anticipatory of those later found in Orwell's *Animal Farm,* her farm animals, like Potter's, suffer the evils of what is essentially domestic abuse. The introduction to *Strike at Shane's* asserts that the relation between man and his domestic animals is less that of employer and employee than "that of master and slave" and urges "educators . . . to appeal for an amelioration of their condition . . . until the law-making power takes some measures to regulate and restrain man's dominion over them."

Like today's ecofeminists, Stratton-Porter knew that Shane's treatment of his stock rose not from an evil nature but from the economic pressures of a culture whose basic ethic is rooted in exploitation and expansionism. When Shane is injured by a horse he has beaten, his hired hand Mike is left in charge of the farm. Mike's golden rule—"I'm just tratin' 'em like gintlemen"—works miracles. First Shane's son, Tom, and later Shane himself are converted to Mike's ecofeminist paradigm.

Potter's depiction of the lives of nonhumans threatened by both human and nonhuman neighbors led Alison Lurie to title her chapter on Potter "Animal Liberation." Everything about Potter's little books, from picture to text, leads readers to identify with the weak (rabbits) rather than with the dominant (human farmer). Potter succeeds in this by reversing the devices—backgrounding, hyperseparation, incorporation, objectification, and stereotyping (see Hawkins 161)—by which dominance has always been maintained. Domestic abuse is exposed in Potter's little tales, particularly in *The Tale of Pigling Bland* (1913) and *Little Pig Robinson,* and it emerges as a major theme in *The Fairy Caravan.* However, it is in the depictions of her wild nonhuman characters that Potter's ecofeminism is most clear.

The landscape in which Peter Rabbit and his relatives live, like most wild places in England, is very near a farm. Though the furnishings of his mother's warren are anthropomorphic, the site itself is realistic—"a sand-bank underneath the roots of a very big fir-tree" (11). Both children and rabbits may learn from the tale that it is wise to obey Mother, but as a cautionary tale for rabbits, *The Tale of Peter Rabbit* (1902) teaches the wisdom of wild animals avoiding human beings and staying in the safety of the wild.

Potter makes Peter her protagonist, forcing the reader to see from his point of view. Anthropomorphic touches like clothes, speech, and household furnishings serve as a shorthand to suggest that in terms of "nest" and care of young, rabbits are not unlike humans. Neither Peter nor his family is seen as less "self-existing entities" than are the McGregors—in fact, it is the human characters who lack substance and complexity. They become Potter's background characters. The result, as Roger A. Caras observes in *A Perfect Harmony,* is that the tale has led generations of readers to "venerat[e] the 'bunny rabbit.'" Indeed, in British and American culture, thanks to Potter, the rabbit has become an "icon" (185, 186).

When Peter's story continues in *The Tale of Benjamin Bunny* (1904), the setting is again the wood "full of rabbit holes" near McGregor's farm. Benjamin's mother and siblings inhabit "the neatest, sandiest hole of all" (56). Here Peter and his cousin, Benjamin, encounter the farm cat, who traps them under a basket. Benjamin's father saves them by luring the cat into the greenhouse and shutting the door. Again the message commonly drawn—depend on grownups—keeps adults happy while young readers learn the wisdom of pitting the strengths of the community of wild nonhumans against those of the community of domesticity as humans have most often defined it. That ecofeminist "community ecology" is again evoked in *The Flopsy Bunnies* (1909), the third tale in which Peter appears.

Benjamin, now "married" to Peter's sister Flopsy, has so many offspring—the Flopsy bunnies—that Uncle Peter has to help feed them. When Peter and Benjamin take the newest litter to McGregor's compost pile, they all consume so much lettuce that they fall asleep. The farmer, arriving with grass clippings, scoops up the babies, gleeful at the thought of selling them and using the money to purchase tobacco. Their little skins will be added to others to make his wife a fur coat. He leaves them in a sack to pick up on his way home. Fortunately, "Thomasina Tittlemouse, a woodmouse with a long tail" (201), sees what has happened, nibbles a hole in the sack, and saves the babies—again, the community of the wild rescuing its own.

Of Potter's twenty little tales, nine feature wild characters like Peter. They—squirrels, hedgehogs, rabbits, mice, insects—share a habitat with the more sinister but essential predatory creatures, badger and fox. Badger and the fox, Mr. Tod, are among the most interesting of Potter's animal protagonists since, like McGregor, they constitute a threat to the well-being of other woodland creatures. The Flopsy bunnies become his victims in *The Tale of Mr. Tod*. Although the fox is dangerous (Potter undoubtedly chose the name Tod because it means death), he merely eats to live while the farmer and his wife kill wantonly, even resenting the woodland creatures eating at their refuse heap. Tod introduces Potter's reader to the predator, an essential ingredient of a balanced ecosystem—but Mr. Tod is another persecuted species as well.

Foxes, considered "vermin" by farmers, were persecuted in the hunts of the landed gentry. Potter insists that although Tod appears "bad" from the perspectives of his potential prey, he is not an evil character. Sheila Egloff notes that Potter is

> the greatest realist of the Edwardian age and possibly of all time. All of the animals are shown in their natural surroundings, which are as accurately portrayed as her interiors, and in spite of being "dressed animals," they are more frequently shown in their own fur, feathers, and skin. She was too clear-eyed and clear-headed an observer of animal life to ignore its predatory aspects, and from these stem most of her plot lines. Peter Rabbit has been consumed in Mrs. McGregor's pie dish, the rabbits are afraid of Mr. Tod, the trout is food for Mr. Jeremy Fisher . . . and Simkin the cat yearns after mice in the tailor of Gloucester's kitchen. (96–97)

Carpenter includes Potter's *Peter Rabbit* in his discussion of realistic animal novels, concluding that her theme is "of predator and victim" (147). By the time this became clear with the publication of *The Tale of Mr. Tod* in 1912, Potter, unlike Stratton-Porter, was in control of her own work. Her publisher placed no pressure on her to avoid a darker vision.

Despite her publisher, Stratton-Porter, too, refuses to stereotype her animals as heroes and villains. She wrote: "You know I have a theory that one must not upset the balance of nature. One must leave her in her natural state to work out her own salvation" (quoted in Brooks 179). Stratton-Porter's Limberlost community, although larger than Potter's Lake District, its ecology and salvation less benign than Potter's seem, is actually quite similar. The original titular character of *Freckles* was the vulture, seen, like Tod the fox, as ominous and associated with death. Bertrand Richards, Stratton-Porter's biographer, observes, "Another evidence of her modernity is her championship of birds of prey—the eagles, hawks, and owls—and the vultures, and her stressing of the necessity for the protection and preservation of these species because of their importance in the great scheme of nature" (98–99). *Freckles* was written soon after Stratton-Porter had spent three months in the great swamp, "making a series of [photographic] studies of a black vulture" (Saxton 30), a species even then endangered. The Limberlost novels, like Stratton-Porter's nonfiction nature writings, "seem almost eulogies for lives and places now lost forever under the bulldozers of American social progress" (Plum 878).

Despite the deaths of the cardinal's nestlings, the near tragic history of his little mate, and the dangers they face from hunters, critics have insisted on labeling Stratton-Porter's *The Song of the Cardinal* sentimental as well as anthropomorphic. As recently as 1980 Bertrand Richards questioned the wisdom of giving the bird protagonists "human characteristics and human emotions." He wants to see *The Song of the Cardinal* not as a novel but a fable like "Aesop and ... [Richard Adams's] *Watership Down*" (74).

Adams's novels, like Potter's little tales, benefit from an ecofeminist reading; their verisimilitude and themes and use of what is usually called anthropomorphism are consistent with Potter's and Stratton-Porter's efforts to foreground indigenous wild animals at risk because of the harm done to them and their natural habitats by humans. The characters' abilities to think and feel (and even to talk) is meant to provide proof of their sentience and, by extension, of what might be gained by humans if they appreciated nonhuman neighbors as individuals. Patrick Murphy suggests that the most basic tenant of ecofeminism is recognition "of the 'other' as a self-existent entity, a thing-in-itself" to be appreciated and respected rather than dominated or exploited (148). All ecofeminist novels share that recognition with their readers.

Stratton-Porter's nonfiction writings (*Tales You Won't Believe* and *Homing with the Birds*)—"nature studies coated with fiction" (Saxton 23)—appeared in *Metropolitan* while she served on the natural history staff of *Outing*, producing for the latter periodical straight nonfiction essays that testify to her knowledge of both nature and the works of contemporaries like Thoreau, Fabre, Muir, and Burroughs. The *Metropolitan* essays preserve the first of her wild animal characters. For example, in "The Last Passenger Pigeon," later included in *Tales You Won't Believe* (1925), the title character is allowed to give his own ideas about conservation and compassion. *After the Flood* (1911) explores the "various experiences of the animals and birds in adjusting to the new life, or in one case failing to adjust because of a bitter experience on the Ark" after landfall (Richards 70).

Acutely aware of the power of the so-called rainbow covenant of Genesis, which gives man—as Abram puts it in the earlier *Song of the Cardinal*—"dominion over the beasts 'o the field, an' the fowls o' the air"

(125), Stratton-Porter, like Potter, uses anthropomorphism as a device to level the playing field. The animals in *After the Flood*, like those in *The Cardinal*, are characters as individual as any human character. Those sharing the ark are as important in establishing Stratton-Porter's version of the biblical drama as Noah or his family. Since Stratton-Porter "was writing at a time when there was a good deal of latent anxiety about the kinship of humans with animals," it is not surprising that *After the Flood* stirred controversy (Plum 882).

In *A Girl of the Limberlost*, the title character, Elnora Comstock, "grew from childhood to womanhood just as her creator . . . had done" at the edge of the swamp. Elnora's father, lost in the Limberlost's quicksand when she was three, left a wife, bitter and remote, who seemingly blamed their daughter for the loss. Nonetheless, Elnora finds beauty and joy in the swamp: "As a child, Elnora falls in love with nature—with all living things, and the Limberlost provides the antidote to her loneliness and emotional deprivation" (Perkins vi).

An ecofeminist reading of the Limberlost novels reveals that humans who become a part of the swamp and of the lives of the endangered nonhumans dwelling there develop a bond with and empathy for nature through what Phillips refers to as epiphany. Elnora's mother, Kate, once she realizes how she has wronged her daughter, experiences such an epiphany while deep in the swamp, searching for the rare moth Elnora needs to complete her collection. Kate prays:

> "This way, O Lord! Make it come this way! Please! You know how I need it" (245). But when she catches it, she realizes it is not the one Elnora is trying to find. . . . Yet this moth brings her something of even greater value: *Just there the Almighty was kind, or nature was sufficient, as you look at it, for following the law of its being when disturbed, the moth again threw the spray by which some suppose it attracts its kind, and liberally sprinkled Mrs. Comstock's dress front and arms. From that instant, she became the best moth bait ever invented. Every Polyphemous in range hastened to her. . . . She could see more coming, and her aching heart, swollen with the strain of long excitement, hurt pitifully* (246).
>
> The spray that falls on her serves not only as a physical means of enabling her to achieve her goal but also as a baptism bringing a soothing balm to her heart and soul. . . . This incident serves as the beginning of a series of steps Kate makes toward becoming an active participant in her community. (Phillips 154–55)

When Freckles, a one-armed orphan from Chicago, first finds employment guarding the logging company's claim in the Limberlost from thieves, the great swamp strikes him as a hostile, feminine beast: "The Limberlost . . . shook herself, growled, and awoke around him" (22). But as he becomes familiar with her very real dangers, he also wakens to her beauties, developing what Natov calls "a projected empathy for the swamp." Indeed, according to Natov, "Porter asserts that 'nature can be trusted to work her own miracle in the heart of any man whose daily task keeps him alone among her sights, sounds, and silences.' 'The only way to love nature,' she once said, 'is to live close to it until you have learned its pathless travel, growth, and inhabitants'" (249–50). The swamp and its creatures become his friends. Having them "to think for and to talk to," as another of the novel's human characters observes, prevents Freckles from going mad during the long hours he spends alone in the Limberlost.

Soon Freckles refers to the birds who follow him on his rounds as his chickens, bringing them scraps of food, delighting in their company, and asking for books that will teach him about their ways. Once he has become a familiar, the swamp begins to reveal its secrets—the black vultures mating and raising a rare fledgling, the frog in one of its "large, green pools, filled with rotting logs and leaves" to which Freckles is guided by the falling black vulture feather that was originally to provide the novel's title, and who advises the boy to "Fin' dout! Fin' dout! Find out!" (44)

Beatrix Potter and Gene Stratton-Porter have, by bringing generations of readers into this kind of intimate relationship with nature, had immeasurable influence on the developing attitudes toward conservation of land and animals in the twentieth century. Potter was a factor in the growth and thought of writers like Richard Adams, Maurice Sendak, and Grahame Green, while Stratton-Porter has influenced writers such as Mary Cantwell, Annie Dillard, and Scott Russell Sanders. Cantwell, interviewing Dillard, alluded to her own passion for Stratton-Porter. Dillard "all but ignited" with enthusiasm: "'*Okay!*' she yelps. 'Gene Stratton-Porter! *Now* you're talking! Have you read her lately? She's *wonnn-der-full! A Girl of the Limberlost. Freckles . . . Moths of the Limberlost* set me onto science, and I've been on science ever since I read it in the seventh or eighth grade'" (36). Sanders admits to having been lured by "her words and photographs" (80) to update the story of the reclamation of a part of the Limberlost. The group involved in restoring Loblolly Creek to the marshland it was in Stratton-Porter's day testifies that "Stratton-Porter is 'the reason the Limberlost has survived in the minds and hearts of so many people'" (Sanders 84). Commenting on the county digging out beaver dams, Sanders writes: "I can't help feeling that Gene Stratton-Porter would have rooted for the beavers. . . . In spite of the hazards, she celebrated the fecundity and beauty of the Limberlost, which appears in her books as a kind of eden. . . . Everywhere the waters glisten, overshadowed by trees, fringed by flowers, teeming with marvelous creatures" (82–83).

Stratton-Porter's defense of this watery paradise against the powers of those who would rape and destroy it, like Potter's defense of Britain's Lake District, used fiction to ensure that readers loved and valued both the place and the wild animals whose habitat it comprised. Both women trusted that their readers would, like the group who is currently returning Loblolly Creek to what it was in Stratton-Porter's day, become their emissaries to the future—an ecofeminist legacy, indeed. "A. Harry Griffin, a naturalist who has written about the Lake District for most of his 90 years, said many people underestimate what is at stake. If [Potter's] Herdwicks disappear, he said, . . . 'The Lake District will disappear.'" Paul Tiplady, National Park chief officer, wished, wistfully, that "Beatrix Potter was still around" (Cullen).

Ronnie Zoe Hawkins, building on the work of Val Plumwood, describes the goal of ecofeminism as the establishment of a "community ecology" that would restore the "continuity of human with nonhuman life" by deconstructing the "mutually exclusive oppressor and oppressed identities" that persist in patriarchal thought (161). Potter and Stratton-Porter sought, in life and art, to influence readers to conserve both the "wild," where nonhumans might flourish free of human domination, and the borderlands, pastures, and farmlands, places where humans and nonhumans might benefit from the presence of the "other." Their animal characters serve essentially as what Patrick Murphy calls "emancipatory strategies" (148). The voices and stories of these characters are intended not to elicit sentimental clichés, but to move audiences to actively engage in dialogues with nonhumans set in habitats specific to the animal character evoked, and to become advocates of conservation strategies to save such areas.

Works Cited

Blount, Margaret. *Animal Land: The Creatures of Children's Fiction.* New York: William Morrow, 1975.
Brooks, Paul. *Speaking for Nature: How Literary Naturalists from Henry Thoreau to Rachel Carson Have Shaped America.* Boston: Houghton Mifflin, 1980.

Cantwell, Mary. "A Pilgrim's Progress." *New York Times Magazine,* April 26, 1992, 34+.

Caras, Roger A. *A Perfect Harmony: The Intertwining Lives of Animals and Humans throughout History.* New York: Simon & Schuster, 1997.

Carpenter, Humphrey. *Secret Gardens: The Golden Age of Children's Literature from Alice . . . to Winnie-the-Pooh.* Boston: Houghton Mifflin, 1985.

Cullen, Kevin. "Potter's Cherished Sheep Lack a Storybook Ending." *Boston Sunday Globe,* April 15, 2001, A19.

Egloff, Sheila. *Worlds Within: Children's Fantasy from the Middle Ages to Today.* Chicago: American Library Association, 1988.

Hawkins, Ronnie Zoe. "Ecofeminism and Nonhumans: Continuity, Difference, Dualism, and Domination." *Hypatia* 13 (winter 1998): 158–97.

Lurie, Alison. *Don't Tell the Growups: Subversive Children's Literature.* Boston: Little, Brown, 1990.

Murphy, Patrick D. "Ground, Pivot, Motion: Ecofeminist Theory, Dialogics, and Literary Practice." *Hypatia* 6 (spring 1991): 146–61.

Natov, Roni. Afterward to *Freckles,* by Gene Stratton-Porter. New York: Signet, 1990. 247–55.

Perkins, Patricia Barrett. Foreword to *A Girl of the Limberlost,* by Gene Stratton-Porter New York: Gramercy, 1991, v–ix.

Phillips, Anne E. "Of Epiphanies and Poets: Gene Stratton-Porter's Domestic Transcendentalism." *Children's Literature Association Quarterly* 4 (winter 1994–95): 153–58.

Plum, Sydney Landon. "Gene Stratton Porter." In *American Nature Writers.* Ed. John Elder. New York: Scribner's, 1996, 2: 877–91.

Potter, Beatrix. *The Complete Tales of Beatrix Potter.* London: Frederick Warne, 1989.

———. *The Fairy Caravan.* New York: Puffin Books, 1986.

Richards, Bertrand F. *Gene Stratton Porter.* Boston: Twayne, 1980.

Sanders, Scott Russell. "Limberlost and Found." *Smithsonian* (May–June 2001): 78–84.

[Saxton, Eugene Francis]. *Gene Stratton Porter: A Little Story of the Life and Work and Ideals of "The Bird Woman."* Garden City, N.Y.: Doubleday, 1915.

Stratton-Porter, Gene. *After the Flood.* Indianapolis: Bobbs-Merrill, 1911.

———. *A Daughter of the Land.* Garden City, N.Y.: Doubleday Page, 1918.

———. *Freckles* (1904). New York: Signet, 1990.

———. *A Girl of the Limberlost.* New York: Grosset & Dunlap, 1909.

———. *Homing with the Birds.* Garden City, N.Y.: Doubleday Page, 1919.

———. *The Song of the Cardinal* (1903). Garden City, N.Y.: Doubleday Page, 1915.

———. *The Strike at Shane's.* Gold Mine Series, no. 2. Boston: American Humane Education Society, 1893.

———. *Tales You Won't Believe.* Garden City, N.Y.: Doubleday Page, 1925.

Taylor, Judy, Joyce Irene Whalley, Anne Stevenson Hobbs, and Elizabeth M. Battrick. *Beatrix Potter, 1866–1943: The Artist and Her World.* London: Frederick Warne and the National Trust, 1987.

Wakeford, Tom. *Liaisons of Life: From Hornworts to Hippos, How the Unassuming Microbe Has Driven Evolution.* New York: John Wiley, 2001.

5

Arthur Ransome and the Conservation of the English Lakes

Karen Welberry

Arthur Ransome (1884–1967) set five of his twelve *Swallows and Amazons* books (1930–47) on or near a slightly fictionalized version of Windermere in the English Lake District. While the *Swallows and Amazons* books continue to be popular both in England and abroad, few readers outside England even realize that their setting is quite specific and that Ransome himself had a profound influence on this environment. In keeping with the general tendency to marginalize children's literature within the academy or to refer it only in terms of a notion of "classics" problematized with respect to most adult fiction, Ransome's work has been received within "universal" rather than "regional" or "environmental" frameworks.

And yet, very clearly, the Lakes were tremendously important to Ransome. As a child, he spent holidays in the Lakes with his family. After finishing prep school at Windermere Old College, Ransome left the area to work for a publisher—but returned to the Lakes on his very first vacation. It was there, in the middle of Copper Mines Beck near Coniston, that he met his mentor, W. G. Collingwood (1854–1932). The story goes that Collingwood found Ransome lying on a rock in the middle of the stream and, fearing the worst, called out something like "Are you alive, young man?" After learning that Ransome had spent the day failing to write poetry, Collingwood invited him to call in at Lanehead, the Collingwood family home. Collingwood became like a second father to Ransome. He encouraged Ransome to write and gave him additional reason to return again and again to the Lakes and finally to settle there in 1925.[1] All of these facts have been seen as crucial to the framing of Ransome's career as a writer by his biographers, with the "Copper Mines incident" becoming something of an established "turning point" (for example, Brogan 42; Townend 54; Wardale 9).

But despite acknowledgment of the Lakes' effect on Ransome, little has been written about Ransome's effect on the Lakes. Within the discourses of cultural geography, his name has been mentioned in connection with the nascent youth hostelling movement of the 1930s and the increasing popularity of the Lakes as a destination for adventurous pursuits (for example, Appleton 120; Barcus; Feaver 94). But no one from within cultural geography has linked Ransome to an environment movement per se, nor have literary scholars placed him within a broad environmental/ historical analysis. Ransome's status as a children's author is central to this exclusion.

This essay examines the way in which Ransome has been omitted from ecocritical discourse about literature and the battle to make the English Lake District a national park. In making the case for Ransome's relevance to the national parks movement, I intend to argue against the historical orthodoxy of the Lakes established by Jonathan Bate in *Romantic Ecology: Wordsworth and the Environmental Tradition* (1991). Bate positions William Wordsworth (1770–1850), John Ruskin (1819–1900), and Canon H. D. Rawnsley (1851–1920) as the "apostolic succession of heroes" to which the 1951 designation of the Lakes as a national park can be traced (Richards 123). In doing so, Bate seeks to establish a new "pragmatic and populist" basis for literary study: one that emphasizes literature's direct links with environmental change in the real world (Bate, *Romantic Ecology* 10). Many have taken this perspective to be one of the "inaugural" statements of ecocriticism (Kerridge and Sammells xiii–ix). Literature is valued by Bate in *Romantic Ecology* for its representation of and relation to environmental issues—a representation that is seen as inherently "socialist," along "green" rather than "red" lines. In Wordsworth's case, this means establishing a line of descent from Wordsworth to Ruskin, from Ruskin to the National Trust and the Lake District Defence Society, and from these early environmental organizations to the "democratic" phrasing of the National Parks and Access to the Countryside Act of 1949 (Bate, *Romantic Ecology* 48).

Such a case omits the complicating evidence that Ransome was at least as important as Wordsworth in "preserving" the Lakes with the 1949 act and remains potentially more pertinent to their ecologically and sociologically sustainable future. Ransome's case is especially significant because Ransome created in his children's texts a poetics of belonging in the Lakes that can be read as an explicit commentary on—and alternative to—Bate's "Wordsworthian" and "socialist" paradigm. Although rarely considered in a literary context,[2] Ransome's vision of the Lakes as a "playground" was hugely influential in "pragmatic and populist" terms in the 1930s and 1940s. His engagement with the politics of representation in the Lakes not only disrupts what this essay characterizes as the celebratory teleology of much ecocriticism, but raises many important questions about the kinds of authors and audiences supporting this theoretical stance and their relationship to material culture.

The English Environmental Tradition

The omission of Ransome from the national parks story would not be so surprising except that several other writers who lived in the Lakes and represented it in their work have recently been accorded an extraordinary degree of environmental significance. William Wordsworth and John Ruskin have both been positioned as writers who, through their writing and personal activism, directly inspired the first conservationist organizations in the Lakes: the Lake District Defence Society (LDDS), founded in 1883, and the National Trust (NT), founded in 1895. It is argued that, because the first memberships of both societies were drawn from the Wordsworth Society and the Ruskin Society, and because forms of both the LDDS and the NT continue to be proactive in the Lakes today, we have in this region a literal monument to the power of literary achievement. "From Wordsworth Society to National Trust" is a typical formulation (Gill 235–60; see also Bate, *Romantic Ecology* 47–58).[3]

One could take issue with many aspects of this argument for literary transmission,[4] but this essay concentrates on the central feature of the argument: that both Wordsworth and Ruskin are "indigenized" as Lakes writers as they are validated by ecocriticism. Wordsworth in particular is portrayed by Bate as a Cumbrian native, "made" by this landscape and purely motivated by "bioregional" concerns in his relation to it.[5] Similarly, Ruskin's Brantwood years, 1871–1900, have been highlighted by recent Ruskin scholarship and several new Ruskin institutions in the Lakes.[6]

The indigenizing of both Wordsworth and Ruskin is a necessary part of Bate's "green" socialist agenda. If a usable "English environmental tradition" is going to emerge from Wordsworth and Ruskin, Bate needs these men to speak for "the people" about "the land," as opposed to projecting cosmopolitan ideas onto them. It is therefore profoundly fortuitous for Bate that H. D. Rawnsley had, for his own reasons, already written Wordsworth and Ruskin up in precisely this way. Rawnsley wanted to garner national support for his campaign to protect the Lake District from development and so presented the Lakes as producing figures of national importance. Bate follows Rawnsley's practice in books like *Literary Associations of the English Lakes* (1893) and *Ruskin and the English Lakes* (1901) in emphasizing Wordsworth and Ruskin's relationship with their local communities and the strength they each derived from Lakeland scenes. With respect to Wordsworth this was a fairly easy task. Wordsworth's poetry and prose from 1793 onward is full of reference to his being at heart a "mountain Youth" or "northern villager" (*Prelude* 3.32–33). Many Wordsworthian scholars have, however, questioned the veracity of this autobiographical presentation.[7]

Wordsworth was indeed born in the Lakes and lived there most of his life; Ruskin was influenced by a tour there as a child and settled there for his last thirty years. Both men undoubtedly self-identified with the Lakes. But there are other aspects to these men's lives that were strategically elided by Rawnsley and are consequently not dwelt on by Bate. It must suffice here to point to such things as: Wordsworth's formative years outside the Lakes (1787–99); the "madness" that afflicted Ruskin during his Brantwood period; Rawnsley's penchant for attaching "big names" to his own causes; and Wordsworth and Ruskin's tacit acknowledgment at times that they constructed the Lakeland they wanted to see. Far from being "made what he was" by the natural sublimity of the Lakes, for example, there is reason to suppose that Wordsworth considered one of the greatest charms of the Lakes to be their suitability as space in which to play out ideas about belonging and identity. This side of Wordsworth can be seen most clearly in his otherwise anomalous relationship with Hartley Coleridge and with the "Madras" school experiments in Grasmere.[8]

The point of interest here is that it was this "practical" Wordsworthian legacy that Ransome's mentor, W. G. Collingwood, picked up via Ruskin and developed in his own widely influential Lakeland guides. In the "Wordsworthian-practical," the Lakes are "used" by the subject as an arena for self-invention, in contradistinction to the "Wordsworthian-divine," in which the subject is "made" by the Lakes. The "practical" Wordsworth presented by Collingwood in *The Lake Counties* (1902; rev. ed. 1932) and *Lake District History* (1925) is inspiring as a poet on "universal" themes but decidedly irrelevant to the contemporary efforts to defend the Lakes.

W. G. Collingwood was an almost exact contemporary of H. D. Rawnsley and in many ways led a parallel life. It would be fair to say that they were equally active in local projects to conserve, remember, and improve the quality of village life in the Lakes, the one as a clergyman and propagandist, and the other as an artist, historian, and more quietly committed activist. In some circles, Collingwood is the one whom history has remembered (Brogan 42–48; Hall 18–19). But when it comes to the story of the national parks movement in the Lakes, Collingwood's importance has been completely overshadowed by Rawnsley's. He is not mentioned in Bate's account. This is despite the fact that Collingwood was a member of the LDDS from the very beginning, particularly involved with the central footpath campaigns, and one of the driving forces behind the Armitt Museum, a parallel attempt to conserve Lakeland heritage (see Jay 38–48).

In contrast to Rawnsley, Collingwood knew Ruskin as a friend rather than a "master." In his memorial to Ruskin, *Ruskin Relics* (1903), he highlighted the things Ruskin loved doing and the "games" that he liked to play in the Lakes. This view of Ruskin's relationship with the Lakes was diametrically opposed to the picture painted by Rawnsley in *Ruskin and the English Lakes* (1901). According to Collingwood, the Lakes (and Wordsworth), though much beloved by Ruskin, were always seen as removed from—and diminutive in comparison to—the world stage on the Continent. Collingwood did not see Ruskin as a "twin soul" of Wordsworth, nor did he perceive Wordsworth's *Guide to the Lakes* (1835) to be the be-all and end-all of conservationist paradigms. That this perspective was even possible around the turn of the century, let alone held by someone with such intimate knowledge of both Ruskin and the Lakes, should make one wary of taking Rawnsley's contrary account to be mainstream.

While Collingwood played an active part in many of the campaigns to protect the Lakes from inappropriate development, he held a wide geographical and historical perspective on their cultural importance. Consequently, Collingwood disassociated himself from the conservation group he referred to as "the Romanticists" (*Lake District History* 129). Most pointedly, he never joined the National Trust, the organization Rawnsley formed to buy land and "hold" it unchanged for perpetuity. Collingwood's historical research informed him that the Lakes landscape had been sculpted by an array of mining and agricultural enterprises in the past: by people who had chopped trees and dug holes. He was not therefore categorically against its ongoing development. On the contrary, Collingwood's guides to the Lakes open his readers' eyes to the multiple and varied past uses of this land and the possibilities still open for the future. In their virtual avoidance of both

Ruskin and Wordsworth, they must be read as a direct counter to Rawnsley's account of the region. Collingwood replaced anecdotes illustrative of the Wordsworthian-divine with simple comments such as "[here in Eskdale] you can play at being lost, and imagine a great lone land" (*Lake Counties* 79). These are the kind of imaginative suggestions, the alternative Wordsworthian legacy, taken up by Ransome.

The *Swallows and Amazons* Saga

The Copper Mines moment in which Ransome met Collingwood is perhaps one of the most important recorded incidents in Lakeland environmental discourse. Here, in 1903, the lives of two people were for a few minutes perfectly aligned. On the face of it, the map of the Lakes in Ransome's mind, as revealed by the volumes on English prosody in his knapsack and his melodramatic posture in the middle of a stream, was pure Wordsworthian-divine: a landscape in which solitary men uncover great thoughts or conceal in their person unheralded passions and tragic histories. The map of the Lakes in Collingwood's mind, as revealed by the canvas under his arm and melodramatic reaction to the sight of Ransome, was precisely the same. Given this perfect coincidence of timing, motivation, and expectation, it is not surprising that the two men found an instant rapport and continued firm friends until Collingwood's death. That such an event could happen seemingly testifies to the efficacy of Rawnsley's campaign to present the Lake District as productive of Noble Men and Great Thought. Both Ransome and Collingwood were brought up under relatively privileged conditions (Ransome, *Autobiography* 41, 138) and were exactly the middle-class literary audience Rawnsley was targeting with his Lakeland appeals.

And yet there is something ironic about the way in which Ransome and Collingwood met under a Wordsworthian flag. Ransome had totally failed to write the poetry he set out to write, and Collingwood had turned the picturesque scenery into art for practical rather than aesthetic reasons.[9] Wordsworthian-divine mystique presides over their encounter, but it does not account for what they took out of it. On the contrary, this historic incident reveals that what looks like an illustration of the dominance of the Wordsworthian-divine paradigm in the Lakes at the turn of the century might actually be a self-conscious "quoting" of its imputed stature. In this case, there is good reason to argue that the most significant thing that Ransome took from the encounter was not renewed respect for Wordsworth's cultural valency, but the incident itself as motif of a shared set of expectations about the Lakes. And what we find is that Ransome used the structure of this encounter to develop a paradigm for Lakeland representation in *Swallows and Amazons* (1930) and *Winter Holiday* (1933) that was "post-Wordsworthian" in the sense that Collingwood inherited the Wordsworthian-practical from Ruskin. It was a paradigm that would open experiences like the one Ransome and Collingwood shared at Copper Mines to a far greater range of people. Significantly, it was also a paradigm based on the education of children and conducted outside the public realm.

Swallows and Amazons, the first book in Ransome's saga featuring the adventures of the Swallows (John, Susan, Titty, Roger, and sometimes Bridget Walker), Amazons (Nancy and Peggy Blackett), and D's (Dick and Dorothea Callum), is set on a slightly fictionalized Windermere in August 1929. The story opens with the Walkers who, with their mother and baby Bridget's nurse, have taken lodgings at Holly Howe, a farm with lake frontage and a boathouse. From Holly Howe they can see an island which, to the children of a commander in the navy, makes "nothing but a sailing voyage of discovery . . . worth thinking about" (16). Having obtained permission from their father by telegram, the four elder children sail to the island, set up tents, and plan to make a chart of the unexplored waters and surrounds. The steamers, motorboats, and rowing boats also on the lake do not pose a problem to the children's game of "discovery" because "after all there was no need to notice any of these things if one did not want to" (38)

Significantly, however, there are a few things that the Walkers (or "Swallows," after their boat) cannot ignore. When they get to the island they find that "someone's had a fire here before" (43) in the very place that they would have chosen themselves. When John tries to find the better harbor for *Swallow* that he thought he glimpsed from the lake, "almost it seemed to him that someone had been that way before" (46). And then the children see another sailing boat, "about the same size as *Swallow*, only with a white sail instead of a tanned one" (87). Because this boat, the *Amazon*, is the same as theirs, it cannot be ignored or treated as a "native vessel." It is now inevitable that the Swallows will meet the Amazons. Their game of discovery is ruptured by the presence of another boat occupying not just the same physical but the same mental space. This needs to be resolved before narrative progression can continue.

The meeting that Ransome thus prepares takes place on the island. The Swallows are having a council after breakfast when "something hit the saucepan with a loud ping, and ashes flew up out of the fire" (104).

It is an arrow with a green feather. Initially the Swallows think it has been sent by the man whom they have characterized as pirate Captain Flint, who lives on a houseboat nearby. But then they see the Amazons and realize that not only do the Amazons have a boat like theirs, they are also the prior inhabitants they have been suspecting on the island. Given that the two groups of children are now in the same place at the same time for the same reason, it is not surprising that they know exactly the terms on which to proceed:

> "Let's parley first and fight afterwards," said the leader of the Amazons.
> "It's no good our parleying with you if the houseboat man has got *Swallow*," said John.
> "But he's got nothing to do with it. He's a native, and very unfriendly."
> "Well, he's unfriendly to us too," said John.
> Susan pulled John by the sleeve. "If the houseboat man isn't with them," she whispered, "they must have taken *Swallow* themselves, and the only place they could put her is in the harbour. Their own ship must be there too. So if they have got our tents we can take both ships."
> "If he's unfriendly to you, too, we had better parley at once," said the elder Amazon.
> "Where is *Swallow?*"
> "She is a prize, and we have taken her into our harbour."
> "It's our harbour," said John. "And anyhow that's not much good to you. You can't get out from this end of the island against the four of us. The harbour end of the island is in our hands, so really it's the *Amazon* that's a prize, and we've got both ships. You've only got our tents." (109–10)

There are many points of similarity between this encounter and the Ransome/Collingwood moment at Copper Mines beck. Both meetings reveal a synchronicity of language and intention concomitant to being in such a place at the same time. *Parley, ship,* and *prize,* for example, are words from the world of naval warfare and are used as a matter of course by both sets of children, actually holidaying on inland water in small boats. In this way, the encounter reveals an underlying shared map of the Lakes. The children understand each other at once because the sight of an island in a lake has conjured in them similar desires (see Erisman 110–11). It is almost inevitable that friendship will follow.

If Ransome had drawn on the Copper Mines incident only once, in *Swallows and Amazons,* it might be tempting to interpret the allusion as playful homage or idle speculation as to other people's Lake District maps. But Ransome goes on to thematize his concept of a shared vision of the Lakes in *Winter Holiday,* where he introduces another set of children, Dick and Dorothea Callum. Although the "D's" are, in one sense, very different kinds of children to either the Swallows or Amazons, having been brought up in a town, they are nevertheless able to answer Nancy's question, "[W]hat are you? In real life, I mean" (39), with barely a flicker of hesitation. Dick identifies as an "astronomer" and Dorothea as a "writer of stories" in precisely the same way that the Swallows identify as "explorers" and the Amazons as "pirates" because they fundamentally inhabit the same mental world. Like the Swallows, the D's have been left at the Lakes by their parents—parents experienced enough in physical adventures to know why they are leaving their children there. These are parents, moreover, who have given their children imaginative tools with which to deal with new experiences. The D's meet the others through the exercise of these tools. The Lakes to all of these children and their families are space in which to play out ideas. By responding in an appropriate way to Nancy's question, the D's pass a kind of "meritocratic" test that initiates them immediately into warm friendship with the others.[10]

The especially significant point here is that, in both these reworkings of his own "primal encounter" in the Lakes, Ransome does not project his own conceptual framework onto the fictional children. Ransome gives the Swallows, Amazons, and D's a shared body of knowledge like that which he found so happily between himself and Collingwood, but he makes Wordsworth notably absent from their cultural baggage. The epigraph to the first chapter of *Swallows and Amazons*, for example, is from Keats rather than Wordsworth, and other literary allusions in the novel are from the genres of colonial adventure and seafaring, not romanticism. There are no references to Wordsworth in any of the five Lakeland novels. Indeed, Ransome underlines a post-Wordsworthian frame of reference in *Winter Holiday* by having Dorothea, his aspiring writer, imagine melodramatic potboilers or historical romances as she learns more and more about the Lakes. Not even Titty, the character with whom Ransome sometimes identified his own "romantic" side, is ever caught trying to write serious poetry.

Far from perpetuating the monolithic Rawnsleyan account of this region as source of English poetry, Ransome, through the different biases of his fictional children, insists on multiple perspectives toward the Lakes. The Lakes are posited as a site for exploration and piracy in *Swallows and Amazons*, mountaineering in *Swallowdale*, polar expedition in *Winter Holiday*, mining in *Pigeon Post*, and the early history of Britain in *The Picts and the Martyrs*, with fiction writing and natural history being additional pursuits in the last three novels. As Titty observes in *Pigeon Post* (1936), "it can't be piracy or even war while we're camped in the garden. What's it going to be? It won't be North Pole again" (25). The children's choice of the "it" is always a self-conscious aspect of the books. The constant in their network of approaches to the Lakes is variety. This playful attitude owes much to Collingwood's record of the varied faces of Lakeland history and his use of these in his historical fiction, and little to Rawnsley's directives regarding poet laureates and literary heritage.

In the context of Ransome's own "Wordsworthian childhood" in Coniston and Windermere, the preeminence of Wordsworth in school curricula in the 1920s and 1930s (see Welberry 32–34), and the imputed centrality of Wordsworth to the nascent national parks movement in the Lakes at that time, the absence of Wordsworth from Ransome's heterogeneous projection of the Lakes can only be deliberate. Here are four middle-class children from a naval family, two girls from a well-to-do local family, and the children of academic parents, who between them possess a multitude of ways of reading this landscape—not one of which resembles Wordsworth. Either Wordsworth's valency at the time has been grossly exaggerated or Ransome is making a point of being historically improbable. Considering the Wordsworthian influences on Ransome's own life, there is a strong case for arguing the latter. Ransome found that Wordsworth was of no use to people like himself in their quest to find a sense of belonging in the Lakes. Wordsworth's *Guide* might be all very well to those content with a visitors' permit but, with its invective against the wave of settlers who arrived in the late eighteenth century, is hardly appealing to those questing for imaginative possession or permanent residency.

Ransome himself did not want to be a "Tourist" in the Wordsworthian sense, and everything he writes presumes that his readers do not want to be either. In the *Autobiography*, for example, Ransome is quite candid about his desire for local friends in the Lake District to "help . . . make me feel that I had a countryside I could call my own" (129). There is also a telling moment in *The Picts and the Martyrs* when Dorothea is asked by the local boy, Jacky, whether they are visitors to the Lakes. Despite the unavoidable truth that they are, Dorothea's answer is, "yes, *in a way*" (107; emphasis added). The information and ideas contained in Collingwood's books were of the utmost utility in helping people like Ransome and fictional characters like Dorothea identify with the Lakes. Herein lay a template for historical revisioning and a reminder of the possibilities in "a great lone land" (Collingwood, *Lake Counties* 79).

Ransome's five Lakeland novels take up the invitation implicit in Collingwood's phrase. They can be read as an alternate guide to the Lakes, addressed not "to Persons of taste, and feeling for Landscape" (Wordsworth 34), but to anyone with a little imagination. By erasing Wordsworth from the Lake District and embedding a fictional history in his place, Ransome instructs his readers as to how they, too, might be able to approach what the conservationists had long argued was an exclusive and fully occupied world.

The *Swallows and Amazons* saga is a way in to the Lakes with inherently popular appeal. Readers of Ransome feel like initiates into a whole world they can walk out and possess rather than participants in a 1930s act of creative fiction. The main reason for this is that Ransome naturalizes an innovative approach to the Lake District by giving it a fictional history. The books are set in the 1930s but they refer back to the last century as if people like the Swallows and Amazons had always been there, as if their labeling of sites was the valid accretion of years. Ransome's representation is also popular because his backward projection of characters is also a forward projection into the future. Not only are there several references to "in thirty years' time" in the books but the repetitions Ransome makes encourage further repetition by his readers. By progressively ruling out the concept of "discovery" in the Lakes in his saga, Ransome makes a concept akin to "renewal" the reigning imperative. Mrs. Blackett, Captain Flint, and Mrs. Walker all work behind the scenes of the books to let the children know what they have known, just as Ransome enthusiasts in the 1990s seek to perpetuate the rituals for their own children. The *Swallows and Amazons* series demonstrates that, by projecting one's own particular coloring onto a landscape, one can have an entirely new experience that is simultaneously the reenactment of thousands of others.

Ransome's paradigm of Lakeland encounter ultimately made the Lakes an attractive destination to vast numbers of people precisely because it was not in itself a preservationist impulse. The kind of relationship with the Lakes that Ransome popularized in the 1930s was entirely compatible with certain kinds of industrial development, with new railheads, innovative farming techniques, conifer plantations, and mass tourism—just to cite a few of the contentious issues for the conservationists. His books accurately and unsentimentally document 1930s tourism in the Lakes, including scenes such as noisy bonfires, fireworks, and hot pies on the ice in *Winter Holiday* (201, 269), crowded shops in Bowness, and motorists who carelessly start fires (*Pigeon Post*

286, 335). With the exception of the careless motorists, Ransome does not judge, preferring simply to leave some things to other tastes and take his elsewhere. By representing such diversity he opens the Lakes conceptually to the kinds of people alienated by conservationist discourse. Like Collingwood and perhaps a wider ambit of ordinary British citizens, Ransome wants a way of owning the Lakes that is dependent on neither birthright nor aesthetic credentials. He proposes a poetics of belonging drawn up on strictly meritocratic lines. Ransome thus familiarized a new, broader-based set of people with the beauty of the Lake District. In doing so, he helped make it incumbent on the Labour government of 1949 to finally pass legislation that had been in the offing for more than fifty years.

Children's Literature, Ecocriticism, and the English Lakes

Ransome, it has been argued, figuratively elaborated in his children's novels many of the aspects of Collingwood's Lakeland that were historically pitted against the Rawnsleyan discourse. This is the basis on which he should be included in narratives of the Lake District National Park. It is worth noting, however, that Ransome did participate in contemporary discussions about what should and should not happen in the countryside to some degree. Some, for example, see him as an "environmentalist" before his time for helping to develop a "countryside code" of behavior (Swift 62). In his regular fishing columns for the *Manchester Guardian,* he railed against the tarring of roads and the speed of motorboats on Windermere (*On Fishing* 235–41). The novels themselves encourage an ethic of burying rubbish, shutting gates, and being careful with fires. These sentiments alone might have earned him a place in Lakeland environmental history with as much justice as Ruskin, whose "environmentalism" was really more universal than specific to the Lakes.[11] But so far they have not. Ransome and the more popularist view of the Lakes he derived from Ruskin and fostered have been elided from the narratives of national park.

Foremost among the reasons for this must be the fact that it has only been in the last decade that Ransome has begun to be "academecized." This is a fate typical of many children's writers. Before the 1990s, knowledge about Ransome was held largely in the grip of fans. With a few notable exceptions (for example, Inglis 126–28), "discussion" of Ransome's work took the form of imitative novels and private expeditions. Few scholarly studies were published before that time; mention of

Ransome was usually within the context of the "classics" of children's literature. Discussion about the "classics" is, of course, a "universalist" rather than a regionally specific discourse. Ransome had, and has, many fans and critics who have no idea that his books were set in real places, or that this might be a significant aspect of their production. On the contrary, they typically recall the way in which they mapped Ransome's "fictional" geography onto their own available topography and played similar games. Whereas the universalism of the classics has now been deeply problematized with regard to most adult fiction, this is not always the case with the (academically marginalized) genre of children's literature.

The advent of the Arthur Ransome Society (TARS) in 1990 did little to change this. While the material published in *Mixed Moss*, the "literary" organ of TARS, might be generally useful as background to "research" on Ransome, in itself it offers little analysis or depth of insight. On the contrary, what it does offer is evidence of a fairly large group of people who are wildly enthusiastic about Ransome and who have a literary journal in which they zealously share knowledge with other initiates (see Hunt, "Academicising Arthur Ransome" 2–4).

Moreover, the inaugural moment of TARS in July 1990 coincided with, rather than preceded, the first scholarly studies of Ransome in 1989 and 1990. To some extent, both TARS and academic interest in Ransome are riding on the same historical imperative: to capitalize on literary heritage and to be a player in its ongoing construction. TARS continues to have a significant influence in these terms. At least one of the founding members, for example, is responsible for curatorial decisions in several of Cumbria's museums and art galleries, and a number of its past proposals have been endorsed by the National Trust. At the dawn of the new millennium, it seems that TARS is actually winning this ideological war over the meaning of Ransome: little is published on Ransome without its endorsement and the critical establishment has left him well alone since those few papers at the turn of the decade.

There are two major consequences to this "grassroots victory" in the context of the environmental history of the Lakes. The first is that, because Ransome was associated with a number of places during his lifetime, TARS has no reason to focus on his specific rather than general impact on a particular region. On the contrary, the branch structure of TARS encourages identification of Ransome equally with several different regions within Britain: the Lakes, the Broads, London, Scotland, and Leeds. As a result of the geographical dissemination of TARS members, Ransome's formative experiences in the Lakes have not received the attention they would have done had a regional institution claimed him as an object of scrutiny. By contrast, Wordsworth's long-term residency in Grasmere and the substantial nature of his material remains (houses, furnishings, manuscripts, and so on) support both a thriving tourist industry and local elite institutions. The sheer number of visitors to Dove Cottage helps validate scholarly research into Wordsworth's cultural importance.[12] Ransome, on the other hand, frequently liquidated his worldly possessions to move elsewhere and has left little worth marketing.

Second, the appropriation of knowledge about Ransome by an enthusiast society like TARS has meant that many people outside this sphere of influence have either never heard of Ransome or dismiss him as a subject of serious inquiry. Much of the information available on Ransome is not accessible through research institutions. To gain access to material such as *Mixed Moss,* transcripts from TARS literary weekends, and even Christina Hardyment's *Arthur Ransome and Captain Flint's Trunk* (1984), it is necessary to make personal purchases direct from TARS. Discussions with various academics and heritage professionals in Cumbria have given the author of this essay the impression that most environmental researchers would not touch this kind of non-scholarly material. However, it seems a catch-22: if TARS controls information about Ransome and no serious researcher will touch TARS, then how can Ransome ever escape the TARS perspective?

The other main reason for the critical neglect of Ransome and the "Collingwood line" of Ruskinian thinking about the Lakes is that unlike Rawnsley, Collingwood did not enjoy the limelight. In fact, on a number of occasions Rawnsley received the accolades for work largely executed by Collingwood behind the scenes. The institution of the Ruskin Museum in Coniston is perhaps the best example of this, but there are many other instances of work "opened" by Rawnsley but designed and/or made by Collingwood.[13] Collingwood, it seems, was quite happy to let Rawnsley have nominal control if it meant that he could get on and do the work that interested him from the base of his family home (R. G. Collingwood).

Indeed, much of what Collingwood transmitted to Ransome took place within his family circle. Historically, domestic traditions have always lost out to the public, "political" ones in academic discourse, and it seems in this sense that Collingwood and Ransome occupy what has often been a "feminine" space in comparison to Rawnsley. It was at Lanehead that Collingwood reared his son, the philosopher R. G. Collingwood, according to Ruskinian virtues (see Johnston 28–30), and at Lanehead that Ransome met W. G. Collingwood's grandchildren, upon whom the Walker children in *Swallows and Amazons* were based. Just as Collingwood imbibed Ruskin's ethic of making the most of the Lakes as an educational resource with his family, Ransome used them as a "school" away from school in his books. The educational experiments both performed in the Lakes can be seen as the direct descendants of those conducted by Wordsworth in Grasmere and his "Pantisocratic" friends in Keswick—and yet without the Wordsworthian-divine connotations of Nature herself as teacher and bestower of power.

Recognizing Ransome's place in the history of the Lake District National Park is therefore important because it removes from Wordsworth the idealizing patina that has settled on him since Rawnsley's day—a patina polished by Bate. In his celebratory account of Wordsworth's impact on a landscape, Bate fails to address many of the problems others have perceived with the Wordsworthian terms of the Lake District National Park. Two of the most recent representations of the Lake District, for example, Jimmy McGovern's *The Lakes* (1997)[14] and Ian McEwan's *Amsterdam* (1998), are far from eulogies of the romantic associations of this landscape. This screenplay and novel join a growing number of sociologically oriented studies of the Lake District that highlight the social and environmental cost of the many "aesthetic" conservation decisions made in the past (for example, Cox 24–33; Croall 1; MacEwen and MacEwen 7; Mandler 467–71). Ransome's presence not only unsettles the celebratory ecocritical teleology, it functions as a potential means for negotiating a less onerous literary heritage for the Lakes.

NOTES

1. Ransome lived at Low Ludderburn on Windermere from 1925 to 1935. He later lived at the Heald on Coniston Water (1940–45), Lowick Hall near Nibthwaite (1948–50), and intermittently at Hill Top in Haverthwaite (1960–67).

2. Both Peter Hunt and William Feaver have gestured toward Ransome's role in creating "the mental image that the British have of the English lake district" (Hunt, "*Swallows and Amazons*" 222; Feaver 94), but neither have pursued this theme or sought to give it specific force. By contrast, Ransome's relationship with the Norfolk Broads has been vigorously explored by David Matless in a recent article (132–36).

3. One must place this kind of argument for the importance of Lakes literature to environment against earlier, less widely convincing models to gauge its full significance. In the late 1980s, for instance, cultural geographer Shelagh J. Squire started a sustained debate in the *Canadian Geographer* about the extent to which a poet like Wordsworth could really be said to have "led" a change in taste for landscape. Squire met fierce attack from two more traditional geographers for her claim about the poet's importance. Despite

the fact that Squire reeled out plenty of statistics on "Wordsworth Tourism," one senses her opponents' discomfort about the impossibility of determining the inner motivations of people doing "Daffodil Tours" (see Dilley; Sitwell; Squire). By tracing the origins of environmental organizations, on the other hand, literary scholars seem to have found a way to quantify literary value that will speak to those outside "cultural" disciplines.

4.   Bate does not consider, for example, that Rawnsley, his "link" between the Wordsworth Society and conservationist societies in the Lakes, resigned from the LDDS in 1889; nor does he take into account ways in which the interwar NT came to depart from the spirit of its founding members. See Cannadine 15; Dowthwaite 53.

5.   Bate develops the concept of a "bioregion" in a later essay, "Poetry and Biodiversity" (54).

6.   The year 1998 saw the opening of a new international research library of Ruskin material at Lancaster University and 1999 the opening of a new Ruskin Museum in Coniston. Note also the focus of *Ruskin and Environment* (1995), edited by Michael Wheeler, especially the essays by Keith Hanley, Jeffrey Richards, and John K. Walton.

7.   For example, in *Wordsworth's Second Nature* (1984), James K. Chandler presents the case that Wordsworth's grounding of himself in the most English "nook of English land" in *The Prelude* must be seen in the context of the complicated ties with French Theory, French women, and French politics that he was trying to untangle at the time (see esp. 50–59).

8.   See Plotz and Taylor for the "cursing" of Hartley by romantic poets who did not really want him to remain a "perpetual child." On the "Madras" school, see Richardson (91–103).

9.   The Collingwoods made their "bread and butter" money by selling pictures of local scenes (Battrick 180).

10.   "Meritocracy" in this instance implies an invented, imaginative order, open to anyone who is competent to embrace it.

11.   Ruskin gave Rawnsley permission to put his name "without asking leave to any petition against the railways anywhere" (letter from Ruskin to Rawnsley, quoted in Murphy 83).

12.   There were 82,511 visitors to Dove Cottage in 1997, making it the tenth most popular tourist attraction in Cumbria (English Tourist Board Research Services 2).

13.   Such as Ruskin's funeral and the Ruskin memorial on Friar's Crag. It is also worth noting that Rawnsley appropriated one of Collingwood's favorite subjects in *Past and Present at the English Lakes* (1916) with two essays on the German miners of Keswick. This book would have reached a far wider audience than Collingwood's publications in the *Transactions of the Cumberland and Westmoreland Antiquarian and Archaeological Society.*

14.   Published as a novel by K. M. Lock in 1997, this BBC series screened in 1998 and 1999 in Australia.

Works Cited

Appleton, Jay. "A Sort of National Property: The Growth of the National Parks Movement in Britain." In *The Lake District: A Sort of National Property.* Cheltenham, England: Countryside Commission and Victoria & Albert Museum, 1986, 113–22.

Barcus, Robert K. Letter. *National Geographic* 186.6 (1994): forum section.

Bate, Jonathan. "Poetry and Biodiversity." In *Writing the Environment: Ecocriticism and Literature*. Ed. Richard Kerridge and Neil Sammells. London: Zed Books, 1998, 53–70.

———. *Romantic Ecology: Wordsworth and the Environmental Tradition.* London: Routledge, 1991.

Battrick, Elizabeth. "Creative Years and the Lake District." In *Beatrix Potter, 1866–1943: The Artist and Her World.* By Judy Taylor, Joyce Irene Whalley, Anne Stevenson Hobbs, and Elizabeth M. Battrick. London: Frederick Warne and the National Trust, 1987, 170–84.

Brogan, Hugh. *The Life of Arthur Ransome.* London: Pimlico, 1992.

Cannadine, David. "The First Hundred Years." In *The National Trust: The Next Hundred Years.* Ed. Howard Newby. London: National Trust, 1995, 11–31.

Chandler, James K. *Wordsworth's Second Nature: A Study of the Poetry and Politics.* Chicago: University of Chicago Press, 1984.

Collingwood, R. G. "Obituary. Mr W. G. Collingwood: Artist, Author, and Antiquary." *The Times,* October 3, 1932.

Collingwood, W. G. *The Lake Counties.* London: J. M. Dent, 1949.

———. *Lake District History.* Kendal, England: Titus Wilson, 1925.

———. *Ruskin Relics.* London: Isbiter, 1903.

Cox, Graham. "'Reading' Nature: Reflections on Ideological Persistence and the Politics of the Countryside." *Landscape Research* 13.3 (1988): 24–34.

Croall, Jonathan. *Preserve or Destroy: Tourism and the Environment.* London: Calouste Gulbenkian Foundation, 1995.

Dilley, Robert S. "'Wordsworth and Lake District Tourism': A Commentary." *Canadian Geographer* 34.2 (1990): 155–58.

Dowthwaite, Michael. "Defenders of Lakeland: The Lake District Defence Society in the Late-Nineteenth Century." In *Windermere in the Nineteenth Century.* Ed. Oliver M. Westall. Lancaster, England: Centre for North-West Regional Studies, Lancaster University, 1991, 49–62.

English Tourist Board Research Services. *Regional Tourism Facts: Cumbria.* London: English Tourist Board; Windermere: Cumbria Tourism Board, 1998.

Erisman, Fred. "Arthur Ransome, Children's Play, and Cultural Literacy." *International Review of Children's Literature and Librarianship* 4.2 (1989): 107–14.

Feaver, William. "Lakeland Trails: Beatrix Potter to Schwitters." In *The Lake District: A Sort of National Property.* Cheltenham, England: Countryside Commission and Victoria & Albert Museum, 1986, 85–104.

Gill, Stephen. *Wordsworth and the Victorians.* Oxford: Clarendon Press, 1998.

Hall, Marshall. *The Artists of Cumbria.* Newcastle-upon-Tyne, England: Marshall Hall Associates, 1979.

Hanley, Keith. "The Discourse of Natural Beauty." In *Ruskin and Environment: The Storm-Cloud of the Nineteenth Century.* Ed. Michael Wheeler. Manchester, England: Manchester University Press, 1995, 10–37.

Hardyment, Christina. *Arthur Ransome and Captain Flint's Trunk.* London: Jonathan Cape, 1984.

Hunt, Peter. "Arthur Ransome's *Swallows and Amazons:* Escape to Lost Paradise." In *Touchstones: Reflections on the Best in Children's Literature.* Ed. Perry Nodelman. West Lafayette, Ind.: Children's Literature Association, 1985, 221–32.

———. "'Tread softly for you tread on my dreams': Academicising Arthur Ransome." *International Review of Children's Literature and Librarianship.* 7.1 (1992): 1–10.

Inglis, Fred. *The Promise of Happiness: Value and Meaning in Children's Fiction.* Cambridge: Cambridge University Press, 1981.

Jay, Eileen. *The Armitt Story, Ambleside.* Ambleside, England: Loughrigg Press for the Armitt Trust, 1998.

Johnston, William M. *The Formative Years of R. G. Collingwood.* The Hague: Martinus Nijhoff, 1967.

Kerridge, Richard, and Neil Sammells. "Notes on Contributors." In *Writing the Environment: Ecocriticism and Literature.* Eds. Richard Kerridge and Neil Sammells. London: Zed Books, 1998, i–ix.

Lock, K. M. *Jimmy McGovern's "The Lakes."* London: Penguin/BBC, 1997.

MacEwen, Ann, and Malcolm MacEwen. *Greenprints for the Countryside? The Story of Britain's National Parks.* London: Allen & Unwin, 1987.

Mandler, Peter. "Politics and the English Landscape since the First World War." *Huntington Library Quarterly* 55.3 (1992): 459–76.

Matless, David. "Moral Geography in Broadland." *Ecumene* 1.2 (1994): 127–55.

McEwan, Ian. *Amsterdam.* (1998) London: Vintage, 1999.

Murphy, Graham. *Founders of the National Trust.* London: Christopher Helm, 1987.

Plotz, Judith. "The *Annus Mirabilis* and the Lost Boy: Hartley's Case." *Studies in Romanticism* 33.2 (1994): 181–200.

Ransome, Arthur. *Arthur Ransome on Fishing.* London: Jonathan Cape, 1994.

———. *The Autobiography of Arthur Ransome.* Ed. Rupert Hart-Davis. London: Jonathan Cape, 1976.

———. *The Picts and the Martyrs; or, Not Welcome at All.* London: Jonathan Cape, 1943.

———. *Pigeon Post.* London: Jonathan Cape, 1936.

———. *Swallowdale.* London: Jonathan Cape, 1931.

———. *Swallows and Amazons.* Harmondsworth, England: Puffin Books, 1962.

———. *Winter Holiday.* Harmondsworth, England: Penguin, 1968.

Rawnsley, H. D. *Literary Associations of the English Lakes.* 2 vols. 3d ed. Glasgow: MacLehose, 1906.

———. *Past and Present at the English Lakes.* Glasgow: MacLehose, 1916.

———. *Ruskin and the English Lakes.* Glasgow: MacLehose, 1901.

Richards, Jeffrey. "The Role of the Railways." In *Ruskin and Environment: The Storm-Cloud of the Nineteenth Century.* Ed. Michael Wheeler. Manchester, England: Manchester University Press, 1995, 123–43.

Richardson, Alan. *Literature, Education, and Romanticism: Reading as Social Practice, 1789–1832.* Cambridge Studies in Romanticism 8. Cambridge: Cambridge University Press, 1994.

Sitwell, O. F. G. "Geography as Criticism: A Comment on 'Wordsworth and Lake District Tourism.'" *Canadian Geographer* 34.3 (1990): 158–64.

Squire, Shelagh J. "'Wordsworth and Lake District Tourism': A Reply." *Canadian Geographer* 34.2 (1990): 164–70.

———. "Wordsworth and Lake District Tourism: Romantic Reshaping of Landscape." *Canadian Geographer* 32.3 (1988): 237–47.

Swift, Jeremy. "A Fisherman's Life." In *Arthur Ransome on Fishing.* London: Jonathan Cape, 1994, 17–112.

Taylor, Anya. "'A Father's Tale': Coleridge Foretells the Life of Hartley." *Studies in Romanticism* 30.1 (1991): 37–56.

Townend, Matthew. "Collingwood and Ransome." *Mixed Moss* 2.1 (1994): 52–54.

Walton, John K. "The National Trust: Preservation or Provision?" In *Ruskin and Environment: The Storm-Cloud of the Nineteenth Century.* Ed. Michael Wheeler. Manchester, England: Manchester University Press, 1995, 144–64.

Wardale, Roger. *In Search of Swallows and Amazons: Arthur Ransome's Lakeland.* Wilmslow, Cheshire, United Kingdom: Sigma Press, 1996.

Welberry, Karen. "Colonial and Postcolonial Deployment of 'Daffodils.'" *Kunapipi* 19.1 (1997): 32–44.

Wheeler, Michael, ed. *Ruskin and Environment: The Storm-Cloud of the Nineteenth Century.* Manchester, England: Manchester University Press, 1995.

Wordsworth, William. *The Illustrated Wordsworth's Guide to the Lakes.* Ed. Peter Bicknell. New York: Congdon & Weed, 1984.

6

E. B. White's Paean to Life

The Environmental Imagination of *Charlotte's Web*

Lynn Overholt Wake

[A]ny writer who sees the world in ecological perspective faces a hard problem: how, despite the perfection of our technological boxes, to make us feel the ache and tug of that organic web passing through us, how to situate the lives of characters—and therefore of readers—in nature.

SCOTT RUSSELL SANDERS, "SPEAKING A WORD FOR NATURE"

E. B. White's masterpiece, *Charlotte's Web,* has been a best-seller since it appeared in 1952. White called his novel "an appreciative story. . . . It celebrates life, the seasons, the goodness of the barn, the beauty of the world, the glory of everything" (*Letters* 613). Because the particular farm lifestyle White depicts predates the book by a generation or more, older readers often respond to his text with nostalgia, and critics have generally seen the book as a well-wrought pastoral, but if we read this story of "how a pig shall be saved" as an invitation to life's dance—the way White advises us to read his own favorite book, *Walden*—then *Charlotte's Web* emerges as a comedy of survival. Regardless of the reader's age, this book seen though an ecocritical lens beckons as a major text in American environmental literature.

The barn in *Charlotte's Web* functions as its own ecosystem. Sheep, geese, and pigs, though "production agriculture" animals, are respected and their lives are celebrated. Templeton, though "wild," is a rat, an introduced species. The gray spider, Charlotte, the one indigenous creature, and Fern, a Euro-American girl, inhabit almost opposite ends of the nature/culture spectrum, their existence in the same story mediated by White's barn. Drive any distance across Nebraska or Iowa today and try to imagine a girl quietly sitting and watching the animals in one of the sterile, spider-free, hog confinement buildings spreading over the landscape. As Gary Paul Nabhan observes in *The Geography of Childhood:* "That sensibility—that the presence of other creatures can keep one from feeling lonely or isolated—is apparently becoming a scarce commodity among children today" (90); yet fifty years after his familiar story first appeared, E. B. White invites us to situate ourselves more attentively and more harmoniously within both culture and nature, which together comprise the web of life. White's novel, like the barn that inspired it, is built to nurture and to house a regenerative experience of nature.

Lawrence Buell calls for such a regenerative experience in *The Environmental Imagination*. Although Buell concentrates on nonfiction, *Charlotte's Web* exemplifies his four criteria for an environmental text (7–8): "the non-human environment" is not only present in White's book but it dominates the story; biocentricity prevails while human interest recedes; a child's question regarding environmental ethics initiates the plot in the first sentence of the book; and the natural processes of birth, growth, death, and seasonality give the novel its form.

Pointing out the possibility of "many kinds of environmental imagination," Joseph Meeker might have had E. B. White in mind when he described environmental writers as sharing a "profound love of the natural world," a fascination with its complex processes, and an understanding that the "high integrity" of the natural world is not dependent for its value on human use (address). In *The Comedy of Survival*, Meeker, like the spider he describes flying a kite across a forest path to anchor the web it soon weaves across the gap (74), provides a useful bridge between children's literature and ecocriticism. The distinctions he draws between the pastoral and the picaresque patterns of response to the world are especially relevant. Although *Charlotte's Web* has some affinity with the pastoral mode, pastoral elements in the story are framed by a broader, more biocentric, picaresque pattern. Meeker's sense of the picaresque hero as being one small organism surviving within his or her ecosystem parallels not only the animal characters of much of children's literature, including *Charlotte's Web*, but also young readers' and ecologically minded older readers' life experience.

A Summary of the Story

Fern Arable makes such a fuss the morning she sees her father about to dispatch a newborn pig (the runt of the litter) that he gives her the pig to raise. But after five weeks she is told she must sell Wilbur, and her

Uncle Homer Zuckerman buys the pig for six dollars. Now the scene shifts to a wonderful old barn, where Fern sits for hours, watching Wilbur and listening to the animals talk. Wilbur learns what boredom feels like and briefly escapes from his pen, but is lured back by Lurvy, the hired man, with a bucket of slops. Wilbur realizes he is lonely, and a gray spider named Charlotte announces she'll be his friend; the next morning, with her musical "Salutations!" the salvific relationship begins.

When the old Sheep lets slip that Wilbur will become bacon at Christmastime, Charlotte promises to save him, and does. She weaves SOME PIG into her web, which is taken for a miracle, and after she extends her successful advertising campaign with the words TERRIFIC, RADIANT, and HUMBLE (the latter two located by the crafty rat, Templeton), Wilbur's life is saved. Charlotte produces her own "magnum opus," her egg sac, and dies, alone. Ever more thoughtful and mature, Wilber promises to take the egg sac back to Zuckerman's barn, where he rejoices to see her 514 children emerge in the spring, but none of the new spiders ever takes Charlotte's place. "It is not often that someone comes along who is a true friend and a good writer. Charlotte was both" (184).

E. B. White, Another Scribe for All Nature

With White, one encounters a connoisseur of humor; a masterful and prolific writer of letters; the author of at least ten books of prose, two books of poetry, and three children's books; a man who was the editorial voice of the *New Yorker* for decades; an author and general editor of Roosevelt's *Four Freedoms*; and a writer who literally wrote the book on style—that is, *The Elements of Style,* which John Griffith calls "the most popular English composition handbook of all time" (xii). Readers may know White as an amusing, urbane essayist and editorial writer, or they may think of him as the author of talking animal fables for children; however, neither of these roles conflicts with seeing E. B. White as a nature writer. The full effect of E. B. White on the landscape of American literature has yet to be measured. White's lifelong writing career should not be divided into separate provinces; his accomplishment was more holistic than it was fragmented. While it might seem surprising that a man who found the *New Yorker* magazine a congenial place in which to work and publish is indeed a nature-oriented writer, a closer look at White invites us to expand our understandings of the nature of nature writing.

White fits Henry David Thoreau's vision of a writer as the scribe of all nature. As Scott Russell Sanders points out, "Thoreau situated himself *within* nature, and drew upon all the senses . . . to convey what was going on around him in the green world" (189). Although Sanders is speaking specifically of Thoreau when he writes, "The forces at work in pond and forest he found also at work in himself," I believe he describes the seamlessness with subject and world that defines a nature writer. When Sanders quotes Thoreau's journal: "A writer, a man writing, is the scribe of all nature; he is the corn and the grass and the atmosphere writing," he puts his finger on a helpful way to understand what nature writing is—a blurring of the boundaries between self and world, an understanding that humans do not, in fact, live their lives separate and apart from the life of a living world, an intuitive determination that one's writing must not deny the interconnectedness of living things. One way or another, nature writing affirms the web of life. E. B. White situates himself within human culture as well as within the green world of pond and forest, recognizing, as do ecocritics, that culture and nature comprise one world. By having a gray spider physically write words in her web, by having the barnyard animals meet to suggest words, and by having Templeton the rat bring words from the dump, White functions in a double sense as the scribe of all nature.

An Almost Virulent Sympathy

One way in which White functions as a writer of environmental texts is through his lifelong attention to animals. The earliest sample we have of White's writing is a letter he wrote to his brother Albert, on October 21, 1908, when he was nine: "I wrote a poem about a little mouse Sunday. It is on the next page" (Elledge 30). His biographer points out that "White's long and interesting literary association with mice began early. In the spring of 1909 he won a prize from the *Woman's Home Companion* for a poem about a mouse" (30). Thirty-six years later his first children's book chronicles the adventures of Stuart Little, described as very much like a mouse, although not literally declared to be one.

Apparently the youthful White continued to win prizes for writing about animals. Following a friend's suggestion, he put plenty of "kindness-to-animals" into his submissions to *St. Nicholas Magazine* to increase his chances of winning. White later recalled: "As I look through the back numbers and examine my own published works, I detect running through them an amazing note of friendliness toward dumb creatures, an almost virulent sympathy for dogs, cats, horses, bears, toads, and robins. I was kind to animals in all sorts of weather almost every month for three or four years. The results were satisfactory" (quoted in Elledge 31). White's subtly self-deprecating tone does not obscure the fact that he was indeed kind to animals all his life, enjoying their companionship, concerning himself with their well-being, and making use of his observations of them in his work.

Elledge's biography of White details a myriad of affectionate relationships with animals. Required to keep his dog Mac in the cellar, White later wrote of "gloomy guilt" over that (18). The large Victorian house where White grew up in Mount Vernon, New York, had a stable that at various times housed pigeons, ducks, geese, and a turkey, as well as horses, of course. "Under the stable lived rats and, occasionally, a wild cat. Like Wilbur in *Charlotte's Web*, [White] was lucky to be surrounded by such various and sensuous manifestations of life—by 'everything'" (19). *Everything*, in White's long experience with living things, included a specific interest in birds and their eggs, with spring and the promise of new life. "Life is always a rich and steady time when you are waiting for something to happen or to hatch" (*Charlotte's Web* 176). In the beginning of White's third novel for children, *The Trumpet of the Swan*, Sam Beaver finds the nest of a trumpeter swan and deliberately does not tell his father, who asks repeatedly if he's seen anything. For White, to approach a nest with eggs is to come close to the miracle of life itself. Nests, like barns, are sacred places where life begins. White was inevitably a biophilic writer, regardless of the age or the level of sophistication of his intended audience.

Other critics have also noted E. B. White's love of animals. In the only full-length treatment of *Charlotte's Web*, John Griffith writes: "White's feeling about animals seems to have been an unusual mixture of the naturalist's love of pure observation, the farmer's businesslike concern for care, feeding, and harvesting, and the pet-lover's pleasure in animals' companionship, enriched by a certain imaginative projection onto them of human personalities. *Charlotte's Web* contains signs of all these attitudes, and (perhaps as a result) it falls somewhere in between the major categories of animal stories" (55). This type of unusual mixture of attitudes toward animals is also fully evident in White's well-known essay "Death of a Pig," which appeared in January 1948 in the *Atlantic Monthly* and which Solheim, Neumeyer, Griffith, and Elledge all recognize as a precursor to *Charlotte's Web*. In that essay, White describes three to four days he spent caring for a pig with a fatal case of erysipelas.

Coming between *Stuart Little* and *Charlotte's Web*, the piece reveals White's empathy for animals as fellow creatures and his emotional ties to their fate, as well as the genius of his writing when he fully engages his deep affinity for animals.

In "Death of a Pig," White employs three different voices, blending them together subtly, so that his reader has the experience of one dynamic but seamless essay. First is his matter-of-fact, *Farm Journal*, businesslike approach to the raising of a pig: "I spent several days and nights in mid-September with an ailing pig" (243); but before that first sentence is finished ("and I feel driven to account for this stretch of time"), he has already shifted into his second attitude toward his subject, this one personal and reflective. White, the consummate wordsmith, pivots on the word *accounting*, moving from agribusiness concerns to his personal musings on the mortality of the pig in relationship to his own: "[T]hings might easily have gone the other way round and none left to do the accounting," a tonal shift from efficiency to eschatology. The third variety of White's voice in this essay involves his use of metaphor based on literary and dramatic concepts; he speaks of tragedy, murder, scripts, lines, actors, and performance. By the third paragraph, we read, "The classic outline of the tragedy was lost." White mentions not only tragedy and melodrama, but comedy, farce, and slapstick as well, shaping his story and his thoughts through reference to the vocabulary of literature and drama. Writing a quarter-century before Joseph W. Meeker's classic study in literary ecology, White celebrates in this essay "the comedy of survival" with gemlike brilliance and clarity.

Helene Solheim notes White's ability to sustain a tone both serious and lighthearted in "Death of a Pig": "The reader is compelled to share White's perspective, and his dualism. Paying attention to the untimely death of a pig is absurd, a colonic carnival, but we come to see it is the untimely death itself, rather than its victim, which occasions a greater loss—a disruption in the community of things" (146). Actually, considering the role he creates for Fred, his dachshund, White's essay goes beyond dualism to find a way to restore that disruption in the community of things; his artful attention to the dog who survives the death of a pig testifies to the continuity of the animal kingdom.

White so easily moves among various levels of writing, one can hardly tell if he's taking the animal's demise seriously and the art of writing lightly, or the other way around. It's an amazing piece of writing: compelling narrative, satisfying detail, compassion and sympathy, all delivered with laugh-out-loud humor. Within all of this, Fred steals the show. The pig, as foreknown, dies; but Fred lives, to become a vaudevillian character in this artful essay, as well as a real dog owned by a real person. Reading about him confers such pleasure, one can infer that White, who seems to be actually grieving over the death of the pig, must have taken comfort in the ongoing life of his dog.

Connected empathetically with the life of other creatures, White in "Death of a Pig" honors one animal's death and celebrates the survival of another. In fact, the dog gains literary immortality. Seven years after his death, Fred makes an important appearance in "Bedfellows" *(Points of My Compass)*, where the dog becomes a unifying element, bringing the presence of the natural world, including the concept of death, into White's essay on school prayer and the freedom of the press: a good example of White's highly integrative style of nature writing. One can conclude that perhaps White's own pleasure and satisfaction in creating Fred's part in "Death of a Pig" may have helped inspire him to begin the writing of *Charlotte's Web*.

Points of His Compass

Alongside the matter of White's affinity for animals comes another component of environmental writing: an author's sense of place. While other up-and-coming American writers of the twenties were gathering in Paris and steaming between New York and London, White, who graduated from Cornell in 1921, drove across America in a Model T with a friend in 1922. They traveled through New York state to Ohio, Kentucky, and Indiana; northwest to Minnesota and North Dakota; on to Yellowstone, spending about ten days on a Montana ranch before motoring on to Glacier National Park; and finally west to Seattle (Elledge 70–80). As they journeyed they wrote. White's later essay based on this trip, "Farewell, My Lovely!" is widely anthologized.

One can hear echoes of this youthful odyssey written into White's ending of *Stuart Little*, with its mouselike protagonist simply headed north, searching for his true love, a pretty brown bird with a streak of yellow on her breast. When Margalo appears in the Little household, Mr. Little and George, the elder son, cannot agree on what type of bird she is—a walleyed vireo or a young wren. Contrasting with their interest in scientific nomenclature, a human construction that actually adds nothing to their knowledge of her, Stuart greets Margalo directly, "Hello. . . . Who are you? Where did you come from?" The bird is not an object to be identified but a fellow creature, a potential friend. Stuart seeks to connect with her, not to classify her, and asking about the place she came from is the natural way to strike up a friendship.

By way of introduction, Margalo says, "I come from fields once tall with wheat, from pastures deep in fern and thistle; I come from vales of meadow-sweet, and I love to whistle" (51). Not only is a sense of place vital to E. B. White's mouselike, humanlike hero, Stuart Little, but the lyrical beauty of Margalo's answer is indispensable as well. Of course a bird would answer in song, so White uses a ballad stanza for Margalo's answer. Stuart's response is to sit bolt upright in bed and ask her to say that again; at that instant he falls in love with Margalo.

White was a man in love with the real world, the natural world, the world of real places, and when he wrote of place, he wrote lovingly. The following passage, which I first found in *Stuart Little* over thirty years ago, still seems a small gem of environmental writing. The scene is Ames' Crossing, a stop on Stuart's journey northward:

> In the loveliest town of all, where the houses were white and high and the elm trees were green and higher than the houses, where the front yards were wide and pleasant and the backyards were bushy and worth finding out about, where the streets sloped down to the stream and the stream flowed quietly under the bridge, where the lawns ended in orchards and the orchards ended in fields and the fields ended in pastures and the pastures climbed the hill and disappeared over the top toward the wonderful wide sky, in this loveliest of all towns Stuart stopped to get a drink of sarsaparilla. (100)

At the end of the book Stuart's search is left unresolved, but "he somehow felt he was headed in the right direction," words that environmentally minded readers might claim as direction indeed.

After his trip across the country, White wrote, "To an American, the physical fact of the complete America is, at best, a dream, a belief, a memory, and the sound of names" (quoted in Elledge 81). White, like Thoreau, sought a place from which to write. His life story is, in part, the story of a man finding ways to situate himself within human culture as well as within the green world of pond and forest.

From 1925 to 1976, White contributed to the *New Yorker* in various capacities. When he published a collection of essays in 1962 called *The Points of My Compass: Letters from the East, the West, the North, the South,* he used his desk at the magazine as the midpoint of his compass, since he "seldom went anywhere or did anything":

> My activities smelled of the hearth. Instead of being in London, I was home. Instead of being in Karachi, I was in the barn, or in the bathtub. My life was

uneventful, my habits were fixed, and my thoughts to an alarming degree ranged back and forth over my small immediate affairs. I regretted this but saw no likelihood that I would suddenly change my ways or leave my haunts. Clearly, if I were to serve as a foreign correspondent to a responsible publication I would have to alter the world itself, and rearrange geography to give me a wider range. (*Compass* xii)

This whimsical approach to geography, and to himself as well, shows the nature writer's attention to place and his need to situate himself in the physical world.

In fact he had rearranged his personal geography decades earlier. Helene Solheim observes that White "for most of his adult life has had one foot on his Maine farm while the other remained firmly planted in Manhattan; he writes equally well from both places, despite the precarious equipose" (150). It was White's own barn, a human-built shelter, that became the personal place that allowed him to celebrate the "glory of everything," and to weave a particularly imaginative web involving both nature and culture.

The Goodness of the Barn

White's family had summered in Maine when he was a boy, and he and his wife, Katharine, had rented cottages in the Blue Hill area for three years. Elledge describes how the Whites first encountered the farm they purchased in 1933:

> On a little cruise out of Blue Hill they anchored one night in Allen Cove at a point from which they could see, up beyond the flats and a pasture full of stone outcroppings, the barn that *Charlotte's Web* would make famous. The following day, as they drove along a road running south from Blue Hill, they passed a house with a FOR SALE sign in front. It was connected, Maine-fashion, to the beautiful barn they had spotted from the boat. The Whites bought the twelve-room house . . . , the barn and other outbuildings, and forty acres of land that ran down to the cove. (Elledge 183)

This is the place that E. B. White loved for the rest of his life, the place that become the inspiration, the setting, and the location for the act of writing *Charlotte's Web*. The barn was what first attracted the Whites to the property at Allen Cove—not the house, and not the land itself. In a letter to Bennett Cerf, for use in his column for the *Saturday Review of Literature*, White explains the genesis of *Charlotte's Web* this way: "Well, I like animals, and it would be odd if I failed to write about them. Animals are a weakness with me, and when I got a place in the country I was quite sure animals would appear, and they did" (quoted in Griffith 35–36). The significance of the barn as shelter for whatever animals might "appear" is clearly implied. I believe that for White, barns represented a crossroads of human culture and biological nature. Here was a human-built structure designed for the nurturing and sustaining of natural life, the life of animals both wild and domestic.

An Invitation to Life's Dance

Shortly after *Charlotte's Web* was published, White wrote to a young reader: "As to your notion of an allegory, there is none. *Charlotte's Web* is a tale of the animals in my barn, not of the people in my life. When you read it, just relax. Any attempt to find allegorical meanings is bound to end disastrously, for no meanings are in there. I ought to know" (*Letters* 373). This advice is reminiscent of the warning Mark Twain posts at the beginning of *Adventures of Huckleberry Finn*—"Persons attempting to find a motive in this narrative will be prosecuted; persons attempting to find a moral in it will be banished; persons attempting to find a plot in it will be shot." But White is not being coy or sardonic. It makes sense to take him literally here; his suggestion to simply relax and read is harmonious with the nature of his book.

He recasts the idea years later in another letter: "I just want to add that there is no symbolism in *Charlotte's Web*. And there is no political meaning in the story. It is a straight report from the barn cellar, which I dearly love" (*Letters* 614). If we take him at his word and use restraint in pursuing allegory, symbolism, and political meaning, the experience of reading *Charlotte's Web* as "a straight report from the barn cellar" opens as widely as a barn door; the book is meant to be an invitation.

White provides solid information on how to read his most famous book in remarks he made about his own favorite book. "*Walden* is the only book I own," he wrote in 1953, "although there are some others unclaimed on my shelves. Every man, I think, reads one book in his life, and this one is mine" (Dale 44–45). He believed that youth was the best time to encounter *Walden*, and because his passage in "A Slight Sound at Evening" clearly explains his sense of what it can be for a young person to read a book with such impact, I quote at length:

> I think it is of some advantage to encounter the book at a period in one's life when the normal anxieties and enthusiasms and rebellions of youth closely resemble those of Thoreau in that spring of 1845 when he borrowed an ax, went out to the woods, and began to whack down some trees for timber.

Received at such a juncture, the book is like an invitation to life's dance, assuring the troubled recipient that no matter what befalls him in the way of success or failure he will always be welcome at the party—that the music is played for him, too, if he will but listen and move his feet. In effect, that is what the book is—an invitation, unengraved; and it stirs one as a young girl is stirred by her first big party bid. Many think it a sermon; many set it down as an attempt to rearrange society; some think it an exercise in nature-loving; some find it a rather irritating collection of inspirational puffballs by an eccentric show-off. I think it none of these. It still seems to me the best youth's companion yet written by an American. (*Compass* 15–16)

Scholars and critics of children's literature generally find a centuries-long evolution in the purpose of literature for children, a movement from instruction to delight (Darton 1–3). E. B. White understood a third important function of a book for young people—to keep them (all of us) company. Because *Charlotte's Web* is such excellent company, it and similar books belong in our college and university classrooms. Received at such a juncture, they could help preserve the web of life.

Close to Holy Ground

White spent two years writing his story of a pig's salvation (the phrase is John Griffith's subtitle), and Fern Arable always had a role in the story. In a famous review in the *Horn Book*, Anne Carroll Moore wrote, "The story got off to a fine start . . . [but] Fern, the real center of the book, is never developed." Moore seems unaware of the new approach White was taking toward a children's story. The human child is definitely not the center of the book, although her role is vital. White was not writing the usual anthropocentric story; instead, he offers a biocentric hymn that celebrates all of life. *Charlotte's Web* is one of the "New Stories" Joseph Meeker and others are calling for, a story creating connections across boundaries.

In his second draft, White began the novel: "A barn can have a horse in it and a barn can have a cow in it, and a barn can have hens scratching in the chaff and swallows flying in and out through the door—but if a barn hasn't got a pig in it, it is hardly worth talking about" (Neumeyer 196). Even before completing his first draft, White sought a better way to begin the story. Manuscripts indicate that he wrote the beginning many times before finding his dramatic first line, "Where's Papa going with that ax?" Elledge explains that for some time White "tried to let the story begin at midnight, when Fern's father goes out to the hoghouse and by lantern-light finds that his sow has littered eleven pigs, one more than she has teats to feed them with" (295). Elledge notes that the problem with all White's "variations on that opening was that they lacked dramatic action and failed to introduce the girl whose perception and sensibility would gradually lead the reader into the world of the barn."

In chapter 3 White found the right spot for his revised description of Zuckerman's barn, "the kind of barn that swallows like to build their nests in . . . that children like to play in" (14). With Wilbur present, the barn is definitely worth talking about: "Fern came almost every day to visit him. She found an old milking stool that had been discarded, and she placed the stool in the sheepfold next to Wilbur's pen. Here she sat quietly during the long afternoons, thinking and listening and watching Wilbur. The sheep soon got to know her and trust her. So did the geese, who lived with the sheep. All the animals trusted her, she was so quiet and friendly" (14–15). Holding my copy of *Charlotte's Web* in my left hand as I copy the lines above, I find that White's book forms a kind of corner, and I sit here in the opening it makes. On the left is a young pig, head down, his rounded back and ears echoing the curves of his wooden trough. On my right sit Fern and the sheep and the goose, all three of them composed of the same curving shapes. And here am I, in the middle, included in the warmth of White's cellar, the south side of his own barn, as Garth Williams drew it.

Fern sits on a three-legged milking stool, leaning on a low fence, watching Wilbur and listening quietly. She is flanked by creatures not of her species. No one is talking now, but Fern's patient waiting, her thinking and listening and watching Wilbur, whom she loves, is somehow transmitted not just into my mind but into my being as well, and I know I am not alone. We are all in this together. The animals and Fern are keeping me company. Fern does lead the reader into the barn, and what we find there with her is essentially a sacred experience.

In a letter to a filmmaker White wrote about Fern's reunion with Wilbur in the barn in some detail: "An aura of magic is essential, because this is a magical happening. Much can be done by music of the right kind, as when the moment arrives when communication takes place between the little girl and the animals in the barn cellar. This is truly a magical moment and should be so marked by the music. (I hear it as a sort of thrumming, brooding sound, like the sound of crickets in the fall, or katydids, or cicadas. It should be a haunting, quiet, steady sound— subdued and repetitive)" (*Letters* 613–14). Fern's ability to understand the language of other living things is hymnodic; their communication is sacred music. With Fern's help, White ushers his readers into the sacred place where life begins, where connections across species are experienced and encouraged.

In a letter to Bennett Cerf, White wrote that the theme of *Charlotte's Web* "is that a pig shall be saved" (Griffith 36). The story that White ultimately wrote, weaving the seasons of Fern, of Charlotte, and of Wilbur so inextricably together (Solheim) also includes Templeton the rat, the one barnyard animal missing from the editorial meeting in which the lifesaving writer, Charlotte, asks for input from all present. In White's fully integrative nature story, even Templeton's assistance is vital. Early in the story, he brings words from the dump, and in the end, he agrees to climb up in the rafters at the fair booth and carry the dying spider's egg sac down to Wilbur.

In between comes the seemingly small incident of the rat and the rotten goose egg. White liked geese, wrote often about his personal experiences with geese, and gave them humorous—sometimes cacophonous but always significant—parts to sing in his barnyard choir. He also loved eggs, and loved the idea of eggs. The goose in *Charlotte's Web* lays eight eggs, but only seven goslings are hatched, and Templeton asks for the unhatched egg, hiding it under his trough.

Four chapters later, "heavily armed" Avery, Fern's brother, tries to capture Charlotte, loses his balance, topples onto Wilbur's trough, and the lifeless egg explodes. In using a rotten egg to foil a mindless scheme of destruction, White weaves several layers of lifesaving into his magnum opus. Not only is the newborn pig saved in the story's opening lines, saved again when sold to Uncle Homer, saved from loneliness through his friendship with Charlotte, saved from becoming Christmas bacon through the spider's skill with words, but the lifesaving plan itself is saved. The fact is that White deals with life and death both alternately and together; the web they make is sacred. Reading this story, one comes close to holy ground.

Seeing the world through an ecological perspective and hearing the music of an ecocentric world, White rises to Scott Russell Sanders's challenge to nature writers "to make us feel the ache and tug of that organic web passing through us . . . to situate the lives of characters—and therefore of readers—in nature" (194). After spending time in White's barn, the lives of these characters, and of us as readers, have indeed become more clearly situated in nature. As we read *Charlotte's Web*, something is urging us to slow down and observe, to listen to nature and to watch; this is not a sermon, not a lesson, but an invocation, an evocation of the actuality of the lives of these other animals. We receive an affirmation that it is all right to be content with our place as one species among many. Fern's quiet contentment affirms our own delight in the life stories unfolding before us.

Fern Arable is the key—not that *she* keeps us company, but that she enables *us* to keep company with the animals. She shows us how things are done in her uncle's barn, ushers us into a sacred place, and shows us how to behave ourselves there. As our liaison with the idyllic life evoked in Zuckerman's barn, she extends our personal invitation to a biocentric comedy of survival, the life-affirming dance. In *Charlotte's Web*, White shows us that we, too, are welcome at the party.

WORKS CITED

Buell, Lawrence. *The Environmental Imagination: Thoreau, Nature Writing, and the Formation of American Culture.* Cambridge: Harvard University Press, 1995.

Dale, Rebecca M., ed. *E.B. White: Writings from the New Yorker, 1927–1976.* New York: HarperCollins, 1990.

Darton, F. J. Harvey. *Children's Books in England.* 3d ed. Ed. Brian Alderson. Cambridge: Cambridge University Press, 1982.

Elledge, Scott. *E. B. White: A Biography.* New York: Norton, 1984.

Griffith, John. *Charlotte's Web: A Pig's Salvation.* New York: Twayne, 1993.

Meeker, Joseph W. Address given at the International Cather Seminar, Nebraska City, Nebraska, June 18, 2000.

———. *The Comedy of Survival: Literary Ecology and a Play Ethic.* Tucson: University of Arizona Press, 1997.

Moore, Anne Carroll. "The Three Owls' Notebook." *The Horn Book,* December 1952, 394. Rpt. in *The Annotated Charlotte's Web.* Ed. Peter F. Neumeyer. New York: Harper, 1994, 246.

Nabhan, Gary Paul, and Stephen Trimble. *The Geography of Childhood: Why Children Need Wild Places.* Boston: Beacon Press, 1994.

Neumeyer, Peter F., ed. *The Annotated Charlotte's Web.* New York: Harper, 1994.

Sanders, Scott Russell. "Speaking a Word for Nature." In *The Ecocriticism Reader: Landmarks in Literary Ecology.* Ed. Cheryll Glotfelty and Harold Fromm. Athens: University of Georgia Press, 1996, 182–95.

Solheim, Helene. "Magic in the Web: Time, Pigs, and E. B. White." In *Critical Essays on E. B. White.* Ed. Robert L. Root Jr. New York: G. K. Hall, 1994, 144–57.

White, E. B. *Charlotte's Web.* New York: Harper, 1952.

———. "Death of a Pig." *Atlantic Monthly,* January 1948. Rpt. in *The Second Tree from the Corner,* by E. B. White. New York: Harper, 1954. 243–53.

———. *Letters of E. B. White.* Ed. Dorothy Lobrano Guth. New York: Harper, 1976.

———. *The Points of My Compass: Letters from the East, the West, the North, the South.* New York: Harper, 1962.

———. *Stuart Little.* New York: Harper, 1945.

———. *The Trumpet of the Swan.* New York: Harper, 1970.

ecoLewis

Conservationism and Anticolonialism in *The Chronicles of Narnia*

Nicole M. DuPlessis

In 1993, reflecting on the state of criticism on C. S. Lewis, Colin Manlove indicated that much Lewis criticism is thematic in nature, dealing primarily with the presence of Lewis's Christian beliefs in his texts (11). In the decade since the publication of Manlove's *"The Chronicles of Narnia": Patterning of a Fantastic World,* very little has changed: critics evaluate Lewis's *Chronicles of Narnia* largely on the basis of their agreement or disagreement with the moral views, often conflated with "worldview," expressed in his fantasies for children. However, the rhetorical force of a text may reach beyond the strict intentions of its author to connect with contemporary issues—in this case, issues of justice that involve humankind and nature. Close examination of C. S. Lewis's diaries and his scholarly writing demonstrate his appreciation of the beauty of nature and his concern for the transience of nature—and often for humanity's part in nature's demise.[1]

In *The Chronicles of Narnia,* the "worldview" embodied in the fantasy world of Narnia may productively be considered from an ecocritical perspective. Such a perspective connects the interest Lewis had in issues of his day, including vivisection and colonialism, to his use of "enchanted woods" as a metaphor for the human experience of nature in his criticism of fantasy and his children's fiction, demonstrating that while Narnia is utopian, its environmental troubles are meant to translate to the real world. *The Chronicles* variously depict deforestation, exploitation of natural resources, and the political and social evils of colonialism, which have implicit ecological consequences because the indigenous population of Narnia are talking animals. Although Lewis would not have allied himself explicitly with protoenvironmental movements, his work thus anticipates the theories of ecoanarchist Murray Bookchin, who argues that "the very notion of the domination of nature by man stems from the very real domination of human by human" (1), as well as the work of more recent ecofeminists and advocates of environmental justice, who identify destruction of the earth with the modern industrialist obsession with power that leads to the exercise of control over both nature and fellow humans.[2]

While C. S. Lewis is seldom considered an environmentalist by his critics and biographers, his connection with nature is never denied. In the past decade, Kath Filmer's *The Fiction of C. S. Lewis* has addressed the political implications of Lewis's children's fiction, including his "conservationist views" (79), and articles by Nancy-Lou Patterson (1994) and John Laurent (1993) have explored Lewis as a "nature mystic" and an early animal rights advocate interested in evolutionary theory, respectively. Laurent, whose work focuses on Lewis's *Space Trilogy*, sees Lewis's concern for animal experimentation, which has sometimes been taken as an affront to science, as a belief in soulfulness in animals, specifically in regard to the "kindliness of one species toward another: the very antithesis of self-centeredness, and surely having something to do with morality" (49). Patterson traces Lewis's "nature mysticism" primarily through his nonfiction writing and the *Space Trilogy*, demonstrating Lewis's anticipation of twentieth-century "Green theology" (7), also known as ecotheology or the Christian "stewardship" movement. *The Chronicles of Narnia* are not addressed at length in either Laurent's or Patterson's article, though each contributes admirably to an understanding of Lewis's concern for nature and how this is demonstrated in his writings for adults.

Similarly, discussions of *The Chronicles* themselves do not treat the representations of nature or animals as such. As anthropomorphic beasts are a standard feature of fables, fairy tales, and children's fantasy, the presence of talking animals in Lewis's stories does not automatically lend the novels to an ecocritical reading. Rather, many environmentalist critics might find this treatment of nature suspect, as making animals more like humans, in the case of a fairy tale or fable, may effectively diminish their affinity with the natural world, promoting an anthropocentric rather than biocentric view of existence. It is necessary to consider how nonhuman creatures function in Narnia in order to understand that Narnians, who include talking animals and supernatural creatures (such as naiads, dryads, fauns, and centaurs) traditionally linked to nature and the natural, are not simply "not nature." Although they are natural and anthropomorphic, their status as part of nature is not compromised by their having human and nonhuman characteristics; rather, they are doubly endangered by this synthesis as demonstrated by the contact they have with human conquerors.

In *The Magician's Nephew* and, to a lesser extent, *The Lion, the Witch, and the Wardrobe,* Lewis establishes that the legitimate monarchs of Narnia are humans; however, the indigenous population of Narnia is not used for the benefit of humans as colonizer. Indeed, there is no sanctioned "colonization" of Narnia by its original human inhabitants, who provide a model of stewardship by protecting the indigenous inhabitants without subjugation while Narnia remains largely wild. Nevertheless, in several of *The Chronicles,* specific characters may be identified with colonial or imperial impulses, and in *The Lion, the Witch, and the Wardrobe, Prince Caspian,* and *The Silver Chair,* Narnia must be rescued from illegitimate rulers, usurpers, and colonial rule. In *The Last Battle,* colonization is finally the instrument of Narnia's destruction, as the Talking Beasts are sold into slavery to the tyrannical Calormenes.

Kath Filmer, who devotes a chapter in *The Fiction of C. S. Lewis* to a discussion of the politics of Lewis's children's fiction, mentions colonialism in her treatment of *Prince Caspian* and *The Voyage of the Dawn Treader* in particular. A recent biographer notes that having grown up in Ulster, Lewis was familiar with postcolonial Irish politics from an early age, even writing a school essay on "Home Rule," in which "he states that he will defend home rule when he grows up while also acknowledging that it is a 'matter of mighty weight not to be answered in a moment'" (Bresland 16). That Ireland was still a part of Lewis's consciousness when he wrote *The Chronicles of Narnia* is evident from *The Lion, the Witch, and the Wardrobe*: there is a room in the Professor's house that is "all hung in green, with a harp in one corner" (3).

Lewis introduces colonial control of nature as early as the first published book, also the most widely read, of *The Chronicles: The Lion, the Witch, and the Wardrobe.*[3] The White Witch practices a particularly environmental form of evil, controlling the inhabitants by making it "always winter but never Christmas" (14) in Narnia; her evil power resides in her ability to interrupt the cycle of the seasons. However, the first fully developed character who can be clearly identified with a colonial impulse is Eustace in *The Voyage of the Dawn Treader.* An obnoxious—though not fully evil—character, Eustace participates in the "experimentation on animals simply out of curiosity" (Laurent 46). The product of "very up-to-date and advanced people . . . , [Eustace] liked animals, especially beetles, if they were dead and pinned to a card" (*Dawn Treader* 1). This initial description of Eustace establishes that he is "a young proto-vivisectionist" (Filmer 80). Filmer notes that "vivisection is not only included in the activities which Lewis condemns in his non-fictional polemical writing, it is also associated with the devilry of the 'modernist' political structure of the NICE [N.I.C.E., National Institute of Co-ordinated Experiments] in *That Hideous Strength,* and the demon-possessed Un-Man in *Perelandra* who mutilates small creatures in a manner which differs from Eustace's only in degree." The negative portrayal of Eustace in the first chapter of the book illustrates Lewis's pro-animal leanings; however, Eustace's enjoyment of bullying those over whom he has an advantage also suggests Lewis's antipathy toward colonialism. "Eustace extends his cruelties (albeit petty ones) to humans of a particular religious and ethical persuasion antipathetic to his own . . . . the cruelty with which Eustace treats his beetles extends to humans of a particular kind—that is, those who do not pander to him" (Filmer 81). This condemnation of Eustace's behavior in *The Voyage of the Dawn Treader* suggests toleration of differences and an admonition not to bully—that is, not to exercise unfair authority over others simply because one has the advantage.

Eustace's taste in books becomes bound up with the idea of colonialism: "He liked books if they were books of information and had pictures of grain elevators or of fat foreign children doing exercises in model schools" (*Dawn Treader* 1). The mention of grain elevators suggests general food production, but may be interpreted as the product of a colony, which would then be consumed by the wealthy colonial power. In his discussion of Eustace, Dabney Adams Hart asserts: "Surely Lewis meant that pictures of foreign countries should portray something unusual and fascinating about them rather than illustrate what propagandists have identified as progress: the Great Wall of China or the golden domes of Samarkand, rather than mass calisthenics for Communist youth" (90). Hart suggests that rather than being interested in consumerism or what a country or culture could become through the influence of progress and a colonial power, Eustace should have been interested in the culture of a people: who they were rather than what they produced. It is notable that, although Eustace claims to be a "Republican" (25), he aligns himself ideologically with the country of Calormen, which is a tyranny rather than a benign monarchy like Narnia.

What is mere bad breeding and childishness in Eustace, who has the possibility of redemption, emerges as a fatal flaw in Digory's Uncle

Andrew in *The Magician's Nephew*. Uncle Andrew, a "greedy capitalist" (Filmer 86), has colonial designs on Narnia on the day of its creation. Andrew Ketterly is a petty, evil magician who feels himself to be above moral and natural law. Through him, "Lewis provides a frightening suggestion of the destruction that can occur if power is given over to the hands of immoral experimenters" (Ford 6). His experimentation on guinea pigs, "some of [which] only died. Some of [which] exploded like little bombs" (*Magician's Nephew* 21), allies him with those scientists and vivisectionists who, disrespectful of animals, experiment with them out of mere curiosity. Like many Lewis villains, Uncle Andrew's lack of respect for living things extends to humans, which he demonstrates when he sends a little girl, Polly, and his nephew Digory into the unknown where he himself is afraid to venture.

Uncle Andrew's treatment of Polly more than justifies an ecofeminist critique. Uncle Andrew relies on the cultural perception of females as weaker and in need of protection, exercising his control over her by exploiting her "natural" vanity,[4] relying on his nephew's sense of social convention and gallantry to rescue her from the unknown. In his experimentation, he makes no distinction between human and animal; nevertheless, the initial human object of his experimentation is gendered female. Lewis reveals that Uncle Andrew suffers psychologically for his experiments: "He had never liked animals at the best of times, being usually rather afraid of them; and of course years of doing cruel experiments on animals had made him hate and fear them far more" (*Magician's Nephew* 128). However, he remains largely unaware of this mental suffering or its connection to his "high and lonely destiny" (18) as a magician. Because of his instinctive fear and rejection of the animals, he is "estranged from the Narnian creatures, whose speech he cannot understand" (Manlove 91). As a result, Uncle Andrew's experience of Narnia is mainly a traumatic one.

Lewis also translates Andrew's greed for magical power and hatred for animals into a capitalistic desire to exploit Narnian resources for personal gain at the expense of its inhabitants. Ford notes Uncle Andrew's "inability to understand anything that doesn't directly relate to his own needs" (8): hence his inability to understand the talking beasts. However, this characteristic also relates to his discovery of the commercial possibility of a land where everything grows. After seeing the bar of a London lamppost "grow" into a whole lamppost, Uncle Andrew exclaims: "I have discovered a world where everything is bursting with life and growth. Columbus, now, they talk about Columbus. But what is

America to this? The commercial possibilities of this country are unbounded. Bring a few old bits of strab iron here, bury 'em, and they come up as brand new railway engines, battleships, anything you please" (111–12). This invocation of Columbus evokes America as a colony; critics (Meilaender; Filmer) also see a connection between Uncle Andrew's desire to exploit Narnia and the designs of Lewis's Devine, "the greedy capitalist from *Out of the Silent Planet*" (Filmer 86). Because he fears the lion, Aslan, who is the creator of Narnia, his first order of business will be "to get that *brute* [Aslan] shot" (*Magician's Nephew* 112; emphasis added). Like Devine's, Uncle Andrew's fear and hatred of the "other," here the animals, combined with his inability to relate to or understand anything beyond selfish gain, lend a particular violence to his designs of exploitation, and he plots the destruction of the creator of Narnia and, presumably, any other creatures of Narnia who hinder his objective.

In addition to connecting capitalistic impulses to negative views of nature in specific human characters, Lewis introduces his readers to notions of exploitation and oppression of indigenous peoples through the "silencing" of nature in *Prince Caspian*. Arguably the most overtly political of *The Chronicles*, *Prince Caspian* deals not only with usurpation versus legal—indeed, divinely bestowed—kingship, but also gives thorough treatment to the concepts of colonization, suppression, and the fear of the environment that both results from and perpetuates mistreatment of animals and other beings. The Telmarines, an ethnic group that is sociopolitically dominant, function in the same way as Uncle Andrew, but on a larger scale. As with Uncle Andrew, whose fear of animals is the result of cruel experimentation, the Telmarines' fear of the sea and the woods surrounding it is related to their tyranny and suppression of true Narnia. Their suppression of the spirits of the water (Naiads) and trees (Dryads) provides examples of the environmental damage resulting from their illegitimate rule: "In the divided Narnia to which Prince Caspian is heir in the second of the Narnian *Chronicles*, humans under the rule of the usurping King Miraz have been 'felling forests and defiling streams' so that the Dryads and Naiads have 'sunk into a deep sleep'" (Filmer 79). In her discussion of the political nature of Lewis's fiction for children, Filmer notes that "Lewis clearly associates such activities with evil; they take place in a state of enslavement" (79). One might extend this further to note that these actions are the result of enslavement, and that the actions of the dominant group in turn enslave the oppressors, who are unable to function effectively, even as oppressors, because of their fear of nature.

A useful way to describe the political situation in *Prince Caspian* is Colin Manlove's term *displacement,* which he recognizes in the transportation of the children from London into Narnia as well as in their displacement from the scene of the conflict when they arrive in Narnia. More important, he uses *displacement* to refer to "the way the Old Narnians have been conquered by the invading Telmarines; [and] the rightful King Caspian's flight from court into exile" (46–47). This displacement involves the environment, which includes, and *is,* the indigenous population of Narnia, since the Talking Beasts are unknown to the human inhabitants of Narnia except through legends. "The Telmarines are levelers of forests and builders of towns, roads, bridges, and schools—not out of a desire to civilize, but out of the more negative urge to suppress wildness, that characteristic of Old Narnia" (Manlove 49). Motivated by fear, the Telmarines, by separating themselves from nature, allow the wilderness to become wilder and deny the existence of beings who blend wildness and sentience.

Like historical conquerors, colonizers and imperialists who use "cultural programming" to "promot[e] the occupiers'... culture" (Kiberd 5), the Telmarines use education as part of their strategy of suppression/oppression. Caspian has been taught by his uncle, King Miraz, and his traditional Telmarine tutors that there were no inhabitants of Narnia before the Telmarines, Caspian's people. Doctor Cornelius, Caspian's half-dwarf, half-human tutor, teaches Caspian the true history of Narnia, revealing Caspian's ancestors as colonial conquerors and tyrants:

> All you have heard about Old Narnia is true. It is not the land of men. It is the country of Aslan, and the country of the waking trees and visible naiads, of fauns and satyrs, of dwarfs and giants, of the gods and the centaurs, of talking beasts. It was against these that the first Caspian fought. It is you Telmarines who silence the beasts and the trees and the fountains, and who killed and drove away the dwarfs and fauns, and are now trying to cover up even the memory of them. The King does not allow them to be spoken of. (*Prince Caspian* 41–42)

The environmental element of Telmarine domination is emphasized in Doctor Cornelius's lecture. The word *silence* is an appropriate description of a conquering people's invalidation of native culture by forbidding indigenous peoples the practice of their traditions, which often includes the suppression of a tongue. However, a "silencing" of nature describes human encroachment upon the environment so that the animals are forced either to adapt to sudden changes in the environment, migrate, or become extinct. Because the Old Narnians function as both animals and indigenous population, both readings of the Telmarine conquest are applicable.

Doctor Cornelius himself represents the racial tension produced by colonization. When Caspian guesses his dwarf ancestry, he reveals himself as racially mixed, suggesting the social problems of colonialism as they exist in human contexts. Dwarfs are shown to be privileged in this construct; though they have lost their community—and, in a sense, their identity—through normalization, they have survived in a sentient form and can remember. Talking beasts, who could not become "normalized" in human society, could only revert to their nontalking state, thereby losing sentience. The less anthropomorphic sentient beings, therefore, have less chance for survival. This suggests the need to respect nature and beasts in our own world, and may be used to show the responsibility humans have to preserve from extinction those species affected by human encroachment upon their territory.

The displacement of Old Narnians by the Telmarines has created imbalance, fear, and hatred. To achieve order and reconciliation in *Prince Caspian*, Manlove argues, further displacement must occur: "Miraz must be deposed and Caspian enthroned in his stead" (47). Likewise, human "civilization" must give way to wild nature, and the two must become productively integrated. "The Narnia that has been seized and 'civilized' into bridges, roads, and towns must be released to find its own equilibrium once more: the river god asks to be freed from his chains, and is so by the destruction of the bridge over Beruna by the disjointing power of Bacchus and his ivy." In this instance, the wild liberates itself—as presumably, over time, the traces of man's domination are destroyed by natural forces such as the ivy. Lewis redefines "civilization" by creating a human culture in Narnia that is free from signifiers of domination: as "maps"—markers of "civilization"—are reevaluated in postcolonial criticism, so one must question the appropriateness of Telmarine "bridges" and "roads"—things that can be mapped by the colonizer—as appropriate markers of civilization. Silenced nature in Narnia must be awakened by divine agency and not the actions of humans. This is made clear in the case of the Dryads. Although she calls to them and is able to feel a faint stirring, Lucy is unable to awaken the spirit of the trees (*Prince Caspian* 96–97). Aslan's intervention is necessary to liberate them and restore their speech. Although it is not explicit in the text, this may suggest that conservation is necessary *before* the trees are silenced—since in this world, unlike in Narnia, there is no magic that may bring them back.

The theme of displacement, found throughout *The Chronicles*, "is a means always of shaking loose the self from settled assumptions, of undercutting human appropriations of reality" (Manlove 47). In *Prince Caspian*, the settled assumption is the "natural" domination of humans over nature. Though it is established by Aslan that correct, just rule in Narnia is human rule, respect for the Talking Beasts and other natural forces is an understood condition of this rule. When Caspian, with his respect and appreciation for "Old Narnia," is restored to the throne, as when the trees are wakened and the bridges removed, the natural order is restored: with humans and wild and sentient nature harmonized under a benign monarchy.

Lewis continues the theme of unjust treatment of indigenous peoples in *The Silver Chair*. The fourth book in the series involves an attempted attack on Narnia which, if successful, would result in an enslavement of the Narnian population. It is different from *Prince Caspian*: the attack is thwarted, and the Narnians face exploitation, not eradication, by their would-be ruler. The agent of evil in *The Silver Chair*, as in *The Lion, the Witch, and the Wardrobe*, is a northern witch. Her plan involves the capture and magical enslavement of Prince Rilian of Narnia, son of Caspian X. "Rilian is to be the witch's tool for gaining power in Overland, which is actually, unbeknown to him, his own country of Narnia, the realm he in any case has the lineal authority to govern" (Manlove 70). In *The Silver Chair*, Lewis shows the domination and exploitation of indigenous peoples in the witch's control of the Underland and its inhabitants, gnomes. She plans to lead the gnomes, who labor under her command, to conquer Narnia, in spite of the gnomes' intense fear of the Overland. These figures suggest the fate of Narnia under the witch's rule: "Loss of power characterizes the Underland. The Earthmen there work silently, without animation, in virtual darkness, the vegetation is sickly, and whole caverns are full of motionless, sleeping creatures"(Manlove 70). The glumness that characterizes the Underland gnomes is revealed as a by-product of their enslavement. When Rilian kills the witch, the Earthmen begin to mobilize, presumably to avenge her. However, it is soon revealed that the Earthmen were not willing servants of the witch, and, unaware that she has been killed, are mobilizing for an attack against the witch, in order to return to their homes in the deeper land of Bism. Her control, which Manlove defines as tyranny, had effectively robbed them of their selfhood; the witch "destroys selves and allows no free will" (Manlove 70). Though, unlike the Telmarines, the witch does not seek to populate either Narnia or the Underland, her exploitation of the inhabitants of Bism and her intended exploitation of Narnia point to the establishment of rule so that the controlling power may reap the benefits of labor as a natural resource.

Environmental exploitation, including mistreatment of animals, is more often mentioned than portrayed in *The Chronicles*, although Lewis demonstrates repeatedly that harming animals is wrong, as in the examples of Eustace and Uncle Andrew. Only in *The Last Battle*, which chronicles the "last days of Narnia," does colonial exploitation reach its extreme. The rightful ruler, King Tirian, must confront the infiltration of his country by a hostile power, the deforestation of the land by these invaders, and the enslavement of Narnia's free inhabitants. Early in the book, King Tirian learns of the deforestation, the murder of talking trees, which may truly be termed Narnian genocide:

> "Woe, woe, woe!" called the voice. "Woe for my brothers and sisters! Woe for the holy trees! The woods are laid waste. The ax is loosed against us. We are being felled. Great trees are falling, falling, falling."
>
> With the last "falling," the speaker came in sight. She was like a woman but so tall that her head was on a level with the Centaur's; yet she was like a tree, too. . . .
>
> "A-a-a-h," gasped the Dryad, shuddering as if in pain—shuddering time after time as if under repeated blows. Then all at once she fell sideways as suddenly as if both her feet had been cut from under her. For a second they saw her lying dead on the grass and then she vanished. They knew what had happened. Her tree, miles away, had been cut down. (16–17)

This highly emotional and graphic portrayal of the destruction of nature is unparalleled except perhaps for the White Witch's execution of Aslan in *The Lion, the Witch, and the Wardrobe.* However, the murder of the Dryad lacks the underlying religious purpose of Aslan's death, while the sad tranquility of Aslan's sacrifice is replaced by violence and meaninglessness. Here the tree, representative at once of wild nature and sentience, calls on Tirian for assistance. This emphasizes humanity's role as protectors of the natural environment, while the felling of the trees represents humanity's role in the destruction of nature. The anthropomorphism here is particularly effective. The anguish of the Dryad at seeing her "brothers and sisters" murdered and the pain of her own death provide a vividly human perspective on the horror of deforestation.[5] The tree, a living being, is cut down before the reader's eyes—and unlike the silencing of the trees by the Telmarines, this evil cannot be reversed. In

The Last Battle, as in the real world, the environmental corruption is absolute.

Lewis again links destruction of the environment with colonial issues in *The Last Battle* when King Tirian goes to investigate this atrocity and discovers that his people have been sold into slavery to the Calormenes by the false Aslan. Lewis adds an additional dimension to this injustice by contrasting the beauty of the forest with the ugliness of the clearing made by deforestation, emphasizing that the Calormenes' actions violate moral and aesthetic sensibilities: "Right through the middle of that ancient forest—that forest where the trees of gold and of silver had once grown and where a child from our world had once planted the Tree of Protection—a broad lane had already been opened. It was a hideous lane like a raw gash in the land, full of muddy ruts where felled trees had been dragged down to the river" (20). This is not a unique image in Lewis's fiction; he uses similar imagery to describe the N.I.C.E.'s alteration of an English country landscape in *That Hideous Strength.* The violence of this particular opening of earth, described as a "raw gash" with "muddy ruts," may be contrasted with the image of the earth bursting open during the creation of the animals in *The Magician's Nephew* and the harvesting of earth for the Dryads' feast in *Prince Caspian.* Lewis demonstrates that there are proper and improper ways of using the earth, as the dwarfs' mining is presumably environmentally friendly, while this Calormene industry is a violation.

Children's and adolescent literature, at their best, may be said to pave the way for certain kinds of consciousness in their readers. By emphasizing ecological aspects of *The Chronicles* that perhaps are not as explicit as their Christian imagery, it is possible to introduce to their study concepts that ultimately expand the relevance of the texts. Throughout *The Chronicles,* the negative effects of colonial exploitation and the themes of animal rights and human responsibility to the environment are emphasized in Lewis's construction of a community of living things. Through the negative examples of illegitimate rulers, Lewis constructs the "correct" relationship between humans and nature, providing examples of rulers like Caspian who fulfill their responsibilities to the environment.

Several factors indicate that C. S. Lewis would not have been an environmentalist by today's standards. Although Lewis approaches concepts that are dear to contemporary environmentalists, because his worldview is hierarchical, emphasizing one's proper place in the scheme of things, his work is at odds with many contemporary perspectives, although it can be argued that by favoring a hierarchical vision Lewis is approximating the concept of the ecosphere or the food chain. Many theorists argue that the realization of "responsible stewardship" may only mature in a democratic society (Binde 23). By implication, the harmonious coexistence of humanity and nature is incompatible with monarchy and other forms of government, though this may require further investigation. Karin Lesnik-Oberstein exposes an impulse toward hierarchy that seems inherent in children's literature while arguing that "[i]deological, political and moral issues are asserted with concentrated force with regard to the 'child,' and find their clearest articulation in books assigned to a child-audience in the prevalent belief (right or wrong) that those books have a unique capacity to affect, and therefore enlighten, their child-readers" (216). Toward this end, Lewis provides a model of human interaction with nature in his *Chronicles,* creating an environmental ideal in the fantasy world of Narnia that reaches for social harmony, though this is necessarily limited by the time period in which Lewis was writing and the sociopolitical factors that influenced the production of the texts. Lewis's love of nature infuses his books for children, illustrating that humans are responsible for nature's continuity and providing examples of human and nonhuman nature existing harmoniously in a community of living things, perhaps stimulating similar appreciation and concern for the wonder of nature in his young readers.

NOTES

1.   For example, Lewis devotes a large part of his discussion in *Studies on Words* to the implications of the word *nature* and the evolution of its meaning.

2.   See, for example, Killingsworth and Palmer.

3.   For a discussion of reading order of *The Chronicles,* see Ford (xxxiv–xxxv).

4.   In his discussion of the word *nature* in *Studies in Words,* Lewis, invoking Aristotle, cites historical social injustices to define *nature* as what really is, as opposed to what is ordained purely by law, custom, or society: "The claims made by women when the suffragist movement began, or by native Africans in parts of Africa, could in traditional language have taken the form 'Our inferiority to you (men or whites) is legal or conventional, not *natural*'" (58). Here Lewis analyzes the term *natural* as it is used rhetorically by oppressed groups, including women. In *The Chronicles,* he actualizes this rhetoric, demonstrating by his use of animal nature that oppression is not natural, and that nature is disrupted by oppressive control and coercion.

5.   This scene is also interesting in comparison to Whitman's "Song of the Redwood-Tree" (1874), which contains the implicit argument that the departure of the spirit

of the forests (dryads and hamadryads) as the great forest meets the ax is a necessary tragedy, making way for the superior human race. See M. Jimmie Killingsworth.

Works Cited

Binde, Per. "Nature in Roman Catholic Tradition." *Anthropological Quarterly* 74 (2001): 15–27.

Bookchin, Murray. *The Ecology of Freedom.* Palo Alto, Calif.: Cheshire, 1982.

Bresland, Ronald W. *The Backward Glance: C. S. Lewis in Ireland.* Antrim, Northern Ireland: W. and G. Baird, 1999.

Filmer, Kath. *The Fiction of C. S. Lewis: Mask and Mirror.* New York: St. Martin's, 1993.

Ford, Paul. *Companion to Narnia.* San Francisco: Harper San Francisco, 1994.

Hart, Dabney Adams. *Through the Open Door: A New Look at C. S. Lewis.* Tuscaloosa: University of Alabama Press, 1984.

Kiberd, Declan. *Inventing Ireland.* Cambridge: Harvard University Press, 1996.

Killingsworth, M. Jimmie. "The Voluptuous Earth and the Fall of the Redwood Tree: Whitman's Personifications of Nature." In *Walt Whitman, East and West.* Ed. Ed Folsom. Iowa City: University of Iowa Press, 2002.

Killingsworth, M. Jimmie, and Jacqueline S. Palmer. "Ecopolitics and the Literature of the Borderlands: The Frontiers of Environmental Justice in Latina and Native American Writing." In *Writing the Environment: Ecocriticism and Literature.* Ed. Richard Kerridge and Neil Sammells. London: Zed, 1998, 196–207.

Laurent, John. "C. S. Lewis and Animal Rights." *Mythlore* 71 (1993): 46–51.

Lesnik-Oberstein, Karin. "Children's Literature and the Environment." In *Writing the Environment: Ecocriticism and Literature.* Ed. Richard Kerridge and Neil Sammells. London: Zed, 1998, 208–38.

Lewis, C. S. *The Last Battle.* 1956. New York: Macmillan, 1986.

———. *The Lion, the Witch, and the Wardrobe.* 1950. New York: Macmillan, 1988.

———. *The Magician's Nephew.* 1955. New York: Scholastic, 1988.

———. *Prince Caspian.* 1951. New York: Macmillan, 1986.

———. *The Silver Chair.* 1953. New York: Macmillan, 1986.

———. *Studies in Words.* 1960. Cambridge: Cambridge University Press, 1967.

———. *The Voyage of the Dawn Treader.* 1952. New York: Macmillan, 1986.

Manlove, Colin. *"The Chronicles of Narnia": Patterning of a Fantastic World.* New York: Twayne, 1993.

Meilaender, Gilbert. *The Taste for the Other: The Social and Ethical Thought of C. S. Lewis.* Grand Rapids, Mich.: Eerdmans, 1978.

Patterson, Nancy-Lou. "The Green Lewis: Inklings of Environmentalism in the Writings of C. S. Lewis." *Lamp-Post of the Southern California C. S. Lewis Society* 18 (1994): 4–14.

8

Playing Seriously with Dr. Seuss

A Pedagogical Response to *The Lorax*

Bob Henderson, Merle Kennedy, and Chuck Chamberlin

Education which fails to clarify our central convictions is mere training and indulgence. For it is our central convictions that are in disorder. If disorder prevails, education is not our greatest resource, but an agent of destruction.

E. F. SCHUMACHER

Our attention to physical pollution may distract us from the fact that much of the debate is over the perception of moral pollution. . . . To the environmentalists, what is at risk is the very possibility of leading a good life. To the industrialists, what is at risk is the very possibility of leading a good life. The debate, it appears, is actually about what constitutes a good life. The instance of physical pollution serves only as the means of persuasion, a staging ground for the underlying debate.

NEIL EVERNDEN

An environmental/ecological spirit versus an entrepreneurial/industrial spirit: is it really that simple? Are our central convictions concerning how we dwell on planet Earth the root cause of our social and ecological disorder? If so, how do we as educators engage with our students—of any age— concerning the dysfunctional binaries we as a culture have created? How do we begin to scrutinize our central convictions; what constitutes a good life? *The Lorax,* written by Dr. Seuss, is directly concerned with such issues. Judging from the extensive use of the story in classrooms of all kinds and containing all ages, it is clear that *The Lorax,* Dr. Seuss's favorite book (Morgan and Morgan 211), resonates with educators.

We have presented *The Lorax* in both elementary and university classrooms. We have seen it presented as early as third grade and as the opening or final presentation in environmental inquiry and forestry classes. However, we have rarely seen the book or the video production of the story discussed or elaborated in any way. There was no need for discussion; the book's message was obvious. That lack of discussion became a springboard for our study group, three educators who met weekly to discuss environmental issues and their implications for education. We began to discuss various moments in the story, wondering if Dr. Seuss had envisioned the possibility of this detailed an investigation when he wrote the book. *The Lorax* was published during the early environmental movement of the 1970s, and we were adding a 1990s spin to its reading based on a wealth of more recent environmental thought.[1] We were surprised at how our Dr. Seuss discussions became both playful and serious. Eventually, we realized that we were developing a new approach to working with *The Lorax* in our classes. Our study group discussions became the forum from which this chapter developed.

Our questions were many. How best to present *The Lorax* in environmental education or social studies classes? How might the story itself provide for a respectful and generous hearing of both the entrepreneurial Once-ler and the environmental Lorax, one in which they are both moved in new directions of thought and action? How, for example, to move beyond the rhetoric of the Lorax and the Once-ler to ask who benefits from acting on each of these positions and how do these two frames of reference answer ontological questions of "Who am I?" and "Who am I becoming?" for children and adults?

Opportunities for dialogue between the Lorax and the Once-ler are present in *The Lorax,* but they are not realized. Our pedagogical response develops these dialogic opportunities, dialogue that would also help to correct "the errors of the Lorax" (Marshall 91), an ecopolicelike character, and make the Lorax a more effective spokesperson for nature. We also revisit the ways of the Once-ler. These proposed dialogues across difference would model the kind of open-minded thinking that we, students and teachers, need to engage in together in order to evaluate our central convictions concerning how we dwell on this planet Earth. We expand upon the dialogues by situating them in the literature of contemporary environmental thought.

Ted Geisel (Dr. Seuss) was asked "if, after all the messages in his books, something remained unsaid" and he responded, "The best slogan I can think of to leave with the kids of the U.S.A. would be: 'We can . . . and we've *got* to do better than this.' Then he drew a line through three words, *the kids of.* After books with pleas against the arms race, prejudice, pollution and greed, and after a lifelong war on illiteracy, he was talking to everyone" (Morgan and Morgan 286–87). Our pedagogical response offers, we believe, possibilities for doing more with this seminal work in environmental education and thus better honoring the story and its intentions. We are interested in using the videocassette version of the story; however, the story line develops differently (mainly through elaboration by Dr. Seuss himself), and therefore in the work that follows we will note video (V) to indicate that medium. All other quotes are from the book.

Introducing the Themes for Discussion

In the *EPA Journal*, Jennifer Zicht writes that "for many young children *The Lorax* may be a first introduction to environmental education" (27). If Zicht is right, then the introduction would, unfortunately, be in keeping with the rhetoric of unfinished and unexamined thinking that leaves polar opposition intact and allows foundational, cultural assumptions and practices to go unchallenged. Soon into our examination of *The Lorax*, one of the present authors read the story to his ten-year-old daughter. She observed matter-of-factly, "Oh, this is a pollution story." We wonder what is so matter-of-fact about pollution. Her father was uneasy as he read the story; he thought, "I know too much to enjoy this. Do I really want my kids internalizing this message? And what message is that precisely?"

Among the many things to be considered here are the important issues of ethics, embodied knowing, and lifestyle. The discussion that follows is centered on themes that probe our thinking more deeply and challenge some of the matter-of-fact, taken-for-granted notions. These themes are individual greed or community caring, progress, ecopsychology, abdicating responsibility, and dialogic barriers. We have compiled a list of reading material to introduce each theme and help develop students' thinking about it. For each theme we quote passages from the literature that can be used at the points of interruption in the story so that a new dialogue can take place between the Once-ler and the Lorax. We also "seriously" acknowledge the power of children's literature to serve the purpose exemplified by Dr. Seuss's Lorax/Once-ler story, a power we are certain Dr. Seuss understood. To this end, we have also developed an annotated list of picture books on each theme.

We hope to interject into the book and video version of the story a dialogue that is not there but should be if "our" Lorax is to be an effec-

tive environmental advocate. We hope to provide, through these interruptions in the story, inroads to dialogue that are framed by the poignant
questions only hinted at in the story. It is even rarer to find these inroads
in the real-world binary opposition of the environmentalist and entre-
preneur, which casts the environmentalist for nature (for them) and cor-
respondingly against humanity (against us) (Quinn).

The Lorax Character as Ecopolice: A Response to Ian Marshall

Before we begin developing themes for inquiry and dialogic possibility,
we must revisit our study group dialogue with Marshall's "evenhanded"
treatment in his article "The Lorax and the Ecopolice." We discussed
Marshall's concern that the Lorax is an ineffective spokesperson for
nature, one who "hardly earns the respect of his audience" (89) given his
"sharpish and bossy" persona and insulting manner. Agreed, Dr. Seuss
has not offered us an ecohero here. Indeed, "there's a lesson for the
Loraxes of the world" (Marshall 90) who speak for all life and against
habitat destruction. We think the lessons to be learned are an intriguing, valuable part of the story—and easily missed. These lessons include
acting with temperance and tact to move beyond dogmatic certainty and
seeking common concerns and possibilities for dialogue through resonance rather than the dissonance that accompanies the assertive
denouncing of another's views.

In Marshall's efforts to show the more "complex and subtle" (86)
telling of the story, he may have overstated his case. For one, the Lorax's
assertion that the Once-ler is "crazy with greed" seems less an insult than
an accurate statement. Similarly, the Lorax's anger, at least initially,
seems an appropriate response for one who genuinely experiences a personal identification with the tree that is hacked with just "one chop."
Most important, however, is the easily missed point that the narrator of
the story is the Once-ler himself. No surprise, then, that we meet a Lorax
who is "sharpish and bossy" and, in Marshall's description, "obnoxious"
(89). Finally, Marshall takes the meaning of the possessive pronoun
"my," used by the Lorax to denote his relationship with the life in his
habitat, to imply ownership, indicative of the Lorax's belief that the
habitat is "his" property and sole responsibility. "My" might also denote
identity, a sense of oneness with the life in the Truffula forest. (A word
count in the book reveals that the Lorax uses "my" three times and "the"
six times when referring to the trees, bears, swans, and fish.) Marshall

suggests that the Lorax's use of "my" in describing the "truffula tuft" frees the Once-ler of any need to feel concern because it is not his own property, nor need he feel any concern for the Lorax who claims the habitat as property. This allows the Once-ler to state, "There's no cause for alarm. I chopped just one tree. I am doing no harm."

There is an intriguing teaching and learning moment here. Why must "my" denote property? Could "my" not equally imply a personal identification with life in the habitat? Rather than the conventional marketplace association that the trees are mine—the property is mine—could the "my" not imply that the trees are me? For example, naturalist John Livingston has suggested that the so-called territoriality of song birds in a marsh, a claim of territory exhibited by aggressive flight paths against invading others and the "shrill" call of these song birds, may not mean "this marsh is mine—stay out" but rather may be the playful, celebratory response of an extended self-identity acknowledging that "this marsh is me" (92–97). It is possible that we humans see in nature only what we see in ourselves and therefore have erroneously cast onto the nonhuman world our own image of ourselves as competitively driven for "limited resources" (70). Could Dr. Seuss have had the notion of extended self-identity in mind? His Lorax declares: "But I'm *also* in charge of the Brown Bar-ba-loots," which suggests the Lorax is solely responsible, freeing the Once-ler from equal responsibility, as Marshall suggests.

All this debate over "my," "the," and "in charge of" all too easily misses the pedagogical response we seek, though we relish the debate for debate's sake itself—the story deserves such attention to detail, follow-up that probes its deeper meanings. Within this debate are larger questions of identity and how we are in relationship with the earth. Perhaps the Lorax is not as obnoxious as he appears in Marshall's view. Perhaps the Lorax's environmental rhetoric reflects such an alternate way of being, of dwelling *with* habitat, perhaps this "within-ness" is misunderstood by Marshall, the Once-ler, and others. Certainly, new dialogic opportunities are opened with this line of questioning (see Livingston; Naess; Fox).

As for the Once-ler, Marshall is commendably open-minded. We suggest overly so, though we still value his insight. Marshall praises the Once-ler for his admirable traits: self-reliance with "scarce resources" (87), hardworking nature, family values, hands-on approach, and general care for society in providing a thneed that everyone needs. Are the resources scarce at the outset? They appear plentiful, certainly adequate to meet the "vital" needs of species that inhabit the terrain. Is the Once-ler's ethic of care in producing the thneed indicative of concern for society or, rather, a scheme to dupe the general public by advertising a product that is more of an imposed "want" than a "need," and certainly not a "vital need"? (*Needs* versus *wants* is discussed more fully later in the chapter.) What, precisely, is the personal identity of the Once-ler? Is he a shallow self, self-absorbed within a narrow tribal community or family? Or is he an expanded Self, able to identify with the total milieu of his surroundings? Arne Naess has referred to this distinction as the difference between the small "s" self-realization and the large "S" Self-realization. The Self that is Self-realizing within an expanded sense of community, a greater enterprise of life, is not just a *human-centered* being but rather an *ecocentric* being. These are just a few of the questions that expose the fundamental nature of the inquiry into human consciousness and relationships with which Dr. Seuss is playing seriously.

Individual Greed or Community Caring: If You're Willing to Pay

Let's start at the beginning. Why must the boy who wanders into the scene pay for the Once-ler's story? "He'll tell you, perhaps . . . if you're willing to pay." The Once-ler, now a pitiful reflection of his former self, demands payment for his story despite his apparent self-sufficiency. Is this not a gesture of a most miserly sort, underscoring the addictive nature of capitalistic greed? Throughout the story we are reminded of biggering and biggering: "I had to grow bigger." Two questions might logically follow. Is capitalism inherently based on greed? Is humanity's basic instinct greed?

Canadian novelist Wayland Drew's response, made casually in an interview to a question regarding his central concern for humanity, is brilliant in its simplicity. "How do we learn to stop?" Here we have a fear of our socioeconomic schema as one rooted in greed. The real problem is that once we are grounded in such a way of knowing and being, what elicits the response needed to change, to STOP? *Simple in Means, Rich in Ends,* a book by Bill Devall, is titled from a phrase first used by Norwegian philosopher Arne Naess. Naess and Devall are concerned with how people can reconnect to their place—rethink how they dwell in their place, shape relations with others with attention to communal, cooperative ventures, and find ways to engage themselves in simpler pleasures. Preceding Devall's book was Duane Elgin's seminal *Voluntary Simplicity*

(1981). These books reflect a tradition of thought and conduct that challenges the Once-ler's greed.

The Once-ler's greed, however, is seen as a given, as common sense. There is no ethical consideration, no moral content to the steady advertising pitch aimed at an unwitting public. Certainly there is nothing unconventional in this practice. The advertising of wants, not needs, is embedded in our culture. The misinformed Lorax claims, "Sir, you are crazy with greed. There is no one on earth who would buy that fool thneed." But the Lorax's brand of common sense is not that of the more socially sophisticated Once-ler. Of the Lorax, Erich Fromm would have us say "that the sane person in an insane world . . . is precisely the revolutionary character" (*Dogma* 117). It is the Once-ler and the public who live with an insane sensibility that reflects a "common sense which repeats the same non-sense over and over and makes sense only because everybody repeats it" (113–14). Fromm calls this a "pathology of normalcy" (*Sane Society* 6). Throughout the story the Lorax remains ignorant to the pervasive entrepreneurial—one might say conformist—"common sense" around him. He is not disobedient to the common sense. He is dumbfounded.

The Once-ler, on the other hand, does have moments of doubt or disobedience about his actions. One time his conscience, presented as an alter ego, admonishes: "The things that you do are completely ungood" (V). Following a pause of silence and a h-m-m-m from the Once-ler, the response is, "Yes, but if I didn't do them, then someone else would." This response is enough to end the one pause for a questioning of and disobedience to the common sense of the profit motive of the corporation. For the Once-ler, his friends and relations in the factory, and the unseen public, Fromm reminds us that obedience today is camouflaged as the way things are: "obedience is not recognized as obedience because it is rationalized . . . as accepted objective necessity" (*Dogma* 114). Fromm asks, "How can you think of disobeying when you are not even conscious of being obedient?" Here is a question that haunts our thinking when remembering one of our children's matter-of-fact acknowledgment of the story as a pollution story. Has this story of greed as common sense become so commonplace as to go unchallenged? This was certainly not Dr. Seuss's intent in 1971. So while his lyrics tell us that the Once-ler "came here on a horse and cart to do this sacred mission" as a manifest destiny on the "frontier" (V), we must examine the mission, gone amok by 1971 and more so today.

Just before the news comes in of soaring stock market profits (V), there is another opportunity to interrupt the story. The Lorax has broken through the entrepreneurial thick skin of the Once-ler with evidence that the other species must leave the Truffula forest. In this dialogue the Once-ler asks the standard question, "Do you want me to close down my factories, put people out of work?" (V). The Lorax responds, "I see your point but I wouldn't know the answer." Here, we suggest, the Lorax refers the Once-ler to a broader conceptual picture offering principles of community dwelling such as the platform principles of deep ecology drafted by Arne Naess and George Sessions (McLaughlin 173–74). The principles that pertain to corporatist greed and authority are:

1. The well-being and flourishing of human and nonhuman life on Earth have value in themselves (synonyms: intrinsic value, inherent value). These values are independent of the usefulness of the nonhuman world for human purposes.
2. Richness and diversity of life forms contribute to the realization of these values and are also values in themselves.
3. Humans have no right to reduce this richness and diversity except to satisfy *vital needs* [emphasis added].
4. The flourishing of human life and cultures is compatible with a substantial decrease in human population. The flourishing of nonhuman life requires such a decrease. . . .
5. Those who subscribe to the foregoing points have an obligation directly or indirectly to try to implement the necessary changes.

This, perhaps, is a difficult answer for the Once-ler's immediate concern, but it is an answer necessary from the environmentally minded Lorax, who must engage the Once-ler to realize the "idealism" of the industrial/resource extraction mind-set—for surely it is idealism that promotes infinite growth in a reality of finite resources. The Lorax, in this instance, lets down the environmental/"specieskind" cause with his lack of a response. We must explore "vital needs" and "wants" in ways that transform consumptive, competitive practice. Or, in the words of a school board president from northern California as he attempted to close the public debate over a local effort to ban *The Lorax* in redwood country, "We are insulting our children. Who do we think we are kidding?" (Morgan and Morgan 278). While we seek an interruption of the video at this important point, we can still give the last word to Ted Geisel/Dr. Seuss: "The Lorax doesn't say lumbering is immoral, . . . I live in a house made of wood and write books printed on paper. It's a book about going easy on what we've got. It's antipollution and antigreed" (Morgan and Morgan 278).

Progress: I Had to Grow Bigger

In a chapter appropriately titled "The Vanishing New World" in an equally appropriately titled book, *Beyond Geography: The Western Spirit against the Wilderness,* Frederick Turner offers the particular historical context hinted at throughout *The Lorax.*

> The old chronicles that tell of these [cancerous travels of New World discoverers, explorers, and settlers] seem traveller's tales to us now, though we have no doubt that we are in the presence of tremendous industry and power. For most of us, even more unsuspected and irrecoverable are the forces that nerved and sinewed our industry and that still drive us toward the acquisition and consumption of more and more power. For what underlay our clearing of the continent were the ancient fears and divisions that we brought to the New World along with primitive precursors of the technology that would assist in transforming the continent. Haunted by these fears, driven by our divisions, we slashed and hacked at the wilderness we saw so that within three centuries of Cortes's penetration of the mainland a world millions of years in the making vanished into the voracious insatiable maw of an alien civilization. (255)

Dr. Seuss draws parallels to the American expansion story, the "opening" of the West. The Once-ler arrives in a Conestoga wagon to a "new" world. In a song of tribute (V) to the frontiersman Once-ler, he is likened to George Washington: "Georgie Washington of the Thneeds." *The Lorax* maintains a general sense of place (the video less so), but there is no doubt that this place exists and is modeled on the American frontier. Turner begins his epic treatment on the "biggering and biggering" of the American frontier sharing the same notion as Dr. Seuss, "that the real story of the coming of European civilization to the wilderness of the world is a spiritual story" (xi)—a story of faulty spirit, we must add (see Wright; Ehrenfeld).

Ecopsychology: A Great Leaping of Joy in My Heart

> Of all the texts that must be read to understand the human condition, the body is the most eloquent. . . . People in different eras and places have read it differently, or made every effort to deny access to parts of the story, to its alternate readings, or to the wider learning that flows from it, so it becomes

the justification for mutual suspicion and for alienation from the natural world.

MARY CATHERINE BATESON

In both the book and the video, there is a moment or a tease of latent spiritual impulse for the land, seen in the Once-ler's rejuvenated spirit of well-being. When he experiences the touch, sight, and smell of "those Truffula Trees!" the Once-ler proclaims in unbounded enthusiasm, "I felt a great leaping of joy in my heart." This is a moment to interrupt the story. Here we ask the question: is the Once-ler expressing his repressed biological being to identify an interconnectedness with all life? This is the biological, genetic inheritance on which supporters of the deep ecology movement such as Shepard, Livingston, and Roszak hinge their faith in humanity. Theodore Roszak has helped launch a branch of applied practice and thought to the deep ecological view with his attention to ecopsychology.

Even if not intended as such, the Once-ler's embrace of the Truffula tufts (V) might suggest vestiges of a deep-rooted biological connection experienced in the fleeting moment before being displaced by the overwhelming entrepreneurial spirit of instrumental value. "Uses" for the Truffula tufts is clearly the way of the Once-ler, but in that moment of embrace was a deeper, intrinsic value in nature about to, perhaps, confuse the issue, if only momentarily? Ecopsychology overtly acknowledges and promotes our biological connection with nature as a therapeutic recovery from our misguided detachment from the earth. Roszak writes: "Just as it has been the goal of previous therapies to recover the repressed contents of the unconscious, so the goal of ecopsychology is to awaken the inherent sense of environmental reciprocity that lies within the ecological unconscious. Other therapies seek to heal the alienation between person and person, person and family, person and society. Ecopsychology seeks to heal the more fundamental alienation between the person and the natural environment" (321). Readers should turn to the book *My Name Is Chellis and I'm in Recovery from Western Civilization*. Here Chellis Glendinning asks, "In the face of this overwhelming onslaught [environmental degradation and social ills], an equally overwhelming question arises: What on Earth is wrong with us?" (ix). Glendinning provides directions for our reenchantment with the earth and "our journey home" irrespective of our particular generation.

A part of the journey home is reconnecting with our embodied knowing in order to (re)connect with the natural world. Alienation from the natural world is evident in *The Lorax* but when the Once-ler feels and smells the Truffula trees and experiences "a great leaping of joy in my heart," however brief the experience, it is possible that his embodied knowing is taking precedence, momentarily, over than his rational knowing. Sharon Butala identifies this experience in her own life as she writes about her apprenticeship in nature: "What I could remember about that natural world from which our family had been separated by so little was a combination of smells, the feel of the air, a sense of the presence of Nature as a living entity all around me. All of that had been deeply imprinted in me, but more in the blood and bone and muscles— an instinctive memory—than a precise memory of events or people. I remembered it with my body" (9). Our connection to the natural world exists in our "blood and bone and muscles" and, alienated as we are from the natural world, requires triggers—the smell and feel of Truffula trees, for example—to awaken our primordial impulse. It is important to ask what sustains these responses. How does this connected knowing become a part of the dialogue? The educator may also ask: Why do I not need to tell students that the loon's call is hauntingly beautiful?

The Once-ler rationalizes his work in a conversation with himself when he says, "I cringe. I don't smile as I sit here on trial asking, 'aren't you ashamed you old Once-ler?' . . . The things that you do are completely ungood. Yes, but if I didn't do them then someone else would. . . . Progress is progress and progress must grow" (V). The Once-ler identifies with the natural world when he realizes what his "cursed" factory has done to the Bar-ba-loots, Swomee-Swans, and Humming-Fish. He says, "Now at last I understand" (V). With the arrival of the stock market report, however, he rationalizes his work; disconnected knowing takes the place of a deeply suppressed connected knowing.

Abdicating Responsibility: Unless Someone Like You Cares

The frequently quoted ending of *The Lorax* demands attention. "Unless someone like *you* cares a whole awful lot, nothing is going to get better. It's not" (emphasis added). The Once-ler says this to a wide-eyed, wondering young boy. The Once-ler saves his revelation of action until now, "now that *you're* here, the word of the Lorax seem perfectly clear." Is the Once-ler, as an adult, not simply abdicating responsibility to the younger generation? The Once-ler's anguish for what he has done, for he does show remorse (mainly in the video), leads to no personal volition other than to pass on the responsibility of righting his wrong to a young boy. Is this a common practice of adults, such that children are burdened? Surely, both adults and children need to share responsibility, to work together, unless . . . Paraphrasing Jean-Paul Sartre, existentialism makes individuals aware of who they are, along with the need to assume full responsibility for their existence; responsibility means being responsible for one's own individuality as well as for all others (36).

The Once-ler exemplifies a standard adult practice here. Certain indigenous cultures speak of an awareness of decision making as a "seven generation" concern. That is, will the decisions made today be fruitful and sustaining for our children's children's children, and so on? This intergenerational equity for the resources, the Truffula tree habitat, is not a part of the Once-ler's ethos; it is left for the next generation to resolve, with no guidance from the generation that used the resources. This unhappy ending is a common response by adults like the Once-ler.

Perhaps Dr. Seuss, Ted Geisel, was right when he said, "Adults are obsolete children and the Hell with them" ("The Doctor Beloved by All"). Certainly, for Geisel, the message of moral pollution in *The Lorax* is clear and does connect generations despite the fact that the story is open to interpretation in terms of the Once-ler's conduct. Geisel also stated: "It's wrong to talk about what's wrong with children today, they are living in an environment that we made. When enough people are worrying enough—about war, the environment, illiteracy—we'll begin to get those problems solved."

Amid the playfulness of the story, there is a serious role evident for both youth and adults. Thinking beyond *The Lorax* to *Yertle the Turtle*, *The Butter Battle Book*, and other Seuss tales, the reader receives clear, forceful messages laden with moral responsibility. Are we missing such moral messages in our society, a society that seems more secular, more unaware of its own mythology? Also, is Dr. Seuss too forceful with the particular antipollution, antigreed moral message in *The Lorax*? Does he wrongly burden youth while letting adults off the hook? Either way, the need not to abdicate responsibility is a strong message. In response, it is best to quote the full passage from David Ehrenfeld's essay "A Turtle Named Mack."

> The message that an order, a pattern, exists in the world is immensely reassuring to children, and essential, I believe, for their healthy development. Imagine yourself placed in a totally alien landscape throbbing with strange and sometimes menacing activity and dotted with important-looking signs

written in a language that you cannot read. How grateful you would be to a kindly, bilingual stranger who could teach you to read the signs and get your bearings. There are landmarks that show us the pathways and limits of our place—all species have them. But humans, far more than any other species, must actively acquire knowledge of these landmarks through learning. And only humans are free to ignore the landmarks, to pretend that they are not there. It was the lifework of Dr. Seuss to teach these landmarks to children, and in so doing to show them and us how to identify both the safe roads and the boundaries that must not be passed in a living world of wonders and pitfalls. (44)

Dialogic Barriers: Shut Up, If You Please

The dialogic barriers in *The Lorax* parallel the dialogic barriers described by Janet Pivnick in her article "Speaking from the Deep: The Problem of Language in Deep Ecology Education." The Lorax represents the "ecological worldview" and the Once-ler represents the "dominant, modern worldview." Neither the Lorax nor the Once-ler attempts to explain the basic principles governing his practices, and so their attempts at dialogue are based on an assumption that they each "hold the same basic understandings of the world and that they differ only in their priorities" (Pivnick 54). Dialogue in the story illustrates the frustration and futility of this dialogic mode. The speech of the Lorax is punctuated with exclamation marks, "as he shouted and puffed," and the Once-ler is dismissive: "I laughed at the Lorax, 'You poor stupid guy!'" They are situated in the world in different ways and "may not share assumptions about knowledge, life priorities or the human place in the world" (Pivnick 53). To engage in dialogue would require that the Lorax and the Once-ler openly express their respective worldviews.

Peter Elbow, in his book *Embracing Contraries,* asks the question, "What really goes on when people start out with positions completely at odds and end up in agreement?" (255). He explores positions that encourage and discourage dialogue: "To doubt well we learn to extricate or detach ourselves; to believe well we learn to invest or insert ourselves" (264). The Once-ler and the Lorax play the doubting game. To break through the dialogic barriers this doubting presents, they need to play the believing game, the purpose of which is to "transmit an experience, enlarge a vision," rather than to "construct or defend an argument" (261). There is one moment when an experience is transmitted. The Once-ler does hear what the Lorax has to say about the loss of habitat for the Barba-loots, Swomee-Swans, and Humming-Fish, but to close the factory would mean the loss of jobs. The Lorax responds, "I see your point but I wouldn't know the answer" (V). They do not move beyond this to develop a multivoiced understanding of the situation in which they find themselves. The Lorax does have important information about the time required to germinate and grow a Truffula seed (V), but he does not share this with the Once-ler. He had tried earlier but his effort was in vain. Nor does the Once-ler share his doubts about his work with the Lorax, choosing instead to have a conversation with himself. They exhibit varying degrees of resistance to opening their minds to another's point of view. They (and we) need to explain their (our) beliefs and probe the immediate consequences and the consequences seven generations hence.

Conclusion

Working with Dr. Seuss, storyteller and lyricist, we have focused primarily on his words. But Seuss is also a powerful illustrator. We note the rich potential for interruption in the images themselves. One opportunity for reflective dialogue appears in the video with the image of a blue sky and fluffy white clouds on a window blind that is lowered to avoid the reality of "smogulous smoke." Students can be challenged to offer similar examples of avoiding reality, of the tendency toward facade that they experience in their own lives.

Lest anyone think of *The Lorax* as an imaginary tale, let us remind readers that the story of the Lorax is, to a large degree, Ted Geisel's story,[2] and it is also omnipresent in our communities. The classic environment versus business/progress debate is played out with tragicomical regularity. One recent example will suffice. The mayor of St. Albert, an Alberta city adjacent to Edmonton, explained her decision to support a contentious bypass highway that will cross a natural conservation area noted for its bird life: "My decisions have always favoured growth . . . this will be a hallmark of efficient growth of our city" (Hryciuk). The apparent "pragmatic" view in the four to three city council vote in favor of the road's construction had one pro-road citizen state, "This city will wither and die without a good route to Edmonton and the airport." An anti-road spokesperson noted, "It will drive away birds from a significant wetlands area." These comments exemplify economic growth/consumer ethos versus an environmental persuasion—the Lorax and the Once-ler personified!

In 1989 in Laytonville, California, parents involved in the logging industry protested the inclusion of *The Lorax* on a school reading list because its message is "make sure that another tree is never cut" (Lebduska

170). Here we would suggest that the "anti-logging" message is a misrepresentation that lacks an understanding of the depth of the issue. As Lebduska states: "The Lorax's criticism of materialism and pollution need not be interpreted as insisting on a choice between economic and environmental health, though extending its logic would lead to a reexamination of American lifestyles."

Canadians need look no further than the vacant or nearly vacant towns (Schefferville in northern Quebec and Ocean Falls on the British Columbia coast) scattered across the country to see the Once-ler's story being played out again and again. "No more trees. No more thneeds. No more work to be done." These are common stories of wanton greed, stories about our culture's convictions. These are stories of resource extraction of a finite "supply" and its ultimate consequences that give an edge to Dr. Seuss's story and have created a climate for banning the book in certain regions. In short, we all know the story.

On a more uplifting note, one of us recently had an opportunity to attend a forum for young Albertans, a government-sponsored educational initiative to introduce secondary students from across the province to contemporary issues. In the role of environmental critic, the author used *The Lorax* as a vehicle to question central convictions of our society vis-à-vis the environment and the interconnectedness of all living things on earth. Students knew the story and it acted as a catalyst for a dialogue both valuable and inspirational. Without *The Lorax* and other resources aimed at a youthful audience and without intergenerational dialogue, it is too easy for the concept of *citizen* to shift in our perception, or even our reality, to *consumer* and/or *client*. Intergenerational involvement in difficult community issues helps to keep Edward Abbey's wry definition of *pragmatism* from gaining a hold in our psyches: "Among politicians and businessmen, pragmatism is the current term for to hell with the children" (100).

We have considered another ending to *The Lorax*. Wouldn't it be grand if the Once-ler emerged from his Lerkim, returned the boy's payment for the story, and joined the boy in planting the last Truffula seed to ensure the Truffula forest's regeneration? The message now becomes one of intergenerational action, concrete and participatory, to right a wrong—to transform our understanding of ourselves in the way of Naess's Self-realization. It is not the chore of the ever-present next generation to solve the mistakes of its predecessors. Rather, the project is one of celebrating a proactive stance, taking action to work intergenerationally against a greed that benefits only a few in the short term, and being awake to our "ecological unconscious," our inherent connection *with* the earth, and our organic reality, being *of* the earth. "The seeds of an effective and radical ecocentrism live in those who somehow awaken to the exhilaration of being human in harmony with the rest of nature.... While the search for purity is admirable, its attainment is impossible and the fruits of action are uncertain. The point is the action, not its fruit. Such an understanding can sustain us through the hard times with a joy in all existence and an appreciation of our fellow travelers. As Norman Cousins put it, none of us 'knows enough to be a pessimist'" (McLaughlin 224).

The Lorax demands a pedagogical response. Beyond enjoying the wordplay, illustrations, and story line, we are suggesting direct interruptions that question cultural assumptions and practices. And so, to all readers and viewers of *The Lorax* we offer this thought from Jacob Needleman: "Our culture has generally tended to solve its problems without experiencing its questions. That is our genius as a civilization, but it is also our pathology. Now the pathology is overtaking the genius, and people are beginning to sense this everywhere" (7).

Let us hope that we *are* beginning to sense this everywhere. If so, then Ehrenfeld's concern for landmarks, Turner's claim of a crisis of spirit, Evernden's attention to moral pollution, and Schumacher's concern for our central convictions, all evident in *The Lorax*, will reveal ourselves to ourselves in ways that begin to promote genuine change. We salute *The Lorax* as a powerful story for teaching and learning, as a story that can promote transformational ideas in educational practice. Indeed, unless someone like all of us, teachers and students, cares a whole awful lot, nothing is going to get better. It's not.

Notes

1. For an overview of environmental influences when *The Lorax* was first published (1971), see Lebduska (173).

2. Biographers Judith and Neil Morgan report that from his San Diego coastal studio Ted Geisel watched the once empty coastline as it "teemed with condominiums and look-alike houses" (209). Geisel, frustrated with "dull things on conservation, full of statistics and preachy," was having trouble making the subject amusing. "[*The Lorax* is] one of the few things I ever set out to do that was straight propaganda. . . . It was also the hardest thing I have ever done." Seeking a break from the mental logjam that prevented the book from being written, he escaped on a trip to Kenya. While lounging by a swimming pool at the Mt. Kenya Safari Club, he saw elephants walking across the mountain

and that became the catalytic image for the story. The logjam broke. He said of this experience, "I had nothing but a laundry list with me, and I grabbed it. . . . I wrote ninety per cent of the book that afternoon. I got some kind of release watching those elephants" (210).

Works Cited

Abbey, Edward. *A Voice Crying in the Wilderness (Vox Clamantis in Deserto): Notes from a Secret Journal.* New York: St. Martin's Press, 1989.

Bateson, Mary Catherine. *Peripheral Visions: Learning Along the Way.* New York: Harper-Collins, 1994.

Butala, Sharon. *The Perfection of the Morning: An Apprenticeship in Nature.* Toronto: HarperCollins, 1994.

Devall, Bill. *Simple in Means, Rich in Ends: Practising Deep Ecology.* Salt Lake City: Gibbs Smith, 1988.

"The Doctor Beloved by All: Theodore Seuss Geisel, 1904–1991." *Time,* October 7, 1991, 65.

Ehrenfeld, David. *Beginning Again: People and Nature in the New Millenium.* New York: Oxford University Press, 1993.

Elbow, Peter. *Embracing Contraries: Explorations in Learning and Teaching.* Oxford: Oxford University Press, 1986.

Elgin, Duane. *Voluntary Simplicity: Toward a Way of Life That Is Outwardly Simple, Inwardly Rich.* 2nd ed. New York: William Morrow, 1993.

Evernden, Neil. *The Social Creation of Nature.* Baltimore: Johns Hopkins University Press, 1992.

Fox, Warwick. *Toward a Transpersonal Ecology.* Albany: State University of New York Press, 1995.

Fromm, Erich. *"The Dogma of Christ" and Other Essays on Religion, Psychology, and Culture.* New York: Holt, Rinehart and Winston, 1963.

———. *The Sane Society.* New York: Rinehart, 1955.

Glendinning, Chellis. *My Name Is Chellis and I'm in Recovery from Western Civilization.* Boston: Shambhala, 1994.

Hryciuk, Dennis. "Bypass Opponents Vow to Keep Fighting." *Edmonton Journal,* April 23, 1997, B3.

Lebduska, Lisa. "Rethinking Human Need: Seuss's *The Lorax.*" *Children's Literature Association Quarterly* 19 (winter 1994–95): 170–76.

Livingston, John. *Rogue Primate: An Exploration of Human Domestication.* Toronto: Key Porter, 1994.

Marshall, Ian S. "The Lorax and the Ecopolice." *Interdisciplinary Studies in Literature and Environment* 2 (winter 1996): 85–92.

McLaughlin, Andrew. *Regarding Nature: Industrialism and Deep Ecology.* Albany: State University of New York Press, 1993.

Morgan, Judith, and Neil Morgan. *Dr. Seuss and Mr. Geisel: A Biography.* New York: Random House, 1995.

Naess, Arne. *Ecology, Community, and Lifestyle: Outline of an Ecosophy.* Trans. D. Rothenberg. Cambridge: Cambridge University Press, 1989.

Needleman, Jacob. *The Heart of Philosophy.* San Francisco: Harper and Row, 1982.

Pivnick, Janet. "Speaking from the Deep: The Problem of Language in Deep Ecology Education." *Trumpeter: Journal of Ecosophy* 14.2 (1997): 53–56.

Quinn, Daniel. "Is It Time to Give the E Words a Rest?" In *Environmental Literacy and Beyond.* Eds. Bruce Wallace, John Cairns Jr., and Paul A. Distler. Blacksburg, Va.: President's Symposium, Virginia Polytechnic Institute and State University, 1993, 5: 25–31.

Roszak, Theodore. *The Voice of the Earth.* New York: Simon and Schuster, 1992.

Schumacher, E. F. *Small Is Beautiful: Living As If People Mattered.* Abacus Books, 1974.

Seuss, Dr. [Theodore Geisel]. *The Butter Battle Book.* New York: Random House, 1984.

———. *The Lorax.* New York: Random House, 1971.

———. *The Lorax.* Columbia Broadcasting, 1972.

———. *"Yertle the Turtle" and Other Stories.* New York: Random House, 1958.

Shepard, P. *Nature and Madness.* San Francisco: Sierra Club, 1980.

Turner, Frederick. *Beyond Geography: The Western Spirit against the Wilderness.* New York: Viking, 1980.

Wright, Ronald. *Stolen Continents.* Toronto: Penguin Books, 1990.

Zicht, Jennifer. "In Pursuit of the Lorax: Who's in Charge of the Last Truffula Seed?" *EPA Journal* (September–October 1991): 27–30.

Children's Literature

The following titles, grouped according to the themes in *The Lorax,* offer one interpretation of how these picture books might be used in a pedagogical response to *The Lorax.*

INDIVIDUAL GREED OR COMMUNITY CARING: IF YOU'RE WILLING TO PAY

Eyvindson, Peter. *Jen and the Great One.* Winnipeg, Manitoba: Pemmican, 1990. Jen has a special relationship with an old tree she calls the Great One, who talks to her about long ago, when he was part of a vast forest community. Now the Great One stands alone, a single tree. He tells Jen about the arrival of Big Businessman in the valley, and how "he did not see the beauty of green boughs being tossed in the wind. Instead he saw only a sea of green, green money." Jen and her friends devise a plan to do something about the devastation, to help ensure the longevity of the Great One.

Mendoza, George. *Were You a Wild Duck, Where Would You Go?* New York: Stewart, Tabori & Chang, 1990. Mallard describes past journeys through a world wild and free and present journeys through a polluted world. "What frightens a wetland bird? Greed. Mankind needing everything bigger, with no thought of what would make a better world."

PROGRESS: I HAD TO GROW BIGGER

Baker, Jeannie. *Window.* New York: Greenwillow, 1991. The message in this wordless picture book is developed in collage constructions that begin with a mother and baby viewing the wilderness from a window in their home. Urban development is documented over the course of the baby's lifetime.

Brown, Ruth. *The World That Jack Built.* New York: Dutton, 1991. The beauty of nature surrounding the house that Jack built is juxtaposed with the degradation of nature surrounding the factory that Jack built.

George, Jean Craighead. *Everglades.* New York: HarperCollins, 1995. A storyteller tells a group of children the story of "this river, the miraculous Everglades of Florida." They learn about the formation and destruction of the Florida Everglades.

Stone, A. Harris. *The Last Free Bird.* London: Prentice-Hall, 1967. The story describes the natural world before and after inhabitation by people, and the life of birds in these two different environments.

Ecopsychology: A Great Leaping of Joy in My Heart

Baylor, Byrd. *I'm in Charge of Celebrations.* New York: Charles Scribner's Sons, 1986. A dweller in the desert celebrates the richness and diversity of life there, with "one hundred and eight celebrations—besides the ones that they close school for."

George, Jean Craighead. *To Climb a Waterfall.* New York: Philomel, 1995. Instructions on how to climb a waterfall accompany the artwork. Arriving at the top of the waterfall becomes an experience that connects the climber and the waterfall in such a way that the climber will not be the same again.

Kidd, Nina. *June Mountain Secret.* New York: HarperCollins, 1991. Jen spends the day trout fishing with her father but there is no sign of the rainbow trout. Thinking like a trout helps them to land it. From this experience Jen becomes a part of the secret of rainbows that hide in the river.

McFarlane, Sheryl. *Eagle Dreams.* Victoria, British Columbia: Orca, 1994. The story is best summed up in the author's dedication, "to a world where bald eagles flourish along with the dreams they continue to inspire."

Parnell, Peter. *The Rock.* New York: Macmillan, 1991. "To some, the Rock is just there; just a huge lump on the forest floor . . . in the way." So begins this story that describes how the rock is much more than that and how it endures after a fire.

Ryder, Joanne. *Winter Whale.* New York: Morrow Junior Books, 1991. Readers are invited on "a journey of imagination" to become a humpback whale.

Abdicating Responsibility: Unless Someone Like You Cares

Caduto, Michael J., and Joseph Bruchac. *Keepers of the Earth.* Saskatoon, Saskatchewan: Fifth House, 1991. This collection of North American Indian stories and related activities helps children to "feel a part of their surroundings" and to understand their impact on the environment.

Cherry, Lynne. *A River Ran Wild.* San Diego: Harcourt Brace Jovanovich, 1992. The history of the Nashua River is documented from the time of Indian settlement until the river's ecological death and its eventual restoration.

———. *Flute's Journey.* San Diego: Harcourt Brace, 1997. A young wood thrush migrates over thousands of miles and meets many challenges along the way.

Leger-Haskell, Diane. *Maxine's Tree.* Victoria, British Columbia: Orca, 1990. On weekends five-year-old Maxine and her father camp in the Carmanah Valley, where her father builds trails so people can visit the ancient rain forest while Maxine plays in "her" tree. Upon discovery of a clear-cut across the valley, Maxine revisits her tree, talked to her Nannie, and thinks about what she can do. Her plan receives support beyond her expectations.

Van Allsburg, Chris. *Just a Dream*. Boston: Houghton Mifflin, 1990. Walter has no time for environmental concerns; he lives for a future of technological advances. His wish to live in the future comes true in a dream—but the future is not as he'd imagined it. His dream changes how he lives in the present.

DIALOGIC BARRIERS: SHUT UP, IF YOU PLEASE

de Paola, Tomie. *Michael Bird-Boy*. London: Prentice-Hall, 1975. Michael Bird-Boy loves the natural world. One day a black cloud pollutes his world and he sets off to find its source—an artificial honey syrup factory in the city. Michael Bird-Boy shows the factory owner how real honey is made.

LeBox, Annette. *Wild Bog Tea*. Toronto: Douglas & McIntyre, 2001. A grandfather introduces his grandson to a wild bog, and over the years they learn about the many plants and animals that are a part of this ecosystem. When the young boy becomes an adult he moves away. When he returns he visits the bog alone because his grandfather is unable to make the journey—but brings back the ingredients for wild bog tea, which he makes for his grandfather.

McFarlane, Sheryl. *Waiting for the Whales*. Victoria, British Columbia: Orca, 1974. Every summer a lonely old man who lives by the ocean watches the orcas, waiting for them to come in close to shore. One day his daughter arrives with her baby girl and so begins a relationship across generations. He teaches his granddaughter about the land and the ocean. When he dies his legacy lives on in the relationship between his daughter and granddaughter.

Suggested Readings

INDIVIDUAL GREED OR COMMUNITY CARING: IF YOU'RE WILLING TO PAY

Hardin, Garnet. "The Tragedy of the Commons." *Science* 162 (1968): 1243–48.

Hutton, W. "The State We're In." In *The State We're In*. London: Vintage, 1996.

McLaughlin, Andrew. "Nature as Privately Owned: Capitalism" and "Nature as Owned by Everyone: Socialism." In *Regarding Nature: Industrialism and Deep Ecology*. Albany: State University of New York Press, 1993.

PROGRESS: I HAD TO GROW BIGGER

Ehrenfeld, David. *The Arrogance of Humanism*. New York: Oxford University Press, 1978.

Russell, Andy. *The Life of a River*. Stillwater, Minn.: Voyageur, 1987.

Turner, Frederick. *Beyond Geography: The Western Spirit against the Wilderness*. New York: Viking, 1980.

ECOPSYCHOLOGY: A GREAT LEAPING OF JOY IN MY HEART

Butala, Sharon. *Perfection of the Morning: An Apprenticeship in Nature*. Toronto: Harper-Collins, 1994.

Fisher, Andy. *Radical Ecopsychology: Psychology in the Service of Life*. Albany: State University of New York Press, 2001.

Fox, Warwick. "Arne Naess and the Meanings of Deep Ecology." In *Toward a Transpersonal Ecology: Developing New Foundations for Environmentalism.* New York: State University of New York Press, 1995.

Glendinning, Chellis. *My Name Is Chellis and I'm in Recovery from Western Civilization.* Boston: Shambhala, 1994.3.

Roszak, Theodore. *The Voice of the Earth.* New York: Simon and Schuster, 1992.

Abdicating Responsibility: Unless Someone Like You Cares

Chamberlin, Chuck. "The Practice of Citizenship as Support for Deep Ecology." *Trumpeter: Journal of Ecosophy* 14.2 (1997): 82–85.

McLaughlin, Andrew. "For a Radical Ecocentrism." In *Regarding Nature: Industrialism and Deep Ecology.* Albany: State University of New York Press, 1993.

Milbrath, Lester W. *Learning to Think Environmentally: While There Is Still Time.* Albany: State University of New York Press, 1996.

Naess, Arne. "Fact and Value: Basic Norms." In *Ecology,*

Community, and Lifestyle: Outline of an Ecosophy. Trans. D. Rothenberg. Cambridge: Cambridge University Press: 1989.

Sartre, Jean-Paul. *Essays on Existentialism.* New York: Citadel Press, 1965.

Dialogic Barriers: Shut Up, If You Please

Elbow, Peter. *Embracing Contraries: Explorations in Learning and Teaching.* Oxford: Oxford University Press, 1986.

Fay, Brian. *Critical Social Science: Liberation and Its Limits.* Cambridge: Polity, 1987.

———. "How People Change Themselves." In *Political Praxis and Social Theory.* Ed. Terrance Ball. Minneapolis: University of Minnesota Press, 1977.

Habermas, Jurgen. *Knowledge and Human Interests.* Oxford: Polity, 1972.

Pivnick, Janet. "Speaking from the Deep: The Problem of Language in Deep Ecology Education." *Trumpeter: Journal of Ecosophy* 14.2 (1997): 53–56.

9

"The World around Them"

The Changing Depiction of Nature in *Owl Magazine*

Tara L. Holton and Tim B. Rogers

> The most moving look I ever saw from a child in the woods was on a mud bar by the footprints of a heron. We were on our knees, making handprints beside the footprints. You could feel the creek vibrating in the silt and sand. The sun beat down heavily on our hair. Our shoes were soaking wet.
>
> BARRY LOPEZ

Hands dirty, water sloshing between wet toes, the child in this excerpt is fully engaged in nature. Her body is in dialogue with the world, sensing its very corners and crevices while exploring human-to-heron comparisons. The "moving look" on the child's face is due, in no small measure, to this rich and sentient engagement in the world around her. Here we see a way of knowing nature that affords a lifetime of passion and understanding.

Yet this fully embodied way of coming to know nature is not the only one possible. For example, nature can be known from a distance, through the penetrating and objective gaze of the scientist, or mediated by spiritual concerns, breathing supernatural character into its living soul. This confirms the observations of scholars that discourses of nature are numerous and varied (Cronon 23–68; Macnaghten and Urry 1–74; Evernden 1–36; Manes), each with long-standing historical, intellectual, cultural, and moral content (see, for example, White). How we choose to present the world to our children is deeply influenced by the discourses recruited to know it, suggesting that examination of the discourses revealed in children's literature is critical in coming to understand ecological literacy.[1]

In response to this observation, the present essay addresses the changing discourses presented in *Owl Magazine,* an award-winning Canadian nature publication for children. Our goal in this exploration is to explicate the publication's particular notions of nature and how these have changed over the last quarter of a century. We draw on these findings to consider social practices—some condoned and some occluded—in *Owl.* This is done with an eye to considering alternate possibilities in addressing the increasingly important project of changing and improving some of our problematic practices in dealing with the world around us. Our study begins by examining several thematic analyses of children's environmental literature that sketch out the predominant discourses of nature found in this canon. We then do a careful analysis of the discourses of nature in *Owl,* followed by a discussion of some implications of our findings.

Thematic Analyses of Children's Environmental Literature

While environmentally themed stories for children of Western culture can be traced as far back as the eighteenth century, there has been a significant increase in the occurrence of environmental or ecological content since the first Earth Day in 1970 (Sigler 148). This growing literature has revealed a number of consistent themes. For example, in their examination of award-winning children's literature between 1960 and 1982, Kirk and Karbon found that sixty-six of seventy-two books contained environmental content, ranging from very general to highly specific. They organized their findings into themes, three of which are relevant to this essay. First, the most common message involved people interacting with and demonstrating a dependence on nature and in some cases on animals. Many of these books contained a "cause and effect" theme and suggested the need for balance or a sharing interdependency with the environment (5). A second theme involved survival, in which the characters depended directly on the environment for shelter, clothing, food, and water. The third theme exemplified the dichotomy between good and evil and how evil may destroy the "collective interplay" or balance of all living and nonliving things.

In contrast to these more general discourses, Lenz found three detailed and interrelated themes (or modes) in children's environmental literature. The first related to anthropocentrism, often involving a demonstration of the damage human beings may inflict on the environment through selfish practices and ignorance of the balance of give-and-take that is needed to maintain the health of the environment. The second theme portrayed humans as caretakers of the planet. Third, Lenz found a "harmonic" theme (162) in which the characters exist in harmony with nature, most often demonstrated by someone living within and depending upon "the land."

These studies suggest that discourses of interdependence, resourcism, anthropomorphism, stewardship (caretaking), and harmony/balance predominate in environmental children's literature. Notable by their absence in these studies are the authoritative discourses of science, spiritualist perspectives, and the kind of embodied, dialogical orientation sketched out at the beginning of this essay. Perhaps these omissions are recent additions to the literature, suggesting that examining changes in the literature is indicated.

Surprisingly, very little research has looked at changes in the depiction of nature to children over the years. One exception is Sigler, who looked at such changes in her discussion of environmentally themed children's books from the late eighteenth century to the present day. She found that the eighteenth century portrayed nature as idealized (as seen in gardens and parks) and simplistic—an embodiment of all that is good and natural. Reflecting nicely the concerns of the Victorian era, this early environmental literature maintained the eighteenth-century view of the "perfect" environment as well as the portrayal of nature as an escape from growing industrialization and civilization (150). Also present in the Victorian era was the foreshadowing of present-day environmental concerns, portrayed as the devastation of idyllic nature through the cruelty and selfishness of humankind.

In contrast, early-twentieth-century children's environmental literature began to depict nature in a more "realistic" manner and not merely as an illusion or fantasy. Nature became something wild, something that changed, something with which children may interact, not merely sit prettily within. According to Sigler, current environmental children's literature has begun to reflect the views of various groups, such as aboriginal people, ecofeminists, deep ecologists, and others. It depicts nature as complicated, changing, as something for which the child must fight to save from the anthropocentric actions of humanity (151).

Although Sigler's work focuses directly on the changing depictions of nature, her work spans a wide time frame, perhaps purchasing breadth at the expense of depth. This suggests that a more restricted time frame might provide a different view of the discourses enacted in children's literature. One such study is Glenda Wall's, which examined the changing depiction of nature in the Canadian television show *The Nature of Things*. Although not directly related to the issue of children's environmental literature, Wall's research uncovered changing themes or depictions of nature over the three plus decades the show has been running. During the 1960s nature was presented within a traditional scientific framework, as a resource to be exploited. By the 1990s nature came to be defined in a spiritual voice, as something ancient and intelligent, a victim of our earlier exploitation.

The present essay is similar to Wall's work, only we have chosen to examine the depictions of nature for children in *Owl Magazine*. By examining roughly the same time frame in the same cultural context, we gain an interesting comparative vantage point that is revealing about the versions of nature presented to adults and children in what might be considered mainstream media outlets.

Owl Magazine

Beginning with its first issue in 1976, *Owl* has been endeavoring to interest children in "the environment and the world around them."[2] It contains articles on wildlife or domestic animals along with questions and answers about environmental science, primarily (although not exclusively) stemming from ecology, chemistry, biology, zoology, botany, archeology, meteorology, physics, and astronomy. Although there have been other topics and features in the magazine over the years,[3] wildlife and science have remained primary. The magazine is void of advertisements or promotions, save for information regarding *Owl*'s sister magazine series, web site, and television program.[4] Published in ten months out of every year (July and August are excluded) and targeted toward children nine and older, *Owl* has gone from being "the Canadian outdoor and wildlife magazine for children" to "the discovery magazine for kids." *Owl* has a circulation of seventy-five thousand and has enjoyed over twenty-five years of uninterrupted publication, from 1976 to 1997 by the Young Naturalist Foundation and from 1997 to the present by Bayard Presse Canada.

OUR METHODOLOGY

We restricted consideration to feature articles explicitly dealing with nature and the environment in five randomly selected magazines from each year of publication between 1978 and 1998—one hundred magazines in total.[5]

We explored commonalties and changes in the depiction of nature using content analysis.[6] Briefly, in this approach, texts are coded for recurring themes, beginning at a general level and gradually increasing in complexity and specificity as themes are confirmed, refined, and expanded. This process continues until a point has been reached at which no new themes are found in the texts. We found seven major themes that we believe communicate the general character of the texts in *Owl Magazine*. Of course, our list is not exhaustive, but rather serves to organize our overall impressions. The examples and excerpts presented below are the best illustrations of these seven themes, representing what might be considered prototypical examples.

Of our seven themes, four changed over the twenty-year study period and three remained relatively consistent. While our focal concern is with the changes, it is important to consider those elements that remained stable. Hence, we first discuss the three themes that were common to all of the *Owl* magazines we examined.

UNCHANGING DISCOURSES IN *OWL*

SCIENTIFIC LENSES

Although the formatting and presentation of *Owl* has changed somewhat over the years, more often than not, the main articles and the cover of the magazine are dedicated to scientific discussions of the environment and wildlife. *Owl Magazine* has consistently discussed these topics from the fundamentally "objective" perspective of the scientist. Thus, the presentation and general tone of the magazine, and indeed perhaps one of the most consistent and pervasive characteristics we found, is the emphasis placed on nature as something to be understood and examined through scientific discourses.

SCIENTISTS IN CONTROL

If *Owl*'s main means of examining nature is through science, it is not surprising that scientists are the main authorities in most of the texts. There are usually a few articles in every magazine that pose questions—some asked by readers, others made up for the sake of the articles—that are answered by referencing scientists. For example, in an article from an early issue of *Owl* discussing the difference between frogs and toads, the reader is told that "fortunately, scientists have sorted them all out into 20 families" ("Frogs"). Similarly, in a later issue discussing animals in the zoo, readers are told that while "many people think its wrong to keep animals captive, [a zoologist] however, says that animals don't understand our idea of freedom. Most wild animals live their entire lives without once stepping outside their limited home range" ("What's New?"). Scientists, as cited in *Owl*, are viewed as the authority on all issues, regardless of other possibilities that might exist. More than any other group of individuals involved in environmental work, they are referred to as experts, interviewed by child reporters, and invited as guest writers. They are written up as modern-day heroes and adventurers who, among other things, "collect fossils of plants . . . to solve the big mysteries of science" ("Pollen"), save manatees from extinction ("Operation Rescue"), and study giant pandas "living wild in China" ("Wild Panda").

Indeed, the scientific perspective offered in *Owl Magazine* is so encompassing that if scientists have not placed a stamp of authenticity on a given issue in nature, the credibility of the issue is often drawn into question. For example, in a 1994 article on lightning, readers are told that an unusual form called ball lightning is so rare that "scientists still don't know if it exists" ("Lightning"). Thus, the existence of nature/natural phenomena appears dependent upon scientific pronouncement.

STUDYING NATURE

While *Owl* has steadily (although to varying degrees) carried a message indicating the importance of enjoyment and responsibility regarding the environment, its main emphasis in teaching children about nature has always been primarily from the perspective of *studying* nature in order to understand and enjoy it. For example, in an early issue of *Owl* discussing rain, it is explained that one can look for signs of rain in order to determine whether it is safe to plan a picnic. Readers are informed that the "marshy smells" that emerge before a rainstorm are due to a decrease in air pressure ("Looks Like Rain"). Similarly, in a later issue readers are invited to conduct an experiment to determine why "snowflakes float and raindrops fall" ("Snowflakes"). Certainly there are articles on games, sports, activities, and other manners of involving oneself in the outdoors without studying it, but these are not the norm, nor are they given the same importance as the articles that study the environment. This is not to say that *Owl* does not encourage children to "get outside" ("Get Outside") and involve themselves in the outdoors. On the contrary, *Owl* has encouraged these activities (to varying degrees) from the first magazine we examined, particularly in its "Hoot" news section, where *Owl* reports what other children are doing to help the environment. However, particularly in the main articles, studying and helping nature/the environment is privileged over simply enjoying it and interacting with it. There is a sense that the richly embodied discourse with which we began this essay is relatively underemphasized in *Owl*.

It seems clear that *Owl Magazine* has functioned consistently as a vehicle for teaching young children the importance of the scientific voice in coming to know the world around them. This, of course, is a particularly important lesson for children to learn, given the cultural authority of science. *Owl* appears to be well entrenched within this means of understanding nature, as it follows a naturalist framework that has its roots in natural history (Yearley 177). However, there are other groups, such as environmentalists, who portray other means of understanding nature, and indeed of utilizing and portraying science (186). This voice and others are less well represented on the pages of *Owl*.

Changing Discourses in *Owl*

DECREASE IN WONDER

While it must be emphasized that *Owl* has always maintained an environmentally friendly message, it has over the years decreased its more "spiritual" references regarding the "wonder" and "beauty" of nature. A good example of this can be found in a 1980 article in which the main character travels to a remote area to study wolves. The reader not only learns to "study" wolves scientifically through the eyes of the narrator but is also told about the beauty of wolves and their existence in the wild. There is a message about being a part of nature: the narrator watches the wolves as he builds an igloo and tells of his loneliness once the wolves have disappeared from view. The narrator also explains that he felt the wolf howl was a song of "terrible hunger and hardship, but it was also about hope and survival. And it was the most beautiful song I had ever heard, I would remember it forever" ("When Wolves Sang").

Our reading of the magazine indicates that the frequency of stories such as this one, which foreground involvement in nature, feelings, and emotional links to the world, decreases over the study period. In part, this is linked to a decrease in the narrative or "storytelling" format and an increase in "sound bites" ("sight bites") of information, where small pieces of information are scattered about the page. Readers are no longer romantically "transported" to the situation by a story. Rather they are kept at arm's length and given names and facts. Even when stories are told in later years, they are often from the objective perspective of someone who is simply studying nature, and stories of involvement or emotion, if present at all, are secondary to studying.

This can be seen clearly in articles about whales, which are a fairly popular topic in *Owl*. In a 1978 article, the reader is told a true story of a young killer whale named Miracle, harmed by hunters, who had been rescued and saved from death. When she was first found, injured and motionless, she was described as resilient: even though she was "obviously waiting to die, she happily accepted all the herring [a fisherman] threw in the water for her." Miracle is further described as intelligent, because she "somehow knew she was being helped" and "allowed herself to be loaded into a sling." Thus, Miracle is given a personality—intelligent, resilient, and later, when she heals, playful ("Miracle!").

In contrast, later articles about whales deal with the equipment scientists use to study and track whales in the wild and other informational tidbits such as how much food killer whales can eat in a day and their life span ("Whales"). In a 1988 article, a researcher tells of a humpback whale named Speckles whom she has been studying in the wild since the whale's birth. However, the stories told by the researcher are objective in tone, examining how Speckles catches food and turns it into "insulating blubber" and describing how she studies Speckles's interaction with other whales and waits for his return each year ("Guess"). There is a detached and objective aspect to the researcher's story, just as there is in the scientific tidbits of information on killer whales. The raw wonder about the presence and complexity of these huge mammals seems to be disappearing from the pages of *Owl Magazine*.

INCREASED PRIVILEGING OF SCIENCE AND OBJECTIVITY

While the scientific voice has always been well represented in *Owl*, its presence appears to be increasing, especially as regards the value of objectivity. In part, this is related to the decrease in wonder discussed above, but it also appears to represent the emergence of an even more scientized view of the world. This is clearly demonstrated in a 1998 article that discusses an artist who paints murals of killer whales. The painter indicates that he sees whales as individual creatures with physical and spiritual qualities. He mentions that he attempts to "paint not only the great whale, but its great spirit" ("Whaling Walls"). This seems in line with the more wonder-ful story about Miracle, told in 1978. However, *Owl* informs readers that although it is "incredible how human-like" the whale's eye looks in the mural, the painter "does not try to personify whales. He consults scientists, and dives with whales regularly to paint them as accurately as he can." The reader is informed that the painter's way of seeing whales is "unusual" and is what allows him to "transform plain walls into windows on the sea." It seems that the personification of nonhuman creatures, an unacceptable attribution for an objective scientist, is denounced, and the reader is told that the artist's behavior is unusual. Through all of this, the cultural authority of the scientific voice is clearly strengthened and privileged.

Another example demonstrating the preference for objectivity in *Owl Magazine* involves a question from a reader asking if the earth is alive. The reader is told that "by definition, something is alive if it can grow and reproduce the way people, plants or animals can. Since our planet can't do this, most scientists say that Earth isn't alive." The reader is then informed that "other scientists look at Earth another way," whereupon the Gaia hypothesis is introduced ("You Asked"). Here we see that the reader is not denied knowledge about possible alternatives such as the Gaia hypothesis. However, the hypothesis that *most* scientists follow, and the one seen to be usual and privileged, is the "objective" one. From our analysis, we believe that the foregrounding of an objective epistemology has been on the increase in *Owl Magazine*.

DECREASED FREQUENCY OF "WE DON'T KNOW"

The preference for objectivity appears to be linked to an increased preference for scientific explanations and the possibilities afforded by science.[7] Discourse in earlier years was more likely to include the possibility of the unknown, something science was not yet capable of understanding, whereas in later years, faith in "today's" science prevails. For example, in a 1982 article a reader asks, "Why do some flowers close up at night?" and is told: "Scientists aren't sure. It may have to do with the plant's shape" ("Things"). While there are references to scientists not having a definite answer in later years, they are less frequent and usually just implied by phrases such as: "scientists think" instead of "scientists have shown" or "proved." Indeed, if something is unknown, it is often explained that this is due to extraneous circumstances or a need to advance further scientifically before we inevitably find the answer. This theme is not unrelated to the privileging of science discussed above, to the extent that admission of the unknown can be seen as a challenge to the scientific project. What is particularly interesting, and a point we will pick up later, is the clear indication that environmental scientists themselves are increasingly admitting the "unknown" (Suzuki and McConnell), suggesting a degree of inconsistency between the contemporary scientific discourse and what is appearing in *Owl*.

INCREASE IN CARETAKING

Another theme that has increased over the twenty years examined is the view that nature is something intricate that humans have damaged and something that must be protected/preserved. This message is reminiscent of the caretaker theme found by other researchers examining children's literature (for example, Lenz 162; Sigler 150). As mentioned earlier, this theme has always been a part of *Owl*, especially its news sections, which describe what other children have been doing to help the environment. However, in *Owl*'s articles, the number of references to the notion of saving the environment/wildlife and acting responsibly toward nature increased dramatically between 1978 and 1998. This is particularly true of the main articles, whose purpose is not specifically to carry a caretaker message to the readers, as the news sections of *Owl* often are. Of course, this is not to say that this message was completely absent in the main articles of early issues. For example, in 1981, *Owl* featured their "superkids" of the year, a group of elementary school students who had cleaned up a stream "choked by pollution" and reintroduced the fish population ("*Owl* Superkids"). Further, in another article from the early 1980s, readers are encouraged to take action against acid rain by "writing letters to both Prime Minister Trudeau and President Carter or any other Head of State telling them that you also care about stopping acid rain and hope that they will treat it as the most important problem of the 1980s" ("What Is Acid Rain?").

However, the presence of the caretaker theme in the main articles discussing wildlife or other aspects of the environment changed dramatically in the latter decade, particularly in the last three years we examined. In the late 1990s nearly every issue made reference to the damage humankind has done to wildlife and the environment and the necessity and integrity of taking care of what is left and replenishing what is gone. For example, in a 1992 article, readers are told that the best zoos make people aware of the need to conserve animals and protect endangered species. Readers are informed that future zoos may become "'bioparks' that explore the many connections in nature," and readers are encouraged to write *Owl* and tell them what they think about zoos ("What's New?").[8] In other articles, readers are told that all living things on earth are part of an intricate system, and that we need to "keep this system clean and unpolluted so that Earth will continue to teem with life" ("You Asked"). They are told that when we destroy forests, we can harm animals such as monkeys ("Snow Monkeys") or rare birds ("Very Wary Cassowary") and cause the extinction of plants ("Pollen"). Individuals who do protect the environment are praised. In a 1995 article discussing the "comeback" made by the stilt, a Hawaiian bird, readers are told that "in the past 30 years, Hawaiians have been protecting wetland areas—and the *stilt* population is more than five times larger today" ("Hawaii").

Even animals that contribute to the environment are honored, such as the bat, which "plays an important role . . . eating night flying insects and spreading seeds." Readers are told it is "holy bat appreciation time, bat friends" ("Hanging Out"). In a related vein, readers are encouraged to do what they can for the environment, such as recycle paper, which fills 34 percent of landfills ("Zedhead"). Similarly, *Owl* featured an article on schoolchildren working in many ways to protect trees, such as planting them and putting on plays that promote awareness of what humankind has ignorantly done to damage trees ("A Play"). Further, the increased message of taking an active stance in caring for the environment is demonstrated in the cartoon "The Mighty Mites." In early issues (1970s–80s), the emphasis was on the "Mites" exploring the world and having fun, while in later issues (1990s), they act as "superheroes" who, among other things, save the environment and rare wildlife from the evil "Blade," who would conduct such crimes as selling endangered baby birds over the Internet ("Mighty Mites").

So while the caretaker theme is not new to the pages of *Owl*, it is clearly on the upswing in more recent issues, particularly in the main articles, reflecting perhaps the increased "greening" of society (see Harré, Brockmeier, and Muhlhausler).

A Discursive Crossover

Comparison of our seven themes with those noted in Glenda Wall's work with adults suggests some disparity between the two domains, although they were studied over roughly the same time frame. Wall noted an *increase* in discourses of unknowability, mystery, and spirituality shown in the more recent version of nature presented to adults.[9] With passing time, David Suzuki, the scientist-turned-media-personality who hosts *The Nature of Things,* has abandoned his earlier traditionally scientific stance and begun to adopt more sacred, harmony-based and balance-oriented discourses. This is fully realized in Suzuki and McConnell's book, the title of which, *The Sacred Balance,* clearly instantiates this change. Reflecting some developments ushered in by new understandings of the world such as chaos theory, enhanced multicultural awareness, and a revitalized appreciation that full understanding and prediction of ecosystems may be impossible, the Suzuki discourses are increasingly in tune with emergent trends in some corners of environmental science and in our culture considered more broadly.

Yet the discourses we identified in *Owl* were somewhat different from those documented by Wall. Rather than the increased wonder presented in the adult world, we found a decrease in *Owl.* Rather than the decreased privileging of the traditional scientific discourse noted in Wall, we found it on the upswing in the children's magazine. And rather than an increased understanding of the unknowability of nature articulated by Suzuki, we found less acknowledgment of it in *Owl.* There appears to be a kind of crossover here, wherein the children and adults are being presented with different, almost oppositional, visions of nature. This crossover is dynamic and changing because, as noted above, the earlier issues of *Owl* showed a willingness to admit "we don't know" when confronted with difficult questions. At the same time the Suzuki scripts were caught up in a deterministic, science-knows-it-all discourse. Fast-forwarding to the mid-1990s, this opposition is reversed. The adults now are presented with an unknowable world and the children with a more objectivistic, deterministic one. It is as though the children are presented with a complementary or oppositional discourse to that offered to the adults, with this difference flip-flopping over the study period. While some of the themes have remained consistent (for example, caretaking), there is a sense of incongruence between the notions of nature being presented to children and to adults, and this incongruence has survived major changes to the discursive environments.

There are a number of possible reasons for this discursive crossover. First, it may be a simple cohort effect, with some of the current adult viewers, who as children were exposed to the "unknowable" and mysterious views through media such as *Owl,* simply responding to a familiar perspective in the recent television programs. Second, perhaps the shift from narrative to more fractionated "sight bite" presentational formats has made it increasingly difficult to articulate the subtle and nuanced "mysterious" perspective. If this format shift is more pronounced in the children's world, it could set the stage for privileging the deterministic view. Third, the crossover could reflect a "lag," with visions of nature being presented to children a decade or so behind that to which adults are exposed. A fourth potential contributor to the crossover is the possibility that children are being offered discourses that reflect their relatively powerless status. All four of these possibilities, each in its own way and in complex interaction with the others, more than likely contribute to the discursive crossover we have noted. No matter the reason, the differences in the two discourses suggest a number of possible implications for the examination of ecocriticism and ecological literacy.

Some Implications of the Seven Themes

Our examination of *Owl Magazine* between 1978 and 1998 revealed a number of general trends. The discourses reflected on the pages of this publication were built on a strong foundation of valuing science, revealed in consistent privileging of the scientific voice and the view that studying nature and the environment was primary. We noted an increase in the privileging of objectivist views of nature and in the already familiar caretaker theme. At the same time "discourses of wonder" began to recede, as did the frequency of admitting "we don't know." We also noted some discursive changes that were complementary to changes shown in the adult world, demonstrating a kind of crossover or interaction. Taken in total, these observations suggest some important changes are taking place in the way in which nature is being portrayed to children in *Owl*. While our analysis is based on a clearly limited set of texts compared to the discourse-saturated worlds of both adults and children, it does point toward a number of interesting observations.

Perhaps the most important point to highlight is the cultural significance of the discourses revealed in *Owl*. The predominant themes in this magazine are clearly grounded within a naturalist framework in which the most valued approach to understanding the world involves somewhat detached, empirical observation/study. In a society in which this style of relating to the earth, the scientific voice, has almost exclusive warrant in delineating the "truth," the emphases noted in *Owl* are clearly appropriate and important. Youngsters reading this magazine will gain a deep understanding and appreciation of the significance of this particular approach to knowing and relating to the world. Here we find a clear congruence between *Owl* and the cultural context in which it is embedded. The finding that the caretaker discourse is consonant with changes in general society, such as increased greening, further indicates the fit between *Owl* and its surrounding social context. These congruent elements between the magazine and the more general context in which it is embedded suggest at least one reason why it has won many awards and continues to be a worthy and successful publication.

Yet, as noted in the discursive crossover we found, this congruence is not complete. Rather, there are elements of nature that are presented differently to children than they are to adults in the sources we have reviewed here. At a general level this incongruence reinforces the point made by a number of authors that nature is a contested discursive terrain (for example, Harré, Brockmeier, and Muhlhausler; Ehrlich and Ehrlich). Phil Macnaghten and John Urry have argued that these contests are played out through specific social practices that "produce, reproduce and transform different natures and different values" (2). These practices are discursive, embodied, spaced, and timed and involve models of human activity. Put differently, the practices and discourses of the kind we've noted in *Owl* represent more than "mere words" in the presentation of nature. They implicate specific forms of social practice that have tremendous importance to the manner in which we conceptualize and articulate our conceptions of nature—and indeed, they set the framework for how we treat the world around us.[10]

In the case of *Owl*, the recommended social practices are those that foreground a somewhat distancing study/observation of the world, as we might find in a scientific community. The visual sense is foregrounded in the spectatorlike pose implied in these particular "study-based" practices.[11] If, as argued by several authors (such as Ong; Kidner), such ocularcentric, "distancing" practices contribute to our troubled relationships with the world,[12] the discourses and implied social practices foregrounded in *Owl* can be seen as problematic. This emerges not so much in terms of the social practices these discourses condone as in the possibilities that they conceal from view.

The most notable occlusion we identify in *Owl* takes us back to the Lopez quotation with which we began this essay. Interchanges of the kind on the mud flat, comparing heron to human, are not foregrounded on the pages of *Owl*.[13] Embodied experience of the world, born of active dialogue within it, are, at least to a degree, occluded. Rather, the less engaged practice of examining or observing nature is what we see emphasized. There is a sense in which the discourses and implied social practices of *Owl* normalize studying the world from a distance as a spectator, in contrast to getting our hands dirty by coming into embodied engagement with it. Embodied dialogue with the world, often demeaned as "play" within our adult, scientized world, has been hidden somewhat on the pages of *Owl*. Active involvement of all the bodily senses—seeing, listening, smelling, touching, moving—is not the primary focus in the discourses/social practices emphasized in this particular magazine. In the same way that science education strips away the "felt" passions we hold for the earth (Rogers and Holton), so too has this children's magazine tended to replace passion with reason, felt subjectivity with objectivity, and embodied involvement with visually focused study. In so doing, the problematic split between humans and nature is reinstated, subtly inserted into the discourses and social practices offered to our children.[14] Not unrelated to this is the diminution of wonder and spirituality that accompanies this scientization of nature. Acts such as imagining, fantasizing, and frolicking appear to have been underemphasized in the interests of presenting a scientized view.

Our intent here is not to paint a picture of some kind of sinister adult plot to subvert our children's ways of coming to know the world. Rather, we wish to suggest that certain kinds of social practices and ways of knowing the world can readily fall between the cracks when particular discourses are privileged. This observation does not deny the possibility that children, in their own inimitable creative ways, will overcome these occlusions, nor do we suggest that they are not exposed to other possibilities in other media. Rather, our point here is to note that in this particular magazine, there is a clear privileging of one particular discourse, that of the scientist. And while this emphasis is appropriate to the cultural context in which the magazine is embedded, our analysis does serve to highlight the manner in which alternative, possibly more nature-friendly ways of visioning the world are inadvertently shunted into the background.

This suggests a kind of tension between science and more fully embodied approaches of coming to know the world. Our view is that the latter pole in this tension is particularly important for children, and that some presentations of nature fail to give this pole the attention it deserves. Perhaps in emphasizing, even more than we do at present, playful, embodied engagement in the world, we will be able to foster deeper understandings of the complexity and interrelatedness of ourselves with nature. Perhaps these deeper, embodied understandings will help to establish more sympathetic and nature-friendly ways of dialoguing with the earth.

"The quickest door to open in the woods for a child is the one that leads to the smallest room, by knowing the name each thing is called. The door that leads to the cathedral is marked by hesitancy to speak at all, rather to encourage by example a sharpness of the senses. If one speaks it should only be to say, as well as one can, how wonderfully all this fits together, to indicate what a long, fierce peace can derive from this knowledge" (Lopez 151).

Barry Lopez articulates the importance of recognizing this tension between scientized and embodied orientations toward the world. Thinking in terms of scientific discourse as "knowing the name each thing is called" and embodied dialogue as revealing a "sharpness of the senses," he notes a reluctance to speak at all as children are getting their hands dirty during their engagements with nature. Through calculated silence and its implicit sanctioning of embodied dialogue, we, along with Lopez, sense some tremendously positive possibilities for helping children come to know the world around them.

NOTES

The authors would like to thank Yoshiharu Okawara for his insight and his help with data collection. We would also like to thank the rest of the student and faculty members of the Theory Program in Psychology at the University of Calgary for their valuable comments and suggestions. Correspondence should be addressed to T. L. Holton, Department of Psychology, University of Calgary, Calgary, Alberta, T2N 1N4, Canada.

1. Our approach here is grounded in discourse analysis, which presumes that talk, or discourse, whether spoken or written, is responsible for the construction, alteration, and portrayal of our cultural and historical worlds (Billig; Edwards). It is the instrument through and within which we create and sustain knowledge about our own culture, our environment, our society, and ourselves (Edwards and Potter).

2. This subtitle later changed to "Nature, Science and the World around Them."

3. Examples include discussions involving outer space; "The Mighty Mites"; "Dr. Zed," a scientist who provides the readers with experiments they can conduct; "From Eh? to Zed," a page of interesting facts; and "Hoot," *Owl*'s news section, which often includes information on what children are doing for the environment.

4. *Owl* also has two "sister" magazines, *Chirp* and *Chickadee*, aimed at children between the ages of three and six and six and nine respectively. These magazine contain age-appropriate games, puzzles, crafts, and information regarding animals and the environment. Information about these magazines may be obtained through *Owl*'s web site: http://www.*Owl*.on.ca/.

5. We have chosen not to include an in-depth examination of the cartoon "The Mighty Mites," which involves three children who can shrink down to a small size to explore their environment, including animals, insects, and so on, from this detailed per-

spective. We will briefly discuss some changes in the depiction of nature present in this cartoon, but "The Mighty Mites" is so rich a resource that the attention it deserves is beyond the scope of the present chapter.

6. Content analysis is considered to be the application of grounded theory to pre-existing archival texts and data (see Coffey and Atkinson).

7. It should be noted that while the present essay deals with the depiction of nature in *Owl Magazine,* the trend of increased faith in science appears to be evident in other articles as well. For example, in an article on UFOs from the late 1970s, the unknown is emphasized: readers are told that we just do not know enough yet to understand or explain UFO sightings. ("UFOs"). In contrast, an article on UFOs from the late 1990s tells the reader that many scientists do not believe that UFOs are alien visitors from outer space, but that this should not stop people from imagining ("UFO Files"). While both articles leave the door open for the possibility that UFOs are aliens from another planet and both emphasize the importance of science in determining what UFOs are, the earlier article allows for the unknown and does not give the reader a definite, scientific opinion as the later article does.

8. Encouraging readers to write in and give their opinion is nothing new for *Owl.* They have been soliciting reader feedback for the entire twenty years examined. Indeed, in regard to the 1998 UFO discussion addressed in note 7, readers were asked to write in and explain what they thought UFOs were. Several children wrote in claiming UFOs were visitors from another planet, whereupon *Owl* indicated that while scientists may not think UFOs were evidence of alien life, the readers certainly did ("Hoot").

9. It should be noted that this was only part of Wall's findings. She also found that early discussions of nature referred to it as a resource to be exploited, while later discussions concentrated on the damage humans have inflicted on the earth and how we must act to undo the damage and preserve what we have left. In our examination of *Owl,* while we did find an increase in the caretaker theme over the twenty years examined, we did not find that early articles discussed the earth as a resource for humans to exploit—"environmentally friendly" messages regarding the importance of undoing the harm done to nature by humans have been present in *Owl* from the beginning.

10. The notion of spatial and social practices and the complex relations between them and discourses have been elaborated by Lefebvre; de Certeau (especially 1–42, 91–130); Ingold; and Macnaghten and Urry (172–211).

11. The ocularcentric aspect of both science and our more general social practices has been elaborated by, among others, Evernden (57–103); Macnaghten and Urry (104–33); and Kidner (27–39, 107–58).

12. The argument here is that the visual is particularly congenial to the exploitationist/industrialist orientations toward the world seen as underlying our troubled relationships with it. Walter Ong (72), for example, has noted how sight isolates and divides. Kidner (27) suggests vision contains "ideological quicksands" that both overwhelm other senses and contribute to a fractionated, divided perspective about the world.

13. There are examples in *Owl* suggesting embodied dialogue with the world, such as getting active and planting trees. But our reading of the magazine indicates that study is clearly the most frequent and privileged mode of interaction with nature. The concept of "embodied dialogics" has been developed more fully in Rogers.

14. The problematic aspects of the split between nature and humans hardly need rehearsal here given the extensive critical literatures in ecocriticism (White), philosophy

(Rogers), geography (Cronon 19–56), psychology (Kidner), and sociology (Macnaghten and Urry 1–31). We take this critique as a given in our argument here, seeing the split as one of the major contributors to environmental problems.

WORKS CITED

Billig, Michael. "From Codes to Utterances: Cultural Studies, Discourse, and Psychology." In *Cultural Studies in Question*. Ed. Marjorie Ferguson and Peter Golding. Thousand Oaks, Calif.: Sage. 1997, 205–26.

Coffey, Amanda, and Paul Atkinson. *Making Sense of Qualitative Data: Complimentary Research Strategies.* Thousand Oaks, Calif.: Sage, 1996.

Cronon, William. *Uncommon Ground: Rethinking the Human Place in Nature.* New York: W. W. Norton, 1996.

de Certeau, Michel. *The Practice of Everyday Life.* Trans. Steven F. Rendall. Berkeley: University of California Press, 1984.

Edwards, Derek. *Discourse and Cognition.* Thousand Oaks, Calif.: Sage, 1997.

Edwards, Derek, and Johnathan Potter. *Discursive Psychology.* Thousand Oaks, Calif.: Sage, 1992.

Ehrlich, Paul R., and Anne H. Ehrlich. *Betrayal of Science and Reason: How Anti-Environmental Rhetoric Threatens Our Future.* Washington, D.C.: Island Press, 1996.

Evernden, Neil. *The Social Creation of Nature.* Baltimore: Johns Hopkins University Press, 1992.

Harré, Rom, Jens Brockmeier, and Peter Muhlhausler. *Greenspeak: A Study of Environmental Discourse.* Thousand Oaks, Calif.: Sage, 1998.

Ingold, Tim. "The Temporality of Landscape." *World Archaeology* (1993): 152–74.

Kidner, David. *Nature and Psyche.* Albany: State University of New York Press, 2001.

Kirk, Kerry Ann, and Jerry Karbon. "Environmental Content in Award Winning Children's Literature: 1960 through 1982." *Journal of Environmental Education* (1986): 1–7.

Lefebvre, Henri. *The Production of Space.* Trans. Donald Nicholson-Smith. Oxford: Blackwell, 1991.

Lenz, Millicent. "Am I My Planet's Keeper? Dante, Ecosophy, and Children's Books." *Children's Literature Association Quarterly* 19.4 (1994): 159–64.

Lopez, Barry. "Children in the Woods." In *Crossing Open Ground.* New York: Vintage, 1988.

Macnaghten, Phil, and John Urry. *Contested Natures.* London: Sage, 1998.

Manes, Christopher. "Nature and Silence." *The Ecocriticism Reader: Landmarks in Literary Ecology.* Ed. Cheryll Glotfelty and Harold Fromm. Athens: University of Georgia Press 1996, 15–29.

Ong, Walter J. *Interfaces of the World: Studies in the Evolution of Consciousness and Culture.* Ithaca: Cornell University Press, 1977.

Rogers, Tim B. "In Search of a Space Where Nature and Deep Ecology Comes Alive." *Trumpeter* 16.1 (2000). http://www.icaap.org

Rogers Tim B., and Tara L. Holton. "How Advanced Science Education Contributes to the Environmental Crisis." In *Green Education: Learning for the Earth and Posterity.* Ed. Tim Boston. Winnipeg, Manitoba: Wuertz, forthcoming.

Sigler, Carolyn. "Wonderland to Wasteland: Toward Historicizing Environmental Activism in Children's Literature." *Children's Literature Association Quarterly* 19.4 (1994): 148–53.

Suzuki, David, and Amanda McConnell. *The Sacred Balance: Rediscovering Our Place in Nature.* Vancouver: Greystone Books, 1997.

Wall, Glenda. "Science, Nature, and *The Nature of Things*: An Instance of Canadian Environmental Discourse, 1960–1994." *Canadian Journal of Sociology* 24 (1999): 53–88.

White, Lynn, Jr. "The Historical Roots of Our Ecologic Crisis." In *The Ecocriticism Reader: Landmarks in Literary Ecology.* Ed. Cheryll Glotfelty and Harold Fromm. Athens: University of Georgia Press 1996, 3–14.

Yearley, Steven. "Nature's Advocates: Putting Science to Work in Environmental Organizations." In *Misunderstanding Science?* Ed. Alan Irwin and Brian Wynne. New York: Cambridge University Press, 1996, 172–90.

Owl Magazine Articles Cited

"Frogs and Toads Together." *Owl*, summer 1981, 14.

"Get Outside." *Owl*, summer 1998, cover.

"Guess Who's Coming to Dinner." *Owl*, May 1988, 12–15.

"Hanging Out Like a Bat." *Owl*, October 1996, 15.

"Hawaii Then and Now." *Owl*, May 1995, 7.

"Hoot." *Owl*, November 1998, 28–29.

"Lightning." *Owl*, summer 1994, 23.

"Looks Like Rain to Me." *Owl*, summer 1980, 25.

"Mighty Mites." *Owl*, summer 1998, 24–27.

"Miracle!" *Owl*, February 1978, 6–7.

"Operation Rescue." *Owl*, October 1995, 10–11.

"*Owl* Superkids." *Owl*, January 1981, 4–5.

"A Play with a Purpose." *Owl*, November 1991, 6.

"Pollen Power." *Owl*, March 1997, 12.

"Snowflakes: From Eh to Zed." *Owl*, September–October 1997, 18.

"Snow Monkeys." *Owl*, December 1993, 6–9.

"Things You Always Wanted to Know but Didn't Know Who to Ask." *Owl*, September 1982, 27.

"The UFO Files." *Owl*, May 1998, 4–7.

"UFOs." *Owl*, February 1978, 24–27.

"The Very Wary Cassowary." *Owl*, May 1998, 12–15.

"Whales." *Owl*, February 1995, 16–17.

"Whaling Walls." *Owl*, April 1998, 20–13.

"What Is Acid Rain and What's Being Done about It?" *Owl*, September 1980, 6.

"What's New at the Zoo?" *Owl*, January 1992, 4–9.

"When Wolves Sang." *Owl*, October 1980, 14.

"Wild Panda Search." *Owl*, February 1985, 11.

"You Asked about Your World." *Owl*, March 1992, 12.

"Zedhead: From Eh to Zed." *Owl*, March 1995, 19.

10

Still Putting Out "Fires"

Ranger Rick and Animal/Human Stewardship

Arlene Plevin

> How we image a thing, true or false, affects our conduct toward it, the conduct of nations as well as persons.
>
> LAWRENCE BUELL, *The Environmental Imagination*

A black rhinoceros, a roseate spoonbill, a European hare, a grass frog, and a fennec (small fox of North Africa): these are some of the faces of *Ranger Rick* magazine for the year 2000. This National Wildlife Federation publication has been offering its full-color cover shots of animal eyes and faces for thirty-four years, influencing millions of children aged seven to twelve—and their parents. The nation's oldest and largest nature and outdoor discovery magazine for children, *Ranger Rick* has a circulation of 525,000 with an estimated "pass-around" readership of 200,000 and more. These numbers suggest that at least three-quarters of a million people each month discover which animals like what habitat and food, what is possibly endangering their existence, and just what, for example, Scarlett Fox has to say about "Should I keep feeding birds after winter?" (March 2000, 38).

Scarlett Fox, Ranger Rick's sidekick and cohort, has been dispensing advice for approximately fifteen years. She is one of several animal characters who have introduced young children to the world and concerns of animals and insects. Like Ranger Rick, she has a voice—a column—and a mission. Her mission is similar to her compatriot's: to articulate a way of life that is less anthropocentric, or human-centered. Ranger Rick himself was originally created as a forest ranger and made his debut fighting a forest fire. As Gerry Bishop, who has worked with *Ranger Rick* magazine for thirty years, serving as editor for the past fifteen, explains: "As a ranger, he was the enforcer of good laws and regulations and good policy toward wildlife." Although that image, as Bishop puts it, kind of "dates the character," currently "Ranger Rick is the hero that leads the others to investigate an environmental problem and to sort of figure out what the solution might be." He is a kind of raccoon steward, working to put out fires when needed, but more likely to engage with complicated environmental degradation.

Ranger Rick's success is unquestionable, its popularity assured by older generations of readers who look forward to sharing the magazine and its cast of animal characters with their own children. The mix of full-color photographs, interactive exercises such as completing rhyming poems about baboons, and regular features, including "Reader Riddles" and "Ask Scarlett," is intriguing enough for most adults to read on their own—after they've shared it with their children. After all, there are stories about animal families, invitations to imagine oneself receiving "a big bear hug from a wild giant panda" ("Big Bear Cat," December 1999) and, for those who enjoy scatological humor, sections of "Animals Eat the Weirdest Stuff" (February 2000), with its vivid photographs of "poop tarts" (animals eating droppings of other creatures) and "eye sips" (moths and other insects that drink animals' tears and so on).

But what kind of interaction with the environment is *Ranger Rick* magazine encouraging? What kind of activism is created by its mix of talking animals of both genders, animals under stress from human encroachment, and animals portrayed as in need of human intervention? Whose culture is valorized, and how is *Ranger Rick*—published by one of the world's largest environmental groups (three million members)—disrupting what is usually considered fairly wasteful, the overall North American use of resources, arguably the dominant paradigm of its readers and their families?

Beginning with these questions, I suggest that *Ranger Rick* has been a forerunner of ecocriticism, anticipating and even directing, to some degree, some of that criticism's perceptions of humanism and stewardship. I argue that *Ranger Rick* uses animal "characters"—both its beloved cast and other anthropomorphized and personalized animals—to teach a less anthropocentric worldview (yes, ironically), and I discuss the magazine's recent shift in its narrative and representational style, which highlights its desire to be more accessible and current while criticizing resourcism and monumentitis, both ways of perceiving nature that is tied to human-defined use. Importantly, there are distinctions made in *Ranger Rick* between various levels of human resemblance and responsibility that make the magazine a complicated publication, reflecting changing attitudes toward humans' relationship with the world as it challenges sometimes unquestioned lifestyles.

Ranger Rick models a genre of modulated anthropocentric steward-ship. This worldview places humans first, as determinants of meaning in the natural world (and in what survives) and espouses a role of car-ing for the earth. This is sometimes motivated by an ethic of all things deserving a place and space and sometimes by a human-centered value system, which places everything nonhuman as a resource for everything human. It is a worldview complicated by *Ranger Rick*'s monthly creation of animals that speak and act, who are capable of affecting their environment in ways traditionally considered human. Interestingly, this reinforces a tenet of green ethics that is seldom considered: that the nonhuman can be valued. Ranger Rick, Scarlett Fox, and other char-acters emphasize that nonhuman presence in the realm of the inter-pretable; the usual boundary between nonhuman and human is dissolved in the wash of words. While the magazine's cover features a graphic of a paw print just below its title, it is human imprints of all sorts that determine meaning and value and, by extension, existence. *Ranger Rick*'s characters and columns negotiate a variety of terrains: introducing children to animals as creatures of feeling, motivation, agency, and thought, the magazine does more than sometimes dress them in clothing. Long before ecocriticism began to be discussed in the university as a way of looking at the connections between nature and culture, as a way of examining human and nonhuman relationships, *Ranger Rick* brought those concepts into conversation.

It is useful to consider what Lawrence Buell in *The Environmen-tal Imagination* calls a "rough checklist of some of the ingredients that might be said to comprise an environmentally oriented work" (7). For Buell, drawing from Henry David Thoreau, the four points of an "envi-ronmentally oriented work" are:

1. The nonhuman environment is present not merely as a framing device but as a presence that begins to suggest that human history is implicated in natural history.
2. The human interest is not understood to be the only legitimate interest.
3. Human accountability to the environment is part of the text's eth-ical orientation.

4. Some sense of the environment as a process rather than as a constant or given is at least implicit in the text. (7–8)

As Buell's words suggest, the environment is not merely a setting or a stage. Humans are actors. To quote Shakespeare's *As You Like It,* we are "merely players," one among many. The world becomes larger than human measurement, embracing the nonvocal. Yet, humans are still the determinants of value: it is *their* "accountability to the environment" that is one of the ingredients of a "text's ethical orientation."

Ecocriticism, as understood by William Howarth in "Some Principles of Ecocriticsm," extends from Buell's working definition above and serves to both complicate and compromise the usual binary positioning of nature and culture. Typically set up as them (nonhuman) versus us (humans, with our signs of human culture), this binary is one of the unexamined assumptions of literature, our culture, and criticism. For Howarth, this points out that "although we cast *nature* and *culture* as opposites, in fact they constantly mingle" (69). Howarth also argues for more rigorous consideration of other boundaries, calling for what can be perceived as the in-depth knowledge from other disciplines, particularly science or, in Howarth's case, a more than glancing awareness of ecology and its principles. Ecocriticism "implies more ecological literacy than its advocates now possess." This is not merely an understanding of some ecological concepts, but a knowledge of the discipline that leads to environmental activism. Referring to David Murray, Howarth adds: "In the darker moments of history, ecology offers to culture an ethic for survival: land has a story of its own that cannot be effaced, but must be read and retold by honest writers" (76). Consequently, ecocriticism can remind us to read for that story; it is essential for our very existence, our "survival," in an *ethical* fashion. It is, as Howarth and others suggest, the domain of other voices, a place where humans can begin to question their positionality, their so-called awesomeness.

Ecocriticism's many purposes can be succinctly represented by Cheryll Glotfelty's introduction to *The Ecocriticism Reader,* where she notes: "Students taking literature and composition courses will be encouraged to think seriously about the relationship of humans to nature, about the ethical and aesthetic dilemmas posed by the environmental crisis, and about how language and literature transmit values with profound ecological implications" (xxv). As Scarlett Fox and Ranger Rick go about their adventures, joined at times by other characters from

Deep Green Wood, their actions and words evoke a complicated, even confusing attitude toward the nonhuman world, the world beyond human bodies, the realm (supposedly) of environmental organizations.

Opening *Ranger Rick* magazine for the first time means getting past the cover. Most issues feature a full-frontal shot of an animal's face: the close-up shot of an arctic fox on the cover of the January 1998 *Ranger Rick* is typical. Looking more like a friendly puppy than a creature of the coldest weather, this fox gazes directly at the viewer, his or her pink tongue the only color against the white surrounding snow. The magazine's name, *Ranger Rick,* appears in a kind of pink-orange color akin to the fox's tongue, prominently centered in the largest font. The overall impression is one of welcome. Whether it is the two barking tree frogs balancing on top of one another, the arch of their mouths suggesting a smile (March 1999) or the snow-dusted face of a cougar shown in close-up detail (January 2000), *Ranger Rick's* covers offer an animal to be discovered, interrogated, and enjoyed. Even the bugs are gorgeous: the August 1998 issue features a large and appealingly lime-looking critter: a "spiky green caterpillar [who] has stopped nibbling a leaf to see who's taking its picture" (2). As the section "About the Front Cover" explains, the caterpillar will soon "spin a cocoon and begin changing into a big and beautiful polyphemus (pol-uh-FEE-mus) moth" (2). For those of us, adult or child alike, who stumble over scientific names, especially multisyllabic ones, there's help like that in every issue. This task of science—the proper naming of the domestic in our lives—is phonetically offered alongside a friendly image of a curious creature, who pauses while eating to see who's aiming a camera at them. Beginning on the cover, they oblige our gaze. Nature is brought up close and personal.

Pages 2–3 of every *Ranger Rick* magazine offer the table of contents and a large color photo spread. In the November 2000 issue, five nutria (large rodents that live near water, native to South America), caught in the act of snuggling down for a nap, "settle down" while one yawns largely, affording us a glimpse of what would be tonsils in humans. These five nutrias lead into an article on sleep and animals, which begins by defining sleep as "nature's 'pause button'" and then includes both people and animals in the explanation (4). Sleep, we learn, is "a regular time of rest when people and many other animals tune out from the world around them. During sleep, the muscles relax. Breathing gets slower and so does the heartbeat." A photo of a hyena who has taken a moment to "kick back and reeeelax [*sic*]" includes the textual sound of sleep emanating from its mouth (5). "Z-z-z-z-z-z"s descending from larger- to smaller-sized font curve above his paws, which are folded on his belly. Positioned above and to the left of a photo of three plump baby wrens in "snuggle-heaven," the sleeping hyena is the picture of vulnerability. The layout brings these two disparate animals into view and invites readers to enter this usually unwitnessed world. The "z-z-z"s continue for four more pages; on the page following the wrens, they emanate from the mouth of a koala, his head cradled by two branches, while he sleeps oblivious to everything. As the photograph's caption explains: "A fork in the branches is a great place for this dozing koala to 'hang out.' A koala on the ground isn't very safe. But high up in a tree, it can rest easily" (7).

There is innocence and a bit of voyeurism in this and other such articles. *Ranger Rick* allows the young reader to experience animal vulnerability and human resemblance. Like people, animals sleep and dream. Relevant information about animals' sleep biology is offered, and animals from the common and harmless wren to the exotic and unfamiliar (perhaps a bit terrifying?) hyena snooze. Both adult and baby animals are depicted; they sleep soundly, no predators—human or otherwise—in sight. It is a disarmingly cozy and enticing scene: joining animals of all kinds (human, hyena, wren) in a common need. There is, of course, the implicit invitation to protect these animals who sleep so adorably in our presence.

Ranger Rick himself appears in the magazine's beginning, serving as a correspondent in the "Dear Ranger Rick" column, which typically follows the first picture-driven article. Drawn along with his furry friends and a usual stack of colored mail (or e-mails shown on computer screens), Rick wears his trademark ranger hat and answers questions. Various animal buddies appear with him, perched among the piles of mail, and help direct readers' attention to the themes of the correspondence. Rick typically addresses the readers, thanking them and acknowledging their concerns. He is receptive and informative.

This positioning was made more apparent in the November 2000 issue, where "Dear Ranger Rick" tackles the recent transformation of the "Adventures of Ranger Rick" from a narrative-driven, realistically drawn feature to a cartoon. In this issue, Rick responds to his repositioning as a comic strip character. Up until the March 2000 issue, the "Adventures of Ranger Rick" had been a four-page mostly textual narration of experiences such as journeying to the Everglades where "[t]he gang finds plenty of sun and surprises in the Florida Everglades" (February 2000, 16). In that particular and representative Ranger Rick adventure, Ranger Rick and friends were detailed drawings—their fins, fur and feathers distinct, more akin to illustrations in a child's storybook than a cartoon. There was a two-dimensionality about these "Adventures of Ranger Rick": not only were Scarlett Fox and Ranger Rick one to four inches high but they were surrounded by columns of text. A certain narrative quality permeated the "Adventures of Ranger Rick" of yore. The animals echoed human reactions: Boomer (the Badger) "grouched loudly," Punky (the Porcupine) "protested," and Scarlett's "good mood was beginning to fade." Here, as elsewhere in the magazine, the animals reacted as might a group of kids. They chanted "No more snow! Nothing but fun in the sun!" (16), and they "teased" and "snapped" at one another (17). If all of the animals appeared in one drawing, it tended to depict one aspect of the adventure, one "frame," so to speak.

In the March 2000 issue, however, Ranger Rick entered the realm of cartoons. The "Adventures of Ranger Rick" became "Ranger Rick's Adventures," with *Adventures* sprawling across the upper lefthand corner of the cartoon, welcoming and positioning adventure as prominent, with the size of the type and the shadow effect designed to provide depth and prominence. Signaling a change in presentation—and, I would suggest emphasis—"Ranger Rick's Adventures" repositions the ranger and his buddies as more contemporary and accessible.

In the September 2000 strip, Ranger Rick revisits the environmental version of the tortoise and the hare. In a story by Rhonda Lucas Donald, Becky the hare is racing Bosley, the box turtle. Wearing sweatbands around her head and wrists and looking like a trim (human) athlete, Becky is determined to avoid temptation and win. Her jacket-clad coach cautions her, "No detours to eat clover or to take naps" (22). However, Becky does succumb to greener grass, so to speak, and pauses for a clover break, "a nibble—just to keep up my energy" (23). She immediately discovers trouble, a crate of box turtles who, sobbing, explain, "We've been caught by humans . . . and now we'll be taken away from our home forever!" Becky's widemouthed and wide-eyed stare indicate her immediate concern. She puts herself on the line, telling the panicky turtles, "I've got to get you out of here before those people see me!" "Those people"—a father and son wearing baseball hats and possibly sunglasses—are faceless and oblivious; they remain distant, rooting in the woods, searching for more profit from animal capture. While the cartoon animals tend to have eyes drawn very large, the humans—including the bulldozer driver on the cartoon's following page—have barely visible faces. This suggests the peoples' less than admirable position in this strip. As the narrative at the bottom of one frame makes clear:

"The turtles didn't know it, but the man and boy were capturing them to sell as pets. What they DID know was that no turtle who had been caught in the past had ever come back!"

In fact, while the animals may not be physically harmed, killed, or used for medical purposes, their fate as pets is equally dire—and they know it, are frantic because of this knowledge. Removal from their home, their habitat, their community, both frightens them and propels Becky into a savior role, one that will seemingly cost her the race win she wants so badly. Critically, it is human voices that wake Becky from her clover-eating reverie: She was "about to chow down on some clover when she heard some human voices. First she froze" (23). This inaction is momentary. Human presence doesn't thwart Becky; she is drawn into saving those turtles against whom she is ostensibly competing. As she asks the box turtles to move to one side of the crate to enable her to free them, her challenger, Bosley Turtle, is making his way toward the finish line. Becky, however, takes the time to hide the turtles she has freed before running furiously toward the finish line, "hoping the turtles would be safe and that another turtle named Bosley hadn't already passed her" (24). As she races forward, Becky encounters other people-created disasters, among them a bulldozer pushing down trees and denuding the earth. Rescuing yet another turtle, Becky places him on her back, noting she will "try to find [him] a new home." Naturally, Bosley wins, but upon seeing Becky's hitchhiking turtle and hearing the story, he, recognizing Becky's sacrifice, forfeits his win and places the medal around Becky's neck, proclaiming, "[Y]ou've show there's more than one way to be a winner!" (25).

Becky is a winner, but this particular cartoon suggests that the animals are losing the environmental race in the long haul. Becky manages to rescue one crate of box turtles from a part of the human economics system, but their habitat, their ecological system, is still threatened by human greed. Becky's distressed cry, "They're wrecking Turtle Grove!" is in response to the bulldozer's claiming of land where animals once were, land that is "being taken over by people!" (24). The turtles are under siege and so, by extension, are all the animals who share their greenwood home. In the magazine, moreover, the various species function as a community: recognizing each other's vulnerability and heroism (all the while dressed like amateur human athletes). Unfortunately, they cannot fight technology, resist economic forces, or combat deadly human encroachment.

The "More Facts" box that follows the cartoon emphasizes their helplessness. It's a rather hard-hitting recitation of human abuse and box turtle woes. "Box turtles . . . lose their homes when people take over the land, and others are run over on highways or by off-road vehicles (ORVs) on trails. . . . people often don't know the law—or they break it anyway. They may think that taking just a few turtles won't hurt anything. But they're wrong. If just one or two box turtles are taken from an area each year, the species may soon be wiped out from that area" (25). Ignorance is not an excuse—it kills turtles and harms the species into future generations. The most common rallying cry of the diverse environmental movement—that you can make a difference and that people should protect the environment for future generations—is employed for a powerful condemnation of thoughtless human behavior. Here it is behavior predicated on the desire to possess, to "own" a turtle as a pet. It is especially poignant in a magazine directed at children, who may have these lines read to them by an adult. As the shortest sentence "But they're wrong" in the "More Facts" box, its impact is heightened by its direct message, especially since it follows a narrative in which humans' treatment of animals has been shown to be harmful. While many *Ranger Rick* readers probably do have a pet, some creatures are off-limits, belonging in a habitat free from human encroachment and meddling. It's a sophisticated distinction, one that suggests that while animals might have humanlike characteristics, some are meant to be apart from human interference or domination.

What's most startling is that the problems created in this comic strip are solved for the moment by animals. The "More Facts" box suggests a way for humans to contribute to animal efforts, even to report to the authorities those who take turtles "from the wild [by writing] . . . down his or her car license plate number." (25). At this point, humans are positioned as secondary problem solvers, although this cartoon has done much to disrupt what David Ehrenfeld describes as the privilege of humanism. In *The Arrogance of Humanism*, published in 1978, Ehrenfeld suggests humanism is a religion in its own "right." He explains: "Humanists are fond of attacking religion for its untestable assumptions, but humanism contains untestable assumptions of its own. . . . If they occurred in others, humanists would call them superstitions, or, more politely, articles of faith" (16). For Ehrenfeld and others, humanism infiltrates most ways of thinking and being. While mostly discussing humanism in terms of Western philosophy and ways of knowing, Ehrenfeld states these "articles of faith" function as "assumptions in mathematical proofs, in short declarative sentences." For him, "[t]he principal humanist assumption . . . is very simple. It says: *All problems are soluble . . . All problems are soluble by people.*" Humanism can be seen to position humans at the center of the universe, as the makers of meaning. It's important to note that while there is an "arrogance of the humanist faith in our abilities," humanism is not without merit (12). Ehrenfeld acknowledges that "belief in the nobility and value of humankind and a reasonable respect for our achievements and competences are also in humanism, and only a misanthrope would reject this aspect of it" (10). Consequently, it is "reasonable respect" for humanity's achievements along with a recognition of humanity's limits that is crucial. Yet humanism is an ideological framework that is seldom questioned; it is "the heart of our present world culture—we share its unseen assumptions of control" (20).

"Ranger Rick's Adventures" certainly disrupts the notion of humans as being the only problem solvers, often reminding readers that their adult/human lifestyles may have caused animals harm. The comic strip uses familiar and beloved animal figures to address complex environmental problems. The April 2000 "Ranger Rick's Adventures" further illustrates this strategy. From the beginning, the reader recognizes that this will not be a normal sightseeing tour—the first narrative frame announces: "California, here they come—the gang from deep green wood, that is. Ranger Rick Raccoon, Scarlett Fox, and Cubby Bear were enjoying some new sights in this big western state, but Boomer Badger had more than sightseeing on his mind" (25). Boomer Badger initially has panning for gold on his mind but rapidly discovers an undesirable feature of a local stream—dead fish. In this strip, the animal visitors discuss pesticides and particularly how "some of them harm other living things besides pests" (28). Traveling as tourists, they encounter the appearance of perfection—thick green grass—about which Ranger Rick warns: "There is definitely something strange about this lawn!" (26). Ranger Rick and his wild cohorts warn a lark about a "housecat," described as a "flea-bitten fur-bag," who's aiming right for her five lark babies. This reinforces a notion that human-owned animals should remain in the controlled human domestic sphere. That the mother lark is not as effective suggests the monstrous power of pesticides. Expressing gratitude to Ranger Rick and his friends for shooing the cat away from her nest, she explains: "Oh, thank you! I should've been more watchful. But I've been feeling so strange today" (28). The strangeness is due to the influence of prevalent pesticides, which "often wash off the land and into streams, lakes, and other bodies of water. There they can poison insects, fish, and other water animals, and the animals that eat these poisoned animals can also be harmed."

This particular strip echoes Rachel Carson's novel *Silent Spring*, with its opening fable depicting the horror of a world infused with toxins: "Everywhere was a shadow of death. . . . The people had done it themselves" (14). However, there is a difference, one that allows readers of both generations to move beyond the unexpected "apocalyptic rhetoric" (Plevin 254–55). There are enlightened people and consequently hope for the future. Set in California, this particular "Adventures of Ranger Rick" ends up praising and promoting organic farmers, who embody the "gold" that Boomer Badger is initially seeking. Tucked in the lower left corner of the last page of this "Adventures" strip, adjacent to the daunting collection of facts about pesticide damage, is literally the song of the lark, the note of hope, the gem left in the proverbial Pandora's box. "Guess what. I have some really good news!" the mother lark exclaims (28). "Here in California there are a lot of organic farmers that don't use pesticides or other poisonous chemicals on their crops!" Lest there be any doubt about this different economy, as Boomer walks off into the sunset, his shovel attached to his backpack, he praises this inversion: "Well, maybe this state has something going for it after all . . . even if there is no gold in sight!" California's gold still comes from the earth, but it is an earth not tampered with, an organic earth that still yields the food humans need. This time, however, California will also acknowledge animal needs as well and go "gold," or organic. Preserving California's reputation as a trend-setting state, this "Adventure" rehabilitates gold and returns to a cherished image of America's frontier days. It is a tonic to the rhetoric of toxic doom, to the images the cartoon has created of Boomer swimming in a stream and coming up, puzzled, his paws holding dead fish.

In this magazine, animals are repositioned as vulnerable and in need of human assistance. It's not just that their fate influences ours, but that we are joined together in an often toxic world. This position helps disrupt aspects of Western ways of thinking, Western philosophy. As Richard Sylvan and David Bennett in *The Greening of Ethics* note: "Throughout most of the brief history of Western philosophy, certain humans have been the sole objects of positive moral concern" (7). Yet, as *Ranger Rick* underscores, humans are not the only object, nor the only agent. This green ethic, which according to Sylvan and Bennett is new in the West, "is the serious contemplation of including the non-human world under the aegis of moral concern, or even more startlingly *doing so*, extending adequate ethical treatment to parts of it" (8). The "Adventures of Ranger Rick" map what environmental ethics might look like and why they are important. The magazine becomes a powerful tool for imagining another way of life, one that includes organic farming, for example, and other more responsible ways of interacting with the land.

In "Cleanup at Otter Creek," featured in the same issue, a group of children join adults in a day of volunteer effort "paddling downstream, picking up all kinds of trash" (16). Here both generations work to undo the mess others have made, creating a rhetoric of cross-generational action—of families both being affected and responding. A feature on humpback whales four pages later trades on their beauty, power, and pod relationships; Doug Perrine's photograph of a calf and mother is described as the humpback calf brushing "against the top of Mom's head—as if to say 'hi'" (23). Information about the mammals' songs, family, physicality, and feeding habits are contextualized by the article's ending, which emphasizes rejuvenation: the whales, "once nearly killed off, seem to be making a good comeback!" (24). Although scientists are involved in the study of these huge animals, they are ancillary to the article and to the whales' survival. Here, as elsewhere in *Ranger Rick,* nature is protected because it is valuable to human life but also because it is valuable on its own terms. Protecting animals and improving the habitat are important above and beyond selfish humanism.

In "Whose Nature? The Contested Moral Terrain of Ancient Forests," James D. Proctor notes: "Environmental philosophers have typically classified systems of environmental ethics . . . principally on the basis of the type of value conferred upon nature. . . . Intrinsic value in nature implies that its worth is independent of its utility to humans; instrumental value implies that its worth depends on its ability to serve a human end. 'Is it good?' is a question of intrinsic value; 'What is it good for?' is a question of instrumental value" (280–81). Proctor offers several other categories of environmental ethics, noting that the above system "leads to a similarly twofold schema of anthropocentric and nonanthropocentric ethics" (281). For Proctor, an anthropocentric ethic revolves around human desires—"where people value nature instrumentally, as a means to human material, aesthetic, or other ends"—whereas nonanthropocentric ethics are those where "people primarily value nature intrinsically, without reference to human ends." However, Proctor is cognizant of the motivation enmeshed in the later, emphasizing the primarily intrinsic aspect of value. Some environmental philosophers, according to Proctor, suggest anthropocentrism can be expressed as "resourcism, in which people value nature as a material resource, or as preservationism, in which nature's worth follows from its inspirational

value." Of course, questions of cultural value complicate these definitions, pointing to, among other things, what has been suggested of John
Muir and other environmentalists who valued the high points of
nature—mountains, vistas, and other more overtly "loveable" sites of
inspiration—devaluing swamps and other lowlands in what has been
called *monumentitis.*

Ranger Rick avoids monumentitis and resourcism. In fact, it argues
(often in a heavy-handed manner) that humans should question our use
of resources, our own alleged needs. Attacking what some might consider a sacred cow—the sports utility vehicle or SUV—the June 2000
instalment of "Ranger Rick's Adventures" takes Rick and Scarlett Fox
"to check up on Rick's cool cousin, Radical Racoon" (37) and highlights
the "road hog" aspect of SUVs, concluding that people should "buy cars
that get better gas mileage and don't pollute as much as SUVs do" (40).
Should anyone miss the message, four of the cartoon's frames situated in
the car dealership feature a big banner "Roadhogs," with a pig's face in
the second "o." Here again is an animal out of its place, so to speak, symbolizing inappropriate resource use by humans and tapping into the typical hog/pig bias. Note that not all transportation is condemned, just the
gas-guzzling, easy-to-tip-over kind. The strip ends with humans of all
types demonstrating at the local city park alongside animals such as a
seagull, bunny, and beaver. Their placards, "We need clean air to live,"
"Bicycle power," and "Clean Air," remind us of our collective needs.

Ranger Rick offers a sophisticated mix of photos, cyberactivities,
information, how-to's, interactive games, and people profiles. Overall,
young readers are imagined as inherently interested in the world around
them, eager to understand animals (especially the "sexy" ones, like octopuses, panda bears, and giant Galapagos turtles), desirous of animal jokes
(there's a "Critter Crackups" cartoon that usually anthropomorphizes
animals), and ready to develop "appropriate" ecological concern. However, Ranger Rick doesn't shy away from complex issues or perspectives.

The overt linkage of humans and animals has been receiving more
emphasis since the late 1990's in *Ranger Rick.* Earlier issues, to around
the end of 1997, were less likely to bring together humans and animals
on the cover. There's a kind of starkness about those issues' covers when
compared with later ones. A gray wolf stares out from the December
1996 cover, the only text the magazine's identifying title and in smaller
print the organization and the date. This format changed; in August
1999, for example, the magazine's title appeared in a font more akin to
human handwriting, Tecton. This less polished font echoes children's

print, and combined with the inked paw print resting over the "R" of Ranger Rick and the inclusion of article titles on the front, *Ranger Rick* illustrates not only its desire to be attractive on the newsstand (the magazine became available in newsstands in 1998) but also to more overtly link human and animal activity. The August 1999 cover even announces this with one article's title prominently displayed: "Eye to Eye with Animals."

It is this eye-to-eye positioning that promotes a form of identification, heightened by the articles and features. M. Jimmie Killingsworth and Jacqueline Palmer's pivotal book, *Ecospeak: Rhetoric and Environmental Politics in America,* offers another way of considering an aspect of what *Ranger Rick* magazine achieves. Killingsworth and Palmer note: "Environmentalism is an outgrowth of the general liberal temperament and ideology. Only recently—and with precious little success—have philosophers, green politicians, deep ecologists, and eco-anarchists sought to reach beyond this political framework to a new discourse and new forms of action" (41). As such, *Ecospeak* addresses some of the language and positioning that can account for the environmental movement's failure to build consensus, to "form adequate identifications" (7). It is with children, through a multitude of activities and a variety of scenarios that feature a threatened world, that *Ranger Rick* seeks to create such identifications, while asking children to consider the ideological framework of capitalism and humanism. From turtles shown as caught in the devastating aspects of economics to whales and other species being members of families, *Ranger Rick* readers are offered information on how others, including animals acting as humans, have made a difference, and they are encouraged to care beyond the boundaries of the magazine. Like the mix of species demonstrating for clean resources for all, *Ranger Rick* readers are invited to participate, invited to hope. They are invited to join Ranger Rick in putting out fires of all sorts, evolving with him into the more complex world of environmental stewardship, perceived as being for the good of all.

Works Cited

Bishop, Gerry. Telephone interview, December 11, 2000.

Buell, Lawrence. *The Environmental Imagination: Thoreau, Nature Writing, and the Formation of American Culture.* Cambridge: Harvard University Press, 1995.

Carson, Rachel. *Silent Spring.* New York: Fawcett Crest, 1962.

Ehrenfeld, David. *The Arrogance of Humanism.* New York: Oxford University Press, 1978.

Glotfelty, Cheryll. "Introduction: Literary Studies in an Age of Environmental Crisis." In *The Ecocriticism Reader: Landmarks in Literary Ecology.* Ed. Cheryll Glotfelty and Harold Fromm. Athens: University of Georgia Press, 1996, xv–xxxvii.

Howarth, William. "Some Principles of Ecocriticsm." In *The Ecocriticism Reader: Landmarks in Literary Ecology.* Ed. Cheryll Glotfelty and Harold Fromm. Athens: University of Georgia Press, 1996, 69–91.

Killingsworth, M. Jimmie, and Jacqueline Palmer. *Ecospeak: Rhetoric and Environmental Politics in America.* Carbondale: Southern Illinois University Press, 1992.

Plevin, Arlene. "Green Guilt: An Effective Rhetoric or Rhetoric in Transition?" In *Technical Communication, Deliberative Rhetoric, and Environmental Discourse: Connections and Directions.* Ed. Nancy W. Coppola and Bill Karis. Stamford, Conn.: Ablex, 2000, 251–65.

Proctor, James D. "Whose Nature? The Contested Moral Terrain of Ancient Forests." In *Uncommon Ground: Rethinking the Human Place in Nature.* Ed. William Cronon. London: Norton, 1996, 269–97.

Ranger Rick. Vienna, Va.: National Wildlife Federation, 1996–2000.

Sylvan, Richard, and David Bennett. *The Greening of Ethics.* Cambridge, England: White Horse; Tucson: University of Arizona Press, 1994.

Environmental Justice Children's Literature

Depicting, Defending, and Celebrating Trees and Birds, Colors and People

Kamala Platt

As citizens of the United States, our apathy, over-consumption and lack of moral political conviction has created situations all over the world similar to the one in Chiapas. This beautiful book [*The Story of Colors*] reminds us that the Zapatista movement is one of dignity that emanates from the grassroots of the indigenous people of Mexico. It is a lesson for all of us in the human spirit.

> AMY RAY OF INDIGO GIRLS, *The Story of Colors* BOOK JACKET

Rani and Felicity's stories [in *Rani and Felicity*] . . . raise important questions that we as consumers have to answer. Our answers will determine the kind of world we will create for ourselves and our animals in the future.

> VANDANA SHIVA AND RADHA, *Rani and Felicity*

Three hundred years ago more than 300 members of the Bishnoi community in Rajasthan, led by a woman called Amrita Devi, sacrificed their lives to save their sacred khejri trees by clinging to them. With that event begins the recorded history of Chipko.

> VANDANA SHIVA, *Staying Alive*

Cheryll Glotfelty defines *ecocriticism* as "the study of the relationship between literature and the physical environment" (xviii). Following this broad definition, some ecocritics choose not to interrogate either the literature or physical environment for an understanding of their links to culture, human society, politics, or history. Ecocriticism in this sense is most often only a form of literary criticism, a tool for literary interpretation, a way of reading texts to find an embedded significance; it is not interdisciplinary and does not engage extensively in the multidimensional reality of text formation and contextualization. The text is not seen as an expressive agent for social change; it may be seen as an artifact that reflects a particular ideological relationship to the physical environment, but if so, that relationship is not itself historicized. I have described one stance on the wide spectrum of work that may fall into Glotfelty's definition of ecocriticism, but it is what I understand to be the self-proclaimed norm in ecocriticism.

In situating my own critical/theoretical work within the generic realm of ecocriticism, it is imperative that I describe it in contrast to that norm, not only in the nature of the process at work but in relation to the purpose. I discuss the texts I describe as "environmental justice poetics," texts that are created to promote both environmental well-being and social justice, texts that expose environmental racism and the closely linked degradation of the earth. I see the relationship of the authors, illustrators and, in some cases, broader publishing collectives as being consciously involved with both the physical and cultural environments they describe. This does not suggest that they are solely explicit in their ideological stances; as always, there are (sometimes contradictory) embedded ideologies in this work. However, I choose the literature that I write about because it clearly falls into a body of environmentally and socially committed expressive poetics. Often, those producing the books may be involved in, or clearly allied with, environmental justice movement activities and organizations. As a theorist and critic, my work is also invested in the promotion of a more environmentally just world.

In order to explain both the why and the how of my investment in environmental justice, let me turn briefly to the work of environmental justice practitioners and scholars before discussing texts in environmental justice children's literature. Dorceta E. Taylor, in suggesting that the environmental justice movement "represents a revolution within the history of U.S. environmentalism" (57) states:

> The environmental justice movement is . . . more ideologically inclusive than more traditional ecology groups. It integrates both social and ecological concerns much more readily and pays particular attention to questions of distributive justice, community empowerment, and democratic accountability. It does not treat the problem of oppression and social exploitation as separable from the rape and exploitation of the natural world. Instead, it argues that human societies and the natural environment are intricately linked and that the health of one depends on the health of the other. (57)

If we value the ideals that she lays out, how might Taylor's delineation of the stance of environmental justice practitioners affect the way we read literary texts—in this case, texts for children? Among other contributions, her words encourage us, as cultural critics, to look for both ideological and empirical links between environmental and social ills and to search for means of transformation. They suggest that our interpretations of the physical environment in literature might also engage an understanding of the roles of activists and artists in social and natural history, of political relations of domination such as colonialism, of structural oppression such as environmental racism. They challenge us, as literary critics, to move beyond a simple critical norm, described above, in order to engage a methodology that allows—and indeed requires—that the texts themselves function as ecocritical, cultural artifacts, as organs of environmental justice, as a transformative poetics.

In the introduction to *Chicano Culture, Ecology, Politics: Subversive Kin*, Devon G. Peña defines ecology in opposition to more conventional scientific approaches and compares the roles of ecology and Chicano studies in interpreting land-based culture and environmental justice struggle, specifically that of residents of the Rio Arriba bioregion. "Ecology respects the situated nature of knowledge. The ecologist locates truth *in place*, within the contextual limits of both natural and cultural landscape mosaics that constitute a bioregion at a given point in time" (3). Ecology counters a "Western scientific worldview [that] privileges expert universal knowledge against the traditional, place-bound, local knowledge" (3). Peña finds that Chicano studies "emerged to challenge the prevailing ways of thinking about things and doing them. It questioned the dictates of the 'cult of objectivity'; confronted racist myths and stereotypical conventions about culture; and championed ideals of social action and change-oriented research" (12). Importantly, he shows how both discourses "offered a critique of capitalist domination and provided an alternative vision of knowledge" as a collaboration between intellectuals and grassroots communities. The "dialogue between ecology and Chicano Studies" (13) that he claims for the essays in *Chicano Culture* might provide a model for approaching "relationship[s] between literature and the physical environment" in what Taylor deems a more "inclusive" way (57).

In *Close to Home: Women Reconnect Ecology, Health, and Development Worldwide*, Vandana Shiva notes that there "is no insular divide between the environment and our bodies" (9). There may also be no "insular divide" between the environment and our cultures, our literatures. My chapter, then, is committed to understanding the relation between literature and physical environment within a context of lived experiences, of the production of cultural identities, social domination, and transformative response.

"When a bird sings to the cherries as they are ripening, it is like a mother singing to her child in the womb. The baby is born with a happy soul. The shaded coffee will put that song inside you—. The sprayed coffee tastes just as good if you are tasting only with your mouth. But it fills you with the poison swimming around in that dark cup of disappointment" (15). These lines from Julia Alvarez's *A Cafecito Story* illustrate the nexus of ecocritical-environmental justice interconnections mentioned above through bird migration and coffee-growing and -drinking practices in a short story that is, as it is subtitled, "A Story for the Americas" and a story for all ages. As described on its web page, "*A Cafecito Story* tells the complex tale of a social beverage that bridges nations and unites people in trade, in words, in birds and in love." It is only one of many recent books that foreground our relation to justice and ecology, to people and nature. Much children's literature presents environmental issues and many young people's books focus on animals, or other aspects of the natural world, from across the globe. Some books introduce social justice issues and social problems in age-appropriate approaches. Among these, a growing number describe environmental justice issues—environmental issues inequitably and negatively affecting human communities. Environmental justice literature for children is not bound by region or language; the examples I discuss were chosen for their accessibility and range, their resonant similarities, and their illuminating differences.

Subcomandante Marcos of the Zapatista National Liberation Army, "the South's best known environmentalist"—as described by the *New Internationalist* on the back cover of Shiva's *Stolen Harvest*—a physicist from India, a Swedish artist, an indigenous artist from Mexico, and a science writer at the University of California–Berkeley have all had a hand in creating the environmental justice children's literature discussed below. They create stories for children that examine how human rights and social justice issues are linked to ecological issues, how environmental degradation affects human communities, and how some human communities have long sustained symbiotic relations with their earth habitats. The writers and illustrators of these books address issues at the nexus of ecological mythologies, environmental devastation, social justice, the legacies of colonialism, and developing realities of corporate capitalism. They draw on legend and science, create political allegory to depict violence toward nature and people and, conversely, describe the creative energies of people and nature in sync—all this in children's books with international settings and audiences, produced in international collaborations.

In examining the portrayal of environmental justice issues in such books for children internationally, I will focus on three stories that use a range of strategies. *The Story of Colors/La historia de los colores: A Folktale from the Jungles of Chiapas* is a bilingual book by Subcomandante Insurgente Marcos of Mexico's Zapatista Army of National Liberation, illustrated by indigenous artist Domitilia (Domi) Domínguez. *La historia de los colores* was first published in Spanish in 1997 by Colectivo Callejero in Jalisco, Mexico. The bilingual edition, translated by Anne Bar Din in 1999, received unexpected publicity when the National Endowment for the Arts (NEA) suddenly revoked a promised $7,500 grant for the storybook.[1] The Lannan Foundation, described on its web site as "dedicated to cultural freedom, diversity and creativity" (http://www.lannan. org) immediately offered Cinco Puntos Press a grant for twice the amount for the publication of *The Story of Colors* (Byrd). The book retells a Mayan legend about how the gods find and distribute colors to the natural world, transforming their black and white and gray existence. In Marcos's telling and Domi Domínguez's illustrations, the ancient legend becomes contemporary (the book jacket contends it is "postmodern"); it is an ecojustice mythology, a political allegory, and a mandate for right relationships among people and between people and earth.

The People Who Hugged the Trees, like *The Story of Colors*, is based on an ancient legend: the Rajasthani folktale about Amrita Devi leading three hundred people to save *khejri* trees by embracing them when they were about to be chopped down. This environmental folktale has been adapted by Deborah Lee Rose and illustrated with Birgitta Säflund's watercolors. The legend has been a motivating force behind the contemporary Chipko movement, which started in the 1970s in the Himalayan foothills when villagers, whose sustainable lifestyle depended on an intact forest, followed the legendary example of protecting the trees in the face of outsider (in contemporary instances, corporate-sponsored) deforestation. The legendary event was commemorated when the village of Khejare in Rajasthan was given India's first National Environment Memorial. The final page (a children's book epilogue) also discusses the contemporary Chipko movement, which received the Right Livelihood Award in 1987 for "dedication to the conservation, restoration, and ecologically responsible use of India's natural resources" (quoted in Rose, n.p.). Widely known as the "Alternative Nobel" and presented annually in the Swedish parliament on the day before Nobel Prizes are presented, the Right Livelihood Award is given to groups or individuals "to honour and support those offering practical and exemplary answers to the crucial problems facing the world today" (http://www.rightlivelihood.se/about.html). Reception of this award signifies the recognition of the crucial need for, and vitality of, the Chipko movement. Announcing such accomplishments of the contemporary movement to the children reading the legendary tale illustrates to them both the continuity of a history of environmental justice and the significance of social action today. It connects readers to history through contemporary South Asian women's environmental justice organizing.

Rani and Felicity: The Story of Two Chickens (1996) presents the environmental justice concerns surrounding abusive corporate animal farming and its implications for sustainable agriculture, the environment, people's livelihoods, and communities. Radha's text, written on the basis of research by Vandana Shiva's Research Foundation for Science, Technology, and Natural Resource Policy in New Delhi, portrays North-South disparity through the lives of two chickens, showing the differences between corporate capitalist agriculture and low-impact family (ecologically compatible) farming that recognizes the chicken's literal and symbolic ancestry in the Indian jungle.

All three storybooks guide readers in viewing and critiquing the world from perspectives that support the well-being of both people and the rest of nature. They tell stories of people protecting nature and living in harmony with it as part of the community; this is particularly evident in *The People Who Hugged the Trees*. *Rani and Felicity* shows how the well-being of nature suffers or is sustained, depending on people's actions (and the lifestyles and institutions they maintain). And in *The Story of Colors*, people are presented mythohistorically and in conjunction with natural colors, spiritual elements, and emotions, in an amicable context that incorporates synesthesia. While each story has its own ideological and formal storytelling strategy, these tales hold a resolute ideological stance in their common ecocriticism. In each, ecocriticism is contextualized historically and politically; readers learn legendary histories of people's resistance to domination of themselves and their natural environments *(The People Who Hugged the Trees)*, of the origins of the natural(ly peopled) world *(The Story of Colors)*, and of the detrimental effects of capitalist globalization *(Rani and Felicity)*. Following an interpretative summary of each story, I will synthesize their larger contextual relations and analyze the implications for children's learning about both the diversity of cultural and environmental histories that are our legacies and the crises of environmental degradation facing humanity today.

The Story of Colors was originally written in its Spanish version as a communiqué to the Mexican people from Subcomandante Insurgente Marcos on October 27, 1994, ten months after the Zapatistas in southern Chiapas publicized to the world their struggle for the rights of indigenous and other economically disenfranchised peoples. This struggle emphasizes the crucial ties between peoples and lands and espouses an ecological ethic that is part and parcel of the demand for human rights. The Zapatistas' public initiation of a small-scale armed insurgence was timed to coincide with the continent's inauguration of the Zapatistas' antithesis—the U.S.-led North American Free Trade Agreement, NAFTA. Communiqués from Subcomandante Marcos quickly became serial e-mail communication from the Lacandon Jungle. With equal interest, literary and political science scholars pored over both Spanish originals and English translations, for Marcos's writing is rich in literary and political allusions and analysis, symbolic language, and the interwoven aspects of multiple traditions. While, like the other stories discussed in this chapter, *The Story of Colors* was originally written down for another purpose, it lends itself easily to the transposition into a children's story. In essence, it is an origination myth, not unlike hundreds of others from around the world. Yet, the adaptation is rendered through melding contemporary indigenous Mexican reality, U.S. children's book publishing reality, and the story's traditional source. This is accomplished partly as Marcos, the initial narrator, introduces the audience to the elder storyteller and subsequent narrator, "el viejo *Antonio.*" Read in the context of the turn of the twenty-first century, the story implicitly advocates ecological sustainability, amiable social interaction that occurs without oppressive structures or domination, and a multicultural coalition bound by difference. Even as the gods are fighting because the black and white and gray world is boring, the earth and its people seem relatively serene: "And that's the way it was. The gods woke up after Night had said to Day, 'Okay, that's it for me—your turn.' And the men and women were sleeping or they were making love, which is a nice way to become tired and then go to sleep." Lovemaking and cigar smoking are presented as aspects of life—instilling a healthy approach to sex and other pleasures that doesn't prioritize the need to consider the behavior potentially abusive. After each of five colors (the primary colors plus green and brown) is discovered, they are flung upon various aspects of nature by the gods from the top branches of a ceiba tree;[2] later, they are all poured onto a macaw for safekeeping. The story ends: "And that was how the macaw took hold of the colors, and so it goes strutting about just in case men and women forget how many colors there are and how many ways of thinking and that the world will be happy if all the colors and ways of thinking have their place." In other words, nature, in the body of the macaw, carries the responsibility of gently and brilliantly reminding human beings to respect biological and cultural diversity.

There is synchronicity involved in the creation of the colors, which are discovered as the gods encounter emotions; this is evident in brown, discovered as a god searches for the "heart of the earth," yellow, which is laughter stolen from a child that is later flung on the sun, and green, the feeling of hope. The story begins with one god finding the first color—red—in his blood, spilled when he trips and hits his head after a quarrel; the violence of the red can be likened to the Zapatistas' public beginning in armed uprising. The god who brings the color blue goes "straight upwards," and becomes blinded when "the color of the world stuck to his eyes," and he thus returns "carrying the color of the world in [his] eyes." The image of blue eyes blinded by their accumulation of the world has implications in the real-world indigenous experience with European (blue-eyed) domination of the continent. As the yellow (the color of the culturally central corn/maize) is stolen from the child, another aspect of life—indigenous land and culture—is stolen from peoples who, in the vehicle of this book, share their culture with the children of those who hold the legacy of domination. What more sophisticated and intricate resistance to cultural domination?

Even as the book is a collective effort by those from within and outside its cultural context and those partial insiders with substantial experience in indigenous Chiapas, the artwork shapes and is integral to our understanding of the story of colors in very crucial ways. In crafting the sense of the legend as an alternative visual history, Domi Domínguez, the Mazatecan artist, paints a story with indigenous roots that speaks visually and symbolically about something beyond literary criticism's banal banter on authenticity. For example, although the narrative lists only five colors that are added to the black, white, and gray palette of the earlier world, the audience sees in the illustrations multiple shades of primary, secondary, and tertiary colors that are deeply textured and toned—brilliant colors. Thus, implicitly, the reader is led to understands as the story unfolds that each shade holds its truth, its narrative, its perspective, its place in the world. Together, words and colors restore or sustain a hope for a healthy order among beings established to respect the well-being of all.

Less utopian in its story line, less abstract in its illustrations, *The People Who Hugged the Trees* nonetheless holds much in common with *The Story of Colors*. It transforms a Rajasthani historical legend into a universalized environmental tale of good conquering evil, of the village people, through their bravery, convincing the maharaja to leave the forest uncut. In *The People* the forest is a benevolent natural force in battle against a natural threat: the desert winds and sands. This is one of the senses in which the retold legend takes on a more universal ecological significance—certainly, in deforested areas across the globe, the destruction of forest has encouraged the encroachment of desert conditions, which fail to support the local level of human existence previously possible.

The last page, the epilogue, explains that in "the original legend, Amrita Devi and several hundred villagers gave up their lives while protecting their forest, nearly three centuries ago." Yet the children's tale itself has a peaceful ending in which no villagers are killed and the trees are saved for subsequent generations. This erases the actual massacre that legendary history commemorates as well as the violence done to forests and their resident protectors in both colonized and present-day privatized India. Presumably, the writer tailored out the violent history to make it more age-appropriate, less disturbing, for a young international audience. Its less abstract plot does not allow *The People* to make the implicit, but bold, statements about human domination that *The Story* makes. Because it stops short of a literal telling of the legacies of violent domination of people and nature, it compromises on its political perspective.

This book is not for the Indian children's audience; the book's price is listed in U.S., U.K., and Irish currency, and many web sites that list the book and its offshoots, creative projects, are from the United Kingdom. (I've not found Indian children's books on Amrita Devi and the Bishnoi massacre suffered as the villagers attempted to save their forest, but they are likely to exist, though few may be in English.) The only direct reference to Asia in *The People* is that, like many picture books, it is printed in Hong Kong, a contrast to the international collaboration that created *The Story* but more representative of the particular kind of multicultural corporate collaboration implemented in the contemporary U.S.-based publication industry.

In line with my earlier critical mention of the concept of authenticity in late-twentieth-century cultural studies, I would not argue for some *fictional* standard of *historical* representation (or vice versa). Such an argument may suggest that there is one authentic story per situation, even if "the Truth" has been multiplied to include a spectrum of cultural contexts. Domi Domínguez's paintings, in their bold floral and bird designs and intense tones of color, reflect her earlier work in embroidery and images from her cultural context expressed in woven and embroidered *huipils* (an indigenous style of blouse). As Domi Domínguez's artistic trajectory shows, culture is maintained not through a static hold on transformation but through self-defined change that reveres, critiques, and synthesizes the cultural past through careful incorporation of shifting opportunities. Nevertheless, I believe we must return to the significance of erasing—erasing not only the original massacre of three centuries back but the intervening years of colonial, and subsequently imperialist, ecocide and violent violation of human rights. *The People* raises most directly a question that each of the three books engages differently but effectively: How does children's literature portray the troubling reality of our world in order to address social issues and to promote a path toward productive resolutions without shattering a sense of hope, without destroying (in the terms of *The Story*) the "green" and replacing it with "gray"? This question is especially relevant when many children recognize that their world is more gray than green, literally and symbolically.

In contrast to *The Story, The People* was written and illustrated by people whose credentials place them outside the cultural or regional context that they portray. Deborah Lee Rose, author of another children's book, *Meredith's Mother Takes the Train,* is a science writer at the University of California–Berkeley. Birgitta Säflund, native of Sweden, lives in West Cork, Ireland, and is known for "exquisitely detailed nature paintings" (Rose, jacket blurb); her watercolor paintings, in their presentation of the dress of the people and the aesthetics of the land, reveal likely study of historical Rajasthani painting. It is likely that, as is often the case in children's book illustrations, the author and the artist did not conceive of the project together. There is little evidence of experiential relationships to the cultural aspects of the story, though both author and artist study (in word and paint) "nature."

As the colors of the universe coalesce in the *The Story*'s macaw, the bird takes on an almost spiritual aspect. The cultural and spiritual aspects, though implicit, are strong in *The Story*; does this correlate with its grounding in a specific cultural context that is shared by the makers of the book? Might these aspects have been stronger in *The People* had it been created from inside the Chipko movement, or at least by those more intimately aligned with it? In the contemporary Chipko movement, spiritual aspects are strong. Women have transferred and transformed gendered Hindu ritual in service to the trees: for example, adapting a traditional ritual in which a sister bestows protection on her brother by tying a sacred thread around the boy's wrists, women tie sacred threads around the trees to protect them. Religious symbolic ritual helped promote leadership roles for women within the Chipko movement. *The People*, even while it erases certain aspects of Indian social environmental history, celebrates the grassroots politics of the contemporary Chipko movement. However, had *The People*'s author and illustrator been more directly in touch with the sociopolitical and contemporary context of the Chipko movement, to which they link the legend, *The People* might have established a stronger regional and geopolitical connection.

Created in India, *Rani and Felicity: A Tale of Two Chickens* nonetheless indicates international collaboration: the photographs are taken from U.S. and U.K. sources. Illustrations and layout were done, presumably locally in Delhi, by Aparna Chakrabarty, and the text was written by Radha (although on web sites selling the book the author is listed as Dr. Vandana Shiva). However, the audience is again, at least predominantly, international, arguably Western, in that the narrative addresses "we consumers," a clearly Western attribute in the dichotomy the story establishes. To convey the sensibility of *Rani and Felicity,* the story of two hens, I must momentarily revert back to the nightly "story times" of my own childhood.

When I was a small child, my father was completing his doctoral dissertation on hognose snakes, and thus I grew up around these gentle, even pacifist, snakes—neither species of hognose my father was studying bites humans, and when threatened, the Western hognose snake will play dead rather than attack. Yet outside of my nuclear family, the socially induced fear of snakes was as rampant in south-central Kansas (where we had only one, very rare, venomous species of snake) as elsewhere. One of my earliest attempts at educating, beyond playing school with my younger brother, was an attempt to convince a baby-sitter that indeed snakes were benevolent and beneficial creatures that were terribly misunderstood by most humans. Upon discovering that this baby-sitter feared snakes, I launched an education campaign by asking that she read to me an "all about snakes" book that I thought would put her fears to rest.

Rani and Felicity reminds me of that childhood reform project because I get the sense that it is written for the adult (perhaps young adult) reader as well as the child listener, and that it is intended to provoke its audience to think critically about current cultural norms in agricultural production and animal husbandry.[3] The concepts of global capitalism's corrosive effects on domestic animals make this a book that would be of interest to a wider age range of children than the other two picture books, as well as to an adult audience involved in progressive, environmental, or "Third World" concerns. However, it is accessible to children, partly through its conversational tone: "Did you know that free range chickens spend 50% of their time pecking for food?" (8). The plot is simple: a corporation owns Felicity; no person is involved. On the other hand, Rani lives in the backyard of her owner Kamala's house. Not only does Rani have a home with Kamala, as opposed to the twelve-by-eighteen-inch cage that Felicity shares with three other hens, Rani, as an Indian chicken, has a heritage: "Poultry was first domesticated in the Indian subcontinent," where there are still "at least 14 indigenous breeds" (4).

Symmetrical illustrations feature the white U.S.-grown Felicity and the dark Indian-grown Rani: whimsical, expressive drawings of the Desi (Indian) chicken's life are juxtaposed with photographs of the gruesome conditions of battery house chicken farms. Readers learn that a laying house may hold sixty thousand hens or more; if they do not die from the conditions sooner, they are "exhausted" after a couple years and butchered "for soup and pet food" while the life span of a free-range hen averages fifteen years (5). The comparisons of the hens' meals are particularly stark: battery house chickens are made into cannibals and fed chemicals and pesticides, while Rani is fed grain, whey, buttermilk, and healthy table scraps. Rani forages in the yard for free pecking at "insects and worms," and thus she and "her friends" act as "agents of pest control" but "unlike pesticides . . . [they] do not cause disease" (5).

Gender issues come into play when we learn that Rani roams with both male and female chickens while the male chicks born alongside Felicity die of suffocation or are killed at one day of age. Even privacy issues are at stake in a comparison that seems to be stretching the application of human emotions. The story's perspective is justified, however, when we are told that the free-roaming chicken will find a dark secluded spot when she is ready to brood, while brooding is being bred out of the corporate laying hens. Not surprisingly, even Rani's waste is wealth that reduces the need for purchased fertilizer, while Felicity and her fellow hens will get "litter burned" and suffer from the ammonia stench when the ammonia and litter collect too long.

In the Indian home, nature is not separate from home, and as indicated in the hen's name in translation, Rani is Queen of her barnyard, Kamala's backyard, while in Felicity's experience, nature is regulated by factory precision, and her name (Pleasure) reads sardonically. The significance of these comparisons is suggested in the introduction: "The difference in their upbringing raises important issues of kindness and compassion towards animals, animal rights, health of humans and animals as well as issues about dignity of life" (from the introduction, n.p.)

Rani and Felicity makes its most explicitly political statements in the urgency with which it portrays the demise of animal—and, less directly, human—well-being at the hands of corporate agriculture; it demonstrates what happens when short-term monetary profit is held above service to, or protection of, the environment and the communities therein. Despite its overt stance, its ideology is softened by its matter-of-fact approach and age-appropriate presentation. That the well-being of both nature and culture should come together as a priority over corporate profit is not a difficult concept or one that conflicts with differently nuanced but relatively universal values taught to, if not practiced in front of, children.

A web search for each of the books turned up only 4 hits for *Rani and Felicity* and 87 for *The Story of Colors;* it registered 33,200 hits for *The People Who Hugged the Trees.* Web presence stems from a variety of factors, which would make another essay, but it is worth noting that the largest presence by far is held by the most "commercial" of the books. *The People* also has the most ties to prestigious Western university settings (as opposed to the book produced in a scholarly but grassroots research center, directed by Dr. Vandana Shiva—who earned a Ph.D. in physics before turning to forest women activists for further postgraduate education). Highest web presence was not given to the bilingual book, but to the book that has been translated into seven languages (again, language use is an issue that is another essay in itself). It is the South Asian story in *The People*—written, illustrated, and produced by individuals largely outside of an Asian context but targeting U.S. and European audiences—that has most web presence.

Both *The Story* and *The People* have won awards: *The People* received the 1990 Jane Addams Award Recommended List Selection from the Women's International League for Peace and Freedom and the Jane Addams Peace Association, which acknowledges children's literature (preschool through high school) that "most effectively promotes the cause of peace, social justice and world community" (http://www.tarleton.edu)

In 2000, *The Story* received the Firecracker Alternative Book Award, which celebrates the best in alternative publishing (http://www.fire-crackerbooks.org).

The children's ecocritical literature for environmental justice that this essay describes suggests that stories of victories over environmental contamination and racism, stories from diverse parts of the world—from chicken farms, forests, and jungles and from urban settings—must be told and retold, must be rephrased for new generations, so that indigenous tradition melds with the postmodern. These stories must be told to children, and by children, until we as a world address the toxic inequities and the threats to all humans and the larger body of life upon which we depend for physical, cultural, and spiritual sustenance. Each of these stories creates a distinctive trajectory that not only includes but goes beyond "the relation between literature and the physical environment" ecocritics identify (Taylor 57). Each text advocates social justice honed by ecological concerns and environmental issues tempered with those of social justice. This complexity is accomplished in an ecocritical literature that is accessible and appealing to children and broadens their critical thinking about their world of nature and people.

NOTES

1.   When a *New York Times* article pointed out that the author of *The Story* was from the leader of the Zapatistas, the director of the NEA must have remembered the U.S. political-corporate ties to the Mexican government, which has maintained an invasive military presence against Zapatista revolutionary reform. The NEA immediately revoked its funding support to the publishers of *The Story,* ostensibly because the NEA was afraid the money might go to the Zapatistas (Byrd). However, Bobby Byrd believes it was primarily because the NEA feared negative media response, in particular from the *Washington Times,* the Reverend Moon–owned newspaper that is a favorite of right-wing pundits. Either way, with the funding withdrawn, Cinco Puntos Press received major prepublication publicity for the book, and the first printing of five thousand copies sold out in three days. Although the publicity was a "boon" for Cinco Puntos Press, Byrd points out that the "real ideas and issues got lost in that frenzy, not the least of which is the indigenous struggle for autonomy and land in Chiapas."

Another issue implicitly raised is freedom of expression as regards cultural diversity. On March 9, 1999, when NEA Chairperson William Ivey revoked funding, it was "the first time that the NEA has censored an art project dealing with cultural diversity" (Press Release). As I write the conclusion to this essay in my current home city of San Antonio, Texas, Judge Orlando Garcia's words—offered in his decision on "The Esperanza Center against the City of San Antonio" resonate: "Once a governing body chooses to fund art, . . . the Constitution requires that it be funded in a viewpoint-neutral manner, that is, without discrimination among recipients on the basis of their ideology."

2. The ceiba tree, or cottonwood, a favorite haunt of La Llorona, the woman who wanders most often along waterways, weeping for her dead children (Corpi 15), is native to the Americas.

3. The Philosophy and the Environment Book Catalogue web site advertises *Rani and Felicity* as a "cartoon and photo book with text, comparing the lives of a Free Range chicken and a battery farmed chicken [that is] [a]imed at older children and adults despite the format!"

Works Cited

Alvarez, Julia. *A Cafecito Story*. White River Junction, Vt.: Chelsea Green, 2002. http://www.chelseagreen.com.

Byrd, Bobby. "American Happened to Us." Latest Censorship News, April 29, 1999. http://www.oneworld.org.

Corpi, Lucha. *Palabras de mediodia/ Noon Words*. Berkeley, Calif.: El Fuego de Aztlán Publications, 1980.

Glotfelty, Cheryll. "Introduction: Literary Studies in an Age of Environmental Crisis." In *The Ecocriticism Reader: Landmarks in Literary Ecology*. Ed. Cheryll Glotfelty and Harold Fromm. Athens: University of Georgia Press, 1996, xv–xxxvii.

Marcos, Subcommandante Insurgente. *The Story of Colors/La historia de los colores*. Trans. Anne Bar Din. El Paso: Cinco Puntos Press, 1999.

Peña, Devon G. *Chicano Culture, Ecology, Politics: Subversive Kin*. Tucson: University of Arizona Press, 1998.

Rose, Deborah Lee, adapter. *The People Who Hugged the Trees: An Environmental Folk Tale*. Cork, Ireland: Roberts Rinehart International, 1990. Reprint, Boulder, Colo.: Roberts Rinehart, 2000.

Shiva, Vandana. *Staying Alive: Women, Ecology, and Development*. London: Zed Books, 1989.

———. *Stolen Harvest: The Hijacking of the Global Food Supply*. Cambridge, MA: South End Press, 2000.

———, ed. *Close to Home: Women Reconnect Ecology, Health, and Development Worldwide*, Philadelphia: New Society, 1994.

Shiva, Vandana, and Radha. *Rani and Felicity: The Story of Two Chickens*. New Delhi: Research Foundation for Science, Technology, and Natural Resource Policy, 1996.

Taylor, Dorceta. "Environmentalism and the Politics of Inclusion." In *Confronting Environmental Racism: Voices from the Grassroots*. Ed. Robert D. Bullard. Boston: South End Press, 1993.

12

(Em)bracing Icy Mothers

Ideology, Identity, and Environment in Children's Fantasy

Naomi Wood

> And Nature, the old Nurse, took
> The child upon her knee,
> Saying, "Here is a story book
> Thy father hath written for thee.
> "Come wander with me" she said,
> "Into regions yet untrod,
> And read what is still unread
> In the Manuscripts of God."
> And he wandered away and away
> With Nature, the dear old Nurse,
> Who sang to him night and day
> The rhymes of the universe.
>
>   LONGFELLOW

> Nature herself is cold, maternal and severe. The trinity of the masochistic
> dream is summed up in the words: cold—maternal—severe, icy—senti-
> mental—cruel.
>
>   GILLES DELEUZE

Longfellow's poem illustrates the romantic tradition inspired by
Rousseau and Wordsworth, a tradition in which Nature is depicted as
the child's mother or nurse, an influence that works for the good and
well-being of the child.[1] This tradition emphasizes Nature's warmer and
more benign aspects. Yet there is another tradition, which instead represents Mother Nature's harshness and coldness. Inspired by the Snow

Queen of Hans Christian Andersen and theorized by John Ruskin, this cold, albeit loving, mother is repeated in the work of British fantasists from Charles Kingsley to Philip Pullman. Bracing, pure, and intimately connected with the poles of life—birth and death—these chilling mothers work as a commentary upon the fashioning of children: the narratives stress submission to irresistible sublime power, the appeal to what Deleuze has called "supersensualism," and mark all of these tales with a masochistic signature, a masochism that lends the submissive child moral if not material power. In these fantasies, the cold mother is beautiful, frequently clad in furs, travels rapidly by flying or in a sled or some combination, and offers the child sublimity, rarified love, and power. The child accepting her gifts understands their danger, yet that danger takes him or her to another developmental level. Under the cold mother's tutelage, the beloved child explores the far reaches of human potentiality and either dies or is translated into new levels of existence—or both.

In addition to its child-rearing implications, the cold mother figure complicates some tenets of cultural feminist ecocriticism, mainly that women have always been symbolically linked with the warmth and fecundity of the earth in opposition to the cold sky. This essay extends Ellen Cronan Rose's critique of any unexamined symbolic fusion of women with the earth. As Rose and other materialist ecofeminists do, this project attempts to situate symbols as historical and cultural constructions rather than essential identifications (Rose 150). Noting the exploitive implications of imagining the earth as female, Rose writes that "whatever 'mother' means to a given culture will metaphorically infect the meanings it attaches to mother earth" (151). In stereotypical Western "earth mother" writing, "Nature, especially the earth, was seen as 'a nurturing mother: a kindly beneficent female who provided for the needs of mankind'" (Carolyn Merchant, quoted in Rose 150).

In contrast, the cold mother tradition renders humanity's relationship to nature differently from this "norm": nineteenth-century writers such as Andersen and Kingsley acknowledge Nature's power but insist upon humanity's supranatural connection to the divine. In their writing, the warm, nurturing mother of romantic lore becomes rather a beautifully austere disciplinarian—a mother who demands submission. Looking to the regions of the globe in which human survival is clearly not "natural" or paradisiacal—in which any survival must be the result of struggle and tenacity—these writers imagine a Mother Nature that challenges humanity through her coldness. For Andersen and Kingsley, nature leads the way, but the final journey is beyond the body; Nature's lessons in submission are learned in order to attain divine transcendence; thus, Nature is God's wet nurse—affiliated with but inferior to the divine. Nature is not an end but a means.

In the late twentieth century, Philip Pullman, reacting to this heritage and to the industrial and ecological developments of the intervening century, reformulates the symbolic relationship to indict previous attitudes toward the environment and reframes the theological-theoretical relationship between Nature's power and humanity's identity. Pullman separates the cold mother image into two distinctly different personae with radically opposed attitudes toward the body: materiality and the world beyond. These mothers embody respectively the hostility Western philosophical and religious traditions have displayed toward the natural and the importance of recognizing the symbiotic and irreducible connections humans have with their environment.

Nature, Geography, and Identity

The trope of the icy mother arises concurrently with the consolidation of the Southern Hemisphere under Northern powers through the imperialism of Britain and the West and the systematic exploration of the Arctic regions of the globe; the icy mother does not mother all humanity but only those born within the bracing cold of northern and mountainous regions. She is born after it became possible, because of developments in aesthetic theory, to see in the "horrid" and "terrific" aspects of Nature the sublime (Schama 447–513). John Ruskin in *The Stones of Venice* defines the "nature" of the Gothic as essentially Northern. Connecting Northernness not only with environmental rigors but spiritual purity, Ruskin writes: "It is true, greatly and deeply true, that the architecture of the North is rude and wild; . . . I believe it is in this very character that it deserves our profoundest reverence" (1281). Identifying productions of the fecund South as corrupt and sensual, Ruskin argues that the peoples of the North create "purer" art and architecture because of the rigors of their environment. Naturally "wild and wayward as the northern sea," the Gothic imagination arises out of "a state of pure national faith and domestic virtue," while Southern Renaissance architecture grew from "a state of concealed national infidelity and domestic corruption" (1280). Ruskin connects natural and Gothic forms, pairing cathedral and Alp in a "look of mountain brotherhood" to suggest that contemplating Gothic forms and the Alps evokes similarly the sublime. Ruskin concludes: "If . . . the savageness of Gothic architecture, merely as an expression of its origin among Northern nations, may be considered, in some sort, a noble character, it possesses a higher nobility still, when considered as an index, not of climate, but of religious principle" (1282).

Following the logic of Ruskin's argument, if northern Europe represented greater character and nobility than southern Europe, how much more virtuous would be Ultima Thule, the farthest north signified by the North Pole? For Ruskin and many other writers of nineteenth-century Britain, the North with its rigors offered an opportunity to transcend the physical and approach pure spirituality by confronting the sublime in all its terror. The North disciplines humanity, exposing it to the unfathomable power of the environment while stimulating it to rise to the occasion or die. The North, as such, becomes the rod, transcendental chastisement for one's ultimate good, teaching, in the words of Francis Spufford, "endurance, perseverance, resignation" (103).

At the height of British Arctic exploration, roughly 1818–59, new facts and discoveries about the North both amplified and formed anew public perceptions about it as a physical place (Loomis 107). This discovery and fact-finding celebrated both the sublime beauties of the North and the gallantry of the men who sought to master it. As Chauncey Loomis recounts, during the initial months following the deployment of the Franklin Expedition, newspapers expressed "the feeling that if Franklin went out into the Arctic and mastered it, man would somehow be enlarged in mind and soul." Traveling to the Arctic, then, functioned in the critical commentary as a spiritual as well as physical pilgrimage. Charlotte Brontë's *Jane Eyre* depicts the fascination of younger readers for northern regions: the book opens with her young heroine poring over the pages of Bewick's *British Birds* as Jane ponders the images of the North:

> Of these death-white realms I formed an idea of my own; shadowy, like all the half comprehended notions that float dim through children's brains, but strangely impressive. The words in these introductory pages connected themselves with the succeeding vignettes, and gave significance to the rock standing up alone in a sea of billow and spray; to the broken boat stranded on a desolate coast; to the cold and ghastly moon glancing through bars of cloud at a wreck just sinking. (8–9)

As much about psychology as about physicality, Jane's investment in the scene echoes her own physical chill and desolation within the Reed family; her description emphasizes mystery and the relative finitude of human artifacts ("the broken boat stranded," "a wreck just sinking") in relation to the cold landscapes they invade. In depictions of Arctic regions, humanity is dwarfed and yet ennobled by its hubristic attempt to penetrate the sublime Arctic realms. At the same time, the lifeless, frozen landscape, littered with the detritus of human effort, compels. Northernness seems beyond human capacity yet is the key to heroic identity.

Nature's unfathomable age and durability, its starkness, implacability, austerity colliding with humanity's relative youth, frailty, fleshliness continues to be an important theme in the discourse of the North into the twentieth century. C. S. Lewis confessed that the "northern" quality he found in Longfellow's lines—"I heard a voice that cried, / Balder the beautiful/ Is dead, is dead"—gave him his first experience of what he called "joy," something he linked with transcendence. Lewis writes that on reading those lines, "Instantly I was uplifted into huge regions of northern sky, I desired with almost sickening intensity something never to be described (except that it is cold, spacious, severe, pale, and remote)" (17). In 1986, Barry Lopez makes Ruskin's connection between icy peaks and cathedrals, but extends it beyond Ruskin's racism: "I think the reasons for it are deeper than the obvious appropriateness of line and scale. It has to do with our passion for light" (248), which he reads as "a humble, impassioned embrace of something outside the self, in the name of that which we refer to as *God,* but which also includes the self and *is* God" (250). And Philip Pullman, who titled the first of his *Dark Materials* fantasy trilogy *Northern Lights* (published in the United States as *The Golden Compass*) is no less sensitive to the lure of the North: his heroine, Lyra, connects her ability to read the "alethiometer"—a truth-divining apparatus—with "the same deep thrill she'd felt all her life on hearing the word *North*" (133). Truth and the North inspire similar intrepidity, a similar thrill of the transcendent. In all of these works, the extremity the North represents suggests ideas beyond materiality, beyond the natural; but for Lopez and Pullman, the geographical integrity of the North is also a theme and of concern.

Thus, the North signifies beyond its geography: the North is identity. From John Ruskin to Philip Pullman, the North inspires awe and self-consciousness in the humans who view it, impressing them with its distinctive stamp. And that stamp, recognized as Other (and perhaps even because of this quality), was also figured as female. The North's unmasterability, even with the latest technology (the Franklin Expedition was notoriously well equipped according to the standards of the time), provoked new considerations about humanity's relation to Mother Nature. Nature was no seductive, pliant lover but a mother who demanded submission from her children as a condition for survival. When nineteenth-century writers personified the North as female (and when personified, it was *always* female), they focused, Francis Spufford observes, on the logic of frigidity: "[W]ith the obvious sorts of physical generosity excluded, these explored varieties of female chill, from cool chastity to deathly seductiveness. They gave their Arctics freezing bodies, whether for good or for ill; bodies from the mildly perverse pages of the personifying grammar, which dealt with imaginary women of power, icily splendid" (138–39). As she is represented in children's fantasy, the North is mother to people who define themselves in opposition to the oriental, what we might call the "boreal."

The Cold Mother and the Boreal Identity

As engenderer and nurturer of a boreal people, the cold mother evolved out of a combination of the cultural and religious values implied by John Ruskin's analysis of the Gothic. Discipline, endurance, self-denial, and physical and mental purity were the self-avowed outcomes of John Locke's influential *Treatise on Education,* which advocated systematic exposure of middle-class children to the cold, and to cold water, to toughen them and habituate them to hardship.[2] Even more, Christian doctrines about child rearing ("spare the rod and spoil the child") advocated teaching children to submit and to forswear any version of carnality that might tempt them to sins of the appetite. These masochistic strands combine in fantasy to produce a mother who demands all these things yet satisfies other desires, a point made in the novels of Leopold von Sacher-Masoch and carefully analyzed in Deleuze's study of masochism, *Coldness and Cruelty,* which delineates the connections between coldness, cruelty, supersensuality, identity, and geography.

For Deleuze, this cold masochistic goddess is an "oral mother," a mother whose authority precedes the father's; she subdues the flesh, requiring more refined pleasures. Her qualities—coldness, severity, iciness, cruelty—personify the harsh steppe country of eastern Russia, Poland, the far north of Scandinavia, Svalbard and Nova Zembla. Her implacable virtue inspires new virtue in her children—a virtue that triumphs over carnal sensuality to "supersensuality." Those who embrace this mother and her cold virtues sacrifice themselves upon cold altars. The multinational resonance of this image is made clear in a 1993 review of *Coldness and Cruelty* in the *Moscow News*. Mikhail Zolotonosov writes of Deleuze's description of the cold, oral mother: "I don't think I need to elaborate, for you must have already recognized in the 'oral mother,' the classic Soviet Motherland as immortalized in stone statues of a woman who forever calls people to death and suffering for her own sake and then adorns cemeteries with her presence. This is no mere coincidence, it is an essential link, an accurate description of the kind of state which we have inherited from the collapsed empire" (5). Conflating Nature's rigor with a national sensibility, racial identity, and calls to sacrificial duty echoes throughout this literature. The cold mother, in other words, has continued to be a recognizable trope by which Northern peoples identify themselves and their relationship to the world. Although Zolotonosov remarks only upon the gendered political implications of this image, the image has ecological implications as well. It assumes and encourages a particular kind of relationship between humanity and the material world.

The urmother of this tradition is Danish writer Hans Christian Andersen's Snow Queen, essence of the cold, a nonnurturing mother whose affinity for the cold figures her inability to rear children. As an antimother, she embodies everything foresworn by Victorian domestic ideology and clearly spells danger to the unwary. As Francis Spufford notes, "It is mythically apt that her roles as anti-mother and anti-wife should be vested in the lineaments of beauty, all emptied to white: white furs, white hair, white skin" (141). Yet this excessive whiteness also signifies the purity of the anticarnal, the site of incorruptibility. Andersen's Snow Queen is seductive, ageless, embodying the dangerous appeal of pure reason, mathematics in particular, uncontaminated by organic physicality. In "The Snow Queen," the young boy, Kai, is struck in his eye and heart by a distorting mirror fragment that freezes his emotive capacities and limits him to the pursuit of the mechanically perfect. When Kai's vision is affected by the mirror splinter, he becomes a naturalist before Zola: he is no longer able to see the beauty of a rose—he can only see the worm at its heart; he ridicules people for their "little peculiarities" and can see beauty only in snowflakes because they seem more engineered, more artificial than softer structures. Snowflakes are "much nicer than real flowers" because they are "quite perfect . . . [and] all flawless as long as they don't melt" (Andersen 238–39). Kai's inability to derive pleasure from organic, asymmetrical, or flawed beauty in natural objects and in his dear playmate, Gerda, demonstrates that his better nature has been frozen.

Kai's introduction to the Snow Queen, before his mishap, frightens him: though she is "beautiful," she is "made of ice, cold blindingly glittering ice"; importantly, he sees in her eyes "neither rest nor peace" (Andersen 237). However, after Kai's accident and when she finally arrives swathed in white fur and driving a sled, Kai is engulfed. The Snow Queen's kisses, dangerous but pleasurable, preserve the mind but freeze the heart and soul. Once kissed, Kai can enjoy the cold without feeling it: "'Are you still cold?' she asked, and kissed his forehead. Her kiss was colder than ice. It went right to his heart, which was already half made of ice; he felt as though he were about to die, but it hurt only for a minute, then it was over. Now he seemed stronger and he no longer felt how cold the air was" (239–40). Kai, having forgotten all his ties to home and to Gerda (when he tries to pray, he can only recall the multiplication tables), thinks he has found in the Snow Queen the perfection he has been seeking: "[H]e could not imagine that anyone could have a wiser or a more beautiful face; and she no longer seemed to be made of ice. . . . In his eyes she now seemed utterly perfect, nor did he feel any fear. He told her that he knew his multiplication tables, could figure in fractions, and knew the area in square miles of every country in Europe, and what its population was" (240). Though the landscape unfolds in mysterious vastness around them as they fly away, Kai can only focus on mathematical abstractions. His heart frozen, he cannot perceive the good, nor can he perceive the sublime.

The bulk of the story is about Gerda's quest to rescue Kai from the Snow Queen's power; when Gerda finally locates him in the far north at the Snow Queen's northern palace, he is futilely trying to spell "Eternity" from ice chips. (The Snow Queen has promised him "the world and a pair of skates" if he can do so; greed rather than piety is his motivation.) But Gerda's simple liquid warmth, expressed in her kiss and tears, melts the ice in Kai's heart and frees him—the domestic, finally, is stronger than the alien Other of the North.

Although Andersen's Snow Queen is icily seductive, Andersen's message about the relative power of cold and warmth is unambiguous: heat, water, love are unquestionably stronger than cold, ice, and intellect. The North for Andersen is a metaphor for a state of mind that chills all humanity's worthwhile virtues. Though Kai's townsfolk say of his ill-natured cynical mimicking, "That boy has his head screwed on right" (238) because of the accuracy of his imitations, Kai has lost the ability to imagine a larger perfection—as demonstrated by his inability to spell "Eternity." The Snow Queen's appeal for Kai's mirror-warped sensibility is her "perfection," but this is a perfection with no life and no future—no "rest or peace," a death without dying, a life-in-death that values intellect over soul. As a Scandinavian, Andersen may have been less prone to romanticize the Arctic regions than his contemporaries in more temperate countries. For while Andersen's influence was profound and long-lasting, and while his images, as we shall see, are recycled continually, the meanings assigned to the Snow Queen become more positive as the figure is taken over by English writers.

Even so, Andersen's description of Kai's journey north hints at the ways in which the cold mother will come to be connected to different moral states than Andersen may have anticipated: "[Kai] looked out into the great void of the night, for by now they were flying high up in the clouds, above the earth. The storm swept on and sang its old, eternal songs. Above oceans, forests, and lakes they flew; and the cold winter wind whipped the landscape below them. Kai heard the cry of the wolves and the hoarse voice of the crows. The moon came out, and into its large and clear disk Kai stared all through the long winter night" (240). Here, although the Snow Queen and her powers are explicitly linked to reason and mathematical perfection, the narrator describes as mysterious and inchoate the vastness of the northern landscape—beyond reason, a "great void" evoking eternity, the overwhelming storm and its "old, eternal songs." The inexplicability of wild nature, suggested by wolves and crows and their incomprehensible voices and the eerie presence of the "large and clear disk" of the moon in the darkness of a winter night hint at depths Kai's superficial mathematics cannot begin to fathom. The significance of these depths, in the work of Victorian British fantasists, turns from Andersen's romantic affirmation of emotion and warmth to a natural theology in which humanity is disciplined by Mother Nature in order to triumph over its own carnality and achieve transcendence over the natural.

Like Andersen's tale, Charles Kingsley's *The Water-Babies* also features maternal nature goddesses from the North, but here they hallow the rarified pleasures of the cold to encourage a focus on this world as prelude to the next. Kingsley's nature goddesses engulf their young protégés too, but their embrace, even if it means the ultimate cold of death, creates better, more spiritual beings. Significantly, Kingsley envisions this evolution as the transformation of Tom from a dirty blackened chimney sweep into a "great man of science . . . [who] can plan railroads, and steam-engines, and electric telegraphs and rifled guns, and so forth" (182), from a servant of industrial power to its—and Nature's—master.

The moral summary to the "little man" reading the book is: "[L]earn your lessons, and thank God that you have plenty of cold water to wash in" (183). Cold water, in fact, *is* the lesson: it is what "cools" Tom as he rests his feverish body in the stream and allows him to leave his worthless "shell" of a body to learn the moral lessons his previous background did not teach him. Mrs. Doasyouwouldbedoneby and Mrs. Bedonebyasyoudid begin the process of reforming Tom through the salutary use of cold water and whipping. Counterfables told in the book demonstrate that soft living leads to devolution—in "The History of the Great and Famous Nation of the Doasyoulikes" (126), Tom learns that only degradation can result from easy living, as in the parable of the Doasyoulikes, who live in a warm paradise; refusing to exert themselves, they eventually either die or devolve into apes. As Mrs. Bedonebyasyoudid says severely, "when folks are in that humour, I cannot teach them, save by the good old birch-rod" (127). She then warns Tom, "[I]f you had not made up your mind to go on this journey, and see the world, like an Englishman, I am not sure but that you would have ended as an eft in a pond" (131).

After learning from these fairies, Tom's final exam involves quests to both North and South Poles. On his journey north, Kingsley's Tom wonders at the spectacle of the inhospitable treatment men receive from the far North: he observes "lying among the ice pack the wrecks of many a gallant ship; some with masts and yards all standing, some with the seamen frozen fast on board. Alas, alas for them! They were all true English hearts; and they came to their end like good knights-errant, in searching for the white gate that never was opened yet" (145). In a passage that would inevitably recall the hubristic confidence of the Franklin Expedition (1845–47), Tom too considers the sublimity and futility of Arctic exploration. In a novel very much about "evolving" the virtuous Englishman, Kingsley celebrates explorers' gallantry while cautioning against hubris. The balanced focus is typical of his work; he seeks not only to educate his readers about the wonders of the natural world but cautions them to be content not to know what God has not revealed. The "white gate" is open for Tom because he has already died and is part of a more elemental existence.

Kingsley so valorizes cold water that the North itself becomes a place of life in the midst of ice and snow. Kingsley revered women as the source of life and custodians of death even as he bowed to a father-god; eschewing masculine supernaturalism, he depicts natural goddesses as the intimate disciplinarians of his fantasies. When Tom comes upon

Mother Carey, he is awestruck. Within this icy environment Mother
Carey generates new life out of old, and though she is utterly still
(described as "the grandest old lady he had ever seen—a white marble
lady, sitting on a white marble throne"), Mother Carey's peculiar power
is to "make new beasts out of old . . . [by] mak[ing] them make themselves" (148–49). Tom "makes himself" by choosing pilgrimages to the
North Pole and then to the South and so embraces cold water, redeem-
ing not only himself but his old master, Grimes. Tom becomes the mus-
cular Christian man of science Kingsley admires.

In their associations with cold water and with ice, Kingsley's nature
spirits are sisters of the Snow Queen, even as they offer a middle road
between reason and faith, the combined effects of "hard work and cold
water" to produce "a true English man" (183, 184). Impervious to cor-
rupting influences, cold mothers stimulate their charges to new feats of
heroic self-denial. Tom does not stay with Mother Carey; instead he
learns from her stillness which direction he should follow. Static women
exert serene influence on men who go out to act. Mother Carey's
remarkable stillness, her very frozenness, is necessary to Tom's achievement, and we recall her chill in the final pages of *The Water-Babies*, where
the narrator adjures the reader: "[T]hank God that you have plenty of
cold water to wash in; and wash in it too, like a true English man" (183).
The good is the cold.

Because the North and cold are good, Victorian children's authors
associate the North with Christianity—a Christianity that forswears
sensuality and celebrates impermeability.[3] Contrary to the sensual goddesses of the South such as Aphrodite or Isis, they invent bracing Northern goddesses who pleasure coldly. Deleuze's study of the work of
another Victorian—Leopold von Sacher-Masoch—describes her affect:
"[T]he trinity of the masochistic dream is summed up in the words:
cold—maternal— severe, icy—sentimental—cruel" (51). The ideal
mother becomes the cold mother. A good part of the North's sublime
appeal is its unsparing demand for a peculiar type of submission. No
matter how rigorous are the North's demands, humans attempt to make
them pleasurable. Spufford's assertion that this cold "pleasure . . . cannot
be named masochistic [because] that label abolishes all delicate grades
of intention" (142) denies the possibility of "delicate grades of intention"
in masochism itself. Deleuze's analysis clarifies the paradoxical power
masochism invests in the "victim." If the social order is oppressive (often
identified in ecofeminism with patriarchy but also connected with the
deity), a victim who embraces rather than seeking to avoid punishment

is subversive of that order. Arctic landscape writing embraces the cold, the discomfort, the austerity, and finds that the embrace elevates the identity to new levels, finally obscuring the power that punishes itself. And although in the writings of Christian fantasists such as Kingsley, the punishing mothers are aligned firmly with the word of God as it may be read in the book of Nature, Philip Pullman, in the twentieth century, reads discipline differently.

In a critique of the implications of Christian cosmology, Philip Pullman's *Dark Materials* trilogy explores another vision of humanity's relation to the North and divides the cold mother in two: Mrs. Coulter, a representative of the church, and Serafina Pekkala, a Finnish witch. Both are mother figures to Lyra, the protagonist. In addition to depicting competing mothers, Pullman also challenges simple personification of the environment by emphasizing the complex web of influence and connection within the world and between worlds. One of the main plot elements involves the scientific-theological study of "Dust," a mysterious substance introduced in the first volume that accretes around humans as they attain puberty and is associated with humanity's rise to consciousness thirty-three thousand years ago and with sexuality. Defined as original sin by the church of Lyra's world, it is called "Dark Matter" by a physicist in our own world and, in *The Amber Spyglass,* it is termed life-giving "sraf" by the Mulefa, a species of sentient beings particularly symbiotically connected with their world. As the series unfolds, it becomes evident that Pullman imagines Dust, or consciousness, as evolving over untold billions of years and connecting with humanity (not making it) as it too evolves into consciousness. The only self-styled creator in the many worlds visited is a fraud and tyrant. Attitudes toward Dust reveal themselves in attitudes toward humans and their relation to the ecosphere throughout the narrative, as the opposed mother figures reveal.

Pullman's fur-clad disciplinarian Mrs. Coulter, like her predecessors, offers the romance of the North, discipline, and purity. She offers love at the cost of sexuality and autonomy. When we first see her luring Street children away from their homes, she is dressed in the same golden fur of her monkey-shaped "daemon" (the soul externalized as a familiar, attending animal). Mrs. Coulter is attractive, glamorous, seductive to children, and evil. She has put extensive time and money into northern exploration and situates her monstrous experimental factory near the Arctic Circle. A representative of religion and the church, she underwrites that world's equivalent of science: experimental theology. Mrs.

Coulter (whose name means "iron blade") kidnaps children to make them oblates to a faith that mutilates them in order to preserve their innocence and prevent them from falling into carnality—sexuality—and independent consciousness. The experimental station "severs" children from their daemons, an unthinkable violation. Mrs. Coulter, however, tells Lyra: "[T]he doctors do it for the children's own good, my love. Dust is something bad, something wrong, something evil and wicked. Grownups and their daemons are infected with Dust so deeply that it's too late for them. They can't be helped. . . . But a quick operation on children means they're safe from it. Dust just won't stick to them ever again. They're safe and happy and—" (282–83).

Like earlier goddess figures, Mrs. Coulter disciplines her charges "for their own good," but unlike his predecessors, Pullman questions the entire premise of the enterprise. Compared explicitly with the castration practiced on boy sopranos by the church (374), "intercision" might be justified by the church but is also evil. Lyra remembers the zombielike state of Tony Makarios, whom she'd met in his "severed" state in the forest; later she reflects: "They were too cruel. No matter how important it was to find out about original sin, it was too cruel to do what they'd done to Tony Makarios and all the others. Nothing justified that" (376). The church and science of Pullman's invented world follows the trajectory of our world carefully, evoking the historical Christian understanding of the relationship between humanity and nature as spirit struggling to overcome the material.

With the denial of spiritual integrity to nature, Lynn White writes in a classic essay, "Man's effective monopoly on spirit in this world was confirmed, and the old inhibitions to the exploitation of nature crumbled" (10). Christianity's severing of pagan animistic ties to nature "made it possible to exploit nature in a mood of indifference to the feelings of natural objects." Against this long tradition, Pullman posits that the very thing the church fears as evil is our best hope of good, of wisdom. Not only must we embrace the materiality and the "Dust" (carnality/consciousness) so feared by the church, but we must redefine discipline as something that must emanate from within, from individual desire, if we, together with our world, are to survive. Mrs. Coulter's tactics may grasp at boreal transcendence but ultimately are revealed as a projection of the life-denying, freedom-killing, world-destroying institutional religion responsible for a great deal of the suffering in that world and this. The attitude that a natural substance, in this case "Dust," can be defined as "evil" without understanding what it does or where it comes from high-lights the hubristic nature of religious and scientific endeavor that does not respect nature's autonomy from human definitions, human concerns.

Pullman's alternate atheology (in the final book of the trilogy, he establishes the "Republic of Heaven" to replace the overthrown "King-dom of Heaven") explores also an alternate ecology based on the assumption that all nature is linked inextricably together and that seek-ing to destroy one part due to culturally defined prejudices endangers the whole. In Pullman's series, the North is not only a place of mystery and transcendence but also a place full of life, beauty, and autonomous beings. This alternative view of the Arctic is well articulated in Pullman's other cold mother, Serafina Pekkala. Though she too is a personification of the northern environment, she is markedly different from other cold mothers: "clad like all the witches in strips of black silk, but wearing no furs, no hood or mittens. She seemed to feel no cold at all. . . . [Her voice was] like the high wild singing of the Aurora itself" (301). So much a part of her environment that she needs no furs as protection from the Arctic blasts, Serafina is compared to northern beauties like the aurora borealis itself. When Lyra questions her about her clothing, Serafina replies: "We feel cold, but we don't mind it, because we will not come to harm. And if we wrapped up against the cold, we wouldn't feel other things, like the bright tingle of the stars, or the music of the Aurora, or best of all the silky feeling of moonlight on our skin. It's worth being cold for that" (313). If the chill is appropriate and natural for witches as a separate species, this does not mean that humans must therefore sub-mit themselves to the cold. Lyra, childlike, wishes to feel the cold as the witch describes it, but Serafina firmly discourages her: "You would die if you took your furs off. Stay wrapped up" (314). Embodying the beauty of the North, the northern lights, and the cold, Serafina, as a witch, does not require others to change their bodies or their beings.

If Mrs. Coulter is a knife that severs children from all hope of wholeness, Serafina Pekkala's name (usually said entire by Lyra) suggests a combination of seraphic and peccant qualities—the union of the spirit and the carnal, redeemed because utterly incognizant of Original Sin. She is the pagan repudiation of the church—resonant with contemporary ecofeminist politics exemplified in the writings of Starhawk, to name only the most prominent critic. "Witches have never worried about Dust. . . . We don't fret and tear things apart to examine it. Leave that to the Church," says Serafina Pekkala (318). In contrast with previous cold mothers, Serafina does not attempt to alter her charge but simply encourages Lyra to fulfill her destiny as best she can, caring for her along the way.

Pullman plays with the stereotypical representation of pious mothers and pagan witches in order to raise questions about the moral impact of the actions of each. The pious mother Mrs. Coulter, working for the church under a version of the Sky God, insists upon hygiene, purity that results in a zombielike existence or death. Serafina Pekkala cooperates with nature as a colleague and thus sees no need to alter it. It gives her what she needs and she in turn respects its autonomy. Nor does she believe that things should work against their natures—Dust is not something to worry about.

Although twentieth-century writers agree with their nineteenth-century predecessors that northern extremes compel sublimity and transcendence, Pullman depicts in his series the new awareness emerging in the last decades of the twentieth century that the North is endangered. The last fifty years of the environmental movement highlights the intimate relationship between the Poles, both North and South, and human activity, which has compromised, perhaps irreparably, the balance of nature. Humans, persisting in the use of fossil fuels with their attendant environmental destruction, contribution to global warming, and the depletion of the ozone layer, are now threatening the North. In Pullman's fictive world, this is figured when the charismatic satanic hero Lord Asriel uses the atomiclike energy generated by severing—and killing—Lyra's best friend Roger to create a bridge to another world. Although Lord Asriel's ambitions are impressive and his goal of overcoming the oppressive tyranny of the Authority (God) laudable, he wreaks untold havoc upon myriad creatures and contributes to the endangerment not only of his own world but of others. Catastrophic climactic changes, floods, drought, melting ice that destroys polar bear habitat, and all the familiar litany of natural disasters attending our own polar meltdown reinforce the parallel.

Submission to the North for Pullman means something quite different from earlier conceptions. It means cooperating with the environment rather than proving oneself by fighting against it. Barry Lopez's statement of the difference between the attitudes of traditional inhabitants of the Arctic and those coming from the South helps identify the culturally generated impulses behind our actions: "[Traditional Eskimos] call us, with a mixture of incredulity and apprehension, the 'people who change nature'" (39). Pullman and Lopez posit that our quest for mastery over nature may compromise our ultimate survival as a species. Pullman suggests that if we do not acknowledge our materiality and love the world that gives us birth, we are doomed to destroy it. This is a different kind of submission from the submission of earlier writers. Pullman asks his readers to embrace the necessity of carnality and the challenge of growth. Even in the frigid extremity of the North our protagonist can save herself and others if she struggles to maintain her complete, unexcised identity, her vibrant humanity and her compassion, accepting her environment rather than attempting to destroy it. Mrs. Coulter's ideologically informed technology of purity only creates puppets. Serafina Pekkala acknowledges diversity and balances claims between living things. Finally, Pullman seems to say, we must reject the seductive masochistic goddess of obedient purity, embrace the material as all there is, and achieve wisdom by acknowledging Nature's independence from us, its otherness, working to discern our place within the equally legitimate claims of the other occupants of our planet—and, indeed, of the planet itself. If, as Lawrence Buell has asserted, "aesthetics can become a decisive force for or against environmental change" (3), studying aesthetics can be a way for us to understand both how we got here and where we might go from here. This genealogy of the cold mother and the boreal identity demonstrates one possible trajectory.

NOTES

My thanks to Lee Behlman, Chris Cokinos, Elizabeth Dodd, Dean Hall, and Donna Potts for commenting on drafts of this essay.

1. The above epigraph, which personifies Nature as "The Old Nurse," is excerpted from Longfellow's 1857 poem "The Fiftieth Birthday of Agassiz." Charles Kingsley used these stanzas as an epigraph to the seventh chapter of *The Water-Babies*.

In this essay I capitalize *Nature* when referring to the external world or personification of its role as a force in the universe; I refer to *nature* when describing the inherent character of a given person or thing.

2. "'Tis use alone hardens [the face] and makes it more able to endure the cold.... I have known it us'd every night with very good success and that all the winter, without the omitting it so much as one night in extreme cold weather; when thick ice cover'd the water, the child bathed his legs and feet in it, though he was of an age not big enough to rub and wipe them himself" (Locke, paras. 10, 12).

3. Other examples can be found in George MacDonald's *At the Back of the North Wind* and, with interesting variations, in the work of his twentieth-century disciple C. S. Lewis.

WORKS CITED

Andersen, Hans Christian. "The Snow Queen: A Fairy Tale Told in Seven Stories." 1845. Trans. Erik Christian Haugaard. In *Hans Christian Andersen: The Complete Fairy Tales and Stories*. New York: Doubleday, 1974, 234–62.

Brontë, Charlotte. *Jane Eyre.* 1848. World's Classics Paperbacks. Oxford: Oxford University Press, 1980.

Buell, Lawrence. *The Environmental Imagination: Thoreau, Nature Writing, and the Formation of American Culture.* Cambridge: Harvard University Press, 1995.

Deleuze, Gilles. *Masochism: Coldness and Cruelty and Venus in Furs.* Trans. Jean McNeil. New York: Zone Books, 1989.

Kingsley, Charles. *The Water-Babies.* 1863. Ed. Brian Alderson. Oxford: Oxford University Press, 1995.

Lewis, C. S. *Surprised by Joy: The Shape of My Early Life.* San Diego: Harcourt Brace, 1955.

Locke, John. "Some Thoughts concerning Education." 1692. In *English Philosophers of the Seventeenth and Eighteenth Centuries.* Ed. Charles W. Eliot. Harvard Classics, vol. 37. New York: P. F. Collier & Son, 1910.

Loomis, Chauncey C. "The Arctic Sublime." *Nature and the Victorian Imagination.* Ed. U. C. Knoepflmacher and G. B. Tennyson. Berkeley: University of California Press, 1977, 95–112.

Lopez, Barry. *Arctic Dreams: Imagination and Desire in a Northern Landscape.* New York: Charles Scribner's Sons, 1986.

Pullman, Philip. *The Golden Compass.* New York: Random House, 1996.

Rose, Ellen Cronan. "The Good Mother: From Gaia to Gilead." In *Ecofeminism and the Sacred.* Ed. Carol J. Adams. New York: Continuum, 1993, 149–67.

Ruskin, John. "The Savageness of Gothic Architecture." *The Stones of Venice,* 1851–53. Rpt. in *The Norton Anthology of English Literature.* 6th ed. Ed. M. H. Abrams. 2: 1280–90.

Schama, Simon. *Landscape and Memory.* New York: Vintage Books, 1995.

Spufford, Francis. *I May Be Some Time: Ice and the English Imagination.* New York: Picador USA, 1999.

White, Lynn, Jr. "The Historical Roots of Our Ecologic Crisis." 1967. Rpt. in *The Ecocriticism Reader: Landmarks in Literary Ecology.* Ed. Cheryll Glotfelty and Harold Fromm. Athens: University of Georgia Press, 1996, 3–14.

Zolotonosov, Mikhail. "The Relevance of Sacher Masoch," *Moscow News,* January 28, 1993. Online: Lexis-Nexis (August 9, 1999).

13

Eco-edu-tainment

The Construction of the Child in Contemporary Environmental Children's Music

Michelle H. Martin

In 1986, I was in the middle of teaching an outdoor lesson on aquatic ecology in the Sierra Nevada Mountains of California, when one of my sixth-grade students lost his shoe, stepping in a cow pie eighteen inches in diameter. The kid screamed, and the other eleven students as well as the high school counselor scattered, yelling "Eeew! Ca-ca! Gross! Nasty!" Unfortunately, this was not a unique event. Since cows shared the nature trails with us, similar encounters had happened before and would happen again. How does one carry on with a lesson after such an encounter?

In an attempt to turn run-ins with scat—the biological name for feces—into something positive at this residential outdoor school, I composed "The Scat Song." The chorus and two representative verses will explain the song's purpose:

> Chorus:
> Scat makes the world go 'round,
> The forest can't survive if it's not on the ground,
> So when I step in a lump of scat,
> I'll jump for joy and tell myself that's where it's at.
> *Verse 2:*
> Coyote scat comes in a neat, grey stick,
> And if you look inside, you will get a kick,
> 'Cause you'll find bones and fur and claws
> From the little critter he had in his jaws.

Verse 4:

If you see some scat lying on the ground,

And you believe it's peanut M&M's you've found,

It's small and round and really dark brown,

You can make a guess a deer has been around.

Final verse:

So next time you walk in a forest green,

Remember all the different kinds of scat you've seen.

Don't scream, but please get it off your shoe,

For scat has some very special work to do. (Martin)

"The Scat Song" soon became a regular part of the weekly repertoire of songs at SCICON (acronym for the Clemmie Gill School of Science and Conservation in Springville, California). Once the song helped students to see scat as data for scientific investigation, their inevitable encounters with scat became more positive and humorous than disruptive. Since bears, coyotes, foxes, raccoons, opossums, ringtail lemurs, and many other wild animals live near SCICON's teaching areas, for the students, learning to recognize different types of scat meant knowing what sorts of animals were frequenting our trails. "The Scat Song" and other ecomusic that we shared with the students reminded the instructors that music can sometimes accomplish what traditional teaching cannot.

The music this essay addresses takes characteristics from both American folk music and certain genres of children's literature. Songs like "The Scat Song" come out of a long tradition of folk songs about nature. "This Land Is Your Land" and "Inch by Inch," for instance, advocate nature appreciation even if their ultimate purpose is to entertain rather than to educate. Children's nature literature and even children's books about scatological topics—*Once upon a Potty* (1979), *Toilet Tales* (1985), *The Story of Little Mole Who Went in Search of Whodunit* (1993), *Everyone Poops* (1993), and *The Gas We Pass* (1994)—entertain while they teach. Because of the work of children's authors such as Jim Arnosky, Joseph Bruchac, Michael Caduto, Jean Craighead George, and Gary Paulsen, ecological children's literature has received notable critical attention. *Wild Things: Children's Culture and Ecocriticism* bears witness to this fact, as does the entire winter 1994–95 special issue of *Children's Literature Association Quarterly*, which was dedicated to "Ecology and the Child."

Although children's environmental music has become as readily available as environmental children's literature, scholars have paid scant critical attention to the music. Combining elements of these musical and literary genres, the songs that I will discuss here I am calling *eco-edu-tainment*: songs that seek to teach listeners and singers specific biological or ecological concepts through the lyrics while they entertain with appealing, artfully crafted, child-friendly music. During my five-year career as a naturalist in three different states, I witnessed repeatedly the power of well-written ecomusic to change the attitudes and sometimes the behaviors of children. These observations have led me to believe that musical eco-edu-tainment is just as deserving of critical investigation as the literature of this genre, and the evaluative criteria that I have developed come directly out of my experiences of sharing ecomusic with young people.

Effective ecomedia entertain while they teach ecology, nature, science, environmentalism, and sometimes peace education, and they instruct in such a way that listeners often retain information without realizing it. While this genre encompasses books, videos, CD ROMS, and other contemporary media, I concern myself here only with the music. The goal of this research harkens back to John Newbery's mantra, *Delectando monemus*: "instruction with delight." To establish a set of criteria for evaluating the success or failure of ecomusic to educate while it entertains, I investigate what kinds of subject positions the lyrics of these songs offer listeners, how the musical elements influence these possible subject positions, and what implications the messages in these songs have for young consumers. Relying on my experiences of using this music in environmental education, I argue that the most successful songs, those most capable of positively affecting children's attitudes toward nature, are those that address children as powerful agents of change and strike a good balance between education and entertainment.

Despite the lack of critical attention paid to environmental music, criticism of children's ecological literature can provide a useful lens for analyzing musical eco-edu-tainment. In her 1994–95 article, "Wonderland to Wasteland: Toward Historicizing Environmental Activism in Children's Literature," Carolyn Sigler identifies three approaches that environmental children's literature has taken to the natural world and the position of humans in it. The anthropocentric view, she argues, exemplified both by the pastoral and the literature of territorial expansion, assumes the primacy of humans, who either sentimentalize or dominate the environment—hence, the domination model. The second view, the caretaking model, which is less so but still anthropocentric, positions humans as caretakers of the earth. In this view, humans should be good stewards so that the earth will continue to sustain human life— hence, the stewardship view. The third, a typically non-Western concept, "decenters humanity's importance in nonhuman nature and nature writing (thus rejecting anthropocentric views) and instead explores the complex interrelationships between the human and the nonhuman (a biocentric view)" (148). This concept undergirds many Native American philosophies about the connectedness of all living and nonliving things. Although this third view seems the least compatible with contemporary American lifestyles, such contemporary practices as organic gardening and using nontoxic household cleaning chemicals show evidence that some Americans do embrace biocentrism.

Because contemporary environmental music arose in the 1960s during a time of heightened environmental awareness, few ecosongs embrace the domination model. Many of them, however, focus on stewardship and biocentrism. In the stewardship model, children are "keepers" or stewards of the earth's resources.[1] As beings separate from nature, they are charged with the responsibility of living in earth-friendly ways to insure that the planet remains a livable habitat for humans. In contrast, biocentric models often use the "web of life" metaphor. As Chief Seattle articulates in his response to the American president who proposed to buy land from his tribe: "Man has not woven the web of life. He is but one thread. Whatever he does to the web, he does to himself" (*How Can One,* n.p.). This metaphor is important because in a web hierarchies don't exist; all strands share the same plane, and movement in any part of the web affects every other part of the web. Music that embraces this model seeks to educate children in a type of ecological consciousness that places humans alongside—not above—other living and nonliving things and seeks to inspire them individually to live more lightly on the planet in whatever small ways they can. These last two sorts of songs—ones that embrace stewardship and biocentrism—are my primary concern.

To evaluate the quality of eco-edu-tainment, I examine both how the text addresses and positions the child and the dynamic relationship between instruction and delight within that text. The instruction/ delight relationship manifests itself in one of three ways, and each of these ways relates to the subject position of the child. First, songs can focus so much on entertainment that they lose all educational value. These songs, which don't teach children enough to help increase their ecological awareness, disempower child listeners by objectifying them as lovers of fun who are incapable of learning complex information. A second type of song concentrates on the didactic delivery of an ecological message to such an excessive degree that the text becomes propagandistic. These songs insult child listeners by addressing them as tabulae rasae who know nothing and who therefore need to be told what to think and how to act. A third type of song effectively balances entertainment and education, addressing children respectfully as subjects and acknowledging them as rational beings, with the expectation that listeners will not only develop an eco-consciousness but will also act on the convictions that develop from it.

Recordings that producers advertise as "environmental" music but that offer entertainment with little or no educational value function in a somewhat harmful way: they encourage listeners to adopt a singular subject position, identifying only with the character through whose perspective the story is told—what John Stephens calls the focalizer. Stephens elaborates: "Identification with focalizers is one of the chief methods by which a text socializes its readers, as they efface their own selfhood and internalize the perceptions and attitudes of the focalizers and are thus reconstituted as subjects within the text" (81). Misleadingly advertised as educational, these productions fail to teach children any ecological concepts. Like "Two Kinds of Seagulls," a song recorded both on Tom Chapin's 1990 *Mother Earth* and his 2000 *This Pretty Planet*, these songs poorly inform, misinform, or mislead the audience. This song is supposed to teach that reproduction requires both a male and a female member of any species, but Chapin tries so hard to entertain— particularly through forced rhymes—that the song loses most of its educational value. Following are the chorus and a few representative verses of "Two Kinds of Seagulls":

Chorus:
Most creatures come in pairs; that's the way they mingle.
One kind only would be lonely; it takes two to tingle . . .
First verse:
There's two kinds of llamas, papas and mamas.
They wear different pajamas, and that's why there's llamas.

Last verse:
There's two kinds of people, he-ples and she-ples,
He-ples like she-ples, and she-ples like he-ples
And that's why there's me-ples and you-ples and peoples.

This anthropomorphic treatment of animals compromises the educational information, a common pitfall for musicians, like Chapin, who approach this genre from an entertainment rather than a scientific background. A poor attempt at sex education, "Two Kinds of Seagulls" invites children to identify with the narrative voice and enjoy his rhymes, but it fails to teach them about the mating habits of seagulls, lizards, llamas, or people. Furthermore, it depicts heterosexuality as the only "normal" option with statements like "One kind only would be lonely"—a message that could have an even more deleterious effect on child listeners than the failed scientific message.[2]

The same problem surfaces in Steve Charney's audiotape included in his dinosaur activity kit. Stella Stegosaurus, an anthropomorphic dinosaur whose falsetto voice I find annoying, speaks directly to the listeners and spends her time speeding around in sports cars. The Rock 'n' Learn series, which I discuss later, provides a much better example of educational music about dinosaurs.

Though written to a catchy tune and as wildly popular with Raffi fans as the rest of his music, Raffi's "Baby Beluga" also entertains more than it teaches. The title song of a 1977 album, "Baby Beluga" tells about a young beluga whale's life in the sea. Raffi's choice of the beluga for the subject of this song rather than the killer whale or another species more recognizable to Americans gives important name recognition to this endangered species. That, however, is the extent of the song's educational value. The song's last verse, which tells about the end of the young whale's day, says:

When it's dark and you're home and fed
Curl up snug in your waterbed.
The moon is singing and the stars are out,
Good night, little whale, good night.

Child listeners can learn from this song that whales use a spout to breathe and that their mothers take care of them when they're young, but Raffi's depiction of this beluga as a semianthropomorphic, cuddly creature makes it more a text for delight than for instruction.[3]

In these songs, Chapin, Charney, and Raffi give priority to entertainment over education. Some ecomusic, however, sits on the opposite
end of the spectrum: didacticism so thoroughly dominates the song that
the music becomes merely a vehicle for ecological propaganda. These
types of songs appeal to what Paulo Freire calls "the banking model of
education," in which "knowledge is a gift bestowed by those who consider themselves knowledgeable upon those whom they consider to
know nothing. Projecting an absolute ignorance onto others, a characteristic of the ideology of oppression, negates education and knowledge
as processes of inquiry" (58).

Bill Oliver's 1986 recording for the National Audubon Society,
Audubon Adventures, features, among other catchy tunes, a short piece
called, "Please Don't Leave the Water Running When You Wash the
Dog," which effectively illustrates the banking model of education:

> Please don't leave the water running when you wash the dog,
> Or when you do the dishes or you're finished with the lawn,
> Install a smaller showerhead and fix a leaky spout,
> If we don't waste the water, the water won't run out.

While Oliver sets these lyrics to a tuneful ditty, the imperative mood
indicates how it addresses its audience: "*Do* these things, and life will be
better." Although Oliver does offer children tips for conserving water
that they can do themselves, some others of his songs, such as "Habitat,
Habitat" (set to the tune of "Lollipop, Lollipop") strike a better balance
between entertainment and didacticism than "Please Don't Leave the
Water Running."

Over the past several decades, the music of the Banana Slug String
Band has evolved from being overtly didactic and musically weak to
being educationally challenging and musically contagious. "Save Mother
Nature," one of the songs on their earliest tape, *Songs for the Earth*
(1985), buys into Freire's banking model:

> Dump chemicals into the sea and make more excuses for industry
> Fish start dying, so will we,
> So we'd better start taking better care of the sea
> Save Mother Nature, save Mother Nature.

Other verses warn against paving the ground, treating people "like dirt,"
waging war, and allowing starvation. This song is problematic not just

because it issues directive after directive to its audience but also because children could easily conclude that these imperatives are not really intended for them since they can do so little to change large-scale problems such as starvation and war. This song creates an implied listener who is much bigger and much more powerful than the real children listening. These directives might therefore make an already disempowered group of people even more aware of their powerlessness as children. Misaddressing the intended audience and doing so from a banking model approach run counter to the ways that effective eco-edu-tainment should function.

Just as the song "We Are the World" resulted from the collaboration of famous musicians to relieve the famine in Ethiopia in the early 1990s *(USA for Africa)*, a few ecomusical anthologies have been created in the name of similar causes. *Peace Is the World Smiling* (originally released in 1989), featuring Peter Alsop, Taj Mahal, Holly Near, and Sweet Honey in the Rock, among others, promotes world peace, and $1.30 from the sale of each CD goes to fund peace-oriented organizations. *Put On Your Green Shoes* (1993), featuring songs by LeVar Burton, Indigo Girls, Willie Nelson, Kenny Loggins, Next Issue with rappers Steffon and Blind Kolor, encourages children to develop environmental lifestyles. All royalties for this album are equally divided between Save the Children, Earth Island Institute, and Songwriters and Artists for the Earth.[4]

A common problem with these types of musical productions, however—as is often true of children's picture books by celebrities who are not writers—is that the didacticism is often unnecessarily heavy-handed. Most of the contributors generally write music for adults, not children; perhaps they feel obligated to preach to young listeners. In other words, these entertainers are often guilty of underestimating the intelligence of children. For example, Rory's "Plant More than You Harvest" from the *Put On Your Green Shoes* recording ostensibly addresses children but really talks over their heads at logging firms and city municipalities:

> Clear the meadows and the highways, but plant tall trees
>   between
> Let the forest hold the hillsides, cover the earth with green . . .
> Take water to the desert, where the clouds dare not go,
> Plant flowers in the cities and make room for them to grow.

Except for planting flowers, most children can't do much about these directives; the speaker in this song isn't really talking to children. And on the *Peace Is the World Smiling* recording, Francine Lancaster sings "We Love Our Home":

> Can you hear the children sing?
> See the light our young ones bring?
> They're the joy we hold so dear;
> Through their songs the way is clear,
> The time for peace on earth is here,
> The time for all to say, "We love our home . . ."
> Can you hear the children's song
> Or have we lived with war too long?
> Love is where the answer lies,
> All life is equal in their eyes.
> We are the ocean, earth and sky,
> We are the children, and we love our home.

Lancaster addresses children in the third person until the last two lines, which suggests that she is singing more to adults *about* children than to children themselves.

Some ecomusic, however, manages to strike a balance between the two extremes of sheer entertainment and didacticism, and this type of music, fortunately, is becoming much more abundant in the market as nature education becomes more commonplace.[5] The songs that I have found most contagious in environmental education programs for children combine innovative, informative lyrics with excellent music to position children as important parts of the web of life who can make a difference, rather than as objects who merely exist in a larger ecosystem. Among its environmental selections such as "I Love Trash" and "Stand by Your Can," the Children's Television Workshop's recording *We Are All Earthlings* (1993) includes a song celebrating multiculturalism called "One Small Voice." Though more about peace and cooperation than ecology, this song encourages listeners to embrace and cooperate with those who are different from themselves. The centrality of children's voices in the song—it features children as both soloists and parts of a choir—positions young people as subjects within this musical discourse. A choir of children begins the song:

> Every song the world sings, each was once unknown,
> Somebody felt a song inside and wasn't afraid to sing alone,

If you feel the music, and you sing it clear and true,
Then the world can sing with you.

The song's chorus begins with the voice of one child; the second line adds another child's voice; the third, a third voice; and the entire choir joins in on the last line:

Chorus:
Oh, one small voice can teach the world a song,
Start with one small voice, till another joins along,
And you'll feel the music, growing full and sure and strong.
One small voice can teach the world a song.

The fact that children themselves (along with a few Muppets) articulate these words of hope and inspiration conveys the message that they are affecting change. Furthermore, the metaphorical implications of the song's message suggest that even if a child who is small and alone speaks a message worthy of attention, others will listen and follow.

While *We Are All Earthlings* seeks to empower listeners by convincing them that they can make a difference, the Rock 'n' Learn series empowers children by teaching them complex scientific information that most students don't learn until college, or at least high school. This series combines contemporary rock music and impressively detailed information about different scientific disciplines. For instance, *Dinosaur Rap* (1996), the cover of which claims, "Cool songs teach about prehistoric times for ages 7 and up," begins with "What Is a Dinosaur," and "Fossils" then takes listeners through the Mesozoic, Triassic, Jurassic, and Cretaceous eras, teaching about carnivorous and herbivorous animals of each geologic time period. Listeners learn about everything from the Pangaea to the small brain of the sauropods to theories about what destroyed the dinosaurs. From the *Spiders and Insects* (1999) recording, listeners learn the parts of a spider, its life cycle, and its hunting techniques, among other facts.[6]

Chris McKhool, Canadian children's musician and traveling environmental educator, has also produced some ecological music that uses fun tunes to teach difficult biological concepts. For instance, McKhool's song "Biodiversity" on his *Earth, Seas, and Air* (1996) recording discusses the need to maintain biodiversity since many of the medicines we take and much of the food we eat daily come from plants. Although I don't find the musical style of either the Rock 'n' Learn series or Chris McKhool's recording terribly compelling because the songs all sound so much alike stylistically, I feel that both succeed in raising the level of complexity in this genre of children's music.

The Banana Slug String Band album *Adventures on the Air Cycle* (1989) is both musically compelling and scientifically sound. This recording features a single continuous narrative detailing a story of the Nature Man, who takes two children for a ride in his flying machine—called the Air Cycle—that runs on fresh air. The following dialogue occurs when the Air Cycle crashes near the home of an insect named Buzz after the children, the Professor, and Nature Man have met some lizards who sing to them about the "cold blood and scaly skin" of reptiles.

Spoken introduction to "No Bones Within":

Girl: That was fun!

The Professor: Did you see any of those Banana Slugs?

Girl: Yeah, I saw four of them, and they were singing!

[The Air Cycle begins to make strange noises, as if running out of fuel.]

Boy: What's happening?

Girl: We're going *down*!

The Nature Man: You're not breathing! Breathe, breathe . . . too late! *[sound of crashing]*

The Professor: It looks like we've crash-landed in a farmer's field.

Buzz, the Insect [in a high-pitched, nasal voice]: Yeah, I wish you'd watch where you're going. You almost hit us, you know.

The Professor: I know these things. Whatever you do, don't call them bugs. They get *very* angry.

Boy: What *is* this? First talking lizards and now talking bugs?

Girl: Insects.

Boy: Oh, right.

Buzz: You bet that's right! We insects deserve a little respect. You humans think we're all bad, but your lives would sure be different without us.

Girl: But you look so strange to us!

Buzz: But that's no reason to want to harm us and treat us like second-class citizens, even *if* our skeletons are on the outside

of our bodies. You only have two legs, but we have six legs and
three body parts.

Boy: I know: head, thorax, abdomen.

Buzz: That's pretty good!

Boy: Yeah, and talking's pretty good for a bug—uh, insect.

Buzz: Let me and my friends here tell you about us. Oh, and you
can stop calling me a bug. My name is Buzz. *[Music begins.]*

Chorus [sung by a nasal-sounding choir of insects]:

Head, thorax, abdomen, we're inside out, no bones within

Head, thorax, abdomen, I'm talkin' about my six-legged friends.

Verse 1:

We go through metamorphic change,

We turn from weird to *really* strange,

Wings to fly, antennae too,

Mouth parts to suck and chew.

Both the spoken and musical parts of "No Bones Within" illustrate several key strategies of contagious eco-edu-tainment. First, the adults in the narrative are not the keepers of knowledge. The children who travel with Nature Man and the Professor already know some things about insects before they meet Buzz, and that knowledge helps them to gain credibility with Buzz, who is accustomed to being misunderstood and maligned by humans. Their encounter with Buzz, then, serves less to educate them than to help change their negative attitudes toward an aspect of the natural world that they already understand intellectually but for which they have never developed empathy or appreciation. Second, "No Bones Within" uses humor and an unusual perspective to coax child listeners into a subject position that they might never have considered before. In this zany world that the Banana Slug String Band creates, insects can not only talk, but they can also get their feelings hurt when others call them derogatory names. Buzz's intelligence and sensitivity challenge the egocentrism of the two traveling children and make them think—from an insect's perspective—about how insects live. This song makes excellent use of anthropomorphism without compromising the scientific facts. Third, the attention to musical excellence in this song makes it memorable enough for children to learn with minimal effort. Before they realize it, singers will have retained that all insects have an exoskeleton, a head, thorax, and abdomen, antennae and wings; that insects undergo metamorphosis; that they help organic matter to decompose; and that, in spite of their nasty reputation, they actually do humans much more good than harm. Hence, children could enjoy this piece as nothing more than a fun song but come away remembering all sorts of important scientific information about insects.

In one of the Banana Slug String Band's most recent recordings, they further build on the technique they use in "No Bones Within." On *Penguin Parade* (1996), "the Slugs" sing an a cappella song called "Croak-a-Ribbit," which goes even further than "No Bones Within" to offer the child a subject position that requires identification with an animal that most humans dislike and misunderstand. Although no written version could possibly do justice to this song, the lyrics of the first verse and chorus are as follows:

> Oh, I'm glad I am a frog, (yes I am a frog),
> Just a-sittin' on a log (sittin' on a log—croak-a-ribbit ribbit),
> The most delightful bugs they fly around me (tasty bugs for me),
> I put out my sticky tongue (stickin' out my tongue),
> And there I catch me one (and I catch me one—croak-a-ribbit ribbit),
> A froggy's life is the best life there can be (best life there can be).
> I used to be a pollywog (*spoken:* I actually had a tail!)
> Now I'm a fat green frog (fat green frog),
> Well, everywhere I wear my froggy grin
> (*spoken:* I've gotta smile with my lips closed!)
> The salamander wears a smile
> (*spoken:* 'cause he ain't got no teeth either!)
> The toad he croaks in style (croaks in style)
> (*spoken:* Stay way from his bad bug breath, though),
> We're a bunch of happy, hoppin', flappy, floppin' mm amphibians.
> *Chorus:*
> Well, croak, croak-a-ribbit ribbit
> Croak, croak-a-ribbit ribbit
> Croak, croak-a-ribbit ribbit, uh-huh.

This first-person narrative of a frog puts frog life "in your face." Like the encounter with Buzz, the insect, this direct address to child listeners brings them eye-to-eye with frogs and gives them an informative but playful and humorous look at amphibian life. Listeners can learn as much about amphibians from these talking frogs as they can from Buzz about insects in "No Bones Within." It's rare that we get to hear a frog talk about his eating habits while badmouthing other amphibians for their bug breath and toothlessness, but the humor and irreverence in this song suggest that learning can and should be fun.[7] Conforming to John Newbery's motto of "instruction with delight," "Croak-a-Ribbit" humorously addresses children as intelligent, educable agents of change.

And although the message is often implicit rather than explicit in songs like "Croak-a-Ribbit," texts that embrace biocentrism invite the child to identify not with an adult narrative voice but with the animals, fungi, rocks, or dirt—as in an earlier Banana Slug String Band song, "Dirt Made My Lunch"—on which the song's content focuses. Helping the child to see the world from the perspective of an insect, a snake, or a tree pushes against an anthropocentric view and encourages children to envision how the way they live might affect the existence of both living and nonliving things. Rather than telling the child, "You should live in earth-friendly ways, and this is how you should do it," these songs equip child listeners with knowledge, nudge them toward empathy, and trust *them* to make the ecological connections between their own niche in the world and the habitats of other living and nonliving things. My experiences of using this sort of music with children has convinced me of its power to help young people see themselves as helpful agents of change for the benefit of the environment.

A choir of children best articulates this idea of child empowerment in a song called "Turn the World Around" on the *Peace Is the World Smiling* recording. The message that the children convey in this song is, after all, one of the most important ideas that children can internalize as a result of listening to and singing effective ecomusic:

> We can make a difference, kids can make a difference.
> Save the place we live in, turn the world around . . .
> Listen to the children, voices of the children.
> Spirit of the children, turn the world around.

NOTES

1. Using both the stewardship and biocentric models, Michael Caduto and Joseph Bruchac have written a series of Native American books that contain stories and related

activities teaching environmental perspectives through Native American culture and beliefs. The titles of these books are *Keepers of the Earth* (1988), *Keepers of the Animals* (1992), *Keepers of Life* (1994) and *Keepers of the Night* (1994).

2.   Tom Chapin and John Forster's *Sing a Whale Song* (1993), illustrated by Jerry Smath, and the accompanying musical single of the same name, recorded by Chapin, provide another example of this dynamic. This book and song make an important environmental statement about whale preservation, but the featured whale is a talking humpback whale who uses his magical abilities to turn the boy protagonist, Timothy, into a whale for a day. As a whale (still wearing his red baseball cap), Timothy accompanies the real whale to clean, beautiful places in the ocean, then to a dark, polluted place beneath a garbage scow. The marine animals all gather in a cave and teach Timothy their "whale song" so that he can sing it to the humans and thereby save the whales. When the whale transforms Timothy back into a boy, he takes up his guitar and his mission of singing the whales' song to everyone he meets, exemplifying the stewardship model. Despite the admirable message, the anthropomorphic treatment of the animals in this story may cause readers to doubt the scientific validity of other details within both the book and the song.

3.   Although only a few of the songs on *Baby Beluga* balance instruction and delight, many of the songs on Raffi's *Evergreen, Everblue* (1990)—such as "Mama's Kitchen" (which sings of solving world hunger), "Clean Rain" (clean versus acid rain), and "What's the Matter with Us?" (a reggae song about ecological complacency)—use singable, memorable tunes to convey strong environmental messages.

4.   Though the focus of these musical anthologies differs slightly from those in the current discussion, Jim Papoulis's *Sounds of a Better World* 2-CD series—*Small Voices Calling* (2000) and *Can You Hear? Small Voices Calling* (2002)—whose world tour is sponsored by Hyatt International, donates all composer royalties to the Foundation for Small Voices, which gives to children's charities internationally. "Small Voices Calling," with contributors such as Odetta, the Boys' Choir of Harlem, the Norwegian Children's Choir, and Martha Wash, launched its world tour on January 11, 2000, at Carnegie Hall.

5.   On television, the Discovery Channel and Animal Planet provide further evidence of the increasing availability of nature education to the American public.

6.   The other titles in this series are *Oceans* (1998) and *The Solar System* (1997); other series topics include early childhood, phonics and reading, math, social studies, Spanish, and French.

7.   And notably, these insults are scientifically accurate: salamanders do eat "bugs," and toads lack teeth. This is a much more useful way to create humor than the earlier example of Steve Charney's Stella Stegosaurus's excessively fast driving.

Works Cited

Banana Slug String Band. *Adventures on the Air Cycle.* Audiocassette. Music for Little People, 1989.

———. "Dirt Made My Lunch." In *Dirt Made My Lunch.* Audiocassette. Music for Little People, 1988.

————. *Penguin Parade.* Audiocassette. Music for Little People, 1996.

————. *Songs for the Earth.* Audiocassette. Exploring New Horizons, 1985.

Caduto, Michael J., and Joseph Bruchac. *Keepers of Life: Discovering Plants through Native American Stories and Earth Activities for Children.* Golden, Colo.: Fulcrum Incorporated, 1994.

————. *Keepers of the Animals: Nature American Stories and Wildlife Activities for Children.* Golden, Colo.: Fulcrum Incorporated, 1992.

————. *Keepers of the Earth: Native American Stories and Environmental Activities for Children.* Golden, Colo.: Fulcrum Incorporated, 1988.

————. *Keepers of the Night.* Golden, Colo.: Fulcrum Incorporated, 1994.

Chapin, Tom. *Mother Earth.* Audiocassette. Sundance, 1990.

————. *This Pretty Planet.* Audiocassette. Sony Music Entertainment, 2000.

Chapin, Tom, and John Forster. *Sing a Whale Song.* Audiocassette. Limousine Music & Last Music, 1993.

————. *Sing a Whale Song.* New York: Random House, 1993.

Charney, Steve. *Stella Stegosaurus: Dinosaur Activity Cassette.* Audiocassette. Metacom, 1993.

Children's Television Workshop, Jim Henson's Sesame Street Muppet Characters. *We Are All Earthlings.* Audiocassette. Western, 1993.

Cho, Shinta. *The Gas We Pass.* Trans. Amanda Mayer Stinchecum. La Jolla, Calif.: Kane/Miller, 1994.

Frankel, Alona. *Once upon a Potty.* New York: HarperCollins, 1979.

Freire, Paulo. *Pedagogy of the Oppressed.* New York: Continuum, 1990.

Gomi, Taro. *Everyone Poops.* Trans. Amanda Mayer Stinchecum. La Jolla, Calif.: Kane/Miller, 1993.

Greenaway, Betty. *Children's Literature Association Quarterly* 19 (winter 1994–95). Special issue: "Ecology and the Child."

Holzwarth, Werner, and Wolf Erlbruch. *The Story of Little Mole Who Went in Search of Whodunit.* New York: Stewart, Tabori, & Chang, 1993.

How Can One Sell the Air? A Manifesto of an Indian Chief. Summertown, Tenn.: Book Publishing Company, 1988.

Martin, Michelle. "The Scat Song." *Big Blue Marble.* Audiocassette. SCICON, 1989.

McKhool, Chris. *Earth, Seas, and Air: Eco-Songs for Kids.* Audiocassette. Ken Whiteley, 1996.

Oliver, Bill. *Audubon Adventures.* Audiocassette. National Audubon Society, 1986.

Ostrow, Leib. *Peace Is the World Smiling: A Peace Anthology for Families.* Audiocassette. Music for Little People, 1993.

Papoulis, Jim. *Sounds of a Better World: Small Voices Calling.* Audiocassette. Vital Records, 2000.

————. *Can You Hear? Small Voices Calling.* Audiocassette. Vital Records, 2002.

Raffi. *Baby Beluga.* Audiocassette. Uni/Rounder, 1977.

————. *Evergreen, Everblue.* Audiocassette. MCA, 1990.

Rock 'n' Learn. *Dinosaur Rap.* Audiocassette. Rock 'n' Learn, 1996.

————. *Oceans.* Audiocassette. Rock 'n' Learn, 1998.

————. *The Solar System.* Rock 'n' Learn, 1997.

————. *Spiders and Insects.* Audiocassette. Rock 'n' Learn, 1999.

Sigler, Carolyn. "Wonderland to Wasteland: Toward Historicizing Environmental Activism in Children's Literature." *Children's Literature Association Quarterly* 19.4 (1994–95): 148–53.

Songwriters and Artists for the Earth. *Put On Your Green Shoes: An All-Star Album Dedicated to Healing the Planet.* Audiocassette. Sony Kids' Music, 1993.

Stephens, John. *Language and Ideology in Children's Fiction.* London: Longman, 1992.

USA for Africa: We Are the World. Audiocassette. Polygram Records, 1990.

Von Konigslow, Andrea Wayne. *Toilet Tales.* New York: Firefly, 1985.

14

"It's Not Easy Being Green"

Jim Henson, the Muppets, and Ecological Literacy

Sidney I. Dobrin

It's not that easy being green;
Having to spend each day the color of the leaves.
When I think it could be nicer being red, or yellow or gold or something
much more colorful like that.

It's not easy being green.
It seems you blend in with so many other ordinary things.
And people tend to pass you over 'cause you're not standing out
like flashy sparkles in the water or stars in the sky.

But green's the color of Spring.
And green can be cool and friendly-like.
And green can be big like an ocean, or important like a mountain,
or tall like a tree.

When green is all there is to be
It could make you wonder why, but why wonder why?
Wonder, I am green and it'll do fine, it's beautiful!
And I think it's what I want to be.
    KERMIT THE FROG

When I was young, my ambition was to be one of the people who made a
difference in this world. My hope still is to leave the world a little bit better for my having been here.
    JIM HENSON

The subtitle of this collection suggests that it examines connections
between children's culture and ecocriticism. Admittedly, each of these

terms is problematic, as noted in the book's introduction. Likewise, the selections in this collection also question any sort of definitive definitions of ecocriticism as either a methodology or an epistemology. In many ways, ecocriticism falls short as a methodology, as a means of examining texts that address environmental and ecological issues. Ecocriticism's approach has traditionally been one of interpretation, one of examination of texts *through* an ecocritical lens. That is to say, ecocriticism sees texts as artifacts that can be examined ecocritically for the sake of better understanding a relationship between a text and a physical environment, and ecocriticism is thus a tool, a critical inquiry that can be applied to a text in order to see the relationships of that text in a particular way. In many ways, this approach to literary interpretation and analysis is strictly an academic maneuver.

Interestingly, Glotfelty (rightly) accuses the field of English studies of having become overly academic, of being "scholarly to the point of being unaware of the outside world" (introduction, xvi). Likewise, in an interview, Glotfelty expresses concern that ecocriticism itself is becoming institutionalized, academic. Hence, I am not drawn to ecocriticism as a methodology for examining literary texts—rather, I am interested in how texts themselves are "ecocritical," are used to foster examinations not only between text themselves but among readers, writers, texts, and environments and organisms. That is, I have become less interested in ecocriticism's agenda of textual examination than in issues of ecological literacy.

Ecological literacy refers to a conscious awareness and understanding of the relationships among people, other organisms, and the environments in which they live. Texts themselves work toward ecological literacy, whether specifically or tacitly. That is, texts, because they are inherently enmeshed with the environments from which they grow, produce particular ecological literacies as readers and writers encounter those texts. The term *ecological literacy* is most frequently associated with the work of David Orr and his book *Ecological Literacy: Education and the Transition to a Postmodern World*, in which he contends that "all education is environmental education" (90), but also that most education now presents environment and nature as resources for people, as products for consumers, as things we as humans act upon rather than within. All texts, all systems of knowledge making, then, for Orr are also structures for producing environmental knowledge. All texts, either directly or indirectly, thus teach us something about places, about organisms, about relationships. For Orr, what texts too often teach about environment is a lesson of resource use. Orr suggests that if we talk about and teach ecology in schools, colleges, and universities in all subject areas, we might be able to change the ways we think about environment, nature, and place by overturning this image of resource with a new way of thinking about our world. Orr posits that ecological literacy requires three things. First is "a broad understanding of how people and societies relate to each other and to natural systems" (3). He adds that we should also consider how those same people and societies might live differently to better sustain those systems. Second, individuals must understand the importance of the environmental crisis that we face and the speed with which it is accelerating. Third, Orr contends that in order for individuals to become ecologically literate, they must develop their own ecological consciousness and contribute to that development in others.

Ecological literacy, then, becomes a more active sort of critical tool. Rather than offering an ecocritical vision of relationships between texts and environments, ecological literacy provides a mechanism for understanding that when texts are produced, read, and analyzed, whether academically or otherwise, they educate about environment, some consciously, others less explicitly. This point becomes especially important in consideration of children's texts. Texts with implicit agendas of ecological literacy development can be examined not simply for how they teach about environment, for how they project images of environment, but for how they themselves become part of a larger ecological literacy. In many ways, Jim Henson and the Muppets have taken on an explicit agenda of ecological literacy promotion, and by examining Henson's rather extensive body of work, we can begin to see how Orr's understanding of ecological literacy shows how all education, all texts, affect ecological literacy. In the case of Henson and the Muppets, ecological literacy, as I will argue, was a primary agenda in textual production.

Only limited critical attention has been paid to Henson projects, and most of that has been directed toward *Sesame Street* from the standpoint of education research, generally asking: does this television show promote learning? I note, for instance, the informative book *"Sesame Street" Revisited* (Cook et al.), to which I will turn in a moment. Hence, most of what I report here is gleaned from my own observations and material supplied by the ever generous Jim Henson Company.

My title, of course, is a reference to the wonderful Kermit the Frog song that encourages children to be happy with who they are. The song, written by Joe Raposo, is considered Kermit's theme song, though it was also sung on *Sesame Street* by Lena Horne and Ray Charles. The song makes some interesting connections between individual identity and nature, equating Kermit's color with tones in nature. Yes, he's a talking frog; Henson's anthropomorphism is problematic in some ways, if also endearing. Many of Henson's projects are critically self-reflexive of this anthropomorphism and depict not only anthropomorphized animals but their "real" counterparts as well. Henson's Muppet animals are by no means "natural." The title of the song has also become a bit of a motto for environmental movements and the struggles they face. In fact, a full-page advertisement for Rechargeable Battery Recycle Centers that appeared in the November 18, 2002, issue of *Time* magazine depicts a small tree frog atop a cellular phone battery with the caption, "It's easy to be green," eliciting not only the image of Kermit but parodying the song title in order to suggest that environmentally sound actions such as recycling have become easier.

I look here specifically at five of Jim Henson's many productions: *Sesame Street, Fraggle Rock, The Dark Crystal,* and *Jim Henson's Animal Show with Stinky and Jake,* and "The Song of the Cloud Forest" from *The Jim Henson Hour.* Of course, I am greatly limiting myself (attention needs to be given to *The Muppet Movie, Emmet Otter's Jug Band Christmas,* and *The Muppet Show,* in particular), yet my goal is to open some doors to thinking about the powerful role Jim Henson and the Jim Henson Company have played in contemporary children's texts. Of course, each of these areas needs to be examined in much more detail (perhaps a book of Muppet criticism? Muppeticism?); for now, I introduce the idea that the Muppets are a deeply ecologically conscious group and that Henson projects deliberately promote ecological thinking and ecological literacy.

A Brief Henson History

In the summer of 1954, the year that he graduated high school, Jim Henson began what was to be a remarkable career as a puppeteer. He introduced his first puppets—Pierre the French rat and Longhorn and Shorthorn the cowboys—to the world on *The Junior Good Morning Show* in Washington, D.C. *The Junior Good Morning Show* was short-lived, but the following year Henson created *Sam and Friends,* which aired nightly in a five-minute live broadcast format. In 1959 *Sam and Friends* won a local Emmy, but more important, it introduced the world to Kermit the Frog, a puppet originally made from Henson's mother's green coat and the halves of a ping-pong ball. Henson attended the University of Maryland, where he met Jane Nebel; the two later married and together developed the Muppets' unique style through their work making characters for *Sam and Friends,* which aired from 1955 through 1961. The Muppets appeared on a variety of shows during the 1960s, including *The Ed Sullivan Show, The Today Show,* and *The Jimmy Dean Show.* In 1969 Children's Television Workshop contacted Henson about a new children's show they were developing called *Sesame Street.* Henson was reluctant at first to join the project, afraid that he'd be "typecast as an entertainer just for children" (Borgenicht 182). But he joined the project and his Muppets have been the central figures of the show ever since.

Henson made it clear in 1976 that his Muppets were not to be typecast as solely children's entertainment when he brought *The Muppet Show* to prime-time television. The show was, as the Jim Henson Company points out, "a phenomenal success, reaching an estimated 235 million viewers each week in more than 100 countries and winning three Emmys and many other awards during its five-year run" ("Biography"). Following the success of *The Muppet Show,* Henson was able to expand his Muppet repertoire, developing new characters and puppet technologies. Henson put his puppeteering talents to work in a host of projects: *The Muppet Movie* (1979), *The Great Muppet Caper* (1981; Henson's directorial debut), *The Dark Crystal* (1982), *Fraggle Rock* (1983–87; the first children's television show created specifically for cable broadcast, in 1989 it became the first American television series broadcast in the Soviet Union), *The Muppets Take Manhattan* (1984), *Muppet Babies* (1984–88; an animated television show that won four consecutive Emmys), *Labyrinth* (1986), *The Storyteller* (1987; this presentation of contemporary versions of folk tales won an Emmy), *The Jim Henson Hour* (1989; this earned Henson an Emmy for directing), *The Witches* (1990; a film based on Roald Dahl's classic children's story), *Jim Henson Presents Muppet Vision 3D* (1991; considered by many to be the best 3D movie ever produced, it appears only in the custom-made theater located at the Disney/MGM Studios theme park in Orlando), *Dinosaurs* (1991; a television show conceived and designed by Henson), and *Jim Henson's Animal Show with Stinky and Jake* (1994–97). In addition, the Jim Henson Company produced *Muppet Treasure Island* (1996), *Muppets from Space* (1999), and *Jim Henson's Jack and the Bean Stalk: The Real Story* (2001).

Henson devoted a good amount of his career to promoting ecological awareness and appreciation for nature. He maintained an agenda of ecological literacy throughout his work, and in producing numerous texts, Henson was greatly influenced by his awareness of and appreciation for environment and ecological literacy. As Henson once said, "I find that it's very important for me to stop every now and then and get recharged and reinspired. The beauty of nature has always been one of the great inspirations in my life. I love to lie in an open field" (quoted in Borgenicht 182). It is also evident that Henson drew much of his inspiration from what he observed in the natural world. Aside from the obvious use of animal characters, Henson was intrigued by the fluidity and movement of nature: "Working as I do with the movement of puppet creatures, I am always struck by the feebleness of our efforts to achieve naturalistic movement. Just looking at the incredible movement of a lizard or a bird, or even the smallest insect, can be a very humbling experience."

Henson's work has had a remarkable effect on the ways in which children and adults encounter nature. Henson died on May 16, 1990, and though his legacy lives on through the work of the Jim Henson Company, it was his innovation that developed into some of the most important ecoeducational texts available to children. In addition to the Muppet texts, with which many of us are familiar, Henson and the Jim Henson Company participated in numerous projects specifically for promotion of ecological awareness, including public service announcements (PSAs) for the National Park Service, appearances on television specials in support of the "Keep America Beautiful" campaign, PSAs for the National Wildlife Federation, PSAs for the U.S. Fish and Wildlife Service, and PSAs for Earth Day, to name just some. I have included at the end of this article an appendix chronicling many of Henson and the Muppets' environmentally based projects from 1969 to 2000.

Sesame Street

Though not Henson's first, *Sesame Street* was the project that brought him recognition and fame, providing him the opportunity to teach millions of young viewers about the natural environment. On February 19, 1968, Joan G. Cooney, then president of Children's Television Workshop (CTW), proposed to Carnegie Corporation a concept for a television program that combined entertainment and education, directed primarily at preschool children. Cooney's proposal noted the need for such programs for children from a diverse range of educational, socioeconomic, racial, and environmental (urban and rural) backgrounds. In this initial proposal, Cooney stressed that such an educational show must "teach children *how* to think, not *what* to think" (12). In the early days of *Sesame Street*'s development, CTW designed four specific goals for the television show:

1. *Symbolic Representation* dealt with knowledge of letters, nubmers, and geometric forms.
2. *Cognitive Processes* was concerned with perceptual discrimination, relational concepts, classification, ordering, and reasoning.
3. *The Child and the Physical World around Him* dealt with knowledge of the natural and man-made environments.
4. *The Social Environment* was related to social interaction. (Cook et al. 47)

I want to concentrate specifically on objective number 3, "The Child and the Physical World around Him." This goal was also reported by Borgenicht to be "Physical Environment: Discovering cycles that occur in nature and identifying living things; also determining how man-made objects relate to the natural world" (14).

First aired on November 10, 1969, *Sesame Street* has been running for more than thirty years. The few other television programs that have lasted this long include: *Meet the Press* (1947), *The Today Show* (1952), *Guiding Light* (1952), *The Tonight Show* (1954), *As the World Turns* (1956), *ABC's Wide World of Sports* (1961), *General Hospital* (1963), *Days of Our Lives* (1968), *60 Minutes* (1968), and *Mr. Rogers' Neighborhood* (1968) (Borgenicht 16). David Borgenicht, in *Sesame Street Unpaved,* also identifies these remarkable facts about the show:

> *Sesame Street* has hosted more than 250 celebrity guests.
>
> *Sesame Street* is shown several times daily on more than 300 PBS stations throughout the United States.
>
> Seventy-seven percent of American school children watch *Sesame Street* at least once a week. More than eleven million people (children and adults) watch the show in an average week.
>
> *Sesame Street* has won more than 100 awards: seventy-one Emmys (more than any show in history!); eight Grammys; two George Foster Peabody Awards; four Parents' Choice Awards; the Prix Jeunesse International; A Clio Award; and an Action for Children's Television Special Achievement Award, just to name a few.
>
> The show has already reared two generations of children, and it shows no sign of flagging. There are now more than seventy million *Sesame Street* alumni. (17)

Borgenicht also notes that *Sesame Street* has local and international production in 19 countries and is aired in more than 140 countries. *Sesame Street,* via the Children's Television Workshop, has published more than six hundred *Sesame Street* books. It also publishes six different magazines that draw more than twelve million readers (both children and adults) each month (17). These figures are amazing in many ways; particularly striking in the present case is that these numbers have to be considered in light of the fact that one of the four primary agendas of *Sesame Street* is teaching children about interaction with the natural and man-made worlds. Through *Sesame Street*, Henson[1] and the Muppets reach a staggering number of viewers, primarily children, and with one of the four goals of the show environmental awareness, it becomes easy to identify a far-reaching ecological literacy impact. It also becomes easy (and necessary) to identify Henson's globalization in reaching such a large audiences worldwide. Though there need to be questions raised regarding Henson's participation in globalization, it must be noted that much of Henson's world reach promotes education, literacy, ecology, and the like—agendas, I recognize, that are not free of political, ideological power.

How Henson promotes environmental education and ecological literacy through the skits produced for the show. Often place-based or focused on short, specific lessons, the skits that Henson's Muppets perform frequently teach about interaction not just with "natural" environments but with urban environments as well. Because many of the Muppets are animals (Kermit the Frog, Big Bird, Robin), and many are people (Bert, Ernie, the Count), and some are even monsters (Grover, Cookie Monster, Elmo, Oscar the Grouch), the Muppets often deal specifically with the interactions between the human and the nonhuman. Granted, most of the Muppets, be they animal, person, or monster, exhibit human-specific characteristics. That is, Henson relies on anthropomorphization to make many ecological points. There is some question about the value of anthropomorphizing animals in children's education, but the Muppets make good use of anthropomorphization in order to specify that real animals, unlike Muppet animals, do not act and function like their Muppet counterparts. Take, for instance, one of my all-time favorite Kermit the Frog skits, in which Kermit discusses frogs with costar Bob McGrath:

Kermit: Hi-ho, Kermit the Frog here. Today we are going to talk about frogs *(Bob enters with something cupped in his hands. Something large and green and slimy.)* Good heavens! What is that?

Bob: It's an American bullfrog, Kermit.

Kermit: (*To camera*) I'm more handsome than I realized. *(Bob goes on to describe the frog to Kermit—he's green, he has strong legs.)*

Kermit: He's got a face that would stop a clock.

Bob: Why don't you tell everyone where frogs live, Kermit?

Kermit: (with authority) Frogs live in apartment houses with furniture and television sets and we sometimes—

Bob: Uh, Kermit, most frogs don't live in apartments in the city. They live in riverbanks, ponds, even in swamps and mud holes.

Kermit: Mud holes! Why, that's terrible! If you lived in a mud hole, your floor would get dirty!

Bob: Kermit, what do frogs like to eat?

Kermit: Oh, that's easy. Fried chicken and pizza and pan-cakes and French fries.

(Bob explains that most other frogs eat different things, like flies, worms, and spiders.)

Kermit: (sickened) If you excuse me, Bob, I think I have to lie down. I'm feeling a little nauseous. *(The bullfrog starts to croak.)* Wait a second, what's that? *(Kermit starts listening to the frog.)* What's that? Oh, that's funny. *(Laughs.)*

Bob: Wait—you mean to tell me, Kermit, that you understand what he's saying?

Kermit: Of course I do. I'm a frog.

    (Borgenicht 95)

Funny stuff. But also educational, ecologically speaking. Here the lessons are evident. Notice the care with which the writers not only identify the differences between Muppet frogs and "real" frogs but manage to maintain Kermit as frog in the final lines of the skit. It's also interesting to note that during the taping of this skit, the frog that Bob was holding urinated all over Henson, who was working the Kermit puppet (Borgenicht 95). I'm not sure if Kermit has ever urinated on screen. Nature, you see, isn't manipulated, controlled by pulling strings and hand gestures. This skit goes to great lengths to teach children that Muppets are Muppets and frogs don't live the lives of Muppets.

    Similarly, in a skit called "Big Bird Meets Little Bird," the Muppets address natural difference and species similarity. I have always been intrigued by this skit: by its roots in Aristotelian thinking, its teaching of theorizing. Quite directly, it asks children to learn to observe, question, and speculate about objects. It also promotes triangulation—Donald Davidson's concept that we come to know the world and each other through conversation, that objects are named and understood only when we come to consensus with others as to what those objects are. Granted, I don't think Henson or the other *Sesame Street* Muppet workers sat down and said, "Let's make a skit about triangulation," but I would be willing to bet they agreed that difference and similarities and observation were important lessons to teach. Of course, this skit could be played out using any number of items of difference, but it was performed between Big Bird and Little Bird and therefore it seems evident that learning about animals is also inherent:

Big Bird: What are you?

Little Bird: I'm a bird, silly.

Big Bird: A bird? You're not a bird. I'm a bird. Birds are big.

Little Bird: We'll, I'm a little bird.

Big Bird: You sure?

Little Bird: Uh-huh.

Big Bird: Umph. I don't think you're a bird at all.

Little Bird: Well, look. Do you have a beak?

Big Bird: Well, of course, I have a beak.

Little Bird: Well, so do I. . . . Do you have wings?

Big Bird: Well, yes, I'm a bird. Birds have wings.

Little Bird: Well, so do I. . . . Do you have feathers?

Big Bird: Sure! I'm covered with them! I'm a bird. Look at you! You've got feathers all over you, too! Why, you are a bird!

Little Bird: Yeah, I told you I was.

Big Bird: Well . . . a little bird.

Little Bird: Yeah, and you're a great big bird.

Big Bird: A big bird and a little bird. Can we be friends?

Little Bird: Yeah, I guess so.

Difference. Similarity. Acceptance. There are lessons here that could be applied to a variety of social circumstances, yet the conversation did not occur between cast members for the sole purpose of addressing racial or gender differences; it occurred between two birds in order to stress that these lessons should be learned about nonhumans as well as humans. Of course, big birds and little birds in nature may not be as accepting of each other's presence as this skit suggests—I've often wanted to see this skit end with Big Bird swooping down on Little Bird and eating him for lunch. Now that would be a lesson in nature and ecology, and one no weirder than other things the Muppets have done. Yet, despite my predatory Muppet fantasies, the message of this skit is one of the overriding messages in *Sesame Street*: that lessons of difference, acceptance, and otherness should be considered in terms of the nonhuman equally with the human.

That is, though I don't believe that Henson or *Sesame Street* sets out with an ecofeminist agenda, they do examine human interaction with nature, environment, and place with a rather ecofeminist approach. Ecofeminist Greta Gaard explains: "Drawing on the insights of ecology, feminism, and socialism, ecofeminism's basic premise is that the ideology which authorizes oppressions such as those based on race, class, gender, sexuality, physical abilities, and species is the same ideology which sanctions the oppression of nature" (1). At its core, ecofeminism seeks to end all oppression and recognizes that any attempt to liberate any oppressed group—particularly women—can only be successful with an equal attempt to liberate nature. In the skit detailed here, Big Bird and Little Bird can be seen discussing differences not just in genetic patterns of bird species—wings, beaks, feathers—but differences in perspectives and how those perspectives give rise to judgments about differences. *Sesame Street*, it seems, is replete with similar messages. There is little question that the initial goal of "The Child and the Physical World around Him"—to address "knowledge of the natural and man-made environments—is maintained throughout much of *Sesame Street*. The mere fact that humans, recognizable animals, and unfamiliar "monsters" (read: unfamiliar organisms) occupy and share the same space on *Sesame Street* is indicative of the ecological message Henson and the Muppets convey: that humans are not the sole occupants of places, and that harmonious, respectful coexistence is necessary.

Though *Sesame Street* is by far Henson's most influential project, it is by no means his only. Many of the ecological messages found in *Sesame Street* carry over into other Henson projects.

Fraggle Rock

In 1981, Henson began developing what was to become the first children's television show designed for broadcast on cable television. Ninety-six episodes of Henson's award-winning *Fraggle Rock* were aired on HBO from 1983 to 1987.[2] The show, which is about a world attached to the human world of which humans are unaware, depicts a specific ecology of Fraggles, Doozers, Gorgs, and even humans, who inhabit "outer space." As Henson explains it, "Fraggle Rock is a world just beyond everyday reality" (*"Fraggle Rock* Synopsis"). *Fraggle Rock,* like many of Henson's projects, makes use of fun story lines, humor, original music, and educational plots to entertain viewers, yes, but also with the intent that "through The Fraggles, young viewers learn a little bit each week about how they can live in harmony with people different from themselves." To accept this statement as literally meaning "people different from themselves" is to slight Henson and his project, for there is little doubt that Henson also intended his young viewers to learn how to live in harmony with all of the world, not only people. That is, there seems to be an agenda of ecological literacy manifest in many of the episodes and the primary characters in the show.

The show focuses on the lives of Fraggles, small creatures that live in an expansive cavern system just beyond the human world. There are five Fraggles around which the show primarily revolves: Gobo (depicted as male), the leader and an explorer; Red (depicted as female), the energetic athlete; Boober (depicted as male), who claims that only two things are certain in the world, "death and laundry"; Mokey (depicted as female), the artist and philosopher of the group; and Wembley (depicted as male), whose name is taken from "an ancient Fragglish verb meaning (roughly) 'to be so unable to make up one's mind that it is ridiculous.' Wembley is indecision personified" (*"Fraggle Rock* Character Biographies"). The Fraggles share their cavern with Doozers, small creatures whose lives are devoted to construction work on elaborate crystalline structures made from refined radish sugar, a favorite food of the Fraggles. Hence, the Doozers provide food for the Fraggles through their construction work, and the Fraggles, by devouring the Doozer buildings, open space for new Doozer constructions, the very thing that sustains Doozer life. Ecological systems and niches are emphasized in this relationship and throughout the show.

In addition to the Fraggles and Doozers, the show features two other primary characters: the Gorgs, fifteen-foot "monsters" who live just beyond the Fraggle caverns, and Marjory, the Trash Heap. Though there are only three of them, the Gorgs have declared themselves rulers of the universe (Ma Gorg is Queen of the Universe, Pa Gorg is King of the Universe, and Junior Gorg is the Crown Prince of the Universe and the only Royal Subject). They grow radishes, the primary food source of the Fraggles. They also hunt Fraggles, though unsuccessfully, as they view Fraggles as pests. The Gorgs, like the Doozers, enter into a consumer/producer relationship with the Fraggles. Though the lessons of niches, food chains, and ecological consumerism are depicted in simple terms, the relationships between these characters are structured specifically to show ecological interdependence. The system is definitively economic and capitalistic. Yet, in looking at relationships between ecological systems and economic systems, we must remember that not only do both words—*economy* and *ecology*—derive from the same root, *oikos* (meaning *house*), but that Ernest Haeckel, who coined the term *ecology* for the study of the relationships between organisms and their environments, was a contemporary of Marx. It is thus familiar and easy to explain ecological systems through metaphors of economics.

Marjory, the Trash Heap, is an interesting character: quite literally the Gorgs' trash heap, she has, over time, come to life. Marjory, composed of Gorg waste and trash, is the Fraggle Oracle, and Fraggles risk their lives venturing into the Gorg property to hear her words. It is interesting that Henson has chosen a trash heap to be an oracle, to be the provider of words of wisdom. As ecologists and environmentalists have long argued, our waste teaches us much about our culture, about our ways of life, about our excess. Marjory is no exception. During the second season of *Fraggle Rock,* in episode 27, "The Trash Heap Doesn't Live Here Anymore," Marjory is transplanted to another location by the Gorgs: waste removal. Unfortunately for the Fraggles, the move disrupts Marjory's wisdom, and the Fraggles find her words to be less meaningful. Likewise, in episode 54, "Blanket of Snow, Blanket of Woe," Marjory is frozen solid when the Fraggles fail to cover her during a hard freeze: care and caution of environmental impact. As a side note, I find it particularly interesting that Henson has named the Trash Heap "Marjory"; three of Florida's primary environmental "oracles" were Marjory Kinnan Rawlings, Marjory Stoneman Douglas, and Marjory Carr. I doubt Henson made this connection, but I find it interesting nonetheless.

The Dark Crystal

Simply put, Henson's *The Dark Crystal* is an ecological masterpiece. From the outset, Jim Henson and artist Brian Froud set out to create an entirely new world with an ecology all its own for this 1982 film. "I remember," recalls Froud, "that in my earliest discussions with Jim Henson, we talked of a pantheistic world in which mountains sang to one another and forests were alive" (Finch 5). Their vision was years in development; they created a new world with new animals, creatures, plants, and an ecology different from earth's. As Christopher Finch explains in *The Making of "The Dark Crystal,"* "On this planet, evolution has taken its own wayward course. Creatures have adapted to a set of demands different from any encountered on earth" (5). Even so, as on earth, on the world of the Dark Crystal, animals eat one another, rely on one another. Plants adapt and move, animals camouflage and hide. That is, niches form, trophic levels exist, ecological relationships are formed and relied upon.

The *Dark Crystal* is the story of five kinds of beings that live in the world of the Dark Crystal. The Urskeks were born of the crystal, long before it darkened. The crystal, from which a shard is shattered during the great conjunction, grew dark with this split and led to the split of the Urskeks. In their attempt to find perfection, the Urskeks tore themselves into two kinds of beings: one, the Mystics, a gentle race that maintained the magic and wisdom of the Urskeks but were limited to using their magic only in their home valley. The Mystics are depicted as simple, in touch with the pulse of their world, living a natural existence. The Mystics, as Finch explains it, "took on the sorrows of the world" (10). The Mystics are environmentally conscious; they find their power and wisdom in the land. For each Mystic that was created when the Urskeks split, a corresponding Skeksis was born. The Skeksis are the epitome of evil, pillaging the world for its resources for their uses, including draining the life force from other beings such as the Gelflings and Pod People in order to prolong their own lives. At its core, the split of the Urskeks into the Mystics and the Skeksis is not simply a split of good and evil but a split couched in terms of environmental harmony and environmental destruction. It is particularly telling that Henson and Froud developed the ecology of the world of the Dark Crystal so that the conflict between its ruling beings is based in the political (and magical) agenda of how the world's resources should be used. Use and depletion of resources, control and abuse of animals are in the world of the Dark Crystal simply bad. Environmental harmony is good. The message is clear.

The two central characters, around whom the plot revolves, are Jen and Kira, two Gelflings who have been hidden from the Skeksis—Jen (male) raised by the Mystics in their valley and Kira (female) raised by the Pod People in their village. Neither knows of the other. They are the last of the Gelflings, who have been made nearly extinct by the Skeksis.

The Skeksis, afraid of a prophecy (there's always a prophecy) that fore-told of a Gelfling healing the split crystal and ending the reign of the Skeksis, slaughtered the Gelflings, using their life essences to prolong their own lives. Jen and Kira, raised to respect nature (Kira, in fact, can speak with animals) are the Gelfling equivalent of Adam and Eve: the future of Gelfling populations and cast from their Edenic gardens to ful-fill the prophecy.

In the fantasy world of the Dark Crystal, Aughra, a character said to be born to be the eyes and ears for the rocks and trees, existed before any of the creatures that inhabit that world. In the fascinating book *The World of the Dark Crystal*, written primarily as an account of the history of the world of the Dark Crystal through the words and eyes of Aughra, many of the animals and beings are taxonomized, described, situated in their roles on their world. Even characters that never appear in the film are discussed. The objective of this book, written by Froud and J. J. Llewellyn, is to show that Henson and Froud so thoroughly planned the ecology of the world of the Dark Crystal that they created organisms and environments that do not appear in the film but need to exist to jus-tify and support the existence of those organisms that do appear. Aughra explains that after the crystal split and the Skeksis and Mystics appeared, so too did other new animals. From *The World of the Dark Crystal*:

> "Strange Beasts": Aughra here lists a dozen creatures not seen before the darkening: golarch, hsilin, yoket khria, vereina, gilyak, cherfas, pbyx, storax, garodemana, khaipokhiu, iosos. Unfortunately, the present state of taxonomy does not allow us to identify any of these names (some of which are clearly formed from languages not found elsewhere in the Book of Aughra) with other known creatures of that world; and only one, Cherfas the Deceiver, is mentioned in other sources so far studied. It would appear to have been a small swamp-dwelling reptilian of loathsome appearance whose imitations of the calls of larger creatures deceived unwary travelers. (34)

This text is surrounded by sketches of these creatures, and the book filled with sketches of other creatures that inhabit the world of the Dark Crys-tal, most of which never appear in the film.

My point here is to note that Henson was so fascinated with ecol-ogy that in developing *The Dark Crystal* he went to extreme lengths to understand the world in which his characters would interact. Couched in this ecological masterpiece is the issue of environmental ethics, of see-ing environmental harmony and protection as good and environmental pillaging and oppression as bad. The message here is clear and only part of Henson's continued attention to ecological concern.

Jim Henson's Animal Show with Stinky and Jake

Of all of Henson's projects, *Jim Henson's Animal Show with Stinky and Jake* most directly addresses issues of ecological literacy and environment. The show, which began in 1994—four years after Henson's death—and ran until 1997 on the Fox network, taught viewers facts about animals. The show was produced by Brian Henson, Jim Henson's son. During the first season, twenty-six episodes were produced and thirteen the following season. Set up in a talk-show format featuring hosts Stinky (a skunk), and Jake (a massive polar bear), the show is directed at a viewing audience of preschoolers but, like most Henson projects, contains elements that appeal to adult viewers as well. Each episode introduces Muppet versions of two animals, presented as guests of the talk show. As with *Sesame Street, Jim Henson's Animal Show with Stinky and Jake*'s agenda was specifically educational. But instead of directing only a quarter of this agenda to ecological literacy, as did *Sesame Street*, this show is completely devoted to environmental education. Each episode, as the Henson company explains, "is themed around a common feature of the two guests, for instance a similar eating habit, parenting method or defense mechanism" ("Show Elements").

Each episode features several segments that teach particular facts about the two guest animals. "That's Amazing" is a thirty-second segment that conveys "amazing" facts about the animals. When sharks were featured on the show, for instance, the amazing fact that "if a shark stops moving, he'll drown" was offered. "Jake's Tale" features Jake the polar bear telling a short story about the animals featured on that episode. Though Jake narrates the segment, live-action footage of the animals are shown (not the Muppet guests). "Animal Awards" mimics a game-show format. In this segment, Ollie the tapir awards winners in weekly contests for the animals: "the fastest runner" or "the ugliest insect" are typical contest parameters. Tizzy, a computer-generated roving reporter bee (who likes "to besiege Stinky and Jake with the latest buzz on the animal world"), asks two questions about the guest animals on each show in "Tizzy Quiz." Questions such as "How big does a giant tortoise get?" are typical. One of the funniest segments (and one of my personal favorites) features live-action footage of baby animals with their parents in wild habitats. The footage is audio dubbed with funny conversations, making it appear as if the animals are "talking." "Habitat Time" features Ollie the tapir and Armstrong the chicken hawk exploring the places where the guest animals live.

During the first two seasons of the show, guest animals included cheetahs and gazelles, linked by predator/prey relationships; dolphins and fruit bats, linked by echo location; koalas and ostriches, linked by parental care; crocodiles and armadillos, linked by armor; aardvarks and chameleons, linked by tongues (interesting way to say that); elephants and hunting dogs, linked by ways of keeping cool; lions and zebras, linked by habitat; rattlesnakes and skunks (Stinky served as his own guest), linked by defensive strategies; gnus/wildebeest and green turtles, linked by migration; sharks and sea lions, linked by the sea; rhinoceros and gorillas, linked by their endangerment; sea otters and vultures, linked by their use of tools; owls and octopuses, linked by eyesight; penguins and kiwis, linked by their flightlessness; giraffes and sloths, linked by their tree feeding; tigers and tiger beetles, linked by their ferocity; beavers and spiders, linked by their ability to make their homes; kangaroos and frogs, linked by locomotion; walruses and warthogs, linked by their tusks; brown bears and hedgehogs, linked by their hibernation; manatees and lemurs, linked by their tails; and whales and soldier ants, linked by their size. What is remarkable about these pairings is how they ask viewers to consider relationships, similarities, differences between animals. Animals, then, are seen not as singular, anomalous organisms, but as relational, adaptable, evolving organisms.

"The Song of the Cloud Forest" from *The Jim Henson Hour*

In 1989, Jim Henson won an Emmy for Outstanding Directing for *The Jim Henson Hour*. This show featured stories, skits, and other Muppet acts. Before developing *The Jim Henson Hour*, Henson had produced *Storytellers*, a show designed to present Muppet versions of traditional myths and stories (Henson's daughter Lisa, who studied mythology and folklore at Harvard, had convinced her father to pursue this project). Nine episodes of *The Henson Storyteller* series were made, but only four episodes aired in the United States (all nine aired in Britain); the remaining five aired as part of *The Jim Henson Hour*. Along with the storyteller skits, one segment of *The Jim Henson Hour* in particular depicts Henson's commitment to environmental education: "The Song of the Cloud Forest." This twenty-five-minute skit, set in the brilliance of a tropical rain forest, tells the story of Milton, the last of the golden toads. Its agenda is clear: to teach "the importance of preserving the environment and protecting endangered species" ("'Cloud Forest' Synopsis").

Milton, aware that his species is soon to be extinct, sings his mating call, hoping to find a female. A female golden toad does hear his song, but she is, unfortunately, kept in a cage by two humans. Using the power of his mating song and turning to his friends, Wilf the howler monkey, Aart the armadillo, Blanche the chameleon, Nick the anaconda, Quetzal the bird, and ultimately two human scientists, Milton sets off to rescue the last female golden toad. Like *The Dark Crystal*'s Jen and Kira, the remaining two golden toads are the only hope for the survival of their species.

Conclusions

At the outset of this chapter I made the claim that Henson's ecological literacy agendas have been crucial in the productions of Muppet texts. My limited survey here of some Henson projects serves to show how Henson has turned to ecology and ecological literacy in the development of educational and entertainment productions. There is little question that projects like *Sesame Street* have influenced millions of viewers. Yet, to leave my claim about Henson supported only by noting a few examples of "how Henson's work can be seen as having an ecological agenda" seems to de-emphasize what Henson really accomplishes in terms of children's texts and ecological literacy. Beyond the few projects I have mentioned here, Henson's Muppets have appeared in many other films, televisions shows, and live performances. Muppet characters are easily identified by just about every preschool and school-age child in America. I would be willing to go so far as to say that more children could identify the Cookie Monster or Elmo than they could Mickey Mouse or Donald Duck. Henson's reach is powerful and influential, providing texts that reach millions of children. One can hardly deny the Muppets' influence. Remember a few years back when Tickle Me Elmo dolls were impossible to keep on shelves? Muppets are a part of education, of daily childhood life.

My point about their influence is only part of what needs to be said about the Muppets. More important in this recognition is the call for further critical examination of Muppet texts: televisions shows, films, publications, commercials, public appearances, museums, products. I hope that this brief glance at Henson, the Muppets, and ecological literacy leads not only to an understanding of Henson and the Muppets as committed to environmental education but ultimately to further critical work addressing Henson projects within the agendas of ecological literacy.

Appendix: A Chronology of
Henson's Environmental Projects

1969	Storyboards and scripts created for National Park Service PSAs (not produced).
March 27, 1973	Muppets appear on NBC ecology special, "Keep U.S. Beautiful."
May 12, 1983	"A Rocky Mountain Holiday" with John Denver and Muppets (taped in Aspen, Colorado, September 1982) airs on ABC. It has an environmental theme.
November 8, 1983	National Wildlife Federation PSAs videotaped in Central Park with Kermit and Fozzie.
1984	National Wildlife PSAs with Kermit and Fozzie are broadcast.
March 18–24, 1984	Kermit is honorary chairman of National Wildlife Week. Gives speech at the National Wildlife Federation annual meeting in Atlanta, "A Frog's View."
December 25, 1984	"An American Portrait," with Jim and Kermit honoring naturalist Roger Tory Peterson, airs on CBS.
1985	National Wildlife Federation PSAs with Eddie Albert and Rowlf.
1987	Kermit appears in clean air PSAs for the National Wildlife Federation.
October 13, 1987	Jim and Kermit attend the New York Park Department's celebration of the printing of the one thousandth "Daily Planet" newsletter, held at the Dairy in Central Park.
1988	Kermit and Animal do a PSA for the rain forests, broadcast at a Grateful Dead concert.

	National Wildlife Federation PSA "Forests Are More than Trees" airs.
1989	Kermit is spokesfrog for the Better World Society, and Jim produces PSAs for their causes.
December 12, 1989	Miss Piggy and Kermit present at the United Nations and Battery Park City Authority's holiday tree lighting for global reforestation.
1990	National Conservation Award, National Wildlife Federation, presented to Jim Henson for Outstanding Contributions to Wise Use and Management of the Nation's Natural Resources.
	Telly Award to Jim Henson Productions for "Better World Society: Waste Deep" PSA.
	Telly Award to Jim Henson Productions for "Better World Society: The War Room" PSA.
April 22, 1990	Kermit does a PSA for Earth Day: "Who Says You Can't Change the World," featuring him singing "Being Green."
1992	Environmental Media Award to *Dinosaurs* episode "Power Erupts" for Best Episodic Comedy, Brian Henson, executive producer, Kirk Thatcher, coproducer.
	Columbus International Film and Video Festival, honorable mention on the TV Short Form category for the National Wildlife "You Can Make a Difference" PSA campaign.
	Kermit, Save the Swamp!, an environmentally minded children's book, is published.
April 1992	"You Can Make a Difference" environmental PSA featuring Robin and the Frog Scouts begins airing (for the National Wildlife Federation).
April 8, 1992	Kermit's editorial with a "protect the environment" message appears in the "Imagine" insert of the *New York Times*.

April 21, 1992	Launch of "Support the Parks" campaign. Kermit is spokesfrog for New York City Parks Foundation.
1993	Environmental Media Award to Brian Henson for *Dinosaurs* episode "If I Were a Tree."
March 31, 1993	Kermit tapes "Save Our Coasts," PSA for the U.S. Fish and Wildlife Service to be shown at the Atlanta Braves opening game.
1995	Save the Bay Lifetime Environmental Achievement Award to Jim Henson.
October 12, 1995	Kermit acts as presenter, with Paula Poundstone, at the Environmental Media Awards.
1996	Robert Rauschenberg print awarded to Jim Henson by Tribute 21 for his environmental work.
October 14, 1996	Kermit is again presenter at the Environmental Media Awards.
October 1999	Kermit hosts *Australia Post*'s Small Pond promotion for national stamp collecting month. Campaign contained an environmental message.
March 29, 2000	Kermit appears on Capitol Hill supporting the Shambala Wild Animal Protection Act (Congressman Tom Lantos) and the Save the Wetlands campaign (Congressman Jack Kingston).

("Archives Chronology," 1–2)

NOTES

I am grateful to Carla Della Vedova, associate archivist at the Jim Henson Company, and to the rest of the Jim Henson Company for providing me with information for this essay. All company documents are cited with permission.

1. Here I use "Henson" not specifically as the man Jim Henson but as reference to the larger "Henson project," as it were.

2. *Fraggle Rock* won more than sixteen awards, including: Ace Award (1984), ACT Award (1985), nomination for People's Choice Award (1985), Gemini Award (1986),

ACE Award (1986), Special Recommendation for *Fraguru Rokku* given by the Central Council of Children's Welfare in Japan (1987), Gemini Award (1987), ACE Award (1988).

Works Cited

Borgenicht, David. *Sesame Street Unpaved: Scripts, Stories, Secrets, and Songs.* New York: Children's Television Workshop, 1998.

Cook, Thomas D., Hilary Appleton, and Ross Connor. *"Sesame Street" Revisited.* New York: Russell Sage Foundation, 1975.

Cooney, Joan G. "Television for Preschool Children: A Proposal." February 19, 1968. In *"Sesame Street" Revisited.* New York: Russell Sage Foundation, 1975.

Finch, Christopher. *The Making of "The Dark Crystal": Creating a Unique Film.* New York: Holt, Rinehart, and Winston, 1983.

Froud, Brian, and J. J. Llewellyn. *The World of the Dark Crystal.* New York: Henson Organization Publishing/Alfred A. Knopf, 1982.

Gaard, Greta. "Living Interconnections with Animals and Nature." In *Ecofeminism: Women, Animals, Nature.* Ed. Greta Gaard. Philadelphia: Temple University Press, 1993 (1–12).

Glotfelty, Cheryll. Interview. "Ecocriticism, Writing, and Nature: A Conversation with Cheryll Glotfelty." In *Writing Environments.* Ed. Dobrin, Sidney I., and Christopher J. Keller. Albany: State University of New York Press, forthcoming.

———. "Introduction: Literary Studies in an Age of Environmental Crisis." In *The Ecocriticism Reader: Landmarks in Literary Ecology.* Ed. Cheryll Glotfelty and Harold Fromm. Athens: University of Georgia Press, 1996.

Jim Henson Company. "Jim Henson—Biography." Company document. New York, N.Y.

———. "Jim Henson Company and Environmentalism: Archives Chronology." Company document. New York, N.Y.

———. "*Fraggle Rock* Character Biographies." Company document.

———. "*Fraggle Rock* Synopsis." Company document. New York, N.Y.

———. "*Jim Henson's Animal Show with Stinky and Jake* Show Elements." Company document. New York, N.Y.

———. "Jim Henson's *Storyteller* Synopsis." Company document. New York, N.Y.

———. "'The Song of the Cloud Forest' Synopsis." Company document. New York, N.Y.

Orr, David. *Ecological Literacy: Education and the Transition to a Postmodern World.* Albany: State University of New York Press, 1992.

Rueckert, William. "Literature and Ecology: An Experiment in Ecocriticism." *Iowa Review* 9 (winter 1978): 71–86.

15

Cartoons and Contamination

How the Multinational Kids Help
Captain Planet Save Gaia

Susan Jaye Dauer

I am sitting at my desk looking at my official *"Captain Planet and the Planeteers* Ecology Kit: Air Quality Test Kit" (1991). The box proclaims that this product is intended for those eight and up. Upon first opening it, I found that it contained several paper cups, some explanatory information, a small pad on which to take "scientific notes," and several objects made of plastic, including two small bottles. One is a bottle of distilled water. The other is something called limewater. A warning on the box tells me that the "liquids may cause eye or skin irritation." As well as teaching children how to check the air quality around "home, school or office," apparently this kit is also teaching them that water, even distilled water, is potentially dangerous. Perhaps this is to encourage the young "planeteer in training" to seek out the water test kit. On the other hand, despite the plastic components, let me assure you that this kit is fully recyclable; I bought it slightly used on eBay. In many ways, this kit is ideal as an introduction to *Captain Planet and the Planeteers,* an extrapolative, ecofictional cartoon series that was one the most popular shows for children in the early 1990s. Attributable to media mogul Ted Turner, who developed it for his TBS Superstation network, *Captain Planet* is today part of the conglomeration we know as the Time-Warner Company.[1]

Extrapolative fiction, which includes science fiction, fantasy, and utopian literature—those literatures that seek to move beyond what is known of the world and predict what could happen, given specific variables—is often concerned with environmental issues; examples include Ernest Callenbach's fine *Ecotopia* (1975) and its sequel, *Ecotopia Emerg-*

ing (1981). In her letter in the October 1999 *PMLA* "Forum on Literatures of the Environment," Ursula K. Heise provides further examples.

> One of the contemporary genres in which questions about nature and environmental issues emerge most clearly is science fiction: from the novels and short stories of Brian Aldiss, John Brunner, and Ursula K. Le Guin in the 1960s and 1970s to those of Carl Amery, David Brin, Kim Stanley Robinson, and Scott Russell Sanders in the 1980s and 1990s, science fiction is one of the genres that have most persistently and most daringly engaged environmental questions and their challenge to our vision of the future. (1096–97)

I believe that it is fair to say that both science fiction and fantasy are at the forefront of the environmental literature movement, dealing as they do in projections of the present into the future, and concerned with forests, medicines, aliens and alienation, and toxins produced by industrial societies. Moving closer to *Captain Planet,* Ken Keesee's "Science Fiction as a Genre in Adolescent Literature" discusses why this genre has often been most popular with younger audiences. "Science fiction appeals to the young reader foremost because it involves adventure. Through science fiction, the reader can explore those 'strange new worlds' that she has never seen nor likely will ever see." Many science fiction writers, particularly those who hold Ph.D.s in the hard sciences and who hold academic and laboratory positions, notably Isaac Asimov, Hal Clement, and David Brin, credit science fiction with giving them the imagination and curiosity to pursue such fields as astronomy, engineering, and biology.

Yet, despite the boost from scientists, extrapolative fiction is not often granted a high place in the literary canon, especially when it takes the form of comic books and cartoons. While it's true that these forms can often be mindlessly violent, like the ubiquitous *Bugs Bunny-Roadrunner Show,* they can also be mindfully didactic, like 1980s Saturday morning *Superfriends* and *Tarzan,* two cartoons that actually announced their morals at the end, like modern-day Aesop's fables,[2] and often focused, at least in part, on environmental concerns. Still in reruns on Ted Turner's own Cartoon Network, *Captain Planet and the Planeteers* uses ecological fantasy to teach children about their responsibilities to the world, staking its claim to the didactic and giving its violence a moral purpose.[3]

From the original episode onward, the lessons are clear. Viewers are introduced to Asian Gi, African Kwame, North American Wheeler,

Eastern European Linka, and South American Ma-Ti, the multinational, multiracial, environmentally aware teenagers chosen (and gifted with special rings) by Gaia, the Spirit of the Earth. Gaia is a female being with dark violet eyes, light brown skin, black hair, and Caucasian (if not Barbiesque) features—allowing her to combine all the races represented individually by the teenagers. The rings give the teens the powers of Water, Earth, Fire, Wind (Air), and "Heart," respectively, for the purpose of making them into a team capable of protecting the earth from a notorious assortment of allegorically named polluters, exploiters, and destroyers.

When viewers first meet these teens, each is either actively showing concern for others or otherwise demonstrating connection to the natural world, even if that connection is not exactly straightforwardly "natural." We may not watch Animal Planet or the Discovery Channel and root for the lion to capture and eat the zebra foal, but the cycle of life is one of the basics of the natural world. Thus, while none of the Planeteers is acting to cause harm, their personal relationships with the world are not completely in tune with the natural environment. Kwame is watering new plants, Gi is swimming with a dolphin in the open sea, Linka is playing music and enchanting the birds, Ma-Ti is freeing a monkey trapped in some vines and about to be caught by a hungry jaguar, and Wheeler is rescuing a human victim from a less human bully. Perhaps it is his distance from an immediate, even if potentially problematic, contact with the environment that makes it harder for Wheeler to control his ring's power as quickly as the other four Planeteers, but his concern for the weak at the mercy of the cruelly powerful is a characteristic that all the Planeteers will come to share, often in surprising ways.

In her essay in *Teaching Children's Literature*, Jeanne Murray Walker notes that "the voices that tell stories in fantasy novels are . . . overtly present and omniscient, solemnly counseling the reader through the images of the narrative. . . . [F]antasy instructs its readers in the norms and truths of an identifiable social community." Walker believes that fantasy helps children learn to be adults but "does not pretend a snapshot of the world that is value-neutral" (116–17), and that allows fantasy to be used to teach other social lessons. As James E. Swan said of the early environmental movement, "the initial position . . . was that of social criticism" (quoted in Waage xiii). *Captain Planet*'s Gaia is clearly meant to be that "overtly present and omniscient" figure, counseling these teens, and by extension the show's child viewers, how to save the world. The social criticism of *Captain Planet and the Planeteers* cartoons is not subtle.

When the five teens, the cartoon Planeteers, are chosen, they actually embody issues raised by Walter H. Clark Jr. when he writes that "environmental education" is, or could be, "a rallying cry around which people with a variety of roughly similar interests join in common allegiance, possibly without having too clear an idea of what it is that unites them" (5). He believes that although environmental literature need not be "moral or political," that which "allows for the raising of such issues is to be preferred for teaching purposes over that which does not" (6). Both students of Gaia and initiators themselves, the Planeteers constantly address a variety of environmental and social issues, which are often indistinguishable, and use those issues to encourage their mostly young audiences, through clear breaks in television's fourth wall, to become initiators and environmental activists themselves.

Moreover, there is another element to these cartoons, Captain Planet himself, a second figure who is "overtly present and omniscient." When the teens recognize or find trouble but are unable to act successfully through lack of knowledge or lack of strength, they can use their rings for another purpose than simply to focus their individual powers. Because of the addition of Heart to the archetypical Four Elements, the teenagers discover that they can invoke this great environmental hero. Except when temporarily weakened by exposure to toxic waste or acid rain,[4] evils that, both ironically and significantly, he can be saved from by the teens while they do not have their special powers, he is the embodiment of the strength of the hearts and wills of the five teens, gifted with all four elemental powers at their strongest and perhaps even more empathically (Heart) than physically powerful.

Beyond the cartoon, the Captain Planet Foundation takes the ideas of the show and encourages young people to get involved and do what they can to help the Planeteers—and Captain Planet—to succeed in their vital work. Viewers are encouraged to emulate the actions of the young heroes and even to apply for grants to help in their own way in their own communities. Suggestions for action and activities are clearly and enthusiastically provided at the end of each of the shows. Oil-hungry men (such as Hoggish Greedly, carelessly polluting a wildlife refuge) and indiscriminate destroyers of wildlife (like whale-killers Blunder and Blight, fiendishly attacking baby as well as adult whales) need to be stopped—whether they are villains of a *Captain Planet* cartoon or real-life polluters.

The lessons the show teaches provide serious social criticism, if recognizably from a determined and mainly liberal perspective. One doesn't need to wonder what Captain Planet would think of oil pipelines through Alaskan wildlife sanctuaries or about global warming treaties.

Yet, while teaching children about the importance of protecting nature from exploitation and the importance of standing up to those who would harm the earth, the *Captain Planet* cartoons are also teaching children other lessons. There are "good" lessons, such as the importance of teamwork and the balance of different people's strengths. Over time, the teens learn to accept help when they need it from each other and from outsiders, and each contributes what he or she can to each situation.

However, there are also "bad" lessons, lessons that reinforce the kinds of gender stereotypes that hurt while subverting stereotypes that empower. One of the more problematic, less overt messages, but one that becomes more and more apparent as one watches a number of episodes, is that although Gaia appears to be a powerful being, appearances can be deceiving. She is, in actuality, almost always trapped in one place, Hope Island, and is thus unable by her own efforts to affect the changes and cures necessary to save herself and the planet she represents and guards. She can appear to the teens when they are away from Hope, but she almost never has a physical form or power anywhere else. Thus Gaia, a type of Mother Earth and Mother Nature, is shown as rather a weak creature, constantly in need rescue. By naming this character Gaia, the creators of *Captain Planet* invoke the Gaia hypothesis—but not exactly as Lovelock had envisioned.

> The Gaia hypothesis is not a simple assertion that could easily be proved or disproved. Instead it is a complex statement with multiple levels of meaning, like a work of art. At the simplest level, it asserts that this planet is characterized by the capacity for self-correction that characterizes living organisms, the maintenance of continuity by corrective variation. . . . The Gaia hypothesis deepens the sense of the planet as developing, as having a history. . . . There are several quite different responses to the idea of the earth as a living organism. Some people feel increased solicitude for a planet newly recognized as vulnerable, intricately beautiful. Others respond with nonchalance, saying Gaia can do her own housekeeping, leaving us free to continue as we are. (Bateson 134)

The five teens, working for Gaia, "feel increased solicitude," but almost everyone else in these shows acts with varying degrees of nonchalance, if not outright hostility, toward the planet. Yet, the Gaia who appears in *Captain Planet* is not "self-correcting." She is a damsel in distress.

Another factor to consider in analyzing the messages of this program is the fact that the teens, three boys and two girls, appear equal to one another, but their numbers are uneven. Furthermore, by assigning "Heart," in so many ways the most important element, to the youngest of the boys, the creators of the show have taken what are often considered to be the among the greatest strengths and virtues of women, especially mothers—namely loving and nurturing—and given those qualities to an adolescent boy, perhaps the person least likely in the real world to be expected to have those qualities. Ma-Ti is credited with the gift of empathy even before he receives his ring, and this strength is repeated and expanded in the male Captain Planet who, incidentally, pushes the male to female action ratio further askew. This show provides the subtle message that the weak female, Gaia (both as female figure and as the earth) needs a strong male, Captain Planet, to save her. She may have handed out the rings, but after having done so, she is relegated to the background, stuck in one place, literally left at home—while Captain Planet, like a medieval knight, ventures forth to do battle to save her and her lands. She speaks; he acts. She chose the teens; he actually works with them. Even the very name of the show, *Captain Planet and the Planeteers,* reinforces her lack of importance.[5] Gaia exists to be rescued; she provides the need for the heroes.

In the first episode of *Captain Planet and the Planeteers,* "A Hero for Earth" (1990), Gaia is rudely awakened from a century-long sleep by the illegal oil drilling of the aptly named Hoggish Greedly. Unfortunately for her, the last hundred years have seen some of the greatest changes the earth has ever known, and certainly the greatest caused by mechanical and technological rather than natural means. The twentieth century was a time of great invention—invention, however, that introduced both real and potential ecological disasters for the earth.

Opening a window to the world, Gaia sees shocking scenes of devastation: deforestation, pollution, and loss of habitat. Realizing that she has indeed overslept, *Captain Planet*'s Gaia recognizes that she is failing in her main task, "the strange property of keeping [earth] always a fit and comfortable place for living things to inhabit" (Lovelock, *New Look* vii). Awakened to her responsibility but clearly unable to do anything on her own to fix her mistakes, Gaia makes the decision to send out five rings she has been keeping, apparently for just such an emergency. Starting with Kwame, who is out planting in the hot sun of his African home, Gaia uses natural (mostly animal) means to get the rings into the right hands, then calls the five ring bearers to her home on Hope Island.

The five, particularly Wheeler, are distressed at finding themselves in such a strange place, but they are quickly persuaded that what they are to do is vital and necessary work. Each is given the opportunity to try out his or her talent, to see what he or she can do. The four who have been given the elemental powers find that their first attempts yield a variety of semisuccesses. However, it is here that Ma-Ti (rescued monkey in tow) proves that his power is closely allied to who he is, for he masters his abilities, including the power to mindspeak with the others, without any difficulty at all. After their one brief practice session, practice that is their only real training, and with Gi (who apparently has the only driver's license) at the wheel, the five are sent out to deal with the first of the many ecovillains they will encounter in their Planeteer roles.

Racing to the rescue, the five find trouble rampaging through a "protected" area; Greedly and his sidekick, Rigger, are riding about in a giant oil-driller reminiscent of the mechanical walking machines used by the Evil Empire in the first *Star Wars Trilogy*. The oil slicks and distressed animals they leave in their wake do not deter Greedly, nor is he at all troubled about protecting his ill-gotten gain by using what in any world but a cartoon would be deadly force against teenagers.

Ultimately recognizing that the danger of their assigned task is beyond their individual abilities, the five discover how to combine their powers to call up Captain Planet. Proving himself a true cartoon superhero, Captain Planet soon twists the villainous Greedly's machinery into unusable knots, seals off the oil leak, and cleans up much of the spill. In one of the show's great ironies, Captain Planet's tag line, spoken when he appears and when he has solved the problems the teens cannot, is: "The Powers Is Yours." The five teens are left to use "the power that is theirs" to clean off the walrus and pelican victims of the oil spill. Wheeler, ever the voice of American pragmatism, wonders why he and his new companions have to clean up a mess that they have not made. The other Planeteers explain it to him; this is their new role in life. With little fanfare, the five leave their homes, their families, their old lives. They leave behind "nonchalance." From that day forth, they are Planeteers, working toward finding ways to coexist—and working, more importantly, to save Gaia.

The actions of these teens, while clearly admirable, nevertheless send a mixed message to the show's mostly child audience. In her essay in *Ecofeminism*, Ruthanne Kurth-Schai claims: "Studies of children's utopian future imagery . . . reveal intense interest, concern, and creativity regarding the status of the environment and the quality of human interaction with nonhuman nature. These finding are reinforced by the growing participation of children around the world in efforts to protect endangered species, promote recycling and energy conservation, and save the rainforests" (207). These comments support the creators of this show and appear to make it reasonable to have a show that focuses on what young people the world over can do about the pollution that threatens their world, both within the framework of the show and without it, in the real world. Further, Donna Lee King, author of *Doing Their Share to Save the Planet: Children and the Evironmental Crisis,* quotes British essayist Rosalind Coward, who claims that "children and ecology are two terms that seem to go naturally together. Much green rhetoric is about our children's future" (1).

However, when the show and its situations are examined further, it becomes apparent that there are problems with this cartoon and its Planeteer program. Kurth-Schai also discusses how children can be exploited by adults, how they are "systematically excluded from meaningful social and political participation," while, "on the other hand, children are asked far too soon to assume adult responsibilities that are not of their choosing" (193). King echoes these sentiments, stating, "I began to consider what the culture of environmental crisis meant to *children,* a social category by definition powerless in myriad ways. Telling children to save the planet seemed utterly contradictory, yet everywhere I looked, the message was going to kids that their job is solve environmental crisis" (2).[6] When Gaia chose these teens, she gave them the incredible responsibility to stand up to and stop dangerous adults and to clean up the messes caused by those same adults. Gaia, Captain Planet, and *Captain Planet*'s creators all ask the children who watch the show to act, putting them in the position of the show's teens vis-à-vis the dangers of pollution and, more importantly, of polluters.

Occasionally one will hear or read about the ways in which our current generation, particularly in North America and the rest of the so-called Western world, is "ruining" the earth for future generations, using up natural resources, blighting landscapes, strip mining, drift net fishing, clearing old growth and rain forests, and appointing people like James Watt, Gale Norton, and even Bruce Babbitt to the post of secretary of the interior. In her contribution to an online forum on ecocriticism, Cheryll Glotfelty quotes historian Donald Worster, noting that

> We are facing a global crisis today, not because of how ecosystems function but rather because of how our ethical systems function. Getting through the

crisis requires understanding our impact on nature as precisely as possible, but even more, it requires understanding those ethical systems and using that understanding to reform them. Historians, along with literary scholars, anthropologists, and philosophers, cannot do the reforming, of course, but they can help with the understanding.(Online)

Many of today's most aware and knowledgeable adults are helpless, but there is nevertheless an idea that we must expect the next generation to experience the brunt of "global neglect and abuse"—and fix it.

As Kurth-Schai continues, "[T]hroughout the world the quality of children's lives . . . is repeatedly assaulted by failure to contain hazardous wastes and to provide safe drinking water and by changes in soil, climate and vegetation related to industrialization. . . . In addition to the highly visible impacts, perhaps as damaging and more pervasive are the 'slow and silent killers,' the hidden environmental toxins to which children are uniquely vulnerable" (197). In this light, sending out the young Plane-teers to fight those who use toxins as weapons, against both the earth and human beings, hardly seems appropriate, yet is somehow deemed acceptable, even admirable.

In focusing the show on the potential for teenagers, and by exten-sion the younger children who watch cartoons, to assume roles and responsibilities (particularly those that we at least like to think are tradi-tionally reserved for adults), the frailties and vulnerabilities of children are ignored. In fact, the five cartoon teens do not escape harmful contact with either the toxins or the villains. Unlike many adult heroes, they do suffer serious illness and injury. As noted above, Greedly tries to kill them in "A Hero for Earth," and they suffer other attacks by dangerous adults in other episodes, notably "Fare Thee Whale." In "Hate Canal," Ma-Ti is bitten by a poisoned and therefore poisonous rat. This bite causes him to suffer from a near fatal case of a plague affecting almost the entire city of Venice. In "Skumm Lord," Wheeler falls into a vat of a toxic fluid, and when Linka and Gi attempt to rescue him, they too are overcome. In "The Conqueror," all five Planeteers fall under the spell of Zarm, an evil counterpart of Gaia, who wants to exploit their powers. He almost suc-ceeds through emotionally abusing them and forcing them into decisions even further beyond their maturity levels than they usually have to face.

The kinds of dangers these children face is addressed in a rather commonsense report entitled "What's Gotten into Our Children?" pub-lished by a child advocacy organization called Children Now. In this report, the authors argue that environmental problems, while affecting everyone, are more harmful to children for several reasons. First, smaller bodies make children more vulnerable when they receive the same doses of toxins adults receive. Also, since they are growing and changing, these toxins can more adversely affect them. Second, children don't have the wisdom or maturity to avoid potential dangers; children are curious. Third, children are younger and will therefore have longer to live in and with toxins which will in turn have longer to act and react within them. (quoted in Kurth-Schai 197–98)

Surely the writers of the *Captain Planet* cartoons could have been more aware of these potential complications in putting these teens in the forefront in the fight against toxins and making them role models for younger children.

Although qualities such as "playfulness, spontaneity, conceptual and behavioral flexibility, unique insight, and energy are more easily accessed and frequently expressed in childhood," the exploitation of these qualities does not seem to be justified even by the good the teens do. The seemingly "child-centered social ethic" of these cartoons, "which promote[s] interaction, interdependence, and collaboration rather than isolation, independence, and competition" (Kurth-Schai 201) may be good, but where is the acknowledgment of "children's very real and different-than-adult needs for nurturance and protection" (200)? Why should children have to sneak onto Blight and Plunder's ship? Why should Gaia and Captain Planet, in loco parentis, be not only willing to allow these young people to go into danger, but downright emphatic and insistent about it?

If the world is to be saved, it will be the next generation that will have to shoulder the great majority of the workload. Teaching children environmentally friendly activities and actions is clearly a necessity. Giving them child role models should also be a good idea. The problem is that these teen heroes are not the ideal role models they seem to be. In each episode, they act against stranger adults, adults who almost always have the advantage of superior technology, weaponry, and numbers, as well as the strange advantage of a lack of empathy. These teens make for dangerous role models because they willingly face perils they are not equipped to handle, even with those magic rings. Karen J. Warren, in "Taking Empirical Data Seriously: An Ecofeminist Philosophical Perspective," points out that "toxic chemicals, largely because of their ability to cross placenta, to bioaccumulate, and to occur as mixtures, pose serious health threats disproportionately to infants, mothers, and the elderly" (10). Teenagers who place themselves in harm's way should be added to her list.

What then is the ultimate message of *Captain Planet and the Planeteers*? Is it that children should risk themselves for the sake of the earth? Should we be training up children who, like Robert F. Kennedy Jr., will name their children after their environmental protest activities,[7] even when those activities bring them into danger from industrial complexes and industrial waste and from government agencies and even from their official "*Captain Planet and the Planeteers* Ecology Kit: Air Quality Test Kit"? Or is the message that we cannot continue to live in a world that is borrowing from those children's future? Monetary debts can be repaid; budgets can be balanced. But what will happen to our children in a world in which we have mortgaged the rain forests, the large mammals on the land and in the seas, and even the very seas themselves?

Perhaps the message of *Captain Planet* is that children are already being placed into danger by the adults who pay so much lip service to protecting them. If Captain Planet is right, and "The Power Is Yours," and if Lovelock's Gaia, as well as *Captain Planet*'s, is in trouble, then perhaps she must turn to children as the final choice before acknowledging "that the planet's capacity for self-correction might well involve the end of the creatures that are making the trouble" (Bateson 134). If children are the last line of defense, teaching them to care and hoping that they will have, find, or create "the Power" are inescapable extrapolations.

NOTES

1. See http://www.turner.com/cpf/. Clicking on this web site, one can follow one set of links to a fascinating list of sponsors of an "eco-friendly" house marketed by Torrey Homes at the "Professional Builder's 2001 NAHB Show Village." Supporters include Dow and Dow Agra Sciences, among others. However, other links show that A-list of stars who lent their voices to the show, working for union scale. Chief among these are Whoopi Goldberg, Sting, Jeff Goldblum, and LeVar Burton.

2. Similarly, "[e]ach episode of *Captain Planet and the Planeteers* ended with a 30-second 'Planeteers Alert,' which taught kids lessons on recycling, vegetarian diets, and other planetary protection measures" ("Captain Planet," *Yesterdayland*).

3. Popular reactions to this show have been, to say the least, rather mixed. I have chosen a sampling of responses to the show from a listserv entitled "Jump the Shark":

"This show was the zenith of american [*sic*] animation. . . . It kicked ass, It didn't just focus on environmental concerns, but social issues (streetgangs [*sic*], drugs, etc) as well. One episode even started off in the 1992 LA riots. I'd say it was comparable to *Sailor*

Moon or *Dragon Ball Z*. If your [*sic*] reading this Ted Turner, with all the issues in today's world (racism, biological agents, etc), I seriously wish you'd bring it back." "Captain Planet was the lamest show on TV! Whoopi Goldberg doing the voice of Gya or whatever her name was." "Great way to indoctrinate our kids, Ted Turner! I'll teach my own kid about protecting the environment, thank you; I don't need a multi-millionaire bigot suffering from liberal guilt doing the job for me."

4. Every time this happens, I think, "Kryptonite!"

5. She may, actually, be even less important than I give her credit for. When Donna Lee King interviewed children about the show, only one "spontaneously mentions the character by name and role." Other children remember her as vaguely connected with the rings or as Captain Planet's mother. Many didn't remember her at all (47).

6. Watching a televised Earth Day contest in 1990, King watched a little boy, standing alone on a dark stage, reciting his reasons why we "need to save the earth": "The earth is dying. We should save the earth for the trees. We have to save it. It is going to waste. There is no other planet to go to. If we don't stop polluting it, we and everybody will die" (2). Is this the kind of subject that a six-year-old should have to contemplate?

7. Aidan Caohman Vieques Kennedy was born July 13, 2001. His father will be serving time in prison for trespassing during protests against using the Puerto Rican island of Vieques as a bomb test site ("Kennedy").

Works Cited

Bateson, Mary Catherine. *Peripheral Visions: Learning Along the Way*. New York: Harper-Collins, 1994.

"Captain Planet and the Planeteers." *Yesterdayland*. http://www.yesterdayland.com (2001).

Captain Planet and the Planeteers: "Fare Thee Whale." Videocassette. Turner Home Entertainment, 1991.

Captain Planet and the Planeteers: "Hate Canal." Videocassette. Turner Home Entertainment, 1991.

Captain Planet and the Planeteers: "A Hero for Earth." Videocassette. Turner Home Entertainment, 1990.

Captain Planet and the Planeteers, the Power Is Yours: "Skumm Lord" and "The Conqueror." Videocassette. Turner Home Entertainment, 1990.

"Captain Planet Foundation." http://www.turner.com/cpf/ (2001).

Clark, Walter H., Jr. "What Teaching Environmental Literature Might Be." In *Teaching Environmental Literature: Materials, Methods, Resources*. Ed. Frederick O. Waage. Options for Teaching. New York: MLA, 1985.

Glotfelty, Cheryll. "What is Ecocriticism." In *Defining Ecocritical Theory and Practice*. 1994 Western Literature Association Meeting, Salt Lake City, Utah, 6 October 1994. In ASLE Online: The Association for the Study of Literature and the Environment. http://www.asle.umn.edu.

Heise, Ursula K. Letter in "Forum on Literatures of the Environment." *PMLA* 114 (October 1999): 1096–97. In ASLE Online: The Association for the Study of Literature and the Environment. http://www.asle.umn.edu.

"Jump the Shark." 1997–2001. http://www.jumptheshark.com (2001).

Keesee, Ken. "Science Fiction as a Genre in Adolescent Literature." http://falcon.jmu.edu.

"Kennedy Baby Will Remember Vieques." *Yahoo News,* July 27, 2001. http://dailynews.yahoo.com.

King, Donna Lee. *Doing Their Share to Save the Planet: Children and the Environmental Crisis.* New Brunswick, N.J.: Rutgers University Press, 1995.

Kurth-Schai, Ruthanne. "Ecofeminism and Meaning." In *Ecofeminism: Women, Culture, Nature.* Ed. Karen J. Warren. Bloomington: Indiana University Press, 1997.

Lovelock, James. *Gaia: A New Look at Life on Earth.* Oxford: Oxford University Press, 1995 (1979).

Waage, Frederick O., ed. *Teaching Environmental Literature: Materials, Methods, Resources.* Options for Teaching. New York: MLA, 1985.

Walker, Jeanne Murray. "High Fantasy, Rites of Passage, and Cultural Values." In *Teaching Children's Literature: Issues, Pedagogy, Resources.* Ed. Glenn Edward Sadler. Options for Teaching. New York: MLA, 1992.

Warren, Karen J. "Taking Empirical Data Seriously: An Ecofeminist Philosophical Perspective." In *Ecofeminism: Women, Culture, Nature.* Ed. Karen J. Warren. Bloomington: Indiana University Press, 1997.

16

Disney of Orlando's Animal Kingdom

Kenneth B. Kidd

Like many children growing up in the 1970s, I was a devoted fan of *Mutual of Omaha's Wild Kingdom,* an educational television show about animals produced on NBC from 1963 through 1971 and subsequently syndicated.[1] Marlin Perkins was its host, and he was aided by fellow naturalists Jim Fowler and Stan Brock. Each week I watched breathlessly as the team tackled yet another exotic, often dangerous beast. Episodes sometimes offered in-depth species profiles, sometimes emphasized the ethical dramas of animal-human interaction. Africa and South America were primary set locations; such is the legacy of imperialist show-and-tell. The genteel Perkins was reminiscent of the armchair anthropologist who directed and interpreted, while Fowler and Brock seemed more akin to the ethnographic "men on the spot" who conducted fieldwork and tagged the natives. Given this division of labor, it's not surprising that Perkins was also the show's narrator, his paternalistic manner easy to parody (as in, for instance, "I'll watch safely from the truck while Jim wrestles with the giant anaconda"). I don't remember much about the native people with whom these men interacted, except that they seemed as much a part of the landscape as the featured animals.

I watched *Wild Kingdom* largely for the spectacle of the show, retaining little knowledge about animals or habitats. This corporate-sponsored series helped set the terms for my own pop-nature appreciation. For many of us exposed to such programming, I suspect, nature is something to be screened rather than enjoyed more directly in the great outdoors and/or studied more intensively. Although I spent years at summer camp, even working as a nature counselor, I've always experienced nature primarily as entertainment and spectacle. It's impossible, of course, to know nature without human framing and manipulation, be it micro or macro: hence "picturesque" landscape painting, wilderness photography, the zoological and botanical garden, the aquarium, the natural history museum, the national park, the ant farm, Timelife

Video's *Hunting and Escaping* series, NOVA documentaries, Animal Planet, and . . . the list seems interminable. Entertainment and education mix and mingle in twentieth-century nature shows. And as *Wild Kingdom* makes clear, persistent in such shows are classic nationalistic and/or imperialist schemes of classification and exhibition.

We know that nature is always already cultural. The issue is how so, with what continuities and transformations? Recognizing that nature is always to some extent a utopian idea or symbolic space, how do we nonetheless evaluate its latest forms and effects? How to understand the mass spectacle of nature, particularly in the current moment, in which the ostensibly kinder, gentler programs of yesteryear have yielded to an intensely corporate theming of nature, not only on screen but in entertainment parks such as Anheuser-Busch's Sea World or its Tampa-based Busch Gardens, themed "Africa: The Dark Continent"? In her study *Spectacular Nature: Corporate Culture and the Sea World Experience,* Susan G. Davis explores together "the problem of public space in an era of advancing corporate privatization . . . with the problem of the representation of nature and the environment in the contemporary mass media" (14). Davis's engaging analysis of Sea World emphasizes both the attenuation of the public sphere in late capitalism and the imperialist nostalgia that often attends mass nature productions. "Present-day tourism," she writes, "powerfully reproduces older imperial and colonial relationships between the first and third worlds, very often through the medium of mass consumption of exotic nature" (11).

Davis's analysis helps us make sense of Animal Kingdom, the most recent addition to the Walt Disney World complex in central Florida. Disney, of course, is the undisputed king of the theme park business, having rejuvenated the field in 1955 with Disneyland in California and then Disney World in 1971 (later rechristened Walt Disney World). In the 1970s and 1980s, other large corporations joined the Mouse in theme park ventures. Along with Anheuser-Busch, Disney led the way in specularizing nature for mass audiences, as in the Magic Kingdom, where animatronic animals and "animated" cast members populate a landscape of fairy-tale, animal, and adventure fantasy. By the 1980s, Walt Disney World had helped establish theme parks as cultural sites that everyone should visit, like the world fairs and expositions before them.

With the opening of Animal Kingdom in 1998, however, Disney embarked on a different nature enterprise, in effect privatizing the civic zoo and drawing from its own tradition of "realistic" and often imperialistic nature representation. Zoos have long been "strong on colonial lessons in identity and difference," as John Willinsky notes in *Learning to Divide the World* (70).[2] The zoo, furthermore, animates nature; the Royal Menagerie of London billed itself as "the grandest National Depot of Animated Nature in the World" (Altick 30) long before Disney aspired to similar greatness.

Theming Nature

Most Disney watchers saw Animal Kingdom as a significant departure from its other theme parks, in that animal behavior cannot be totally controlled. As journalist and novelist Carl Hiaasen salaciously puts it in *Team Rodent: How Disney Devours the World*, "Animal Kingdom is inhabited by real wild animals—not robots, not puppets, not holograms, not cartoons, but living and breathing creatures that (unless Disney starts tranking them) will eat, sleep, drool, defecate, regurgitate, sniff each other's crotches, lick their own balls, and occasionally even copulate in full view of the tourists" (69). Nor can Disney prevent animal death. According to a report by the U.S. Department of Agriculture, thirty-one animals died in the eight months before Animal Kingdom went public. It's difficult to assess these numbers and their significance.[3] In any case, some critics of Disney miss the corporation's history of nature speculation and the degree to which animal behavior can indeed be programmed.

Even if Disney has only recently gotten into the zoo business, long before Animal Kingdom opened—and decades before *Mutual of Omaha's Wild Kingdom* aired—the corporation had already been theming nature on film, producing documentaries that combined information with entertainment. In preparation for *Bambi* (1942), the company embarked on a series of animal studies, conducted first within the studios (deer and rabbits and skunks were brought in), then in zoos, and finally in the wild. These live-action films became the True-Life Adventure films, and their realism was at once derivative of and foundational to Disney's animated features. A postwar expedition inspired the first such film, *Seal Island* (1948), about the lives of fur seals, which won an Oscar. Next came *Beaver Valley, The Vanishing Prairie, The African Lion,* and *The Living Desert,* among others. A primary research tool for these shows was *National Geographic*: "We couldn't be in business without it," declared Uncle Walt himself (cited in De Roos 61).[4] Animal Kingdom pays homage to *National Geographic* inside a fake animal research station, in which issues of the periodical are displayed alongside skulls and other curios.

Like that magazine, Disney presents historical epochs and world cultures in a manner ostensibly comparative/relativist but in fact traditionally teleological, privileging first world rights to invade and "imagine," often in the name of nature study. As Terry Eagleton notes in *The Idea of Culture, imagination* is one of our key words for *globalization,* and almost always a positive term; he proposes that "imagination" is really "a liberal form of imperialism" (46). The True-Life films "imagineered" (to borrow an official Disney term) nature in a manner anticipatory of the theme parks.

Critics of Disney are quick to point out that simulation is the real name of the game, as if Disney's fakeness, indeed the inauthenticity of any cultural form, is evidence of its disinterest in nature. "Simulation" and "simulacra" are dirty words in Disney studies, especially ethnographic scholarship on the parks, and often treated as synonyms for the constructed or the artificial rather than, as in Jean Baudrillard's classic formulation, copies that have no original. In my view, this can be an unproductive line of inquiry. For example, I find EPCOT insidious because it smacks of Eurocentrism and imperialist nostalgia, not because the project of representing another culture is inherently suspect, or because simulation itself is bad, as some readings of that park imply.[5] Critics of Disney vis-à-vis simulation must establish some horizon of authenticity, which is tricky at best. Thus Susan Willis worries that "the simulated trip" of Disney's theme parks has supplanted the "quest for experience" that once inspired family vacations; revisiting Dean MacCannell's *The Tourist* (1976), she writes of "a time when many tourists included the desire for authentic experiences in their travel plans" (Project on Disney 45). "Even nature has been staged," she writes of the Magic Kingdom, "from Discovery Island where pesky native species are trapped and relocated (or exterminated) to the precise marigolds that render every garden perfunctory" (46).

But nature has always been staged, even if the terms of its theatricality or specularity have changed, and even if Disney's supersanitized aesthetic is deeply troubling. When exactly *did* tourists want an authentic experience? How long have we been deceiving ourselves about what we want or find in nature? The irony is that, in the theory of simulation to which Willis here seemingly subscribes—in which the society of the spectacle is ever more totalizing and postmodern under late capitalism— Animal Kingdom might actually look more authentic than the Magic Kingdom.

Authenticity is in the eye of the beholder. It's certainly true that Disney has little truck with local or nonexotic traditions of nature that interfere with its global investments. It devalues, for instance, the indigenous Florida. Hiaasen among others is outraged that Disney wiped out twenty-four thousand acres of orange groves and swamps to create the world's largest and most artificial entertainment complex. A Florida native, he bemoans the "destruction of childhood haunts" (77), opposing his own native childhood to the manufactured childhood (and nativisms) of Disney. Like Willis, Hiaasen calls attention to Disney's outrageous efforts to manage nature, but again the bottom line is that Disney shouldn't mess with nature at all. "Not all birds sing sweetly. Not all lakes are blue. Not all islands have sandy beaches. But they can be fixed, and that is Disney's fiendish specialty. . . . Under the Eisner [Disney's CEO] reign, nothing in the real world cannot be copied and refined" (79). For Hiaasen, simulation is the great betrayal.

Even so, denouncing Disney along these lines yields little insight into its nature work. Pointing to the persistent fantasy that nature is a sphere of purity and noncommercial authenticity, Davis remarks that "a theme park about wild nature is either so peculiar that it makes no sense, or contemporary culture is so thoroughly rationalized that it makes perfect sense" (8). Davis finds Sea World fascinating but worries about corporate appropriation of the public sphere, not simulation per se; she points out that the fantasy of a noncommercial nature often plays into decidedly commercial projects. She examines the phenomenon of incorporated nature, emphasizing that the nature theme park invites faith in spectacle alongside incredulity. Even if there's nothing natural about a nature theme park, she suggests, neither are there clear distinctions between the natural and the cultural, the civic and the corporate, the public and the private sphere.

Davis's observations about Sea World generally apply to Animal Kingdom, another corporate exercise in nature theming that seems at once an incredible enterprise and business as usual. For instance, Davis is astonished by the spectacle of a killer whale performing tricks for human audiences; as such, she writes, "it is an amazing cultural phenomenon" (8) even as it is also a standardized and profitable operation. While Animal Kingdom is not arranged around such epic performances, it does feature several animal shows that likewise seem both natural and scripted, amazing and routine. In the bird show "Flights of Wonder," for example, we're asked by the show's hosts to believe that a parrot singing

"How Much Is That Doggie in the Window?" represents "natural bird behavior," just moments after we're told that birds riding bicycles is the cheapest sort of circus trick. On the African safari, we pretend to be riding through a real savanna even as we know that the whole experience is scripted (on this ride, the guides camp it up). In Conservation Station, even the bathrooms are themed; elephants trumpet, and trivia questions dot the walls ("How much can an elephant pee per day?" "Up to 20 gallons!"). Disney is committed to the spectacle(s) of nature, in keeping with a familiar tradition of zoological exhibition. That Disney's spectacles sometimes seem postmodern or ironic doesn't matter much in the grand scheme of things.

The Kingdom Surveyed

Animal Kingdom opened on April 22, 1998, after three years of intense preparations. In his corporate autobiography, *Work in Progress,* Disney CEO Michael Eisner reports that some company executives worried that Animal Kingdom would adversely affect attendance at other parks. Eisner tells us that attendance was astonishingly strong—despite the actual numbers. In 1998, attendance at Animal Kingdom was the lowest of all four parks at Walt Disney World at only 6 million annual visitors, compared with 15.6, 10.6, and 9.5 million for the Magic Kingdom, EPCOT, and Disney-MGM Studios, respectively (Wasko 161). It's hard to reconcile these statistics with Eisner's buoyant claim that on opening day, Animal Kingdom was so mobbed that the gates were shut to hopeful parkgoers by 9 A.M. Whatever the attendance numbers, or financial gains or losses, Eisner prefers to explain the park as Disney manifest destiny: from the beginning, he knew that the park "had the potential to be to old-fashioned zoos what Disneyland had become to amusement parks—a quantum leap" (233).

At five hundred acres, the park is four times the size of the Magic Kingdom, closer in size to the standard metropolitan zoo. The African savanna of the "Kilimanjaro Safaris" alone spans one-fifth of the Animal Kingdom territory. According to the *Field Guide to Disney's Animal Kingdom Theme Park,* the park is "home" to around three thousand species of flora; other sources estimate the animal population at around fifteen hundred. Animal Kingdom has five major areas: Africa, Asia, DinoLand USA, and Camp Minnie-Mickey, with Discovery Island in the center. Each area offers a combination of live animal displays and assorted shows, rides, and shopping opportunities. Whereas the Magic

Kingdom is separated from the real world through a series of tram and monorail rides, no such isolationist fantasy marks Animal Kingdom. The entrance resembles that of a zoo; only some minimal landscaping separates park from parking lot.

Animal Kingdom's centerpiece is the Tree of Life, an artificial structure fourteen stories (145 feet) tall that looms over Discovery Island and indeed the whole Kingdom. Like Cinderella's Castle in the Magic Kingdom, the Tree organizes the field of vision. More than one hundred thousand man-made leaves adorn the Tree—each attached by hand—along with over three hundred carvings of animals. No doubt the panoptical Tree seems the ultimate affront to nature, being so artificial; it's also colonialist, calling to mind the shorter but still impressive Swiss Family Robinson Tree House in the Magic Kingdom, modeled after a Banyan tree but dubbed by Disney PR folk as *"Disneyondendron eximius,* which means an out-of-the-ordinary Disney tree" (cited in De Roos 63).

Eisner acknowledges the direct influence of the True-Life documentary series on Animal Kingdom, aligning the park with Disney's responsible and professional realist tradition: "Disney films such as *The Living Desert* and the Academy Award–winning *Seal Island* focused on animals in their natural habitats. Re-creating that experience was one of the central goals of the Animal Kingdom" (402). But in the next sentence, he insists that the park was an unscripted and bold new enterprise—real, not simulated—as risky as any corporate errand into the wilderness: "Above all, the park was a leap into unknown territory. . . . Rather than guiding and directing experiences, as we did in our other parks, we would encourage visitors to come to the Animal Kingdom to explore and discover for themselves" (403). Eisner thus resorts to ethnographic idiom in describing the kingdom's chief imagineer as "a striking character with a dramatic handlebar moustache and a dozen exotic earrings dangling from one overstretched earlobe." Eisner's presentation of the park vacillates between the two emphases that mark the park itself: one the one hand, we're assured that everything has been carefully prepared—famous experts consulted (such as Jane Goodall), safety assured—on the other, we're told that anything could happen with live rather than animated animals. The paradox is resolved through magic: "Of course, the Animal Kingdom's ultimate magic derives from the real animals."

Eisner promotes the park as classic Disney animal fantasy as well as classic Disney animal documentary. He acknowledges that the corporation hoped to capitalize on the success of *The Jungle Book* (1967) and

The Lion King (1994) by building attractions around those films. But while the "Festival of the Lion King" did indeed materialize, as of yet there are no *Jungle Book* rides or shows. Instead, the park features a stage show called *Tarzan Rocks!*, a combination rock concert and rollerblade/gymnastics extravaganza, located in DinoLand USA. In any case, of these two films, it's *The Lion King* whose presence is implicit in Animal Kingdom, not only in the savanna, where the largest number of animals are gathered, but also in the circle of life rhetoric that stands in for conservation. To quote Eisner a final time: "The Animal Kingdom takes us full circle. Thirty years ago, all you could find on our Orlando property were vast herds of grazing animals and some rather intimidating reptiles. Today, after billions of dollars of investment, we have unveiled our most original theme park concept yet: vast herds of grazing animals and some rather intimidating reptiles" (404). Here, perhaps, is the most insidious Disney propaganda: that the corporation has restored nature to its former state or has had no adverse impact on local nature. Theme park construction, he'd have us believe, proceeds like the circle of life, replenishing and restoring. Eisner acknowledges that Disney has displaced the natural Florida, but implies the trade-off is legitimate. He wants parkgoers to view Animal Kingdom as an environmental investment, as Disney's effort to preserve nature. No wonder Disney's practices are attacked as unnatural.

Zoo Story

However odious Animal Kingdom may be, it is unfair to treat this park in isolation, or to assume that purer forms of the zoo didn't disrupt the native environment or were less crudely opportunistic. Animal Kingdom seems like a bastardization of the traditional zoo only if we forget that the zoo is a relatively new public institution, and that historically zoos have been more concerned with amusement than with education. Animal collections came to be known as "menageries" during the Renaissance, evolving into "zoological gardens" in the nineteenth century. Scholars agree that these terms are more descriptive than definitive, and that they reflect changing forms and ownership. Menageries were royal and/or private institutions, even when the public had access. The zoological garden theoretically belongs to the people; zoological gardens emerged within urban centers, as urban projects. Zoological gardens, or zoos in short, offer a more comprehensive and systematic approach to animal showcasing than do menageries.

In America, the zoo has been around for roughly a century. The first, the Philadelphia Zoo, was established in 1874, and the Smithsonian-affiliated National Zoo in Washington, D.C. in 1891.[6] By the beginning of the twentieth century, major zoos existed in Philadelphia, Cincinnati, Washington, and New York, alongside twenty-five other smaller facilities, plus two aquariums. The first half of the century witnessed the addition of nearly eighty more such zoos; after 1950, construction continued at a less frantic pace, with emphasis shifting to program development and professionalization of the field. The World Zoo Organization estimates that there are now around ten thousand zoos worldwide (Mullan and Marvin xii).

Zoo directors past and present admit that people come to zoos to be entertained and to escape their daily routines. In his survey essay, "Zoological Gardens of the United States," Vernon N. Kisling Jr. emphasizes the zoo's function as wholesome family entertainment, citing a representative comment from a visitor to the New York Zoological Park in 1904:

> [L]earning natural history . . . is not the greatest good this Zoo does for the multitude. It matters little whether Michael Flynn knows the difference between the caribou and the red deer. It does matter a lot, however, that he has not sat around the flat disconsolate, or in the back room of the saloon, but has taken the little Flynns and Madame Flynn out into the fresh air and sunshine for one mighty good day in which they have forgotten themselves and their perhaps stuffy city rooms. (169)

Like other reconstructed wild spaces, such as the city or national park, the zoo offered relief from the daily urban grind, if not necessarily an authentic experience or even an educational one. Unlike the museum and the art gallery, the zoo is typically understood as a form of mass amusement (Mullan and Marvin 116–26). For many if not most of the zoogoing public, the animals on display needed little if any interpretation.

Thus the zoo bears a close relation to the U.S. national park, established not primarily for educational purposes but rather "for the use and the enjoyment of the American people" (Byerly 57). Alison Byerly points out that only more recently has the public come to expect the National Park Service to preserve the wilderness or to make the wilderness available to the public. She also emphasizes the influence of the picturesque landscape tradition of Britain and America—in painting and photography especially—on the aesthetics of park production and reception, suggesting that the artistic commodification of nature is hardly a new phenomenon and has long driven environmental activism. Simulation has always been par for the wilderness course. "The essential goal was that the park *appear* to be a natural wilderness" (60). National park and theme park may not be so different in this respect, even if the former officially belongs to the people.

Like the national park, the zoo has only recently been charged with the sacred missions of education and conservation. International cooperation among zoos and their directors is one factor in this shift. At home as abroad, zoos with greater resources have developed educational and outreach programs, targeting schoolchildren in particular, although most zoogoers still do not participate in these. The emphasis on conservation was more rhetoric than substance as recently as a decade ago, but we've since seen a major shift. Publications such as *Caring for the Earth* (1991), *Global Biodiversity Strategy* (1992), and the *Guide to the Convention on Biological Diversity* (1992) urged zoos to self-identify as conservation centers as part of a global effort to ensure biodiversity. Organizations like the World Zoo Organization, the International Union of Directors of Zoological Gardens, and the Captive Breeding Specialist Group of the International Union for the Conservation of Nature and Natural Resources have joined forces to produce mission statements that direct "responsible" zoos to support conservation efforts and foster knowledge about local habitat. Even the term *zoo* is losing favor with many in the field. While the traditional zoo remains popular, diversification and specialization have produced new cultural spaces of animal study and interaction, among them conservation parks, bioparks, endangered species rehabilitation clinics, and more specialized centers such as herpetariums, insectariums, aviaries, and butterfly parks. Zoos are at once growing smaller and larger, narrower and more comprehensive. "National parks and wildlife reserves," notes zoo historian Kisling, "are becoming so intensively managed that they are becoming zoogeographic megazoos" (ii).

Animal Kingdom pays homage to the zoo's evolutionary history, at once progressive and retrograde in aim and design. Most of the exhibits, for example, ensure unobstructed views of the animals, in keeping with the no-bars reformist zoo architecture of Carl Hagenbeck, a German animal supplier turned zoo director. Hagenbeck's zoo at Stellinger on the outskirts of Hamburg (which opened in 1907) emphasized open habitats and set the standard for twentieth-century animal display.[7] Not coincidentally, Hagenbeck also exhibited exotic people in these ostensibly more natural settings, pairing native people with native animals—Lapps with Norwegian reindeer, for example. Hagenbeck was not alone in this enterprise, but was joined by many others, including P. T. Barnum; the practice had close ties with anthropology. While most zoos have abandoned this strategy, Animal Kingdom resurrects it, exhibiting native people alongside native animals. I'll return to this unfortunate practice in the last section of this essay.

But while Animal Kingdom updates such outrageous traditions, it debuted during the heyday of conservation centers and biodiversity programs, and it is packaged accordingly. There are still rides and shows, but instead of ignoring nature, as we're encouraged to do in the other parks, parkgoers are asked to conserve it, by going to zoos, by recycling, and by using fewer pesticides. Signs along the pathways urge us to "Go Native!"—to plant native flowers, shrubs, and trees. "Insects are Your Friends," we are chastised. The parkgoer presumably must be urged into awareness, if not action. In Conservation Station we thus listen through headphones to *Song of the Rainforest*, which mixes birdsong with conservation injunction.

Throughout Animal Kingdom, the message of conservation is sounded loud and clear, and along with it, Disney's "active" involvement in preservation through money. Disney sponsors the Wildlife Conservation Fund, which makes contributions to a long list of agencies and organizations, among them the ASPCA, the Center for Ecosystem Survival, the Earthwatch Institute, the Save the Manatee Club, and the National Fish and Wildlife Foundation. I asked several cast members how this money was allocated, but no one seemed to know much about it. And of course Disney ignores its own environmental impact, choosing to focus on the canonical spaces of environmental horror, chief among them the Amazon rain forest. Ironic, then, that just outside the gates is the Rainforest Café, a "Wild Place to Shop and Eat!" Vanishing rain forest yields to themed eatery. Disney doesn't just simulate nature; Disney replaces nature with franchise, with a privatized vision of the consumption of wildness. Disney's take on conservation is, to say the least, problematic. Throughout the park, for example, we're told that the worldwide crisis of deforestation demands the establishment of zoos and the relocation of endangered species—not, tellingly, an end to deforestation.

Nowhere represented are the views of environmental activists, or even scientists working with endangered populations. Instead, we hear about veterinary care. Conservation Station includes a large veterinary center, where visitors can watch "surgical" procedures. Or at least medical procedures. On the schedule during my last visit was a dental exam for a gray fox and radiographs for a ring-billed gull (?). Here, as through-out the park, visitors are told that veterinarians supervise the care and feeding of animals. On-site are seven full-time veterinarians and six vet technicians. I asked about other kinds of experts involved—Disney, after all, recruited top people in the botanical and zoological sciences while developing the park—but none of the cast members knew anything about such experts. All I learned is that the park is accredited by the American Zoo and Aquarium Association and maintains connections with the vet school at the University of Florida in nearby Gainesville.

The veterinarian is the animal professional most familiar to visi-tors and probably the most reassuring as well, which helps explain this selective showcasing of expertise. Also in Conservation Station is an "animal communication research station." When I was last there, several "researchers" were watching split-screen images of elephants. I asked whose these researchers were and what they were doing, but no one could tell me much. Animal Kingdom may be simply paying lip service to the new ethic of conservation and research. Someone finally handed me a flier promoting a half-day, in-depth, behind-the-scenes tour of the kingdom—for a fee of merely $75, I think. (I recycled the flier.) There is, in short, very little acknowledgment of alternative expertise, and no acknowledgment that Disney is part of the problem it bemoans.

I've been emphasizing Animal Kingdom's continuities with the zoo, partly to make the obvious point that zoos are themselves complex, evolving, often bizarre institutions. But the differences are just as instructive. While zoos may have corporate sponsors, they are nonprofit organizations, and they are usually still located near urban centers. Theme parks, particularly Disney theme parks, are lucrative enterprises and usually suburban or posturban in setting, even if Walt Disney World has helped transform Orlando into one of the world's amusement cap-itals.[8] Walt Disney World hasn't just left the traditional city; it has largely replaced it. The complex is a private city, as its infrastructure and legal autonomy make clear.[9] So while Disney is not singularly responsi-ble for nor representative of the decline of the public sphere, the corpo-ration has clearly taken privatization, profit, and corporate control to astonishing levels. Never before has a zoo been part of so powerful a non-civic, corporate entity.

In Animal Kingdom, classic zoo entertainment meets a revisionist ethos of conservation in a highly privatized, posturban remodeling of the public sphere. That remodeling, furthermore, occurs within the para-meters of children's culture, not only because zoos have long furnished family entertainment, but also because Disney has re-presented entertainment as a middle-class form of parenting and family bonding. Good parents don't just educate their children; they take them on quasi-educational vacations, preferably to Walt Disney World. As the twentieth century wore on, zoos became popular and respectable destinations for middle-class families.

There are various other historical links between zoo culture and childhood upon which Disney capitalizes in its latest park. For instance, zoos like to exhibit animals that resemble humans, and especially young humans. At work here is the biological principle of neoteny, as theorized by Konrad Lorenz, which "describes those positive reactions to protecting the young which are released in man by those animals which correspond to the 'child schema'" (Mullan and Marvin 24). We human animals apparently prefer to look at animals that seem childlike—warm, fuzzy, and funny. Favorite features include prominent eyes and foreheads, a rounded body, short extremities, and vertical posture. This would seem to explain the popularity of animals such as primates and giant pandas. Anthropologist Elizabeth Lawrence speculates that neoteny is the driving force behind the "juvenilization of fantasy animals in Disney's Magic Kingdom" (cited in Mullan and Marvin 25). Those costumed animals are usually perceived as friendly even when they tower over the kids. Over time Mickey himself has developed more neotenous features.

Makeovers are more difficult with actual animals, however. Animal Kingdom solves this problem by showcasing animals with neotenous features, by minimizing contact with "ugly" animals, and by domesticating animals through simulated performances akin to those in the other parks. Thus the live bird show "Flights of Wonder" coexists alongside the 3D film "It's Tough to Be a Bug," starring Flik and Hopper from Disney/Pixar's *A Bug's Life*. In fairness, "It's Tough to Be a Bug" is every bit as educational and entertaining as "Flights of Wonder." "It's Tough to Be a Bug" is perhaps the best example of the hybridity of Animal Kingdom; it's an educational show about insects and arachnids, and (naturally) a promotional vehicle for *A Bug's Life*.

This intermingling of high-tech and low-tech exhibit makes it difficult to actually find animal exhibits in the park and on the park map. Animal footprints on the map designate "Animal Viewing Locations," but are interspersed with designations for telephones, restrooms, film centers, and ATMs. In some respects, the park map resembles the classic maps of empire, at once accurate and wildly fanciful. In most zoos, visitors can plan routes based on what animals they would most like to see. In Animal Kingdom, the animals compete with 3D shows, rock concerts, action adventure rides, and so forth, all keyed to regions rather than species or habitats—it wouldn't take long to see only the live animals were they not so scattered across the space.[10]

Moreover, there are very few written texts in Animal Kingdom. In the region of Asia, the Maharajah Jungle Trek furnishes guides to the "Royal Forest's" flora and fauna, but these maps are quite simple, and visitors are supposed to return them at the walking tour's conclusion. Even the gift shops have nothing to offer by way of zoological or botanical elaboration, with the exception of Disney's own *Field Guide to Disney's Animal Kingdom,* whose title affirms Disney's approximation of the natural world. The animal exhibits rarely feature the kinds of written summaries standard in zoos and aquariums. Information about the animals is presented either orally by cast members or through televised or faux-interactive computerized formats.

In his essay "Story Time," Shelton Waldrep argues that the latest Disney parks reflect a shift away from traditional narrative and toward "high-concept production," with rubrics such as "animals" displacing the tidy, coherent story lines of the Magic Kingdom (Project on Disney 96). These larger concepts, he says, make difficult any nuanced sense of sequence or history. Waldrep proposes further that with the construction of EPCOT and Disney-MGM, designed partly if not primarily for adults, childhood has also been displaced. With respect to Animal Kingdom, I'm more persuaded by the second thesis of displacement than by the first. Narrative survives in Animal Kingdom; it's just put to different, more nostalgic use, evocative of the global village political conceit. Bob Mullan and Garry Marvin confirm that zoo planners now emphasize story lines more than themes or concepts. For example, at the Blue Ridge Zoological Park in Virginia, zoo architects Jones and Jones develop story lines from the Lewis and Clark expedition and Livingstone's treks through the African jungle (Mullan and Marvin 59). Animal Kingdom perhaps represents a symbolic restitution of childhood vis-à-vis the child-native correspondences of colonialist storytelling and human display.

Animating Others

In *Deconstructing Disney,* Eleanor Byrne and Martin McQuillan aver that Disney's strategy for representing race in its animated films is exclusive anthropomorphism—showing only animal characters—say, cats *(The Aristocats)* or dogs *(Lady and the Tramp)*—and then differentiating among them along implicit racial and class lines.[11] *The Lion King* (1994), the most successful Disney feature to date and indeed one of the most successful films ever, likewise handles race via an anthropomorphic landscape, ostensibly that of Africa but populated by no African people. While Disney has drawn other non-Caucasian characters, not once has Disney animated an African American man. According to Byrne and McQuillan, the anthropomorphism allows Disney to figure race without representing it more self-consciously. "African-Americans are thus unrepresentable because the representation of African-Americans lies outside the remit of an animal kingdom" (104).

Byrne and McQuillan rightly identify the new park as a simulacrum not only of the traditional zoo and safari park, but of *The Lion King* itself. They also recognize that Animal Kingdom represents the reversal of the usual colonial model of Disney parks: "Disney realizes there is no money in Africa and incorporates Africa into its American theme park" (103). The monarchical metaphor persists in the park as well as the film, the rhetoric of "kingdom" covering up the complex geopolitical realities of the contemporary world.[12] In a sense, their analysis applies to Animal Kingdom, which presents an anthropomorphic African landscape in the form of the savanna, one empty of natives. The Kilimanjaro Safari is perhaps the most successful of all Animal Kingdom's attractions, thanks to its commitment to safari form and global village storytelling.

The preride show consists of a series of animal videos, narrated by British wildlife researchers sporting the usual safari wear. Like much of Africa, the safari area is aged or "ruined" to look colonial, with crumbling stone facades and props like steamer trunks, tribal masks, fishing gear, and camping supplies. The ride itself is not conducted on a track. Instead, visitors board a rugged-looking jeep and are driven through the territory, which looks astonishingly like the savanna we've come to know and love through mass media. This is an impressive feat given the decidedly non-African humidity of central Florida. Fake trees and termite towers abound. The animals—elephants, giraffes, lions, cheetahs, and other classic safari specimens—are separated by hidden barriers and even electric shock lines, but the savanna appears seamless. The ride is structured around a story about the hunt for poachers by African officials—since, of course, Disney's own traffic in animals is rarely understood as poaching. The jeep driver "communicates" through shortwave radio with others searching for the evil poachers, and soon the poachers are caught. The driver himself is usually white but also native—a white South African, the perfect guide.

Ironically, Byrne and McQuillan are so committed to the idea that simulation is a layered and complex reality (contra Hiaasen) that they miss the African and Asian cast members in the park. It's easy to wax deconstructive about the spectrality of film, but less easy to treat the theme park as entirely such. If *The Lion King* is "in keen denial about the politics of representation" around race, affirming an Africa "which is always in excess of what can be represented" (Byrne and McQuillan 101), then Animal Kingdom addresses this problem by representing race in a more imperialist and thus "natural" way, combining animal with human display.[13] In Animal Kingdom, Africans do populate Africa, not as natives in the savanna but as park workers stationed throughout the region. But they are very much on exhibit.

The display of exotic animals has long been allied with the display of exotic people, from the earliest of menageries through *Wild Kingdom* and beyond. One of the first known menageries, that of Montezuma in Tenochtitlan (now Mexico), exhibited human oddities—such as hunchbacks, albinos, and dwarves—alongside animal specimens (Mullan and Marvin 103–5). The zoo helped sponsor the freak show before the heyday of P. T. Barnum. Prisons, insane asylums, and zoos have an intimate historical relation. Jeremy Bentham's Panopticon prison model, Foucault speculates in *Discipline and Punish*, was probably inspired by the design of Louis XIV's menagerie at Versailles (203). Nowhere is the interdependence of human and animal exhibition more obvious than in Animal Kingdom. While it's okay to show animals in their natural habitat, Disney recognizes that thus showcasing human animals is no longer tolerable.

Disney has two internship programs for cast members, one for college students and one for international students. The international students work primarily at EPCOT in the World Showcase and in the Africa and Asia sections of the Animal Kingdom, where they double as natives and as interpreters of native animals. This shamelessly imperialist strategy makes the cast members vulnerable to the cluelessness of the public. On my last visit, I chatted with two young women from South Africa who worked (of course) in "Africa," specifically in Harambe Village. It's widely known that Disney cast members are watched carefully by their superiors and are thus fearful of saying anything critical, but to my surprise, these two women were quick to point fingers. They were unhappy with the working conditions at the park and the living conditions nearby; they reported that their apartment was shoddily constructed and that requests for repairs were ignored. The much-touted free course work at Disney University was also a sham; unlike the college interns, they were barred from many classes. If they complained, they were told they were homesick. Visitors, they reported, often condescended to them, treated them like children. One reported that in the middle of an oral presentation, she was asked by a parkgoer what it was like to finally wear shoes. "I wouldn't do this again for a million dollars," she said.

Disney eschews forms of human display and exploitation that aren't ostensibly educational or cultural. Most of the students work as area guides, but a few put on cultural shows, such as the Indonesian show that my friend Cydney and I saw, which consisted of short dance routines and the singing of the Indonesian national anthem. Native drummers, also international students, roam the streets of Africa and entertain the public. We go to Animal Kingdom to see animals, but there are other attractions, among them the cast members, who function much like the costumed characters of the Magic Kingdom (and who seem equally miserable).

Gone Jurassic

DinoLand USA is the most anomalous section of Animal Kingdom if we understand the park as zoological, and I want to end this essay by speculating about its function. The major attraction is the thrill ride "Dinosaur: Countdown to Extinction"; the area also encompasses the stage show *Tarzan Rocks!* plus a dig site playground called the Boneyards, and Dino-Sue, a replica of Sue, the most complete T-Rex ever discovered. But why dinosaurs in an animal park? It's likely, first of all, that Disney was trying to preempt Universal Studio's *Jurassic Park* attraction, due to open soon. Plus, dinosaurs are now a staple of the children's culture scene. McDonald's sponsorship of DinoLand and the rich array of dinosaur-themed toys, books, and other merchandise in the gift shop make clear that dinosaurs are big business. At least since *Fantasia* (1939), dinosaurs have been associated with children's entertainment. Dino-Land USA is Disney's latest attempt to capitalize on the craze.

The area is positioned opposite Camp Minnie-Mickey, the area designed for young kids; like the camp, DinoLand USA is spatially and ideologically sealed off from Africa and Asia. As Susan Willis points out in "Imagining Dinosaurs," because they are safely extinct, dinosaurs can represent almost anything.[14] Presumably they have no political content. But not everyone sees it that way. Willis emphasizes the gender wars of dinosaur culture and pop-paleontology, while for Joseba Gabilondo, the dinosaurs of Steven Spielberg's *Jurassic Park* movies allegorize globalization, at once acknowledging and repressing the condition of the Hispanic subaltern. According to Gabilondo, these dinosaurs embody not only the monstrous logic of globalization but also the otherness of the immigrant and the illegal alien—an otherness so monstrous as to be beyond traditional representation, and which, we might add, cannot be adequately "themed" like Africa or Asia. Spielberg's creatures, after all, are born in Latin America and exhibited in an ecological theme park in Costa Rica. When that park fails at the end of the first film, the sequel brings the dinosaurs to the United States ("DinoLand USA"). They debark in San Diego, no less, where border/immigration panic has an overdetermined history.

While the *Jurassic Park* films are not Disney fare, Disney has its own legacy of Latin American investment and figuration. Walt Disney and his staff made three trips south of the border between 1941 and 1943 in search of "raw material" for the Good Neighbor initiative of the federal government. With the wartime closing of European markets, Disney stood to profit by this new venture, and did. The company produced several dozen films of various length and format, among them the feature-length *South of the Border with Disney* (1941), *Saludos Amigos* (1943), and *The Three Caballeros* (1945). The central figure here, of course, is Donald Duck; in the good (neighbor) old days, Disney preferred duck to dinosaur. Disney has yet to develop a Latin American–themed park, perhaps because it's not as classic and comfortable a space of empire.

While it might be far-fetched to argue that DinoLand USA is a cryptotext of Latin American exploitation, I'm intrigued by the idea that Disney's sudden enthusiasm for the Jurassic condition is entangled with the monstrosity of globalization and cultural imperialism. Certainly, colonial practices are residual in this section. Why, for example, is the stage show *Tarzan Rocks!* in DinoLand USA rather than Africa (where the Tarzan books and films are set)? Here Tarzan morphs with Fred Flintstone, as if colonialist and prehistoric life are synonymous. The thrill ride "Countdown to Extinction" likewise suggests a colonialist remaking of the dinosaur tradition, with a little help from science fiction (itself often preoccupied with prehistoric or primitive landscapes). After a short preshow, guests board safarilike transport vehicles and are sent back sixty-five million years in search of an iguanodon just before its extinction. But we arrive almost too late and are subjected to meteor showers, dino-carnivores, and fierce jungle underbrush before we escape back to the future. An evil scientist has altered our course and exposed us to danger; this premise resembles that of the "Alien Encounter" attraction in the Magic Kingdom. But unlike "Alien Encounter," "Countdown to Extinction" is an actual ride through space. And a bumpy one, as the car shakes and shudders along the tracks. Still, the ride feels simulated, in the sense that our field of vision is carefully controlled; although we are menaced by giant mechanized dinosaurs, the flashing strobe lights and alternating darkness make the experience seem less real.

The animatronic technology of "Countdown to Extinction" is noticeably retrograde when juxtaposed with the digital "nature" of 3D shows and dinosaur films of late, such as the *Jurassic Park* films and Disney's own *Dinosaur* (2000), for which the ride serves as promotional vehicle. The ride is self-consciously old-fashioned, as must be all rides after the digital revolution. Gabilondo points out that while it depends upon digital technology for its astonishing realism, *Jurassic Park* (1993) concludes with the human visitors escaping from the island in a more traditionally mechanized form of technology—a helicopter. Thus the film "exorcises digital technology at a primary level" (27). We might make the same case for "Countdown to Extinction"; we time travel in a machine with wheels and seatbelts—at once safari jeep, moon rover, and SUV—and experience global monstrosity as a very physical journey. The ride exorcises as much as indulges in high-tech hijinks.

No return of the subaltern marks Disney's ride, however. There is no sequel that acknowledges the Other on American turf. The Disney dinosaur is safely contained within DinoLand, within the Animal Kingdom, a "successful" animal theme park, as opposed to the Costa Rican disaster. And the potentially monstrous spectacle of film itself is managed through old-fashioned thrills and the spatial experience of the park. We exit "Countdown to Extinction" through the gift shop, returning to more soothing dino-attractions that are more resonant with Spielberg's first dinosaur film, *The Land before Time* (1988). Children are endangered species in the *Jurassic Park* films but are safe in Disney's dinosaur productions, even when they walk on the wild side.

It's probably naive to insist that a consistent or discrete ideology underwrites Animal Kingdom. Still, I like the idea that Disney, as an American multinational corporation, must disavow its imperialist investments in Latin America because they are too close to home, whereas the classic themes of Anglo-European colonialism are safe for recycling. This explanation demands some faith in the idea of the political unconscious, and not everyone will agree to this formulation. Nonetheless, DinoLand USA may have more to teach us about Disney's history and future than can the more familiar or intelligible themes of nature-empire (such as the safari, or the jungle cruise in the Magic Kingdom). When it comes to the nature work of Disney or other large corporations, it's worth using the anomalous to think about the politics of theming and to move beyond thematic readings vis-à-vis whatever methodologies are useful, since even the most ironic or critical versions of, say, colonialist nature representation don't necessarily subvert corporate interests and may indeed be vital to those interests.

Notes

1. New shows were produced occasionally until 1988.

2. "For scientists and public alike," writes Willinsky, "animals were interpreted in explicitly imperialist terms; as tokens of conquered people and metonymic extensions of the geography of empire, they were illustrations of racial inferiority and difference" (33). He points out further that the desire to see animals adapt to different climates is itself an imperial project (71).

3. Animal activists were outraged by these deaths, some of which did seem the result of human negligence and carelessness. For example, two West African cranes were run over by two safari jeeps, and four cheetah cubs died after ingesting ethyl glycot, a toxic chemical found in paint thinner and antifreeze. Other animals that died include two rhinoceroses, two mole rats, two litters of baby chinchilla rabbits, a hippopotamus, and a guinea hog. Disney spokespeople insisted that animal deaths at the park were unremarkable relative both to the park's total population (of one thousand animals) and to mortality in the wild. In any case, the USDA concluded that Disney had not violated federal animal-welfare laws.

4. De Roos, incidentally, was reporting in *National Geographic*. Early press coverage of Disney was almost unilaterally positive.

5. See, for example, Alexander Wilson's essay on EPCOT, in which he argues that Disney's policy of hypersimulation leads to a crippling "failure" of the imagination. EPCOT seems to be the whipping boy of Disney studies.

6. In 1716, the lion—or more precisely, "The Lion King of Beasts"—was the first exotic animal exhibited in America, in Boston. Next were camels, tigers, and elephants.

7. The earliest U.S. zoos to use these exhibits were in Denver (1918), St. Louis (1919), and Detroit (1920s). At the time, many directors disapproved of this exhibit strategy or thought renovations would be too expensive.

8. Through his theme parks Walt Disney sought refuge from the city, first in Los Angeles, then more successfully in central Florida, even though he didn't live to see the

Florida park open. In each case, however, the parks have generated urban sprawl, shoring up a different sort of city.

9.   Under the auspices of the Reedy Creek Improvement District, the Disney corporation runs its own utilities, conducts it own planning and zoning, maintains its own fire department and security force. The district has the authority to build its own airport, even a nuclear power plant. "The Vatican with mouse ears," Richard Foglesong calls it (cited in Hiaasen 26).

10.   In Tampa's Busch Gardens, in contrast, the thrill rides are clearly separated from the animal exhibits, even if the whole park is Africa-themed. We know exactly where the animals are and can choose to avoid them. Not so in Animal Kingdom.

11.   In contrast, recent Disney films such as *Pocahontas* and *The Hunchback of Notre Dame* have dealt more "humanly" (if not progressively) with the realities of racial persecution and ethnic cleansing, against the backdrop of post–Cold War global politics.

12.   As Byrne and McQuillan note, *The Lion King* affirms monarchy at the thematic level, even as the film as a global commodity makes clear the decline of that system. So too with Animal Kingdom, which pretends to be less corporate than it really is. Disney's proliferation of kingdoms works to obscure the workings of transnational capitalism.

13.   Writing in the early 1990s, before Animal Kingdom was under construction, Jane Kuenz had this prediction about plans to open a new pavilion at EPCOT for equatorial Africa: "Since Africa now exists at Disney only in the barest of signifiers—a totem pole surrounded by the music of drums marks the future site of the pavilion—its eventual full-fledged appearance may make manifest what the others now only hint at: the use and enjoyment of other cultures, particularly of those whose representation in the park is primarily colonial, as the site for sexual fantasies and desire otherwise unavailable or unrepresented" (Project on Disney 73).

14.   Willis speculates that our fascination with dinosaurs is bound up with complicated feelings about extinction—on the one hand, guilt about our role in the annihilation of species, and on the other hand, relief that this mass extinction, at least, wasn't our fault, and was even necessary for our own evolution.

Works Cited

Altick, R. D. *The Shows of London.* Cambridge: Harvard University Press, 1978.

Byerly, Alison. "The Uses of Landscape: The Picturesque Aesthetic and the National Park System." In *The Ecocriticism Reader: Landmarks in Literary Ecology.* Ed. Cheryll Glotfelty and Harold Fromm. Athens: University of Georgia Press, 1996, 52–68.

Byrne, Eleanor, and Martin McQuillan. *Deconstructing Disney.* London: Pluto Press, 1999.

Davis, Susan G. *Spectacular Nature: Corporate Culture and the Sea World Experience.* Berkeley: University of California Press, 1997.

De Roos, Robert. "The Magic Worlds of Walt Disney." In *Disney Discourse: Producing the Magic Kingdom.* Ed. Eric Smoodin. New York: Routledge, 1994, 48–68.

Eagleton, Terry. *The Idea of Culture.* London: Blackwell, 2000.

Eisner, Michael D., with Tony Schwartz. *Work in Progress.* New York: Random House, 1998.

Field Guide to Disney's Animal Kingdom Theme Park. New York: Disney Editions–Round-table Press, 2000.

Foucault, Michel. *Discipline and Punish: The Birth of the Prison.* Trans. Alan Sheridan. New York: Vintage Books, 1979.

Gabilondo, Joseba. "The Global Phallus: On the Digital and Allegorical Economy of the Hispanic Subaltern in Hollywood Film." *Discourse* 23.1 (2001): 4–24.

Hiaasen, Carl. *Team Rodent: How Disney Devours the World.* New York: Ballantine, 1998.

Kisling, Vernon N., Jr. "Zoological Gardens of the United States." In *Zoo and Aquarium History: Ancient Animal Collections to Zoological Gardens.* Ed. Vernon N. Kisling Jr. Boca Raton: CRC Press, 2001, 147–80.

Mullan, Bob, and Garry Marvin. *Zoo Culture: The Book about Watching People Watch Animals.* 2d ed. Urbana: University of Illinois Press, 1999.

Project on Disney. *Inside the Mouse: Work and Play at Disney World.* Durham, N.C.: Duke University Press, 1995.

Wasko, Janet. *Understanding Disney: The Manufacture of Fantasy.* Cambridge, England: Polity Press, 2001.

Willinsky, John. *Learning to Divide the World: Education at Empire's End.* Minneapolis: University of Minnesota Press, 1998.

Willis, Susan. "Imagining Dinosaurs." In *Girls, Boys, Books, Toys: Gender in Children's Literature and Culture.* Ed. Beverly Lyon Clark and Margaret R. Higonnet. Baltimore: Johns Hopkins University Press, 1999, 183–95.

Wilson, Alexander. "The Betrayal of the Future: Walt Disney's EPCOT Center." In *Disney Discourse: Producing the Magic Kingdom.* Ed. Eric Smoodin. New York: Routledge, 1994, 118–28.

Contributors

Kaye Adkins is an assistant professor of English at Missouri Western State College, where she teaches essay writing, composition and composition theory, and technical writing. Her research interests include environmental rhetoric, the preservationist movement, and ecocomposition. She has presented papers on these subjects at a number of national conferences. Her meditative essay, "Re: The Hunt," was included in a collection that accompanied a 1996 art exhibit at the University of Tasmania. She has also been a contributing editor to the annual bibliography of the Association for the Study of Literature and Environment. She received her Ph.D. in composition and rhetoric from the University of Kansas in 1998.

M. Lynn Byrd is an associate professor of English at Southern University in New Orleans. Her teaching and research interests include gender studies, autobiography, children's literature, and environmental literature. She has published an article on Lord Byron's closet drama *Sardanapalus* and a second on Harriet Beecher Stowe, Lord and Lady Byron, and eugenics. She is currently completing a manuscript on twentieth-century women's hybrid-genre autobiography.

Chuck Chamberlin was a professor emeritus at the University of Alberta. He taught courses in social studies and environmental education to undergraduates and research methodology and critical theory to graduates in elementary education. He was active with the Sierra Club's suburban sprawl campaign in Edmonton.

Marion W. Copeland earned her Ph.D. from the University of Massachusetts–Amherst in 1973 and retired after thirty years of teaching English at Holyoke Community College, Holyoke, Massachusetts. She is currently active as a lecturer and writer and is associated with the

Center for Animals and Public Policy at the Tufts School for Veterinary Medicine. Her field is animals in literature. Her recent publications include "Toward Biophilia: Using Children's Literature to Teach Empathy and Compassion," which was anthologized in *State of the Animals 2003* (Human Society of the United States Press) and *Cockroach* (Reaktion Press).

SUSAN JAYE DAUER teaches in the English department at Valencia Community College, East Campus, in Orlando, Florida. She also teaches an online course based on writing about science fiction and fantasy. She has written and presented widely on issues relating to extrapolative fiction and feminism. She is an award-winning author of short fiction and is currently working on several creative projects. Her article "From Teaching in Class to Teaching Online: Preserving Community and Communication" appeared in *Teaching Literature*, a collection of essays (Palgrave).

SIDNEY I. DOBRIN is an associate professor of English and director of writing programs at the University of Florida, where he also serves on the faculty for the College of Natural Resources and Environment. He has written or edited more than ten books on writing and environment, including *Ecocomposition: Theoretical and Pedagogical Approaches* (coedited with Christian Weisser) and *Natural Discourse: Toward Ecocomposition* (cowritten with Christian Weisser). His most recent book of nonfiction essays, *Distance Casting: Words and Ways of the Saltwater Fishing Life,* explores the long tradition of writing about fishing. Dobrin is most comfortable in, on, or under saltwater. He is on a lifelong quest for the perfect grouper sandwich, the perfect cheeseburger, and the perfect glass of rum punch, which he'd like to enjoy on the perfect boat docked in front of the perfect beach hut.

NICOLE M. DUPLESSIS received her bachelor's degree from the University of New Orleans in 1997 and her master's in 2001 from Texas A&M University, where she is currently enrolled in the Ph.D. program in English. Research interests include children's literature and narrative theory, representations of literacy in twentieth-century literature and film, and metaphor and ecopoetics.

BOB HENDERSON is an associate professor of kinesiology and arts and science at McMaster University, Hamilton, Ontario. He teaches courses in outdoor education and environmental thought. He also writes about experiential education, Canadian travel heritage, and environmental inquiry.

Maude Hines is an assistant professor of English at Portland State University, where she teaches children's literature, American and African American literature and culture, and cultural studies. Her essays appear in *The Lion and the Unicorn* and *Body Politics and the Fictional Double*.

Tara L. Holton is a doctoral student in the theory program of the Department of Psychology at the University of Calgary. Her current areas of interest include the construction of nature in education, postcolonial discourse analysis, and discourse analytic approaches to the study of suicide. Her research is supported by the University of Calgary Silver Anniversary Fellowship and the Social Sciences and Humanities Research Council of Canada Fellowship.

Merle Kennedy is an instructor in the Health and Community Studies Division at Grant MacEwan College, Edmonton, Alberta. She teaches a language arts course in the teacher assistant program. Her research work is nested in narrative inquiry, and her most recent study explored racial identity in the life and work of four white female teachers.

Kenneth B. Kidd teaches courses in children's literature and media at the University of Florida. His book *Making American Boys: Boyology and the Feral Tale* is forthcoming from the University of Minnesota Press. He is the associate director of the Center for the Study of Children's Literature and Culture as well as the associate graduate coordinator for the Department of English.

Michelle H. Martin, an assistant professor of English at Clemson University, teaches children's and young adult literature, women's studies, and laptop composition. Her book *Brown Gold: Milestones of African American Children's Picture Books, 1845–2000* is forthcoming from Routledge. She is also coediting an anthology with Claudia Nelson of Southwest Texas University on Anglophone sex education manuals. Martin has published articles in *Children's Literature Association Quarterly*, *The Lion and the Unicorn*, *Horn Book*, *The Five Owls*, and *Teaching and Learning Literature*. She lives in Clemson, South Carolina, with her two dogs and her husband, whom she married in May 2001, on the twentieth anniversary of their first date.

Kamala Platt is an independent scholar and professor. She currently teaches at the University of Texas–San Antonio and San Antonio College. She has conducted research for San Antonio College's Hispanic Research Center as well as for several community organizations, including the Esperanza Center for Peace and Justice, where she serves as an executive board member. Her interests in cultural and postcolonial studies and social identity and justice focus on Chicana/o and South Asian cultural poetics of environmental justice, public wall art, and independent film.

Arlene Plevin's work has been published in *Technical Communication, Deliberative Discourse, and Environmental Rhetoric: Connections and Directions, The Literature of Nature: An International Sourcebook,* and *Ecocomposition: Theoretical and Pedagogical Approaches.* She has worked as a writer and editor for the National Wildlife Federation and the League of American Bicyclists. Her Ph.D. dissertation, "Writing, Self, and Community: The Ethical Rhetoric of Place," received a Susannah J. McMurphy Dissertation Fellowship from the University of Washington. Plevin has also recently been a Fulbright lecturer at Tamkang University in Taiwan.

Tim B. Rogers is a professor in the theory program of the Department of Psychology at the University of Calgary. He is involved in research dealing with the social and psychological construction of nature and how this affects the ways we interact with the world. Other research interests include explorations of the history and metatheory of methods in psychology.

Lynn Overholt Wake is currently working on her Ph.D. in English at the University of Nebraska–Lincoln, focusing on ecocriticism and children's literature, with an emphasis on the presence of animals. Formerly an adjunct instructor in children's literature, a children's librarian, a school media specialist, and a freelance storyteller, Wake is also a poet. She has led Great Books discussion groups for third through eighth graders and worked with local reading projects. She's interested in Cather scholarship and Great Plains literature. Wake holds an M.L.S. from Simmons College and an M.A. from UNL. She has a daughter and a son, is married to a retired farmer, and has lived in Seward, Nebraska, for twenty-seven years.

KAREN WELBERRY was awarded her Ph.D. from La Trobe University, Melbourne, Australia, in May 2001. Her thesis was titled "'The Playground of England': A Genealogy of the English Lakes from Nursery to National Park, 1793–1951." She is currently teaching literature at RMIT University in Melbourne and working on representations of the Australian brumby (feral horse) in literary and environmental discourse.

NAOMI WOOD is an associate professor of English at Kansas State University, where she teaches children's and adolescent literature and courses in Victorian studies. She enjoys hiking in the Colorado Rockies, though she does not enjoy the cold and submits to it with ill grace. She has published on Victorian fantasy and romance writers such as R. L. Stevenson, George MacDonald, Lucy Lane Clifford, and Charles Kingsley, as well as on Walt Disney and other twentieth-century phenomena. With her children's literature colleagues at Kansas State, she coedited a special issue of the Association for the Study of Literature and Environment's *American Nature-Writing Newsletter* on children's literature and environmentalism in 1995.

INDEX